SIR EDWARD COKE AND THE REFORMATION OF THE LAWS

Throughout his early career, Sir Edward Coke joined many of his contemporaries in his concern about the uncertainty of the common law. Coke attributed this uncertainty to the ignorance and entrepreneurship of practitioners, litigants and other users of legal power whose actions eroded confidence in the law. Working to limit their behaviours, Coke also simultaneously sought to strengthen royal authority and the Reformation settlement. Yet the tensions in his thought led him into conflict with James I, who had accepted many of the criticisms of the common law.

Sir Edward Coke and the Reformation of the Laws reframes the origins of Coke's legal thought within the context of law reform and provides a new interpretation of his early career, the development of his legal thought, and the path from royalism to opposition in the turbulent decades leading up to the English civil wars.

DAVID CHAN SMITH is an assistant professor of history at Wilfrid Laurier University, Canada, where he researches intellectual history and law in the early-modern Atlantic world.

CAMBRIDGE STUDIES IN ENGLISH LEGAL HISTORY

Edited by
J. H. Baker
Fellow of St Catharine's College, Cambridge

Recent series titles include

Sir Edward Coke and the Reformation of the Laws: Religion, Politics and Jurisprudence, 1578–1616
David Chan Smith

Medieval English Conveyances
John M. Kaye

Marriage Law and Practices in the Long Eighteenth Century: A Reassessment
Rebecca Probert

The Rise and Fall of the English Ecclesiastical Courts, 1500–1860
R. B. Outhwaite

Law Courts and Lawyers in the City of London, 1300–1550
Penny Tucker

Legal Foundations of Tribunals in Nineteenth-Century England
Chantal Stebbings

Pettyfoggers and Vipers of the Commonwealth: The 'Lower Branch' of the Legal Profession in Early Modern England
C. W. Brooks

Roman Canon Law in Reformation England
R. H. Helmholz

Sir Henry Maine: A Study in Victorian Jurisprudence
R. C. J. Cocks

Sir William Scott, Lord Stowell Judge of the High Court of Admiralty, 1798–1828
Henry J. Bourguignon

The Early History of the Law of Bills and Notes: A Study of the Origins of Anglo-American Commercial Law
James Steven Rogers

The Law of Treason in England in the Later Middle Ages
J. G. Bellamy

William Sheppard, Cromwell's Law Reformer
Nancy L. Matthews

SIR EDWARD COKE AND THE REFORMATION OF THE LAWS

Religion, Politics and Jurisprudence, 1578–1616

DAVID CHAN SMITH

CAMBRIDGE
UNIVERSITY PRESS

CAMBRIDGE
UNIVERSITY PRESS

University Printing House, Cambridge CB2 8BS, United Kingdom

Cambridge University Press is part of the University of Cambridge.

It furthers the University's mission by disseminating knowledge in the pursuit of education, learning and research at the highest international levels of excellence.

www.cambridge.org
Information on this title: www.cambridge.org/9781107069299

© David Chan Smith 2014

First published 2014

by Clays, St Ives plc

A catalogue record for this publication is available from the British Library

Library of Congress Cataloguing in Publication data
Smith, David Chan, 1976– author.
Sir Edward Coke and the reformation of the laws : religion, politics and jurisprudence, 1578–1616 / David Chan Smith.
pages   cm – (Cambridge studies in English legal history)
Based on author's thesis (doctoral – Harvard University), 2007.
Includes bibliographical references and index.
ISBN 978-1-107-06929-9 (hardback)
1. Coke, Edward, Sir, 1552–1634–Influence.   2. Law reform–England–History–16th century.   3. Law reform–England–History–17th century.   4. Great Britain–Politics and government–1558–1603   5. Great Britain–Politics and government–1603–1625   I. Title.
KD621.C64S65 2014
340′.3094209031–dc23
2014032034

ISBN 978-1-107-06929-9 Hardback

CONTENTS

ACKNOWLEDGEMENTS

This book has been long in the writing and could not have been finished without the guidance and support of many others. Clifford Ando and Richard Hoffman inspired me as an undergraduate with their examples of iconoclastic scholarship. In graduate school Thomas Bisson and Michael McCormick introduced me to the technical demands of meticulous scholarship. My dissertation committee was always patient and forthright: Mark Kishlansky guided me through the pitfalls of writing, research and early career angst; David Armitage was unfailingly kind; and Charlie Donahue introduced me to the intricacies of English law. Friends and colleagues along the way have read parts of the work or shared their own, and I am indebted to Simon Healey for taking a young graduate student under his wing, Ian Williams for sharing his deep knowledge with me, Allen Boyer, Nicholas Popper, Chris Brooks, Robert Palmer, Peter Lake, Amy Milne-Smith, Darryl Dee and John Laband. Paul Halliday has been a friend and a mentor to whom I am also deeply grateful. Finola O'Sullivan, my publisher, has been encouraging throughout and patient with my delays.

The librarians and archivists of the British Library (especially Carlos and James), The National Archives, the Honourable Society of the Inner Temple, the Huntington Library, the Folger Shakespeare Library, the Yale Law School Library, the Georgetown Law Library and the many libraries at Harvard University were generous with their time and patient with my many requests. I gratefully acknowledge the support provided by the Social Science and Humanities Research Council of Canada and Harvard University, who funded stages of this work. The journal *Historical Research* kindly allowed parts of my article, 'Remembering Usurpation: the Common Lawyers, Reformation Narratives and the Prerogative, 1578–1616', 86:234 (2013), to be reprinted in Chapters 4 and 8. Translations from Coke's notebooks and other sources throughout the book are my own unless otherwise indicated.

Louis Knafla and J. H. Baker read the entire manuscript. To them I am not only deeply indebted for their advice and their many corrections, but for taking the time to guide a newcomer to their field who might not otherwise have ever completed this book.

Lastly, Logan Walsh and Yvonne Sheppard patiently endured the many years it took to research and compile the manuscript, and offered encouragement at those moments when enthusiasm flagged.

ABBREVIATIONS

APC	*Acts of the Privy Council of England,* ed. J. R. Dasent (London, 1890–1907; repr. 1974), 32 vols.
BL	The British Library, London
Bodl.	The Bodleian Library, Oxford
Bracton	Henry de Bracton, *On the Laws and Customs of England*, ed. Samuel Thorne (New Haven, CT, 1968)
Bro. *Abr.*	Robert Brooke, *La Graunde Abridgement* (London, 1573), STC 3827
C33	Chancery Entry Books of Decrees and Orders, The Public Record Office at The National Archives, Kew, UK
CJ	*Journal of the House of Commons*, vol. I, 1547–1628 (London, 1802)
Co. *Inst.*	Edward Coke, *The Institutes of the Laws of England* (London, 1817; repr. 2008), vols. II–IV
Co. *Litt.*	Edward Coke, *The First Part of the Institutes of the Laws of England*, ed. Francis Hargrave and Charles Butler (London, 1823)
Co. *Rep.*	Edward Coke, *The Reports of Sir Edward Coke*, ed. John Thomas and John Fraser (London, 1826; repr. 2005), 13 vols.
CSPD	*Calendar of State Papers, Domestic. Elizabeth, James I*, ed. M. A. E. Green *et al.* (London, 1852–72; repr. 1967), 12 vols.
CUL	Cambridge University Library, Cambridge
DNB	*The Oxford Dictionary of National Biography*, online edition
ER	*The English Reports*, ed. A. Wood Renton *et al.* (London, 1900–32), 178 vols.
HEL	William Holdsworth, *A History of English Law* (1903–36; repr. 1982)
HLS	Harvard Law School Library, Cambridge, MA
HMC	Historical Manuscripts Commission, London. Reports and Papers
Holkham	Manuscripts of the Earl of Leicester, Holkham Hall, Norfolk
IELH	John Baker, *An Introduction to English Legal History*, 4th edn (London, 2002)
IT	The Inner Temple, London
LJ	*Journal of the House of Lords* (London, 1767–1832)
LRO	The Record Office for Leicestershire, Leicester and Rutland, Wigston, Leicestershire
NRO	Norfolk Record Office, Norwich, UK

OHLE	*The Oxford History of the Laws of England*, ed. J. H. Baker (2003–), 6 vols.
PP 1610	*Proceedings in Parliament 1610*, ed. Elizabeth Read Foster (New Haven, CT, 1966)
PRO	The Public Record Office at The National Archives, Kew, UK
SP	State Papers, Domestic, Elizabeth and James I, The Public Record Office at The National Archives, Kew, UK
SR	*The Statutes of the Realm*, ed. A. Luders *et al.* (London, 1810–22), 9 vols.
ST	*Cobbett's Complete Collection of State Trials*, ed. W. Cobbett and T. B. Howell (London, 1809–28), 34 vols.
STC	*A Short-Title Catalogue of Books Printed in England, Scotland & Ireland and of English Books Printed Abroad 1475–1640*, ed. A. W. Pollard and C. R. Redgrave (1926)
UCL	University College London, London
YB	The Year Books

Introduction

'Certainty is the mother of quietness and repose', Sir Edward Coke wrote in the first volume of his *Institutes*. Over a century later, Lord Mansfield made a similar observation, explaining that 'the great object in every branch of the law ... is certainty'.[1] Sharing this preoccupation, the two chief justices worked to reform English law during periods of discontinuity. But the imperatives for reform under Coke were different from those that drove Mansfield: they did not emerge from the decrepitude of the law or its need to adapt to new conditions. Instead, Coke worked within a dynamic and chaotic system. The sixteenth-century fluorescence of English law had driven its transformation, and the confessional differences of the Reformation brought new challenges to the practice of the law.[2] This book evaluates the influence of these contexts of legal and religious change on Coke's understanding of the law from 1578 to 1616. His ambition to reform the law explains why Coke simultaneously confronted abuses in royal administration even as he believed he was acting to defend the authority of the monarchy. This book examines this paradox, and in doing so, suggests how otherwise royalist Englishmen reached conclusions that slowly led them into opposition.

Coke remains an enigmatic figure despite the efforts of biographers.[3] Writers have tended to disparage the personality of 'that arrogant genius',

[1] *Milles* v. *Fletcher* (1779), 1 Douglas 234, 99 ER 152. James Oldham, *English Common Law in the Age of Mansfield* (Chapel Hill, NC, 2004), p. 124.
[2] T. G. Barnes, 'Due Process and Slow Process in the Late Elizabethan–Early Stuart Star Chamber', *American Journal of Legal History*, 6 (1962), 221–49; 315–46, at 345.
[3] The biographies of Coke include, Cuthbert Johnson, *The Life of Sir Edward Coke* (London, 1837); C. W. James, *Chief Justice Coke and his Family and Descendants at Holkham* (London, 1929); Hastings Lyon and Herman Block, *Edward Coke, Oracle of the Law* (Boston, 1929); R. G. Usher, 'Sir Edward Coke', *St Louis Law Review*, 15 (1930), 325–52; William Holdsworth, 'Sir Edward Coke', *Cambridge Law Journal*, 5:3 (1935), 332–46; E. A. Hahn, *Edward Coke* (Cleveland, OH, 1950); S. E. Stumpf, 'Sir Edward Coke: Advocate of the Supremacy of Law', *Vanderbilt Studies in the Humanities*, 1 (1951), 34–49; C. S. D. Bowen, *The Lion and the Throne: The Life and Times of Sir Edward Coke, 1552–1634* (Cleveland, OH, 1957); Stephen White, *Sir Edward Coke and 'The Grievances of the*

while interpreting his career as a luminous example of principle succeed-ing over self-interest as Coke moved to oppose royal policies with increas-ing vigour.[4] The legal thought of this 'oracle of the common law' or 'Father of the Law' was part of a set-piece battle between constitutionalists and absolutists that defined the political life of the decades leading up to the 1640s.[5] But those who have studied the technical aspects of his litigation and judicial conduct have differed on specifics. For instance, Charles Gray in a thorough study has described Coke's use of the writ of prohibition against other jurisdictions as 'moderate', a word also used by W. J. Jones to describe the chief justice's opposition to injunctions.[6] Paul Halliday, who has scrutinized Coke's granting of habeas corpus, notes that even dur-ing the dispute over the chancellor's injunction, 'we can see quite clearly

Commonwealth', *1621–1628* (Chapel Hill, NC, 1979); John Hostettler, *Sir Edward Coke: A Force for Freedom* (Chichester, 1997) and most recently Allen Boyer, *Sir Edward Coke and the Elizabethan Age* (Stanford, CA, 2003). A survey of the historiography can be found in White, *Sir Edward Coke*, pp. 14–18.

[4] Barnes, 'Due Process and Slow Process', 318; Boyer, *Sir Edward Coke*, p. 190.

[5] Holdsworth, 'Sir Edward Coke', 333–4; William Holdsworth, 'The Influence of Coke on the Development of English Law', in *Essays in Legal History*, ed. Paul Vinogradoff (London, 1913), pp. 297–311, at pp. 299–300; R. G. Usher, 'Sir Edward Coke', 330–1; Bowen, *Lion and the Throne*, pp. 293–4; Louis Knafla, *Law and Politics in Jacobean England: The Tracts of Lord Chancellor Ellesmere* (Cambridge, 2008), pp. 146–7; James Hart, *The Rule of Law 1603–1660* (Harlow, 2003); J. P. Sommerville, *Royalists and Patriots: Politics and Ideology in England 1603–1640* (Harlow, 1986), pp. 107–75; Glenn Burgess, *The Politics of the Ancient Constitution: An Introduction to English Political Thought, 1603–1642* (Basingstoke, 1992); Alan Cromartie, 'The Rule of Law', in *Revolution and Restoration: England in the 1650s*, ed. J. S. Morrill (London, 1992), pp. 55–69; Alan Cromartie, 'The Constitutionalist Revolution: The Transformation of Political Culture in Early Stuart England', *Past and Present*, 163 (1999), 76–120; Paul Raffield, 'Contract, Classicism, and the Common-Weal: Coke's Reports and the Foundations of the Modern English Constitution', *Law and Literature*, 17:1 (2005), 72–9; Alan Cromartie, *The Constitutionalist Revolution: An Essay on the History of England, 1450–1642* (New York, 2006). For the description of Coke as the 'oracle of the common law', see Thomas Fuller, *The Worthies of England* (London, 1662) Wing F2440, p. 251; William Prynne, *Brief Animadversions on, Amendments of, and Additional Explanatory Records to, The Fourth Part of the Institutes of the Lawes of England* (London, 1669), Wing P3905, p. 3; and 'Father', Edward Bulstrode, *The Reports* (London, 1657), Wing 174, 'Epistle Dedicatory'. Similar comparisons are found in James Spedding (ed.), *Letters and Life of Francis Bacon* (London, 1869; repr. 1989), vol. V, p. 121; John Lord Campbell, *The Lives of the Chief Justices of England: From the Norman Conquest to the Death of Lord Mansfield* (London, 1849), vol. I, p. 239.

[6] Charles Gray, *The Writ of Prohibition: Jurisdiction in Early Modern English Law* (Chicago, IL, 1994), vol. I, pp. 67, 80; vol. II, pp. 207, 399; W. J. Jones, *The Elizabethan Court of Chancery* (Oxford, 1967), p. 463.

in his actions ... the respect Coke maintained for the chancellor's juris-diction'.[7] Although Pocock described him 'as nearly insular as a human being could be', evidence from his library suggests that he was interested in and collected continental sources.[8] Coke participated not in a common law culture notable for its shared 'mentality', but rather for its culture of debate and disagreement.[9] Recent work has also emphasized the serious-ness of Coke's historical analysis rather than his credulity.[10] Nor were his decisions sometimes meant as modern historians have read them, and arguments have been made against seeing an expansive constitutional-ism in *Bonham's Case* (1610).[11] Careful attention to the source and context of dicta attributed to Coke is also in order, as Esther Cope demonstrated in her analysis of proclamations.[12] The posthumous editing and publish-ing during a time of civil war of the later volumes of the *Reports,* where

---

[7] Paul Halliday, *Habeas Corpus: From England to Empire* (Cambridge, MA, 2010), p. 91. Halliday notes that, of twenty instances of habeas corpus to the Chancery from 1613 to 1616, only one resulted in a discharge, while seventeen were remanded.

[8] Coke, for example, relied on Barthélemy de Chasseneux to support claims about the heir's property in funeral monuments. J. H. Baker, 'Funeral Monuments and the Heir', in *The Common Law Tradition: Lawyers, Books and the Law* (Hambledon, 2000), pp. 349–64, at p. 357. His ownership of continental books is listed in W. O. Hassall, *A Catalogue of the Library of Sir Edward* Coke (New Haven, CT, 1950), pp. 38–41, 44–5, 53–7. Cf. J. G. A. Pocock, *The Ancient Constitution and the Feudal Law: A Study of English Historical Thought in the 17th Century* (Cambridge, 1987), p. 56. The 'insularity' of the common law has been debated and rejected. D. R. Kelley, 'History, English Law and the Renaissance', *Past and Present*, 65 (1974), 24–51; Christopher Brooks, Kevin Sharpe and D. R. Kelley, 'Debate: History, English Law and the Renaissance with Rejoinder by D. R. Kelley', *Past and Present*, 72 (1976), 133–46; Sommerville, *Royalists and Patriots*, p. 89; H. S. Pawlisch, 'Sir John Davies, the Ancient Constitution and Civil Law', *Historical Journal*, 23 (1980), 689–702; Linda Levy Peck, 'Kingship, Counsel and Law in Early Stuart England', in J. G. A. Pocock (ed.), *The Varieties of British Political Thought, 1500–1800* (Cambridge, 1993), pp. 91–2.

[9] J. W. Tubbs, *The Common Law Mind: Medieval and Early Modern Conceptions* (Baltimore, MD, 2000), pp. 194–5.

[10] George Garnett, '"The ould fields": Law and History in the Prefaces to Sir Edward Coke's Reports', *The Journal of Legal History*, 34:3 (2013), 245–84, esp. 264.

[11] Ian Williams, 'Dr Bonham's Case and "Void" Statutes', *Journal of Legal History*, 27:2 (2006), 111–28. A similar analysis has also been applied to other 'constitutional' cases of the period; Jacob Corré, 'The Argument, Decision, and Reports of *Darcy v. Allen*', *Emory Law Journal*, 45 (1996), 1,261–327.

[12] Esther Cope, 'Sir Edward Coke and Proclamations, 1610', *American Journal of Legal History*, 15:3 (1971), 215–21, at 216; S. E. Thorne, 'Introduction', in *A discourse upon the exposicion and understanding of statutes* (San Marino, 1942), pp. 85–92, and 'Dr. Bonham's Case', in *Essays in English Legal History* (London, 1985), pp. 269–78; Corré, 'The Argument, Decision, and Reports of *Darcy v. Allen*'.

some of his most 'constitutionalist' statements are made, also suggest caution. David Jenkins, the royalist judge who may well have known Coke, later said the following about these texts:

> After his death, in times turbulent and calamitous to Britain, some of his books were published, in which there are a few passages which ought to be expunged, by which he seems to bridle the sovereign, and give the reins to the people: which few passages (if they are his) that great man ... did not insert with an ill design; and doubtless were he to rise from the dead, he would take care to expunge them.[13]

Charles Gray observed that Coke sought to maintain both the prerogative and the liberty of the subject, and Janelle Greenberg has also noticed this 'tension'.[14] Contemporaries also urged that Coke desired to establish a balance between the prerogative and the rights of the subject. Timothy Tourneur, an admirer of the chief justice, suggested that Coke sought equilibrium: 'because the Chancellor cried up the prerogative and beat down the lawe and Coke's labor was to keep the balance of both even'.[15] Whatever ideological differences he may have held, only a few months after his dismissal in 1616 Coke was with the king at Newmarket and 'was so well and graciously used that he is as jocund and joviall as ever he was'.[16] Stephen White, in his study of the primary sources for Coke's later parliamentary career, conceded that he did not move into 'opposition' until the 1620s and that he was more concerned with 'remedying certain legal abuses than on effecting significant constitutional changes'.[17] The endorsement by the judges (usually attributed to self-interest) of Ship Money and the imprisonment of the 'five knights' hint that the common law relationship to the prerogative was more complex and perhaps conservative than the historiography has allowed.[18]

---

[13] David Jenkins, *Eight Centuries of Reports*, trans. Theodore Barlow (London, 1885), p. xvii.

[14] Charles Gray, 'Reason, Authority, and Imagination: The Jurisprudence of Sir Edward Coke', in Perez Zagorin (ed.), *Culture and Politics from Puritanism to the Enlightenment* (Berkeley, CA, 1980), pp. 25–66, at p. 45; Janelle Greenberg, *The Radical Face of the Ancient Constitution: St Edward's 'Laws' in Early Modern Political Thought* (Cambridge, 2001), p. 141.

[15] BL Additional MS 35957, f. 63r.

[16] John Chamberlain, *The Letters of John Chamberlain*, ed. Norman McClure (Philadelphia, PA, 1939), vol. II, p. 45, though compare Coke's claim about the uncertainty of the king's favour at p. 64.

[17] White, *Sir Edward Coke*, pp. 22–3, 45, 76.

[18] The possibility was noticed by Cromartie, *Constitutionalist Revolution*, p. 212.

This book provides an alternative model to the predominant analysis of English political history as an ongoing friction between liberty and royal power, between the claims of the subjects for their rights and the demands of monarchs to enlarge their prerogatives.[19] Parliamentarians self-consciously adopted this classical model to justify their grievances.[20] The drawing of its tension in the historiography has assumed almost as many forms as explanations for the mid-century civil wars and the Glorious Revolution.[21] While the monarch, especially Charles I, has typically served as the antagonist, the common lawyers as a professional group are considered important agents of the move to secure rights and freedoms.[22] Drawing on the intellectual resources of the common law, it is claimed, they helped to develop a language of constitutional rights to contest royal policies such as arbitrary detention and taxation without parliamentary consent. Their commitment to 'ancient constitutionalism', and the claim that their law emerged from customary roots in time immemorial, established the common law's independence from the king. The eventual

---

[19] For a review of the historiographical approaches in Stuart studies, see R. C. Richardson, *The Debate on the English Revolution* (Manchester, 1998); T. K. Rabb, 'Revisionism Revised: Two Perspectives on Early Stuart Parliamentary History', *Past and Present*, 92 (1981), 55–78; Richard Cust and Ann Hughes, 'Introduction: After Revisionism', in Richard Cust and Ann Hughes (eds.), *Conflict in Early Stuart England* (New York, 1989), pp. 1–46; Peter Lake, Thomas Cogswell and Richard Cust, 'Revisionism and its Legacies', in *Politics, Religion and Popularity in Early Stuart Britain: Essays in Honour of Conrad Russell* (Cambridge, 2002), pp. 1–17.

[20] *PP 1610*, vol. II, pp. 98, 191 drawing on Tacitus, *Agricola*, 3.2; John Rushworth, *Historical Collections* (London, 1721), vol. VIII, p. 662; Edward Hyde, *The History of the Rebellion and Civil Wars in England Begun in the Year 1641*, ed. W. Dunn Macray (Oxford, 1992), vol. I, p. 96; Charles McIlwain, *The High Court of Parliament and Its Supremacy* (New Haven, CT, 1934), pp. 76–7, 82–6, 140; David Hume, *History of England* (Boston, MA, 1892), vol. IV, p. 469; Henry Hallam, *The Constitutional History of England* (New York, 1978), vol. I, pp. 1–2, 46. S. R. Gardiner, *The History of England* (New York, 1901), vol. III, p. 36.

[21] David L. Smith, 'Politics in Early Stuart Britain, 1603–1640', in Barry Coward (ed.), *A Companion to Stuart Britain* (Oxford, 2003), pp. 233–52, at pp. 233–4; R. C. Richardson, *The Debate on the English Revolution Revisited* (London, 1988), p. 50; Howard Tomlinson, 'The Causes of War: a Historiographical Survey', in Howard Tomlinson (ed.), *Before the English Civil War: Essay on Early Stuart Politics and Government* (London, 1983), p. 16; J. S. Morrill, 'The Religious Context of the English Civil War', *Transactions of the Royal Historical Society*, 5th series, 34 (1984), 155–78, at 157. Recent writers have insisted on the integration of the religious and political explanations. D. Alan Orr, 'Sovereignty, Supremacy, and the Origins of the English Civil War', *History*, 87 (2002), 474–90, at 484, and Ethan Shagan, 'The English Inquisition: Constitutional Conflict and Ecclesiastical Law in the 1590s', *Historical Journal*, 47:3 (2004), 541–65, at 542.

[22] Though see Mark Kishlansky's recent attempt at rehabilitation, 'Charles I: A Case of Mistaken Identity', *Past and Present*, 189 (2005), 41–80.

result, placing the king firmly under the law, was confirmed by the trial and conviction of Charles Stuart for treason.

While acknowledging that Coke and other judges insisted on the importance of the liberties of the subject and the security of property, the book's major argument is otherwise contrarian. In 1614 when he addressed the new serjeants, Coke described the 'three adversaries' of the common law: 'wresters and perverters of the lawe', 'Romanists' and 'flatterers'. These enemies undermined the law itself: Wolsey, for example, had sought to establish the primacy of the civil law.[23] Coke's jurisprudence evolved as a means of reform to remedy or repulse these threats to the common law. The danger came less from the monarch above than from among Coke's fellow subjects below, who might plot the overthrow of the government or pervert the law and its process.[24] His complaint was timely. Coke echoed the concerns of many of his contemporaries about the litigiousness of their society, and the work of Christopher Brooks has revealed the outlines of the boom in litigation through which they lived. This growth followed a period of 'regeneration' of the common law and an expansion in the legal system generally.[25] These transformations left lawyers such as Coke to ponder the implications of the preceding decades of substantive and jurisdictional change.

Coke articulated the problems created by the expansion of English law using the language of uncertainty and corruption. The proliferation of legal resources, such as statutes, courts and law officers, often seemed to lack coordination and led to jurisdictional confusion, vexatious litigation, corruption among officers, uncertain law and the misuse of legal power by design or ignorance. Bayless Manning has referred to this problem in the

---

[23] IT Petyt MS 538/51, f. 136r.

[24] The importance of reform as a key dynamic in early Stuart history has drawn renewed attention; see Jonathan Scott, *England's Troubles: Seventeenth-Century English Political Instability in European Context* (Cambridge, 2000), pp. 114–35. An earlier generation explicitly rejected Coke's contribution to reform, White, *Sir Edward Coke*, p. 46n.1, though Donald Veall suggested that many of the mid-century reformers were influenced by Coke, in *The Popular Movement for Law Reform, 1640–1660* (Oxford, 1970), p. 99.

[25] J. H. Baker, *The Reports of Sir John Spelman* (London, 1978), vol. II, p. 23 *et passim*; also Baker, *OHLE*, vol. VI, pp. 3–52. See also Samuel Thorne, 'Tudor Social Transformation and Legal Change', in *Essays in English Legal History* (London, 1985) pp. 197–210, S. F. C. Milsom, *Historical Foundations of the Common Law*, 2nd edn (London, 1981), pp. 60–81. The rise in litigation is variously estimated to have been at least a sixfold increase in litigation in all the central courts. Christopher Brooks, *Pettyfoggers and Vipers of the Commonwealth* (Cambridge, 1986), pp. 48–74, and the revision of Robert Palmer, 'Litigiousness in Early Modern England and Wales', http://aalt.law.uh.edu/Litigiousness/ Litigiousness.html (2014); Richard Helmholz, *OHLE*, vol. I, pp. 283–6.

present-day USA as 'hyperlexis'.[26] In Coke's time these behaviours reflected poorly on the common law, which was criticized as partial, uncertain or open to manipulation. Stephen White has described Coke's parliamentary efforts in the 1620s to remedy some of these grievances, especially his concern that monopolists and patentees used their legal authority to pursue predatory schemes. This book extends White's survey backwards and argues that though much has been written about Tudor despots and absolutist Stuarts, Coke was similarly preoccupied with the abuse of legal power by private individuals. Their misconduct and its everyday consequences affected confidence in the law as an impartial, public benefit.[27] This confidence involved more than a trust reposed in the integrity of the judge and the work of the law officer.[28] As Stephen White has written, people acquired confidence through the knowledge of the actual working of the law, the behaviour of legal officers, and through the enforcement and finality of judicial decisions.[29] Crucially, such confidence was constantly tested by outcomes and the perception of their fairness.

From the vantage of Coke and others at the apex of the legal system at the end of the sixteenth century, this confidence was under threat. Problems of loyalty and allegiance raised by the Elizabethan Reformation undermined obedience to the law. The confessional context shaped Coke's jurisprudence in crucial ways, most notably by placing into relief his commitment to monarchy, as the Tudor–Stuart state faced existential challenges from war, Catholic conspirators and even Protestant nonconformists. In these years Coke helped to continue the religious reform of the Tudor state, writing to uphold the legality of its break from Rome, while developing a draconian treason law to defend the government. Along with other common lawyers, Coke's actions were informed by their interpretations of the history of the Reformation, in which the common

---

[26] Bayless Manning, 'Hyperlexis, Our National Disease', *Northwestern University Law Review*, 71:6 (1977), 767–82. The term has also been used by Steve Hindle in *The State and Social Change in Early Modern England, c. 1550–1640* (Houndmills, 2000), p. 89. See also Cromartie, *Constitutionalist Revolution*, p. 180. Previous accounts have tended to treat the misuse of legal power as an anomaly either reflecting local rivalries or addressed by parliamentary action. Michael Braddick, *State Formation in Early Modern England* (Cambridge, 2000), pp. 88–9.

[27] White, *Sir Edward Coke*, pp. 22, 48n.12, 56–8.

[28] For a recent restatement of the importance of trust to the relationship between king and subject, see Howard Nenner, 'Loyalty and the Law: The Meaning of Trust and the Right of Resistance in Seventeenth-Century England', *Journal of British Studies*, 48 (2009), 859–70.

[29] White, *Sir Edward Coke*, p. 22.

law had protected the monarch from usurpations by the clergy and others long before the break with Rome. The context of confessional difference and treason prosecutions produced some of Coke's most strident claims for the authority of the monarch.

This commitment to royal power produced its own logic that increasingly compelled Coke to pursue his convictions and oppose the Crown's policies, if only to his own mind, to protect the monarch. Coke's strong claims for royal authority rested on an assumption of the queen's moral obligation to preserve and give justice to her subjects. As W. H. Greenleaf and James Daly have described the paradigm, her power was derived from God, distributed to the judicial and administrative apparatus, and then delegated to others.[30] The common law, Coke insisted, performed the justice-giving duty of the prince, and safeguarded the monarch and their moral obligations from those who misused the royal authority delegated to them. Coke justified his superintendence of other courts and the restraint of those who made use of royal authority not by asserting their independence from royal authority. Instead, Coke insisted that the King's Bench was the 'king's court', in which the monarch was presumed to be present, and the common law the most reliable defender of the king and his obligations. Paul Halliday has recently described this strategy as 'prerogative capture'.[31] This book examines Coke's arguments, demonstrating that he accepted that some prerogatives were beyond control and that the common law strengthened royal authority through its supervision of the ordinary prerogative. These ideas allowed common lawyers to proceed to limit the exercise of legal power by the monarch's subjects, while maintaining a genuine commitment to royal power.

These claims for the supremacy of the monarch were unstable in a chaotic system that demanded the moral exercise of power.[32] Judges, officials,

---

[30] Greenleaf did not believe that Coke adhered to these ideas and numbered him instead among the constitutionalists. W. H. Greenleaf, *Order, Empiricism and Politics: Two Traditions of English Political Thought 1500–1700* (Oxford, 1964), pp. 184–5; James Daly, 'Cosmic Harmony and Political Thinking in Early Stuart England', *Transactions of the American Philosophical Society*, 69:7 (1979), 1–41, at 22–31. Broader considerations of the political thought of the period include the following: Glenn Burgess, 'The Divine Right of Kings Reconsidered', *English Historical Review*, 107 (1992), pp. 837–61; Johann P. Sommerville, 'James I and the Divine Right of Kings: English Politics and Continental Theory', in Linda Levy Peck (ed.), *The Mental World of the Jacobean Court* (Cambridge, 1991), pp. 55–70; Sommerville, *Royalists and Patriots*, pp. 9–54.

[31] Halliday, *Habeas Corpus*, pp. 11–28, 64–95. R. W. K. Hinton suggested that the common law enhanced the king's authority, in 'English Constitutional Doctrines from the Fifteenth Century to the Seventeenth', *English Historical Review*, 75:296 (1960), 422–3.

[32] Daly, 'Cosmic Harmony', 10–11, 23–5.

commissioners and others were deputized to fulfil the sovereign's justice-giving role. But an assertion of the moral character of this legal power could combine in incompatible ways with the messy and idiosyncratic exercise of that power by those who administered and used the law. Perceptions of the corrupt or improper use of legal authority eroded confidence in the legal system and cast discredit onto the prince in whose name the actions were authorized and who, by the immunizing logic of the system, 'could do no wrong'.[33] This logic dictated that authority, coloured with the morality of the prince's duty to preserve and protect his subjects, must not be used oppressively.[34] The combination of private individuals delegated with royal power – what A. B. White termed 'self-government at the king's command' – created numerous junctions where self-interest and the public good competed, or were imagined to compete, and incentivized corruption.[35] Misuse of the law not only undermined faith in the legal regime, but also disrupted the coherency and integrity of a legal system that represented the moral exercise of the monarch's power.[36]

Instead, a commitment to the prince's central place in the legal system required an implicit assumption that the monarch would remedy problems arising from the misuse of the law. Where systemic legal wrongs were perceived to pass without reform the ruler's moral obligations resulted in weakness, rather than strength, as responsibility crept up the chain of power to associate with him or her. Coke urged that the common law, as the king's principal justice-giving forum, would ultimately oversee the appropriateness of the exercise of legal power and protect the sovereign from its misuse. Only the monarch, assisted in their judicial capacity in the House of Lords, would review its work.[37] Coke had seen at first hand, as an attorney-general and as a lawyer at the bar, the corrupt, mistaken or

---

[33] Sommerville, *Royalists and Patriots*, pp. 43–6; Janelle Greenberg, 'Our Grand Maxim of State, "The King Can Do No Wrong" ', *History of Political Thought*, 12:2 (1991), 209–28, at 211–12.

[34] For example, John Pym couched his accusation against Strafford in this language; John Rushworth, *Historical Collections*, vol. VIII, p. 104.

[35] Braddick, *State Formation*, pp. 35, 39.

[36] Linda Levy Peck makes this connection in a different context in 'Corruption in the Court of James I: The Undermining of Legitimacy', in B. C. Malament (ed.), *After the Reformation: Essays in Honor of J.H. Hexter* (Manchester, 1980), pp. 75–93; cf. Joel Hurstfield, 'Political Corruption in Modern England: The Historian's Problem', *History*, 52 (1967), 16–34.

[37] *Prohibitions Del Roy*, 12 Co. Rep. 63, 77 ER 1342. James Hart, *Justice Upon Petition: The House of Lords and the Reformation of Justice 1621–1675* (London, 1991); Allen Horstman, 'A New *Curia Regis*: The Judicature of the House of Lords in the 1620s', *Historical Journal*, 25:2 (1982), 411–22.

vexatious use of that power. But Coke's imagining of the law required that the king share a similar vision of the operation of legal power, a perspective lacking in James I. The king not only failed to grasp Coke's explanation of the role of the common law, but he held, alongside many of his subjects, concerns about its proceedings. Coke's aggressive personality exacerbated James's lack of confidence that the common law could remedy the abuses prevalent in the legal system, and led to the chief justice's undoing. This episode among many revealed that perspective was one of the most important brakes on reform. To Coke common law interference was a means to remedy abuse and uncertainty in the legal system, while to others the common law was itself a cause of insecurity.

These arguments contrast both with the general interpretation of Coke's thought and with the history of the common law developed since J. G. A. Pocock's study of English feudalism. His focus on ancient constitutionalism has prompted vigorous debate, but few have questioned the idea's linkage with opposition to the royal prerogative among common lawyers. Of key importance to this claim is the assumption that Coke and others insisted on the common law's immemoriality as a means to assert the law's autonomy and to bridle the king under the rule of law.[38] This assumption, Pocock claimed, was a hallmark of the common law 'mind', a mentality or a shared set of assumptions among common lawyers that was cultivated by their training in the Inns of Court and their professional practice.[39]

This narrative continues to inform studies on the emergence of the early modern English law-state. Recent writers have built on Pocock's analysis through contrasting characterizations of early Stuart political culture.[40] The polarity created by absolutists and constitutionalists is still the preferred explanation for political conflict under the Stuarts, reflected in the turbulence of an adversarial political culture and fears of an expansion of royal power. Following Pocock these accounts identify the common law as one of the principal restraints on the monarch's freedom of action. Lawyers such as Coke drew on the law's intellectual resources,

---

[38] Pocock, *Ancient Constitution*, pp. 46, 51. Now forcefully stated by John Phillip Reid, *The Ancient Constitution and the Origins of Anglo-American Liberty* (Dekalb, 2005), pp. 41–3.

[39] Examined in Paul Raffield, *Images and Cultures of Law in Early Modern England: Justice and Political Power, 1558–1660* (Cambridge, 2004).

[40] Burgess, *Ancient Constitution*, pp. 213–15; Sommerville, *Royalists and Patriots*, pp. 224–65; Cromartie, *Constitutionalist Revolution*, p. 237. Though neither paradigm may be sufficient; see Peck, 'Kingship, Counsel and Law', p. 83.

especially the writings of Sir John Fortescue, to rebut absolutist claims.[41] Alan Cromartie has offered a particularly expansive interpretation of common law thought, tracing the history of those developments that led to claims for a 'law [that] provided for all eventualities', and the judges' insistence that they were competent to answer any number of questions, including those over royal policies.[42] At the root of this 'constitutionalist revolution' was the use of positive law by the English Crown to pursue its policy goals, but which encouraged legalistic interpretations of the government's actions.[43] The common lawyers developed concepts and ideas that were then used to articulate and justify resistance in the 1620s, while their 'aggression' strengthened royalism among their opponents.[44] Coke has long been identified as a leading advocate for this constitutionalist view. While admitting that the 'king had no human superior', Coke nonetheless believed that a subject was bound only to follow the law, not an 'extra-legal command' of the king, and 'a conviction that every type of power should benefit from judicial supervision' motivated him.[45] If it has largely been clear where Coke stood, it is less clear where he was relative to others, and discussion has continued over whether he was 'typical' of common law thought or 'an eccentric, and sometimes a confused, thinker'.[46]

These debates reveal the continuing influence of Pocock's ideas even as subsequent work has modified or refuted several aspects of his interpretation. No longer are the common lawyers, even Coke, 'insular', but instead knowledge of the civil law and European intellectual debates informed their thinking.[47] Whereas Pocock focused on custom as the key characteristic of the common law, subsequent writers have emphasized claims

---

[41] Sommerville, *Royalists and Patriots*, pp. 50–1, 82–8, 138.

[42] Cromartie, 'The Rule of Law'; 'The Constitutionalist Revolution', 76–120; *Constitutionalist Revolution*. A similar argument is found in Holdsworth, 'Sir Edward Coke', at 344–5.

[43] Cromartie, *Constitutionalist Revolution*, pp. 3, 226–7. W. H. Dunham, 'Regal Power and the Rule of Law: A Tudor Paradox', *Journal of British Studies*, 3:2 (1964), 24–56.

[44] Cromartie, *Constitutionalist Revolution*, pp. 226–7, 3, 117.

[45] Sommerville, *Royalists and Patriots*, p. 102; Cromartie, *Constitutionalist Revolution*, p. 211.

[46] Burgess, *Ancient Constitution*, p. 21; J. W. Tubbs, '"Custom, Time and Reason", Early Seventeenth-Century Conceptions of the Common Law', *History of Political Thought*, 19:3 (1998), 363–406, at 386, 404; Alan Cromartie, 'The Idea of Common Law as Custom', in Amanda Perreau-Saussine and James Murphy (eds.), *The Nature of Customary Law* (Cambridge, 2009), pp. 203–27, at p. 219.

[47] Christopher Brooks, *Law, Politics and Society in Early Modern England* (Cambridge, 2010), p. 82.

for the law's rationality.[48] The common law mind is still convenient short-hand for the general framework of ideas that suffused the education and culture of the Inns of Court, but its most careful study has concluded that a 'dominant common law mind' did not exist.[49] J. P. Sommerville's assessment of the political thought of the period depicts a complex intellectual culture where even ancient constitutionalism had only a limited body of adherents, and common lawyers might be found who 'displayed a clear bias towards absolutism'.[50] Glenn Burgess has even conceded that early in his career Coke believed that 'certain royal prerogatives' had 'immunity from interference by any human authority at all'.[51]

While inconsistency has been used to explain discrepancies in Coke's career, some have argued that the chief justice simply changed his views over time.[52] A fixation or 'reverence' for an immemorial common law and the overreaching policies of Charles I shifted his attitude towards royal power.[53] Under the rising sun of absolutism Coke's simple assumptions about the purity and authority of the common law hardened into resistance. Increasingly, however, the assumption that the common lawyers as a group were naturally hostile to the royal prerogative has come under question, a possibility that Pocock himself acknowledged when he wrote that there was a 'common-law case for the crown as well as against it'.[54] Christopher Brooks has noticed how common lawyers were able strategically to align themselves with the royal prerogative when they opposed the clerical courts.[55] Paul Halliday has found the same tactic used in habeas corpus, suggesting that the common lawyers could think of themselves as aiding or protecting the prerogative. In fact, Brooks has argued that rather than claiming a decisive constitutional role in the 1620s and 1630s, the conduct of the judges led to their 'political marginalization' for the rest of the century. Instead of Pocock's image of a man determined to attack, Brooks presents Coke as being on the defensive,

---

[48] Tubbs, *The Common Law Mind*, pp. 141–72.

[49] Tubbs, *The Common Law Mind*, p. 194; Brooks, *Law, Politics and Society*, p. 82.

[50] Sommerville, *Royalists and Patriots*, p. 103.

[51] Glenn Burgess, *Absolute Monarchy and the Stuart Constitution* (New Haven, CT, 1996), pp. 200, 204.

[52] Tubbs 'Custom, Time and Reason', 388.

[53] Glenn Burgess, *Absolute Monarchy*, 194, 198, 200–1.

[54] Pocock, *Ancient Constitution*, p. 55; Margaret Judson, *Crisis of the Constitution: An Essay in Constitutional and Political Thought in England, 1603–1645* (New Brunswick, NJ, 1988), p. 13.

[55] Brooks, *Law, Politics and Society*, pp. 98–102.

seeking to answer unpleasant criticisms of the common law by the clergy and others. In fact, common law motivations appear less principled and more tied up with the everyday realities of litigation and judicial politics. While the judges may have been 'naturally inclined' towards 'jurisdictional imperialism', a base desire for fees combined with puritan influence and claims of omni-competence to fuel their efforts against other courts.[56]

This book argues that Coke's legal thought has been often misunderstood in its orientation. Coke has been a convenient straw man, a stand-in as a constitutionalist leader, as others around him became apprehensive about royal policies. That many were concerned even under Elizabeth about the Crown's policies and even overreach cannot be denied. But, as this book will demonstrate, Coke's road to opposition was not short and straight. The book reframes Coke's early career and jurisprudence within contexts outside of the traditional battle between liberty and prerogative. In particular, Coke's perception of forces operating within the law and his ambition to protect confidence in its proceedings shaped his thinking about public law questions and the rights of the subject. If personally grasping, his project was principled. But his principles differed from the characterization of those who laud him as the 'lion under the throne'. They were principles produced by a conservatism and royalism that first aimed to magnify monarchical authority and then by their own logic led Coke into opposition.

Though not a biography, this book locates Coke at different points in his career. His progression from lawyer to law officer of the Crown and finally to the bench, presented Coke with different perspectives on the workings of the legal system. Chapter 1 situates his professional development within a broad context of reforming thought from the 1570s onwards, including the ideas of his eventual rivals Sir Thomas Egerton and Sir Francis Bacon. While those who sought to reform the law did not form a cohesive party and often expressed contrasting ideas, they shared similar concerns. In particular, they perceived that the adaptation and success of the common law and the legal system as a whole throughout the sixteenth century had produced symptoms of dysfunction. Innovation and the entrepreneurial use of legal power characterized this everyday context as jurisdictions expanded, and the creativity of common lawyers tested the possibilities of legal imagination. No learned lawyer of Coke's time could believe that the procedural workings or substantive learning of the common law had

---

[56] *Ibid.*, pp. 184, 142, 425, 127.

remained unchanged from the medieval period: conservatism developed instead from a commitment to the old law and its reason to settle contemporary questions.[57] But innovation and expansion attracted concern that the law had become a tangle or that the law was confused, uncertain or misused. These complaints – valid or not – were not merely tangential or spoken in a vacuum.[58] This book argues that these complaints influenced Coke and other reformers, and they acted: their insistence on standards and rules in the exercise of legal authority was directed at ensuring that subjects had confidence in the fairness and certainty of the law.

Coke's own reforming proposals developed from his early professional experience, described in Chapter 2. As he rose from a practising lawyer to become an attorney-general, he confronted the dangers and uncertainties that vexed both individuals and the government. Legal power was a lucrative resource that could be used to punish personal enemies or build private fortunes. Officials, patentees and informers might misuse the authority delegated to them to pursue private violence or entrepreneurial self-enrichment. Evidence of such abuse weakened the normative claim that law was rational and reached just outcomes. Coke, in particular, accepted the view that all legal authority was a delegation from the monarch who received it from God. Early in his career Coke insisted on holding those trusted with royal authority to account using the Star Chamber and the common law. From these efforts to punish corruption and restrain abuse emerged his articulation of a nascent public law as a response to the harm that subjects did to each other using the law.[59] During this time the conditions of the Elizabethan war-state also influenced Coke's thinking about the law. The regime's opponents contested the queen's right to rule and threatened the state with overthrow. In response to these dangers and the demands of public order Coke developed the treason law and inflected it with his own ideas about royal power. The context of his treason prosecutions exposes Coke's assumptions about sovereignty and obedience,

---

[57] Charles Gray, 'Introduction', in Matthew Hale, *The History of the Common Law in England* (Chicago, IL, 2002), pp. xxv–xxvi; Tubbs, 'Custom, Time and Reason', 377.

[58] Brooks, *Pettyfoggers*, p. 111; followed by Braddick, *State Formation*, p. 158; Brooks, 'The Place of Magna Carta and the Ancient Constitution in Sixteenth-Century Legal Thought', in Ellis Sandoz (ed.), *The Roots of Liberty: Magna Carta, Ancient Constitution and the Anglo-American Tradition of Rule of Law* (Columbia, MO, 1982), pp. 57–88. Hindle acknowledges that these complaints may have represented a more fundamental problem; Hindle, *Social Change*, pp. 83–93.

[59] The growth of official accountability to the House of Commons is considered by Clayton Roberts, *The Growth of Responsible Government in Stuart England* (Cambridge, 1966), pp. 4–10.

revealing that he held a belief that the monarch was ultimately irresistible into the reign of James I.

At the heart of Coke's engagement with these practical problems was a commitment to upholding confidence in the law's proceedings. Chapter 3 examines the involvement of commissions of sewers with drainage projects, and the difficulty in maintaining the appearance of judicial integrity. Disputes over whether drainage should be permitted led to the volleying of complaints about corruption and vexatious litigation, revealing the clash of multiple perspectives that complicated reform. The involvement of the common lawyers as investors and their vouching of the prerogative to justify expropriation further complicated the picture. In the middle were the commissioners, accused of partiality and seen as instruments of the drainers. Their involvement in taxation and the expropriation of common lands revealed the difficulty of determining the line between public and private interest, and strained the authority of the commissions. Coke himself worked to prevent this outcome as a judge, and his rulings attempted to limit the commissions to a course that would protect their integrity. His foresight anticipated later problems. When the Privy Council eventually intervened to imprison resisters and force them to release their lawsuits that had delayed the projects, the government limited recourse to the common law.

To buttress confidence in the common law, Coke articulated a professional identity that was rooted in well-established historical ideas. Chapter 4 examines how his histories defended the common law and demonstrated that it had protected against illegal usurpation in the past. Aware of criticisms that the common law was unreasonable, a Norman imposition that was in need of reform, Coke insisted on the immemorial nature of the law and assured his audiences of the integrity of its underlying reasoning. The law's ancient origins did not detach it from royal influence on its evolution and even survival. Coke described how kings and queens were closely involved in augmenting, recording or changing the common law. The common law, in turn, protected the monarch, a point that Coke and other common lawyers most clearly made in their interpretation of ecclesiastical history. Relying on Protestant apologists such as William Tyndale and John Foxe, Coke argued that the common law had long defended the monarch and subject alike from popish plots.

Chapter 5 analyzes how the context of reform shaped Coke's thinking about the law and suggests that his ideas were less simplistic than have been assumed. Explaining the failings of his fellow practitioners and offering them a path to reform the law, Coke emphasized the difficulty of retrieving the reason of the law. Conceiving of the law as knowledge contained within a complex of memory, Coke argued for the importance of method and the practitioner's capacity to reason to discover and apply general principles that would guide decisions. The common law's flexibility and refinement, so Coke urged, ultimately made it superior to other forms of law, such as the civil law. His belief that the common law embodied reason echoed that of other practitioners of his time. Their appeals to reason operated to orient reform of the common law, and to guide the judges' oversight of other courts and proceedings. Illustrating the application of this jurisprudence, the chapter surveys cases involving local customs, culminating in a reinterpretation of *Bonham's Case*.

Chapters 6 and 7 are case studies examining Coke's relationship with the High Commission and the Chancery. These courts had grown through judicial entrepreneurship, and their expansion drew them into conflict with Coke. But his historical perspective and the practical demands of the legal system complicated his understanding of these courts and their functioning. While Coke's concern that the High Commission's expansion was a reprise of the church's encroachment under popery, he also desired to preserve the Commission as an instrument of reformation. Coke's dispute with the Commission was therefore not a challenge to the prerogative, but rather an attempt to protect the prerogative from a renewed usurpation.

Complex motives also informed Coke's actions against the Chancery, where common lawyers populated its practice and masterships.[60] Their adroit movement of cases between the jurisdictions signalled that cooperation by necessity and inclination marked the normal relationship among courts. As it also evolved its own reform programme, the Chancery had become increasingly assertive in its manipulation of common law processes. Coke stood on the issue of *res judicata* while other common lawyers and even serjeants used the injunction to upset decisions, even in the Exchequer Chamber. His struggle with the Chancery in 1616 involved Coke's disciplining his own profession and their conduct, even as it

---

[60] A fact noticed by several others and described as a 'curious bipartition' that led to a 'civil war'. J. P. Dawson, 'Coke and Egerton Disinterred: The Attack on Chancery in 1616', *Illinois Law Review*, 36 (1941), 127–52 at 148; Charles Ogilvie, *The King's Government and the Common Law, 1471-1641* (Oxford, 1958), p. 119; Knafla, *Law and Politics*, p. 180. Noting their practice in prerogative courts, Gerald Aylmer challenged the identification of the common lawyers as 'enemies of the prerogative' in *The King's Servants: The Civil Service of Charles I, 1625-1642* (New York, 1961), pp. 56–7.

ultimately brought to a head the conflict between his reforming agenda and that of Thomas Egerton.

The episode also revealed the underlying rivalry between the King's Bench and the Chancery, each claiming pre-eminence as the king's superior court. Chapter 8 examines Coke's understanding of the royal prerogative and its relationship to the common law. Coke defended the authority of the common law to oversee other jurisdictions by insisting on its close relationship with the king. He understood the legal system to be a chain of delegation from the king or queen: magisterial authority descended downwards from its fountain in the monarch. As God's lieutenant, the ruler distributed his or her power for the purposes of justice giving and protection. Coke believed that the King's Bench – the place where the king was formally taken to be present in his court – should apply a jurisprudence based on reason to police the delegated use of royal power. By superintending this multifarious legal kingdom, the judges would protect the king from the usurpation or misuse of his authority, while imposing order on the complex of legal power. The king who could do no wrong meanwhile should refrain from judging in his own person in order to immunize himself from the moral consequences of an error that had no appeal.

The logic of this system depended on the approval of the monarch, whom Coke vainly sought to convince the common law protected. Coke's concerns about the erosion of confidence in the common law were well founded. An upbringing under Scots law was not the only influence on James's attitude towards the common law: the king shared the apprehensions of many of his subjects about the common law's dysfunction. Coke's jurisprudence, with its reliance on concepts such as 'artificial reason', was incomprehensible to the king. James's loss of confidence in Coke proved decisive in 1616 and also to the struggle between competing visions of the legal order. In Coke's view the common law should superintend the exercise of legal authority on behalf of the king, protecting him from harm. James, however, preferred the organicism of a system where he intervened to correct problems, and favoured the ameliorative role of the Chancery.

By committing to the idea of the central place of the monarch and even his irresistibility, Coke had included a potentially destructive logic into his thinking about the legal system. A system that depended on the moral exercise of the law could break down as corruptions became more and more apparent. Though legal abuse and the misbehaviours of officers and patentees were increasingly criticized in parliament and elsewhere, a financially squeezed monarch might nonetheless tolerate them by necessity. By insisting on the absolute power of the monarch as a consequence of his justice-giving responsibilities and as a means to protect the religious settlement, Coke's political theory tended towards a latent contradiction. When petty tyrants or simply opportunistic individuals made the law itself an instrument of oppression, they eroded confidence in legal proceedings. The toleration of their behaviours brought the monarch into disrepute and weakened the rationale for reposing such authority in a single person. When suspicion of popery joined the failure of reform in the 1620s, a system depending on confidence began to buckle. The limits of the theory were reached, and Coke's constitutionalism could decouple from its dependence on the centrality of monarchy. This was one path from royalism into opposition.

1

Uncertainty and the reformation of the laws

'Sir Edward Coke undertook from thence to prophecy the decay of the common law.'[1]
'Coke's thought does not read like that of a man on the defensive.'[2]

These two judgments, the first contemporary, the second modern, offer very different characterizations of Edward Coke. In the former, the common law is under siege, threatened by a fear that the ecclesiastical jurisdiction could not be controlled with the threat of praemunire. In the latter, Coke speaks for a confident, resurgent common law. The shrill and insistent tone of his writing perhaps contributes to this ambivalence. But it was the context of a rapidly expanding legal system that explains the discrepancy between Coke's potent rhetoric and his apprehensiveness. Coke and other lawyers of his time believed that the growth and even success of the Tudor and early Stuart legal system had introduced considerable uncertainty into the workings of the law. Louis Knafla has described a 'changing pattern of litigation' during this period, which drove a 'renaissance in legal thought'.[3] Yet some of the negative effects of this transformation remain only partially understood. For example, vexatious litigation, 'an important and nebulous subject', is described as mere 'flotsam' in the legal system even as contemporary complaints hinted at larger problems in the courts and their capacity to handle the growing volume of suits.[4] Problems created by an increasingly litigious society were central to the

---

[1] David Lloyd, *State-Worthies* (London, 1670), Wing L2646, p. 423; *Praemunire*, 12 Co. *Rep.* 38, 77 ER 1319.
[2] Pocock, *Ancient Constitution*, p. 32.   [3] Knafla, *Law and Politics*, p. 106.
[4] Hindle, *Social Change*, pp. 85, 83; Brooks, *Pettyfoggers*, p. 111; Braddick, *State Formation*, p. 158; Richard Ross, 'The Commoning of the Common Law: The Renaissance Debate over Printing English Law, 1529–1640', *University of Pennsylvania Law Review*, 146 (1998), 323–461, 368–9. Even in the reign of Charles I complaints suggested that Chancery growth had begun to produce significant delays in its proceedings; BL Hargrave MS 240, pp. 433, 436.

intellectual development and professional agenda of Coke and many among his generation of lawyers.[5] Familiar constitutional questions or the contribution of the legal apparatus to the creation of a modern state tend to structure the discussions of reform in Louis Knafla, Wilfrid Prest and T. G. Barnes and their analyses of some of the ideas of Coke's generation.[6] But if Coke and others ultimately asked larger questions about the workings of political and legal power, their efforts began as attempts to limit the harm that subjects did to each other through their use of legal authority.

From his earliest practice Coke had experience of these problems and he brought to their resolution a characteristic determination that spanned his entire career. Describing the manner of his birth on 1 February 1552 to his friend Sir Henry Spelman, Coke claimed that his delivery was so sudden that he tumbled newly born from his mother onto the hearthstone.[7] Spelman took the story to be a sign of the ferocity of Coke's will.[8] By affinity and upbringing he was well prepared for the legal world that he would attempt to reform, born into a Norfolk legal family connected by marriage and alliance with the leading county gentry, many of whom also had relatives on the bench or at the Bar.[9] Coke received a broad training that prepared him as a practitioner to range across sources both English and continental, classical and contemporary. His copy of Horace, for example, survives from his early days at Norwich Grammar School and

---

[5] Christopher Brooks, *Lawyers, Litigation and English Society* (London, 1998), p. 224.

[6] Knalfa, *Law and Politics*, pp. 105–22; Wilfrid Prest, 'William Lambarde, Elizabethan Law Reform, and Early Stuart Politics', *Journal of British Studies*, 34 (1995), 464–80; Barnes, 'Slow Process', 242–9; 315–32; Christopher Hill, *Intellectual Origins of the English Revolution – Revisited* (Oxford, 1997), pp. 201–36. The historiography for the later period includes Gerald Edward Aylmer, 'Charles I's Commission on Fees, 1627–40', *Bulletin of the Institute of Historical Research*, 31:83 (1958), 58–67; Barbara Shapiro, 'Codification of the Law in Seventeenth-Century England', *Wisconsin Law Review*, 2 (1974), 428–65; Barbara Shapiro, 'Law Reform in Seventeenth-Century England', *American Journal of Legal History*, 19 (1975), 280–312; Veall, *The Popular Movement for Law Reform*; J. S. Wilson, 'Sir Henry Spelman and the Royal Commission on Fees, 1622–40' in J. Conway Davies (ed.), *Studies Presented to Sir Hilary Jenkinson* (London, 1957), pp. 456–70.

[7] Henry Spelman, *Reliquiae Spelmannianae* (London, 1698), Wing S4930, p. 150.

[8] Chamberlain, *Letters*, vol. II, p. 14; Lloyd, *State-Worthies*, p. 826.

[9] Allen Boyer, 'Sir Edward Coke, Ciceronianus: Classical Rhetoric and the Common Law Tradition', *International Journal for the Semiotics of Law*, 10 (1997), 3–36. Robert Coke was the Townshends' family attorney and friend; C. E. Moreton, *The Townshends and Their World: Gentry, Law, and Land in Norfolk, c. 1450–1551* (Oxford, 1992), pp. 48, 109, 125, 127.

includes copious notes that reflected a humanist education in the Latin classics and also Greek.[10] In 1567 Coke matriculated at Trinity College, Cambridge, where he lived a frugal life, and it was later claimed that John Whitgift, who was then Master of Trinity, had been his tutor.[11] Leaving without a degree (though later awarded the MA), he entered Clifford's Inn on 21 January 1571, and then on 24 April 1572 he proceeded to the Inner Temple.[12] Though Coke recorded that it was not until 1579 that he began his own case reports, he had made important connections at the Inns and gathered accounts of cases from others before that time.[13] Some of his acquaintances, such as the Gawdys, were based on familial ties, while others, such as his contacts with Edmund Plowden, were facilitated by the eagerness of the student and the collegiality of the Inns. These connections had long-standing influence on Coke both professionally – Sir Francis and Sir Thomas Gawdy were both prominent common law judges – and intellectually. Sir John Popham, who was attorney-general (1581) and then chief justice of the King's Bench (1592), was a lifelong friend and model, skirmishing with those jurisdictions with which Coke would later contend.[14]

Called to the Bar in 1578, Coke's reputation for brilliance at the Inner Temple was confirmed when he prevailed in his first major suit, *Lord Cromwell's Case* (1579–81).[15] Coke appears in numerous other cases in this

---

[10] James, *Chief Justice Coke*, p. 4; Boyer, *Sir Edward Coke*, pp. 13–16. For Coke's training in classical rhetoric, see Boyer, *Sir Edward Coke*, pp. 2–4, and more broadly, Barbara J. Shapiro, 'Classical Rhetoric and the English Law of Evidence', in Victoria Kahn and Lorna Hutson (eds.), *Rhetoric and Law in Early Modern Europe* (New Haven, CT, 2001), pp. 54–71.

[11] W. W. Rouse Ball and J. A. Venn, *Admissions to Trinity College, Cambridge 1546–1700* (London, 1913), vol. II, p. 68. Not born to a great fortune, Coke's wealth at this time is difficult to discern; see Campbell, *Chief Justices*, p. 242; James, *Chief Justice Coke*, p. 5; Boyer, *Sir Edward Coke*, p. 197; John Aubrey, *Brief Lives*, ed. Richard Baber (Woodbridge, 1982), p. 76.

[12] BL Harley MS 6687A, ff. 13r, 15v, 17r; *A Calendar of the Inner Temple Records*, ed. F. A. Inderwick (London, 1896), vol. I, p. 423. Little is known of his time at Clifford's; C. M. Hay-Edwards, *A History of Clifford's Inn* (London, 1912), pp. 40, 110, 192.

[13] Coke stated that he began reporting in 22 Elizabeth I, between October 1579 and 1580. A notebook of his containing earlier cases survives, but has been overlooked, at Manchester University, Rylands Library French MS 118.

[14] In his *Reports* Coke praised the chief justice and received a silver basin and ewer from Popham at his death. Douglas Rice, *The Life and Achievements of Sir John Popham, 1531–1607* (Madison, NJ, 2005), p. 268; *Drury's Case* (1607), 6 Co. Rep. 75a, 77 ER 369.

[15] Part of his reputation rested on the success of the possibly apocryphal 'cook's case', see Bowen, *Lion and the Throne*, p. 68, and perhaps also, *A Calendar of the Inner Temple Records*, vol. I, p. 305. BL Harley MS 6687A, f. 15v; *Lord Cromwell's Case* (1581), 4 Co. Rep. 12b, 76 ER 877; James, *Chief Justice Coke*, p. 6.

early period, suggesting a thriving practice.[16] His rising reputation was signalled by a readership at Lyon's Inn where he lectured on the Statute of Fines in 1579.[17] Such early recognition soon brought Coke appointment to offices of responsibility, including among others the recorderships of Coventry (1585) and Norwich (1586). Prestige followed: in 1586 he was also appointed as a justice of the peace in Norfolk and by 1593 for Suffolk and Middlesex, and returned as an MP in 1589 (Aldeburgh, Suffolk) and then again in 1593 (Norfolk).[18] He was made a bencher of the Inner Temple in 1590 and gave his first reading there in 1592 on the Statute of Uses.[19] That same year Coke was made solicitor-general and in 1593, having been returned for Norfolk, he was elected speaker of the House of Commons.[20] The patronage that Coke cultivated assisted him in the attainment of several offices. Burghley, for example, may have helped to secure his appointment as solicitor- and then later attorney-general over the vigorous campaigning of Sir Francis Bacon.[21]

In these years Coke experienced the uncertainty of the law first-hand as a barrister. The dispute in *Shelley's Case* (1581), for example, raised fundamental questions about settlements. Even in these early years Coke preferred to explain this uncertainty as a consequence of an imperfect understanding or application of the common law. In his manuscript account of *Shelley's Case* that circulated soon after the decision Coke warned of the corruptions in the law caused by poor reporting and the 'many strange and absurd opinions' in circulation – a criticism of attempts by lawyers to develop the law of property in novel directions.[22] The manuscript was the origin of the preface to the first part of Coke's

---

[16] See, for example, from 1582 to 1584, HLS MS 204, ff. 90v, 73v, 79v.

[17] BL Harley MS 6687A, ff. 13r, 17r. There is evidence that he had given an earlier reading at the Inn, perhaps as deputy reader, as suggested by J. H. Baker, *Readers and Readings in the Inns of Court and Chancery* (London, 2000), p. 207. See the fragmentary record of a reading by Coke on 5 August 1577 on the abatement of writs, BL Harley MS 6853, ff. 238r–v and HMC, *Ninth Report*, p. 373.

[18] BL Harley MS 6687A, f. 13r. *DNB*, s.v. 'Edward Coke'; Alfred Hassell Smith, *County and Court: Government and Politics in Norfolk 1558–1603* (Oxford, 1974), pp. 273–4, 324; P. W. Hasler (ed.), *The House of Commons, 1558–1603* (London, 1981), vol. I, pp. 622–5.

[19] BL Harley MS 6687A, f. 15v.

[20] *Ibid.*, f. 16r. Hasler (ed.), *The House of Commons*, vol. I, s.v. 'Edward Coke'.

[21] It is assumed that Burghley was instrumental in Coke's promotion; though see Conyers Read, *Lord Burghley and Queen Elizabeth* (New York, 1960), p. 496n26. Coke bore the 'great banner' at the funeral of the Earl of Salisbury in 1612. HMC, *Salisbury*, vol. II, p. 374. Spedding (ed.), *Letters and Life*, vol. IV, p. 3.

[22] Holkham MS 251. Copies of the case are numerous, suggesting that Coke's report circulated widely before its publication in 1600.

Reports, a work that continued in an expanded form the project of providing authoritative reports to quiet many of these 'absurd opinions'.

What experience had confirmed for Coke was already known by many others, including his eventual adversary Thomas Egerton. Leading professionals shared unease about how the legal system operated, warned against its lubricities and often focused on its expense or abuse, the confusion of its jurisdictions or the uncertainty of its remedies.[23] Some, such as Coke or Francis Bacon, had a broad perspective and sought systemic reform, while others aimed at piecemeal change.[24] While frequently referring to an abstract notion of justice, they plotted different paths to reach that difficult goal. They responded to a creative, febrile law and recognized the problems inherent in an increasingly law-minded society. William Fulbecke commented on this state of affairs: 'my neighbours, who are so full of Lawpoints, that when they sweat, it is nothing but Law ... The book of Littletons Tenures is there [*sic*] breakfast, their dinner ... Everie ploughswayne with us may bee a Seneschall in a court Baron.'[25] To modern historians, the growing participation in legal process and access to central law are indicators of the spread of the centralized state.[26] But recent work on France suggests that the early modern judicial state remained highly amorphous and decentralized, a tumultuous competition of interests and private manipulation, rather than simply a pacifying instrument of royal control or bastion of ideological resistance.[27] T. G. Barnes wrote that 'litigation was a joyous game' for some gentlemen, and contemporaries were well aware of the law's potential for misuse: 'The law is unto us, as the heavens are over our heads: of their owne Nature they are cleere, gentle, and readie to doe good to man ... But if they bee troubled by brablings and unruly mindes, and be put from their owne smooth and even byas, then doe they plague the world with stormes.'[28]

---

[23] Hill notes the shared interest of Coke and Bacon; Hill, *Intellectual Origins*, pp. 206–7.

[24] Knafla, *Law and Politics*, p. 107.

[25] William Fulbecke, *The Second Part of the Parallele* (London, 1602), STC 11415a, sig. B2.

[26] Hart, *Rule of Law*, pp. 8–17; Braddick, *State Formation*, pp. 155–65.

[27] Michael Breen, *Law, City and King: Legal Culture, Municipal Politics and State Formation in Early Modern Dijon* (Rochester, NY, 2007), pp. 14–18; Malcolm Greenshields, *An Economy of Violence in Early Modern France: Crime and Justice in the Haute Auvergne, 1587-1664* (University Park, PA, 1994), pp. 59–60, 121; for a similar analysis in England, see Cynthia Herrup, *The Common Peace: Participation and the Criminal Law in Seventeenth-Century England* (Cambridge, 1987), p. 162 *et passim*; and Brooks, *Law, Politics and Society*, pp. 279–81.

[28] Thomas Dekker, *The Dead Tearme* (London, 1608), STC 6496, sig. C1v; Randolph Thomas, *A Pleasant Comedy*, lines 271–4.

Thomas Dekker's complaint was related, as other historians have argued, to the belief that formal legal process undermined values of charity and neighbourliness. These values were expressed in formulaic language that settled a suit, such as Coke used with Sir Robert Riche in 1617, agreeing 'that no sparke or shadow of contention or unkindnes may remaine'.[29] 'Unnatural' lawsuits set family and friends against each other, and Coke intervened in a case between his servant and his servant's brother-in-law, warning that they would 'consume' their estates, and urged them to arbitration.[30] The rush of litigation that characterized the period was partly attributed to 'every meane man, being moved with choller, would in their heate seeke after some colour of misdemeanor to exhibit his complaint'.[31] Driven by malice, litigants might engage in sharp practice or worse: in one case it was alleged that the defendant was motivated by anger to entrap the other within the scope of a penal statute.[32] The lawyer James Whitelocke complained that he was 'molested' with suits by William Pope, who also attacked his mentor, the judge Sir David Williams.[33] The commonplace book of Thomas Roberts, with its methodical recording of trespasses against him and legal processes invoked, illustrates the extreme.[34] Litigation was a campaign rather than a battle, demanding strategy and the rallying of allies.[35] Baptist Hicks explained in a letter that though he had 'foyled' his adversary at the common law, 'now he flees to complain in Chancery'. Hicks added that he hoped that the suit would be denied, since he had already commenced proceedings there as well.[36] Unsurprisingly, Coke participated in this culture of aggressive litigation. In 1598 Sir John Hollis alleged the attorney-general

---

[29] BL Additional MS 12507, f. 67r.

[30] PRO C 115/100 7360; NRO 21508/8; similarly Bodl. Tanner MS 285, ff. 25r and 26r; BL Egerton MS 2713, f. 127r. William Prest, *The Rise of the Barristers: A Social History of the English Bar, 1590–1640* (Oxford, 1986), pp. 300–2.

[31] BL Harley MS 141, f. 45v. Egerton urged lawyers towards quiet suits, *Crewe v. Vernon* (1610), BL Harley MS 1330, f. 14r.

[32] PRO STAC 8 6/48; though 'malice is a good informer', John Hawarde, *Les Reportes del Cases in Camera Stellata, 1593 to 1609: From the Original ms. of John Hawarde*, ed. William Baildon (London, 1894), p. 242.

[33] James Whitelocke, *Liber Famelicus of Sir James Whitelock*, ed. John Bruce (London, 1858), pp. 23, 30.

[34] Paul Karkeek (ed.), 'Extracts from a Memorandum Book Belonging to Thomas Roberts and Family', in *Report and Transactions of the Devonshire Association for the Advancement of Science, Literature and Art*, vol. X (1878) pp. 315–29.

[35] Prest, *Rise of the Barristers*, p. 297.

[36] BL Lansdowne MS 107, f. 172r; Lansdowne 91, no. 46. For similar disputes, see Prest, *Rise of the Barristers*, pp. 300–2.

was pursuing an old quarrel over a garden and attempting to pull down the cottages of his tenants.[37] Nor was it entirely clear that the courts could quiet recalcitrant litigants. Sir Stephen Procter and Sir John Mallory spent upwards of a decade litigating even though the President of the Council of the North personally intervened to settle their bitter suits.[38] A master's report in the Chancery tells of John Fletcher in Pembroke, a 'dangerous, troublesome and contentious person', who was outlawed in the sessions and the Common Pleas and stood excommunicated by the High Commission for incest, yet the sheriffs feared to attach him since 'at all tymes [he] stand upon soe stronge a gard and is soe armed'. Fletcher and his allies continued their vexatious litigation in the Chancery, using suborned witnesses.[39]

Such feuding exploited the overlap of legal authorities from local manor courts and the judicial powers of justices of the peace to the distant authority and strange language of the common law courts in Westminster.[40] Those who advocated for reform sought to prune, restructure and consolidate aspects of the system. They probed how its components worked together and how they might curb the unjust exercise of legal power.[41] They found the cause of the troubles in the structure and incentives of the system rather than in the aberrant behaviours of a few immoral litigants. Like some of their contemporaries across the Channel, they sought to reform law and magistracy to create an 'ethical society'.[42] By opening up the question of the operation of power and probing how it was legitimated, law reformers added to the intellectual structures within which the

---

[37] HMC, *Salisbury*, vol. VIII, p. 234.

[38] *Procter* v. *Mallory* (1611), PRO STAC 8 227/35, f. 4v.

[39] PRO C 38/22, 'Petition of William Walter'; see also the difficulty of arresting a justice of the peace in *Gardener* v. *Saint John* (1600), BL Additional MS 25203, f. 305r. Another suit involved the vexatious litigant John Edwards, *Rockerye* v. *Bodill* et al. (1612), PRO STAC 8 57/8. Later litigation suggested that he was a recusant who used lawsuits against his Protestant neighbours, C 38/37 [n.f.], September 1619. Solicitation and vexation often went together: Bacon prosecuted a former alehouse keeper who was sworn an attorney of the Common Pleas, but solicited suits and used deputies of no 'certayne abode'. *Attorney-General* v. *Wallis* (1614), PRO STAC 8 23/8. Another suit involved a vexatious litigant helped by two sons, one an attorney and the other a solicitor, *Capell* v. *Maynard* (n.d.), PRO STAC 8 96/10.

[40] The general cause for the rise in the volume of litigation is often attributed to the low initial costs of a lawsuit. Prest, *Rise of the Barristers*, p. 297 (following Brooks).

[41] Their work was 'jurispathic' as described by Robert Cover, 'Nomos and Narrative', *Harvard Law Review*, 97 (1982), 40–4.

[42] Marie Seong-Hak Kim, 'Civil Law and Civil War: Michel de l'Hôpital and the Ideals of Legal Unification in Sixteenth-Century France', *Law and History Review*, 28:3 (2010), 791–826; 798.

constitutional questions that vexed the 1620s and 1630s might be posed. If those questions, as Margaret Judson and others have argued, led to the basic proposition of where sovereign power lay in the state, this phase of reform had largely more limited concerns.[43] Through their efforts reformers began the shift from a focus on how subjects used law to oppress one another in the pursuit of their private interests into a much larger inquiry into the operation of royal authority.

Coke himself was preoccupied with the consequences of the 'regeneration' of the common law begun under the leadership of Sir John Fyneux.[44] The driver of these changes was the King's Bench and its development of a civil jurisdiction that attracted some of the lucrative business of contract and property litigation from the Common Pleas.[45] Though Magna Carta barred the King's Bench from hearing common pleas, including those related to property and debt, the judges circumvented this restriction by making use of the bill of Middlesex rather than an original writ from the Chancery.[46] Plaintiffs made a fictional allegation of a trespass in Middlesex allowing the defendant to be arrested by a writ of *latitat* from the court. A second bill was then preferred, stating the true complaint. By 1600 one contemporary claimed that over 20,000 *latitats* a year were granted.[47]

Although this procedural innovation was the foundation for the subsequent growth of the King's Bench, it was also a magnet for complaints. The bill of Middlesex made use of a fiction to escape the traditional jurisdictional boundary of the King's Bench. Critics viewed the device as a violation of the ancient law and an instance of unwarranted jurisdictional expansion. They preferred the procedures of the medieval law and those 'Originall writts which in auntient tyme were by great learning advice and industry devised and framed', and warned that 'except the Common Law bee first confined to originall Writts it cannot be kept within its owne lymits'. The overflowing of common law jurisdiction brought jeopardy: 'all is drowned[,] overwhelmed or in great danger'.[48] Lists of these dangers rising from the abuse of *latitats* circulated, and

---

[43] Judson, *Crisis of the Constitution*, pp. 46–7; William Holdsworth, 'The Prerogative in the Sixteenth Century', *Columbia Law Review*, 21:6 (1921), 554–71.

[44] Baker, 'Introduction', in *The Reports of Sir John Spelman*, vol. II, p. 23; *DNB*, s.v. 'John Fyneux'.

[45] Baker, *OHLE* vol. VI, pp. 151–8; Baker, *IELH*, p. 45. For a tabular summary of the new actions, see Baker, 'Introduction', in *The Reports of Sir John Spelman*, vol. II, p. 60.

[46] Magna Carta (1297), 25 Edward I, c. 11.

[47] BL Lansdowne MS 155, f. 35.   [48] BL Lansdowne MS 253, f. 174v.

literary writers mocked the procedure.[49] The underlying fiction was particularly galling as was the opportunity for abuse when the procedure was used to commit individuals from the provinces at their expense.[50] Egerton noted that through the use of fictions, cases that should properly be heard in liberties in Cornwall, Yorkshire or Wales were brought to Westminster.[51] In a case in the Star Chamber he declared 'theise latitats, of late muche in use, but in auntiente time never knowne nor hearde of, have done muche hurte and [lit]tle good; but the original wrytte is the true ... & beste course'.[52] The ingenious reshaping of the King's Bench left the common law open to charges of innovation, charges that would be tied to concerns that the judges were overreaching themselves as they continued to expand their jurisdiction.

Innovation and expansion were not restricted to procedure: substantive changes at the common law drew more controversy. They suggested to some, including Coke, that the protection of property by the common law was more uncertain than under the medieval law.[53] Perhaps the most significant of these changes was the development of remedies based on trespass, a family of actions offering redress for those harmed by a wrong. These were personal rather than real actions, remedying a wrong done to a person, such as an unwarranted eviction.[54] The adoption of trespass by litigants and its eventual acceptance by the judges affected both property and contract, and displaced the medieval real and contractual actions.

Among the most important consequences of this change was the expansion of common law protection to non-freeholders, especially tenants for years and copyholders.[55] By the end of the fifteenth century, debate had already been joined as to whether trespass might be used to

---

[49] BL Lansdowne MS 155, f. 32v; for example, John Webster, *Cure for a Cuckold* (IV.i); Ben Jonson, *Magnetic Lady* (V.iii); Philip Massinger *Fatal Dowry* (I.ii); Randolph Thomas, *A Pleasant Comedy*, ln. 274.

[50] HLS MS 1026, f. 70r. The statute 21 James 1, c. 23 was possibly related to this complaint; see *SR*, vol. IV, pt. 2, p. 1,232.

[51] Bodl. Barlow MS 9, f. 24r. Similarly Egerton in 1610 motioned that the Star Chamber should not hear small misdemeanours and petty riots, but they should be heard in the counties. CUL Ii.5.21, f. 105r.

[52] *Rape* v. *Girlin* (1607), Hawarde, *Les Reportes,* p. 326.

[53] The general problem of property's uncertainty was noticed by laymen such as Sir Walter Raleigh, *The Works of Sir Walter Ralegh*, vol. VIII, p. 254 (Oxford, 1829) and also BL Harley MS 4708, f. 194r.

[54] Summarized in Baker, *OHLE*, vol. VI, pp. 631–50; *IELH*, pp. 301–3.

[55] Baker stresses that while 'some limited protection' had already been extended, the sixteenth century saw the 'more or less complete protection *in specie*, against the lord as well as strangers'; Baker, *OHLE*, vol. VI, p. 633.

recover the term against either the lessor or a stranger, culminating in a decision of the Common Pleas in 1499.[56] During the 1550s Baker observes that ejectment, a species of trespass, came into common use by leaseholders, an 'ascendancy' that was perhaps related to litigation arising from disputes over property that had been rapidly transferred during the Reformation.[57]

Tenants by copy of court roll or copyholders, also began to use ejectment during the second half of the sixteenth century. The traditional common law view, as described by Sir Thomas Littleton, was that copyholders held 'at the will of the lord according to the custom of the manor'.[58] Copyholders sought their remedies in the manor courts and the Chancery: at the common law they were merely tenants at the will of the lord. But even as Littleton stated the conservative view, there were already judicial dicta suggesting a greater openness to entertaining suits from copyholders.[59] Over the sixteenth century the judges allowed remedies against other tenants and then in 1566 for damages against the lord himself.[60] As Simpson and Gray have described the process, the King's Bench permitted the use of ejectment for specific recovery from at least 1573, with the more conservative Common Pleas following reluctantly by the end of the century.[61] The recognition of the copyholder's interest led the judges into consideration of the custom that governed the conditions of the tenure and which might vary from manor to manor. Copyhold litigation thus brought a diverse body of customary law into greater contact with the common law. While the consequences for patterns of judicial interpretation remained to be worked out, the author of *The Compleat Copyholder* observed that

---

[56] Though the issue addressed by the judges in 1499 may have been limited to the use of trespass against a stranger; see Baker, *OHLE*, vol. VI, pp. 635–6; A. W. B. Simpson, *A History of the Land Law* (Oxford, 1986), p. 144; Baker, *The Reports of Sir John Spelman*, vol. II, p. 181. Judicial approval of trespass against the lessor may have been settled as early as 1490; Baker, *OHLE*, vol. VI, p. 636n38.

[57] Baker, *OHLE*, vol. VI, pp. 636–7, 724.

[58] Cited in Baker, *OHLE*, vol. VI, p. 645.

[59] Simpson, *A History of the Land Law*, p. 162; Charles Gray, *Copyhold, Equity and the Common Law* (Cambridge, 1963), pp. 61–5, 68, 93; Charles Reid, 'The Seventeenth-Century Revolution in the English Land Law', *Cleveland State Law Review*, 43 (1995), 221–302 at 249–51.

[60] Gray, *Copyhold*, p. 64. The debates for the first half of the century are surveyed and key cases identified in Baker, *OHLE*, vol. VI, pp. 647–9, and see also the early assertion in 1552 that the tenant would be protected as long as they did their service according to the custom; J. H. Baker (ed.), *The Reports of William Dalison* (London, 2007), p. 7.

[61] Simpson, *A History of the Land Law*, pp. 164–5; Gray, *Copyhold*, pp. 68–76.

'time hath dealt very favourably with copyholders' and worked to settle the law.[62] Copyholders no longer had to fear the discretionary authority of their lords with the availability of trespass: 'for it is against reason, that the lord should be judge where he himself is a party'.[63] Coke agreed that the copyholder might bring trespass against a lord who ejected him against the custom of the manor, since the copyholder held by 'the will of the lord according to the custom of the manor'.[64] Custom 'established and fixed' the estate, and the lord was bound by its rules. In this way, by insisting on principles of accountability and reasonableness, Coke and other common lawyers revealed how they could adapt their law to change and even expand its reach.[65]

The quicker procedure and simplicity of trespass attracted freeholders away from the medieval actions to use ejectment to try their titles. The procedure, which involved the creation of a lease followed by an ejection, appears to have become 'fairly common', beginning in the 1560s.[66] In 1566 a dispute over the title of lands between Sir Henry Cary and a patentee was tried in ejectment between their leaseholders.[67] The action was clearly contrived in *Cooper's Case* (1584), and during the next reign the barriers to its use to test freehold were significantly lowered.[68] But even by 1601 Coke was able to concede, 'at this day all titles of lands are for the greatest part tried in Actions of Ejectments'.[69] Yet he did not welcome this development and warned that the use of personal actions to try freehold ignored prudent rules of the common law. This led to 'infiniteness of verdicts' to the 'dishonor of the common law ... for the receding from the

---

[62] *The Compleat Copyholder in Three Tracts*, ed. W. C. (London, 1764), pp. 5, 4–6, 59–67. The treatise has been ascribed to Coke, but I follow Brooks and Williams in their doubts about the authorship given the style and content. Brooks, *Law, Politics and Society*, p. 336, esp. n. 132. Gray compares the views on copyhold in Co. *Litt.* and *The Compleat Copyholder* at Gray, *Copyhold*, pp. 84–7.

[63] *The Compleat Copyholder.*, pp. 6, 58, 68–9, 118. Gray, *Copyhold*, pp. 87, 94. See also Charles Calthrope, *The Relation Between the Lord of a Mannor and the Copyholder His Tenant* (London, 1635).

[64] *Brown's Case* (1581), 4 Co. *Rep.* 21a, 76 ER 912; Co. *Litt.* ff. 60b–61a. Coke reported a group of copyhold cases in 4 Co. *Rep.*

[65] See, for example, Coke's discussion of unreasonable fines, Co. *Litt.* f. 59b.

[66] Simpson, *A History of the Land Law*, p. 145; Baker, *IELH*, pp. 301–2.

[67] *Griffyn v. Lennard* (1566), J. H. Baker (ed.), *Reports from the Lost Notebooks of Sir James Dyer* (London, 1994), vol. I, p. 124.

[68] Simpson, *A History of the Land Law*, pp. 146–8; Baker, *IELH*, p. 302; *Cooper's Case* (1584), 2 Leonard 200, 74 ER 477.

[69] *Alden's Case* (1601), 5 Co. *Rep.* 105b, 77 ER 218.

true institution of it introduces many inconveniencies'.[70] But the trend was not to be reversed: when in 1607, on a writ of error, the argument was made that ejectment did not lie for a coalmine, the court responded with unanimity that the action was good and refused to discuss the point further.[71] That same year Sir Lawrence Tanfield JKB explained to counsel, who had argued that the action was a trespass 'in its nature', that the 'action is real'.[72]

The judges admitted their innovation even while occasionally voicing reluctance at these changes. Edward Fenner JQB, for example, observed in *Sprake's Case* (1599) that, 'in ancient times ejectment was only in the nature of a trespass'. The issue turned over whether the action of ejectment brought by the lessee of a copyholder would be good. Popham CJQB, articulating a more conservative sentiment, seemed to disagree, but he did not prevail.[73] Popham's dissent reflected ambivalence among the common law judiciary as to how far the remedy might be extended, if at all. In 1573 Sir James Dyer CJCP had also complained about the availability of trespass in King's Bench, declaring that it was drawing causes away from Common Pleas that should properly be heard there.[74] While ejectment offered a unified remedy for freeholders, termors and copyholders, its increasing use signalled the eclipse of the ancient actions.[75] Moreover, the disagreements between the King's Bench, which led many of these developments, and the Common Pleas, which resisted them, indicated that the common law profession could accept, but was not unanimous about change.

The dissension over the replacement of the ancient actions was particularly pointed over another trespassory action, *assumpsit*, which developed as a contractual action that was then extended to the recovery of debts.[76] *Assumpsit* was more flexible than the older actions of covenant and debt, and it eventually superseded both in a process visible from the fourteenth century. For example, while covenant would lie only for those

---

[70] *Ferrer's Case* (1598), 6 Co. *Rep.* 9a, 77 ER 266.

[71] *Currin and Wheatly* (1607), BL Additional MS 25206, f. 51v.

[72] *Browne v. Bank* (1607), BL Additional MS 25206, f. 56v.

[73] *Sprake's Case* (1599), BL Additional MS 25203, f. 76r.

[74] Baker, 'Introduction', in *The Lost Notebooks of Sir James Dyer*, vol. I, pp. xxvi–xxvii. Dyer also rejected the use of ejectment for recovery of the term, which 'did not ever have grounds in law'; BL Hargrave MS 374, f. 125v.

[75] Baker, *IELH*, p. 302.

[76] *Ibid.*, pp. 329–46; Baker, 'Introduction', in *The Reports of Sir John Spelman*, vol. II, pp. 224–6, 255–98; Milsom, *Historical Foundations*, pp. 314–60; D. J. Ibbetson, *A Historical Introduction to the Law of Obligations* (Oxford, 1999), pp. 126–51; A. W. B. Simpson, *A History of the Common Law of Contract: The Rise of Assumpsit* (Oxford, 1975).

contracts made by deed and was limited to specific performance, *assumpsit* also lay for parol or oral promises where there was 'consideration' or a quid pro quo by which the contract was made actionable.[77] This flexibility was attractive to litigants in the commercial economy of the sixteenth century.

Assumpsit was also extended to debt, since the failure to pay a debt might be seen as a wrong.[78] This extension caused significant acrimony in the common law courts when the Common Pleas resisted in preference to the older action of debt. Litigants, mindful of debt's limitations, including wager of law and the need for a sum certain, argued otherwise, and they found support in the King's Bench. The disagreement between the two courts over *assumpsit* created notorious uncertainty by the late sixteenth century: a litigant at assize could not be sure whether a Common Pleas or King's Bench judge would hear the case and how they would direct the jury as to the law.[79] *Slade's Case* (1602) finally permitted *assumpsit* in all the courts of common law and capped a century of development in contract and debt.[80]

While a litigant might face occasional uncertainty in debt, the intricacies of the land law suggested that property might not be as secure as many hoped it to be, especially as lawyers and conveyancers experimented with uses. The use was a beneficial trust developed from the fourteenth century as a means to direct the succession of land and to avoid feudal incidents.[81] Land would be held by a group of trustees to the 'use of' a beneficiary – the *cestui que use* – who was equitably entitled to the profits of the land. Enforcement had originally been through the Chancery, but the Statute of Uses (1536) and the related Statute of Wills (1540) transformed uses into legal estates at the common law. The possibilities opened by the operation of the statutes to shape settlements and landholding encouraged experimentation as well as the development of rules to control uses at the common law. The key question was whether the old common law rules would

---

[77] D. J. Ibbetson, 'Consideration and the Theory of Contract in the Sixteenth-Century Common Law', in J. Barton (ed.), *Towards a General Law of Contract* (Berlin, 1990), pp. 67–124; J. Baker, 'Origins of the "Doctrine" of Consideration', in *The Legal Profession and the Common Law: Historical Essays* (London, 1986), pp. 369–91.

[78] Baker, *IELH*, p. 341.   [79] *Ibid.*, p. 344.

[80] D. J. Ibbetson, 'Sixteenth-Century Contract Law: Slade's Case in Context', *Oxford Journal of Legal Studies*, 4 (1984), 295–317; J. H. Baker, 'New light on Slade's Case', *Cambridge Law Journal*, 29:1 (1971), 51–67, 213–36; A. W. B. Simpson, 'The Place of Slade's Case in the History of Contract', *Law Quarterly Review*, 74 (1958), 381–96.

[81] Milsom, *Historical Foundations*, pp. 200–39; Simpson, *A History of the Land Law*, pp. 173–207; Baker, *IELH*, pp. 248–58.

bind these new constructions: in 1575 Robert Monson JCP, wondered aloud whether or not common law maxims and rules affecting limitations of estates might even apply to uses.[82] Underlying these efforts was a concern over the security of property: some warned that conveyances based on uses would obfuscate rights to the land and result in confusion: 'noe man shall knowe whoe is the tenante to be used or whoe hath the reversion'.[83]

Common lawyers developed the implications of the law surrounding uses in the design of settlements and conveyances aimed at creating the ultimate prize: the perpetuity.[84] The perpetuity would lock up land in a family forever, preserving the patrimony from spendthrift descendants, but curtailing the freedom of heirs to alienate the land. If land were sold, an innocent purchaser might later discover a claim against them from a distant heir, creating uncertainty in the land market. In this way, these constructions encouraged litigation, since those who might have dormant rights to land would seize upon the chance to enforce them. The question of perpetuities generated significant intellectual effort and emotion at the turn of the seventeenth century. The threat was not new: the medieval statute De Donis had also provided the opportunity of creating perpetuities through entails. While these had been limited by the development of the common recovery, attempts to create unbarrable entails continued in the form of contingent remainders into Coke's time.

Later Tudor conveyancers probed how the use might create perpetuities, and so Popham warned that the land law 'begins to be so much troubled with the cases of uses, for which it is also necessary to provide a lawful remedy'.[85] In a case where he was counsel, John Dodderidge described the consequences of uses: 'troubles and vexations are introduced in the commonwealth on account of the tossing and changing of estates of inheritance' and urged that *salus populi, suprema lex* when ruling on these 'innovations and new found conveyances'.[86] These remarks by Popham and Dodderidge responded to those clever settlements and

---

[82] John Rylands Library, French MS 118, f. 33r.

[83] 'Concerning Entayles and Perpetuities' (1601), BL Additional MS 25206, f. 121r.

[84] Simpson, *A History of the Land Law*, pp. 209–10; George Haskins, 'Extending the Grasp of the Dead Hand: Reflections on the Origins of the Rule Against Perpetuities', *University of Pennsylvania Law Review*, 126 (1977), 19–46.

[85] *Dillon v. Fraine* (*Chudleigh's Case*), Popham 83, 79 ER 1195. Joseph Biancalana, *The Fee Tail and Common Recovery in Medieval England, 1176–1502* (Cambridge, 2001). The common law judges continued to protect the common recovery; see *Capel's Case* (1581), 1 Co. Rep. 63a, 76 ER 138; *Sir Anthony Mildmay's Case* (1605), 6 Co. Rep. 41a, 77 ER 314.

[86] *Frampton v. Gerrard* (1604), HLS MS 118(c), f. 27r. Similarly, see *Chudleigh's Case* (1594), 1 Co. Rep. 121b, 76 ER 275.

conveyances, such as 'springing' or 'future' uses, which had raised new possibilities of perpetuities that had begun to appear frequently before the courts by the 1570s.[87]

Attempts to prevent perpetuities revealed the underlying fears about security of property and the disruptive effects of the operation of the common law. The debate over a bill in 1593 to restrict perpetuities and springing uses illustrated the opposing attitudes. Serjeant Thomas Harris, who appears to have been the bill's champion, declared that 'It was against the nature and gravitie of our lande to skipp by waie of transubstantiation, as these uses make it.' Harris explained that uses protecting perpetual settlements bent the rules of the common law, giving the example of arrangements that conveyed land to use if an action were brought against the possessor. Another serjeant, Thomas Hannam, responded that springing uses were a mischief to purchasers who might not know that the use encumbered their land. But Sir Edward Dymocke spoke in opposition to the bill, reminding the House that perpetuities protected the family patrimony and warned that the bill would lead to the 'overthrowe of their howses'.[88] The argument from family could be marshalled both ways: in the preamble to a bill of 1597 limiting future uses, the drafters explained that contingent uses created discord in families as squabbles erupted over property.[89]

Questions arising from limitations by way of uses and contingent remainders vexed judicial opinion in Coke's time. Decisions varied over time: conditions that protected settlements were accepted in *Scholastica's Case* (1571) and followed by *Rudhall v. Milward* (1586).[90] However, in *Chudleigh's Case* (1594) and *Archer's Case* (1595) the judges ruled that an executory interest arising from the Statute of Uses could be extinguished – that the perpetuity could be broken.[91] Coke himself urged that the rules of the common law should strictly limit uses, a point held in *Chudleigh*.[92] Other attempts to create perpetuities using unbarrable

---

[87] J. H. Baker, *IELH*, pp. 248–97; Baker, *OHLE*, vol. VI, pp. 653–86; Milsom, *Historical Foundations*, pp. 178–99, 225–39; J. C. Gray, *The Rule against Perpetuities* (Boston, MA, 1942), pp. 126–190; N. G. Jones, 'Jane Tyrrel's Case (1557) and the Use upon a Use', *The Journal of Legal History*, 14 (1993), 75–93; J. H. Baker, 'The Use upon a Use in Equity 1558–1625', *Law Quarterly Review*, 93 (1977), 33–8.

[88] Terence Hartley (ed.), *Proceedings in the Parliaments of Elizabeth I*, vol. III (London, 1999), p. 118.

[89] HMC, *Third Report of the Royal Commission on Historical Manuscripts*, p. 10 and also William Holdsworth, 'An Elizabethan Bill Against Perpetuities', *Law Quarterly Review*, 35 (1919), 258–63, at 258; BL Additional MS 25206, f. 121r.

[90] Holdsworth, 'An Elizabethan Bill', 262.

[91] Simpson, *A History of the Land Law*, pp. 218–19, 220.

[92] *Fitzwilliam's Case*, 6 Co. *Rep*. 34a, 77 ER 303; Baker, *IELH*, p. 288.

entails culminated in their rejection in *Mary Portington's Case* (1613), described by Coke as that 'funeral of fond and newfound perpetuities, a monstrous brood carved out of mere invention'.[93] While judicial vigilance had thwarted the creation of some perpetuities, the momentum of these earlier decisions would be reversed in *Pells* v. *Browne* (1620) to the exasperation of Dodderidge.[94] His disappointment echoed the foreboding of Popham just twenty-six years earlier: 'But he said plainly, that if the exposition made on the other side shall take place, it will bring in with it so many mischiefs and inconveniences to the universal disquiet of the realm, that it will cast the whole commonwealth into a sea of troubles.'[95] The ultimate acceptance of the strict settlement in the latter half of the seventeenth century revealed the judicial compromise with the continuing pressure of litigants to protect their settlements.[96] Such tumultuous changes touched the very heart of the common law claims to security of property. J. H. Baker cites the words of Oliver Cromwell to describe the land law as, 'an ungodly jumble', and D. J. Ibbetson has bluntly observed that, 'the Common law was now perceived to be in a mess'.[97]

The common law was part of a much larger system of jurisdictions and legal authorities, a system that had also benefited from significant transformation and increased participation. Christopher Brooks records at least a fourfold surge in levels of litigation in the King's Bench during the period between 1560 and 1580, and sixfold if compared to the likely figure in 1500.[98] Between the 1490s and 1640, he estimates that the volume

---

[93] Baker, *IELH*, p. 287; Simpson, *A History of the Land Law*, p. 211. 10 Co. *Rep.* p. x; *Mary Portington's Case*, 10 Co. *Rep.* 35b, 77 ER 976; *Portington* v. *Rogers* (1611), 2 Brownlow & Goldesborough 141, 123 ER 861. Though Carthew has observed that Coke's settlements were drawn 'as strictly as the law would permit him'. George Carthew, *The Hundred of Launditch* (Norwich, 1877–9), vol. III, p. 106.

[94] Baker, *IELH*, p. 288; Simpson, *A History of the Land Law*, p. 222; *Pell and Brownes Case*, 2 Rolle 216, 81 ER 760; *Pells* v. *Brown*, 1 Equity Cases Abridged 187, 21 ER 978; *Pells* v. *Brown*, Palmer 130, 81 ER 1012.

[95] *Dillon* v. *Fraine* (1594), Popham 83, 79 ER 1195.

[96] Simpson, *Land Law*, pp. 194, 222–3, 233–45. Baker, *OHLE*, vol. VI, p. 684; N. G. Jones, 'Trusts in England after the Statute of Uses: A View from the 16th Century', in Richard Helmholz and Reinhard Zimmerman (eds.), *Hinera Fiduciae; Trust and Treuhand in Historical Perspective* (Berlin, 1998), 180–5; Holdsworth, 'An Elizabethan Bill', 263, citing *Manning* (1609) and *Lampet's* (1612) cases.

[97] Baker, *IELH*, p. 289; D. J. Ibbetson, *Common Law and 'Ius Commune': Selden Society Lecture Delivered in the Old Hall of Lincoln's Inn July 20th, 2000* (London: Selden Society, 2001), p. 21.

[98] C. Brooks, 'Litigants and Attorneys in the King's Bench and Common Pleas, 1560–1640', in J. H. Baker (ed.) *Legal Records and the Historian* (London, 1978), p. 43; Brooks, *Pettyfoggers*, pp. 48–74.

increased fourteen times in the Common Pleas and King's Bench.[99] Robert Palmer has argued that Brooks under-counted by perhaps as much as half the amount of litigation in the central courts.[100] The traditional explanation – that business was drawn off from the ecclesiastical and local courts – has not survived scrutiny.[101] The levels of litigation rose in most courts, both local and royal, and a variety of other explanations have been offered for this increase, including the rising prosperity among the gentry and yeomanry, the impact of the credit economy, more efficient procedures and the low cost of litigation in its early stages.[102] Contemporaries, who also noted the growth in litigation, preferred a moral explanation for the growth of litigation as evidence of an increasingly vexatious society and the wiles of lawyers who stirred up suits.

Contemporaries also perceived this juridical landscape with more nuance and detail than modern historians, who have tended to utilize the broad categories of common law and 'prerogative' courts. But matters were not so simple: many courts might be folded under one general rubric, so a contemporary manual described at least three courts in the Exchequer.[103] Though present-day writers often refer to three courts of common law, contemporaries acknowledged a fourth in the Marshalsea. Forms of law were shared across jurisdictions so that manor courts might apply common law principles and rules, as did the Latin side of the Court of Chancery. Although a lawyer might be rebuked for citing authorities in the civil law, in other cases the court consulted with civilians or common lawyers referred to the Code in arguments.[104] While those who staffed so-called 'prerogative courts' might be partisan, they were also often trained as common lawyers. Sir John Dodderidge could appeal to a shared framework of law in his discourse on method: 'out of the civill lawe are taken many axioms and rules which are like wise borrowed and usually frequented in our lawe for since all laws are derived from the law nature and

---

[99] Brooks, *Pettyfoggers*, p. 54.

[100] http://aalt.law.uh.edu/Litigiousness/Litigation.html (2014).

[101] For a discussion of the increase of litigation in the ecclesiasical courts, see Helmholz, *OHLE*, vol. I, pp. 283–6. The rise in litigation in local courts is addressed by Baker, *OHLE*, vol. VI, pp. 291–319, esp. p. 311; W. A. Champion, 'Litigation in the Boroughs: The Shrewsbury *curia parva*, 1580–1730', *Journal of Legal History*, 15:3 (1994), 201–2, 202–7.

[102] Braddick, *State Formation*, pp. 157–8; Craig Muldrew, 'Credit and the Courts: Debt Litigation in a Seventeenth-Century Urban Community', *Economic History Review*, 2nd series, 46 (1993), 23–38; Brooks, *Pettyfoggers*, pp. 75–111.

[103] Thomas Powell, *The Attourneys Academy* (London, 1623), STC 20163, pp. 190–1.

[104] *Wood v. Ash and Foster* (1586), Godbolt 112, 78 ER 69; *Fraunces and Powell's Case* (1612), Godbolt 191, 78 ER 115; *Light v. Ashton* (1609), HLS MS 1192, f. 127r; *Jones v. Bowen* (1611), HLS MS 1192, f. 225r.

doe concure in the principles of nature and reason'.[105] While courts were thus distinct, they might share aspects of substantive and procedural law, and were bound together by the mobility of practitioners and litigants among them.

This growth of the legal system was not accompanied by systematization from above, and instead the Crown's pursuit of additional revenues often shaped its judicial initiatives. Describing the legal changes during the reign of Henry VIII, G. R. Elton observed that 'Court making was an industry in the early sixteenth century.'[106] Several of these courts were created or enlarged to address issues raised by Tudor policy, such as the court of Delegates for ecclesiastical appeals, First Fruits and Tenths, Augmentations and General Surveyors to administer the financial consequences of the Dissolution, and the High Commission to protect the religious settlement.[107] Other courts expanded their jurisdiction, including the courts of Requests and Star Chamber, the Duchy Chamber of Lancaster, the Councils in the Marches, the Marshalsea, the equity side of the Exchequer, and, perhaps most significantly, the Chancery.[108]

This growing system had both soft and hard hierarchies: certain courts were recognized to be inferior to others, while the disputed relationship between the Chancery and the King's Bench led to endemic sparring. As they took the initiative to develop their own substantive and procedural law, the judges of individual courts established their authority relative to others haphazardly: the daily records of the system are littered with the interactions and negotiations among legal authorities. Though the system depended on the cooperation and harmonization of jurisdictions, this was also a system in tension: courts often determined the limits of their business by probing for the resistance of other jurisdictions.[109] Advocates often supported their claims with imaginative readings of medieval precedents, and invented and disseminated accounts of the court's history. These researches advertised not only the authority of the jurisdiction, but articulated its self-identity. The best known of these writings are the prefaces to Coke's *Reports*, but there were many others: works on the ecclesiastical

---

[105]   BL Additional MS 32092, f. 162r. Note his reference to Justinian in *Frampton* v. *Gerrard* (1604), HLS MS 118(c), f. 27r.

[106]   G. R. Elton, *Reform and Renewal: Thomas Cromwell and the Common Weal* (Cambridge, 1973), pp. 141, 129–57; G. R. Elton, *England under the Tudors* (London, 1991), p. 63.

[107]   Baker, *OHLE*, vol. VI, pp. 221–31.

[108]   *Ibid.*, pp. 206–7.

[109]   Jones, *Elizabethan Court of Chancery*, p. 454. See, for example, the rebuffed attempt by the Council at York to intervene in a suit in the Chancery and the common law, BL Harley MS 1576, f. 174r.

jurisdiction by Thomas Ridley and Richard Hooker, Anthony Benn on the Chancery, Julius Caesar on the Court of Requests, Richard Zouche on the Admiralty and Thomas Warre on the Marshalsea.[110]

It was generally assumed that the courts would supplement each other in a mosaic defined by functional and sometimes territorial separation. Such complexities might confuse foreigners, as when judges in Friesland wrote to England to arrest a defendant and execute their judgment, a matter that was referred to the Admiralty.[111] Even Coke accepted that other courts were needed to dispense justice in areas that the common law did not reach, acknowledging that the Admiralty was a 'great necessity' and of ancient origin.[112] He also offered particular praise to the Star Chamber, a forum needed to punish the diversity of evils, declaring that it was the 'most honourable court ... that is in the Christian world'.[113]

Reformers recognized that these circumstances created opportunities for uncertainty in the law. Attempts to determine jurisdictional boundaries led to conflict between courts intent on competing with each other or protecting their judicial business. Litigants might take advantage of this confusion, moving from venue to venue when they were thwarted in one jurisdiction or litigating concurrently in different courts. Both T. G. Barnes and Steve Hindle observed that the Star Chamber, for example, could be an advantageous forum in which to pursue such delaying tactics.[114] Meanwhile the pursuit of lucrative fees collected by judges and their clerks might not have induced corrupt practices, but at the least encouraged them to open their forums to a wider circle of litigants.[115]

The development of the Marshalsea exemplifies the difficulty of reducing jurisdictional competition to a story about the prerogative. Instead, the Marshalsea's ambitions demonstrate the entrepreneurship of its officials and the countervailing tendency to maintain equilibrium in the system. The Marshalsea was undoubtedly an old foundation, some claimed

---

[110] Richard Zouch, *The Jurisdiction of the Admiralty of England* (London, 1663), Wing Z22; BL Cotton MS Titus C I, f. 137v, printed as 'Reasons that the Court of Marshalsea ...' in Thomas Hearn (ed.), *A Collection of Curious Discourses* (London, 1771), vol. II, p. 146. The author was probably Thomas Warre, then steward of the Marshalsea, see BL Additional MS 25247, f. 1; BL Stowe MS 568, f. 57v.

[111] *Anonymous* v. *Wyer* (1605), BL Additional MS 25206, f. 51r.

[112] *Greeneway* v. *Baker* (1612), HLS MS 114, f. 78v.

[113] 4 Co. *Inst.*, pp. 63, 65.

[114] Hindle, *Social Change*, pp. 84–5; Barnes, 'Slow Process', 339.

[115] Wilfrid Prest, 'Judicial Corruption in Early Modern England', *Past and Present*, 133 (1991), 67–95, at 76–8; Dan Klerman, 'Jurisdictional Competition and the Evolution of the Common Law', *University of Chicago Law Review*, 74 (2007), 1,179.

it was the oldest court in England, and applied the common law in its proceedings.[116] The court was empowered to hear causes in the 'verge', or the area twelve miles in all directions from the residence of the king. The *Articuli super Cartas* (1301) formalized its powers, explicitly prohibiting the court from hearing matters of freehold or contract that did not involve members of the king's household. Instead, the statute granted the court pleas of trespass, a move that curtailed its jurisdiction at the time. While attempts had been made in the fifteenth century to circumvent some of these restrictions, it was the common law development of trespass as a remedy for both contract and disputes over land that allowed the court to expand its business.[117] The Marshalsea began to hear *assumpsit* actions and gained a window onto the lucrative business of enforcing contracts and debts in London.[118] This development was strongly resisted by the other common law courts through prohibition.[119] In several cases, culminating in the *Case of the Marshalsea* (1612), the common law judges asserted that the court had overstepped its boundaries and should not hear *assumpsit* except where the parties were both of the royal household.[120]

The historian of the Marshalsea has seen in common law opposition to its hearing *assumpsit* a jealousy of the king and the royal prerogative – the Marshalsea being the 'King's "private liberty"'.[121] But lawyers and judges seldom revealed this jealousy in their arguments when they discussed the 'peculiar and private liberty', which some claimed had its origins in 'time out of mind'.[122] Dodderidge, while defending the jurisdiction as counsel, merely suggested that contract was within the jurisdiction of the court, alluding to the development of *assumpsit* at the common law.[123] When George Croke explained why the court ought to be restrained, he referred

[116] Its errors were reversible by the King's Bench. On the honour and dignity of the court see, *Case of the Marshalsea* (1612), 10 Co. *Rep.* 69b, 77 ER 1029.

[117] These early attempts were barred by 15 Henry VI, c. 2. Douglas Greene, 'The Court of the Marshalsea in Late Tudor and Stuart England', *The American Journal of Legal History*, 20:4 (1976), 267–81, at 268.

[118] *Case of the Marshalsea*, 10 Co. *Rep.* 70b, 77 ER 1030. They may also have been hearing cases touching realty through ejectment; BL Lansdowne MS 486, f. 208v.

[119] *Case of the Marshalsea*, 10 Co. *Rep.* 76a, 77 ER 1038; 2 Co. *Inst.*, p. 538.

[120] *Michelborn's Case* (1596), 6 Co. *Rep.* 20b, 77 ER 284; *Cox* v. *Gray*, 1 Bulstrode 207, 80 ER 893 and *Cox and Gray's Case* (1612) Godbolt 184, 78 ER 112; *Case of the Marshalsea*, 10 Co. *Rep.* 72a, 77 ER 1032. Manuscript reports of the case are found in BL Additional MS 25213, ff. 127v–133r and CUL MS Ii.5.26, f. 26r.

[121] Greene, 'Court of the Marshalsea', 269.

[122] Edward Bulstrode, *The Reports of Edward Bulstrode* (London, 1657), Wing B5444, p. 208, and similarly BL Hargrave 307, f. 41r.

[123] *Hall* v. *Stanley* (1611), HLS MS 114, f. 51v; Bodl. Rawlinson C 643, f. 45v; *The Case of the Marshalsea*, 10 Co. *Rep.* 68b, 77 ER 1027.

to its function: it was 'erect[ed] for a special purpose, and thus has a special jurisdiction', which was to settle matters in the king's house.[124] Croke warned that the court's innovation might lead to trial of freehold there, a clear departure from established practice. Nor did he represent the Marshalsea as somehow standing for the prerogative against the common law. Instead the common law could limit the inferior jurisdiction because it was more closely associated with the king, who was present in the court, whereas the Marshalsea merely 'followed the person of the king'.[125]

The clamour in the parliaments of 1606 and then again in 1610 revealed that the Marshalsea's swelling jurisdiction impinged not only on the senior courts of common law, but on the local courts as well.[126] Alongside complaints that the officers of the court were extorting fees and stirring up suits was the claim that the Marshalsea was taking away business from the civic courts. A petition to parliament in 1605, which was signed by inhabitants of London and surrounding areas, supports the contention that opposition was driven by a concern over the displacement of other jurisdictions, the expense of the court, and the 'multitude and abuses of officers'.[127] This was a familiar pattern: London courts also engaged in this sort of entrepreneurship, and James wrote to London in 1604 complaining that through the use of fictions they were usurping on the Admiralty.[128] In 1611 the Marshalsea was re-established as the Court of the Verge, and the patent suggested that at least some of these complaints were taken seriously, the drafters conceding that there had been oppressions on the part of officers of the court, 'that make a gain upon arrests by stirring of suits upon malice or frivolous causes'.[129]

The Marshalsea had sought to benefit from the common law development of trespass and expand beyond its traditional jurisdiction, but in doing so it disrupted its relationship with other courts. The common

---

124   *Cox v. Gray* (1610), BL Additional MS 25213, f. 128r.
125   *Cox v. Gray*, 1 Bulstrode 208, 80 ER 894.
126   *CJ*, vol. I, pp. 278, 284, 301, 310, 328–9, 333, 369, 371–2; *LJ*, vol. II, p. 436; Robert Bowyer, *The Parliamentary Diary of Robert Bowyer, 1606–1607*, ed. David Willson (1931), pp. 61, 170, 274–5. Copies of bills that were proposed can be found in *Fourth Report of the Royal Commission on Historical Manuscripts* (London, 1874), p. 118; *The Manuscripts of His Grace the Duke of Buccleuch, and Queensbury* (London, 1897), vol. III, pp. 115–16. See also the account in PRO SP 9/209, f. 19r.
127   BL Lansdowne MS 487, ff. 206r–v. The petition is PRO E163/17/11, and a legal opinion from 1607 supported them. Local court rivalries may be underestimated; see a similar complaint involving a vice-admiralty court and the court of King's Lynn, NRO MC 571/4.
128   PRO HCA 30/4, [n.f.]; repeating a complaint of 1598.
129   PRO E163/17/11; reprinted in Spedding (ed.), *Letters and Life*, vol. IV, pp. 263–4.

law judges insisted on the functional purpose of the Marshalsea in their campaign to limit its jurisdiction. Defenders of the court turned to the other major argument at hand: that their jurisdiction would provide better justice and remedy corruptions. When Thomas Warre did appeal to the court's use of the prerogative it was in the context of justifying the entry of the court's officers into liberties where corrupt bailiffs sheltered bankrupts.[130] When the Marshalsea was refounded with Francis Bacon as its first judge, he used arguments about the court's nearness to the king as an exhortation that its proceedings must 'in the execution of justice … be exemplary unto other places'.[131]

Bacon was well informed about the problems in the legal system and he shared with Coke a belief that 'Certainty is so essential to law, that law cannot even be just without it.'[132] Though his later tenure as chancellor proved professionally disastrous, he had sought significant reforms in the law throughout his career. Writing to James I in 1616, he summarized the concerns of many other reformers:

1. That the multiplicity and length of suits is great.
2. That the contentious person is armed, and the honest subject wearied and oppressed …
4. That the Chancery courts are more filled, the remedy of law being often obscure and doubtful.
5. That the ignorant lawyer shroudeth his ignorance of law in that doubts are so frequent and many.
6. That men's assurances of their lands and estates by patents, deeds, wills, are often subject to question, and hollow.[133]

His complaints may have been self-serving, but others also voiced them in surviving texts and parliamentary debate.[134] In his *Lawiers Logike* Abraham Fraunce complained that the 'Law is in vaste volumes confusedly scattered and utterly undigested' and Fulbecke referred to 'an ocean of reportes, and such a perplexed confusion of opinions'.[135] John Davies acknowledged these criticisms, even as he sought to reassure his readers about the efficacy of the common law: 'So are there other vulgar

---

[130] Warre, 'Reasons', p. 146.
[131] BL Additional MS 73087, f. 147v.
[132] James Spedding, Robert Leslie Ellis and Douglas Denon Heath (eds.), *The Works of Sir Francis Bacon* (London, 1858; repr. 1963), vol. V, p. 90; vol. III, p. 319.
[133] Spedding (ed.), *Letters and Life*, vol. VI, p. 64.
[134] BL Royal MS 18.A.36, f. 5r; Hill, *Intellectual*, pp. 203–4. Prest, 'Judicial Corruption', 74.
[135] William Fulbecke, *A Direction or Preparatorie to the Study of the Lawe* (London, 1600), f. 5r; Abraham Fraunce, *The Lawiers Logike Exemplifying the Praecepts of Logike by the Practise of the Common Lawe* (London, 1588), STC 11343, sig. 3v.

imputations cast uppon the lawe and lawiers ... namely 1. that there is much uncerteinty in the reasons and Iudgements of the lawe. 2. that there are extreame and unnecessary delayes in the proceedings of the lawe. 3. that many bad and dishonest causes are wittingly defended by the professors of the lawe.'[136]

Reformers differed on the source of the problems that they identified: was it the law itself or those who practised it? Christopher Brooks and Wilfrid Prest have written at length on negative attitudes towards solicitors and attorneys, and the belief that the underlying cause of frivolous suits was the 'multitude of attornies'.[137] Prest has suggested that complaints rose in tandem with the size of the profession and its increased contact with the population.[138] The lucrative possibilities of lawyering may have attracted less capable candidates and encouraged others to pretend to be lawyers to stir up or profit from suits.[139] Levelling a common charge, one angry litigant in Gloucester faced a slander suit for calling a common lawyer a 'mayteyner of felonyes' who 'use[d] to playe on both hands'.[140] Similarly, Thomas Wilson criticized the common lawyers when he explained that they earned their living by 'seeking meanes to sett their neighbors at varriance'.[141] Nor were the criticisms without effect: Coke is described as having 'galled and glanced' at scholars after *Ignoramus* was performed at Cambridge in front of the king, 'which hath so netled the lawiers'.[142] Even those who praised the common law might warn of the ignorance and corruption of some of its practitioners.[143]

---

[136] John Davies, *Le Primer Report des Cases & Matters en Ley Resolves & Adiudges en les Courts del Roy en Ireland* (London, 1615), STC 6361, sig. *3v–*4r.

[137] BL Harley MS 141, f. 45v. Brooks, *Pettyfoggers*, pp. 48–74; Prest, *Rise of the Barristers*, pp. 49–82 and Wilfred Prest, *The Inns of Court under Elizabeth I and the early Stuarts, 1590–1640* (London, 1972), pp. 50–1.

[138] Prest, *Rise of the Barristers*, pp. 286–7.

[139] PRO STAC 8 5/9, *Attorney-General v. Jones* (1606); STAC 8 201/5, *Litton v. Somerscales* (1610).

[140] *Rich v. Holt* (1609), HLS MS 1165, f. 85r; and other examples of maintenance and ambidexterity: *Dawtrey v. Miles* (1604), BL Additional MS 25213, f. 57r; *Hunt v. Parker* (1606), BL Additional MS 25213, f. 70v; Prest, *Rise of the Barristers*, pp. 293–9. Jonathan Rose discusses defamation suits for claims of ambidexterity against lawyers in 'Of Ambidexters and Daffidowndillies: Defamation of Lawyers, Legal Ethics, and Profession Reputation', *University of Chicago Law School Roundtable*, 8 (2001). Coke brought a defamation suit for the claim that he had taken fees from both plaintiff and defendant in the same case; see *Coke v. Baxter* (1585), discussed by Rose and reprinted in R. H. Helmholz, *Select Cases on Defamation to 1600* (London, 1985), pp. 66–7.

[141] PRO SP 12/280, p. 49. Additional criticisms can be found in Hill, *Intellectual Origins*, p. 203.

[142] Chamberlain, *Letters*, vol. I, pp. 597–8.   [143] BL Additional MS 41613, ff. 82r, 84r.

In their criticisms contemporaries also revealed their ambivalence about legal proceedings, a point suggested by the ironic libel, 'Tis our Comon moane / Lawyers have fowle faultes though the Lawe have none.'[144] The great numbers of councillors who created an 'intollerable charge and delays in law' went 'shifting and roaming bar to bar'.[145] The arguments of these lawyers were 'rather a mayntenaunce of injustice than a furtherer of Justice'.[146] There was long-standing suspicion that clerks and lawyers padded their fees and prolonged lawsuits out of self-interest.[147] Clients retained multiple lawyers to make sure that causes were answered or forwarded in the different courts. Disappointed litigants complained of huge expenses paid towards their suits, such as one who claimed £3,000 spent in the Chancery.[148] The preamble of a bill in the Commons declared that 'the charge of prosecuting suits in law is at this day so excessive that most suitors were better to sit down under the burden of their wrongs then attempt suit for the obtaining of their rights'.[149]

These complaints included concerns about aspects of the law itself. There were long-standing criticisms of the common law's language and arcana, those 'barbarous law-phrase[s]' and especially of law French, culminating in the king's own remarks and Ruggle's *Ignoramus*.[150] There were complaints about sacred common law institutions, such as the

---

[144] BL Additional MS 34218, f. 154r.

[145] BL Lansdowne MS 44, f. 1v. For other complaints about the numbers of lawyers see Huntington Library Ellesmere MS 452; BL Lansdowne MS 43, f. 90v; BL Royal MS 18.A.73, ff. 2r–7v.

[146] Holkham MS 677, f. 423r.

[147] Thomas Starkey, *A Dialogue between Cardinal Pole and Thomas Lupset* (London, 1989), pp. 77–82; PRO SP 1/85 f. 100, cited in Elton, *Reform and Renewal*, p. 139. Though individual fees may not have been as severe as contemporaries alleged, the total costs of a lawsuit could be significant. Wilfrid Prest, 'Counsellors' Fees and Earnings in the Age of Sir Edward Coke', in Baker (ed.), *Legal Records and the Historian*, pp. 165–84, at p. 171. Prest also acknowledges the problem of judicial corruption in *Rise of the Barristers*, p. 311.

[148] PRO C115/100 7571; BL Additional MS 46410, f. 298r.

[149] BL Lansdowne MS 487, f. 203v; and various complaints, Huntington Library Ellesmere MS 2994; PRO 30/26/201.

[150] Chamberlain, *Letters*, vol. I, p. 243; James I, *King James VI and I: Political Writings*, ed. Johann P. Sommerville (Cambridge, 2006), p. 186; Fulke Greville, 'Of Laws', in *Works* (London, 1870), vol. I, stanzas 266–8; Thomas Elyot, *The Book Named the Governor* (New York, 1962), p. 54. For a discussion of the public perception of the common lawyers during the period, see E. W. Ives, 'The Reputation of the Common Lawyer in English Society, 1450–1550', *University of Birmingham Historical Journal*, 7 (1960), pp. 130–61; Prest, *Rise of the Barristers*, pp. 283–326; E. J. F. Tucker, 'Ruggle's *Ignoramus* and Humanistic Criticism of the Language of the Common Law', *Renaissance Quarterly*, 30 (1977), 341–50.

jury.[151] In a debate over tithes, Egerton argued that the matter was best left to the ecclesiastical judge rather than 'the oathes of 12 ignorant and perhapps partiall men, whoe may make it their owne case'.[152] But the suspicion that the law was uncertain and open to abuse drew most concern. Tracts by non-lawyers found fault with legal innovations that had crept in, especially at the common law. Perpetuities were works of pride carried out by 'man castinge aboute howe to make his owne will inviolable lyke gods'.[153] The use of ejectment to try title would 'quyet not possessions'.[154] Even laymen noticed these innovations and identified their significance with precision: 'the Common Law is much fallen from her first grounds … the cause … is the neglecting or wresting of the true nature and use of originall writts … and except the common law bee first confined to originall Writts it cannot bee kept within its owne lymits'.[155] The common law could also be accused of jurisdictional creep, and Sir Francis Kynaston attacked the excessive claims of the common lawyers.[156]

Perhaps the most significant consequence of these criticisms during Coke's time on the bench was their acceptance by the king himself.[157] Knafla has described James as a 'conservative reformer', who attempted to work with his judges.[158] From his earliest days in England James had already received reports of problems in the common law and statute, even as he promised not to alter them unduly. Given James's own highly moralistic statements of his responsibilities to provide justice, and the sinfulness of injustice, he leaned towards an active involvement in addressing the legal system's problems.[159] The king's concern about the state of the law appeared in his speech to parliament in 1607:

---

[151] BL Additional MS 41613, f. 84r; Conyers Read (ed.), *William Lambarde and Local Government: His 'Ephemeris' and Twenty-nine Charges to Juries and Commissions* (Ithaca, NY, 1962), p. 106.

[152] LRO MS 1953 D26/2595, f. 2v; Bodl. Tanner MS 280, f. 121v. See also Fulbecke, *The Second Part of the Parallele*, sig. B.

[153] BL Additional MS 25206, f. 116v.   [154] Bodl. English History MS B 117, f. 40r.

[155] BL Lansdowne MS 253, f. 174r.   [156] BL Lansdowne MS 213, ff. 151v–152r.

[157] F. W. Maitland, *English Law and the Renaissance: The Rede Lecture for 1901* (Littleton, 1985), p. 17ff. Croft suggests that James may have 'paid little heed' to the constitutional significance of the historical and legal debates underway; Pauline Croft, *King James* (Basingstoke, 2003), p. 134. James's early 'absolutist' claims were probably related to resistance theory; Peck, 'Kingship, Counsel and Law', pp. 84–5.

[158] L. A. Knafla, 'Britain's Solomon: King James and the Law' in Mark Fortier and Daniel Fischlin (eds.), *Royal Subjects: Essays on the Writings of James VI and I* (Detroit, MI, 2002), pp. 235–64, at pp. 243, 255–6.

[159] Bodl. MS Ashmolean 1729, ff. 43r; 68r. Knafla, 'Britain's Solomon', pp. 236, 251.

> But as every Law would be cleare and full, so the obscuritie in some points of this our written Law, and want of fulnesse in others, the variation of Cases and men[']s curiositie, breeding every day new questions, hath enforced the Iudges to iudge in any Cases here, by Cases and presidents, wherein I hope Lawyers themselves will not denie but that there must be a great uncertaintie ... Wherefore, leave not the Law to the pleasure of the Iudge, but let your Lawes be looked into.[160]

That these remarks were made in the context of debate over the Union project, which presupposed the joining of the laws of the two countries, may well have added to their pointedness.[161] But James was repeating criticisms frequently made by those worried about the condition of the law, and his call for reform should be placed within this wider context. If union might have supplied the occasion, it was the apprehension of the health of the legal system that had created the need. Nor did James abandon his call for improvement as the Union project collapsed. In 1610, while praising the excellence of the common law, he continued by arguing that the law should be reformed. He urged that the law should be written in English, rather than Law French, which was 'an old, mixt, and corrupt Language, onely understood by Lawyers: whereas every Subiect ought to understand the law under which he lives'.[162] James had already revealed himself to be sceptical of the system of law reporting, perhaps owing to the influence of his Scots law background, and complained that the common law did not have a 'setled text'. He warned that the common law 'hath not in some cases grounds nor maxims but is grounded by reports which is but according the opinion of the judge or reporter. Lastly, there are in the common law contrary laws, precedents and reports'.[163] In 1610 he urged that 'it were good, that upon a mature deliberation, the exposition of the Law were set downe by Acte of Parliament, and such reports therein conformed ... and so the people should not depend upon the bare opinions of Iudges, and uncertaine Reports'.[164] In this parliament James also proposed a programme of fourteen reforms. Many of these

---

[160] James I, *Political Writings*, pp. 162–3.
[161] The king later denied that he had intended to 'conform' the laws of England to those of Scotland; James I, *Political Writings*, p. 209. For concerns over the king's attitude to the law and his dislike of the jury, see CUL MS Additional 335, f. 60v. Brian Levack examines the several meanings of the 'union' of the laws, observing that of the various proposals from 1603 to 1707, 'very few actually called for their fusion'; *The Formation of the British State* (Oxford, 1987), pp. 68–91, at p. 72; Bruce Galloway, *The Union of England and Scotland 1603–1608* (Edinburgh, 1986), pp. 38–41.
[162] James I, *Political Writings*, p. 186; PRO SP 14/57, f. 91r.
[163] James I, *Political Writings*, p. 61.   [164] *Ibid.*, p. 187.

touched on legal matters, suggesting his perception of incompetence or corruption in inferior officers, or tackled specific grievances in law, such as the enlarging of persons upon executions after judgments, the rise in fees and the number of attorney.[165] Later, in 1616, he would repeat the charge that the common law needed reformation, taking issue with its 'incertaintie and noveltie: Incertaintie is found in the Law it selfe … The other corruption is introduced by the Iudges themselves, by Nicities that are used.'[166]

While the king's proposals might have been threatening to some, they were perceptive: his attitude towards Coke and the judges had as much to do with his recognition of the problems in the law as with a disposition towards absolutism. It is likely that he was confirmed in his opinions by Egerton, who also repeatedly described the uncertainty in the system and sought,

> To propounde to the Iudges howe the Incertentye of Iudicature maye be reformed and reduced to more certentye, and how the Infinite multiply-citye of sutes maye be avoyded, with which the people are intollerablye reped, and put to excessiue charge, as by verditte agaynst verditte, and by Iudgement agaynst Iudgement, and by manifoulde sutes in severall Courtes for one and the selfe same Cause.[167]

The causes, he explained, were a consequence both of the growth of the number of lawyers and the innovations in the common law. *Latitats* were 'a noveltye and a tricke newlye devised … and is contrary to the auncyent institucion, and true groundes of the Law, and is the occasion of infinite sutes'. He regretted the decline of the ancient real actions and the rise of ejectment, 'one other of the greatest causes of incertentye of Iudicature, and of multiplycitye and infinitenes of sutes'. Ejectment had eroded the certainty of the ancient actions and 'hath bene a great decaye of the true knowledge and learninge of the lawe in reall accions, and hath almost utterlye ouerthrowne, all accions realle that be possessory'.[168]

Coke joined Egerton in this conservatism and his perception of problems in the law. He explicitly placed his law reporting as a response to

---

[165] *PP 1610*, vol. II, pp. 279–82.
[166] James I, *Political Writings*, p. 211.
[167] Egerton, 'Memorialles for Iudicature Pro Bono Publico', in Knafla, *Law and Politics*, p. 274. For Egerton's contribution to Star Chamber reform, see Barnes, 'Slow Process', 243, 316–19.
[168] James I, *Political Writings*, p. 276.

James's call for law reform, writing that the king had asked that the confusion in the law be cleared: '[he] hath both encouraged and imposed a necessity upon me to publish this Fourth book'.[169] While James had sought remedy in the reformation of the statute law as a foundation on which judicial opinions might be better settled, Coke worked instead to identify that bedrock within the law itself. Coke chose to represent the confusion in the law as a consequence of a departure away from the medieval learning, and warned against judicial entrepreneurship.[170] He cautioned later in his life with the benefit of hindsight that, 'So in the Common wealth (Justice being the main preserver thereof) if one Court should usurp, or incroach upon another, it would introduce incertainty, subvert Justice, and bring all things in the end to confusion.'[171] The decline of the real actions provided a further explanation for uncertainty and the rise of vexatious litigation:

> 1. The multitude of suits in personal actions, wherein the reality of freehold and inheritance is tried, to the intolerable charge and vexation of the subject. 2. Multiplicity of suits in one and the same case; wherein oftentimes there are divers verdicts on the one side, and divers on the other, and yet the plaintiff or defendant can come to no finite end, nor can hold the possession in quiet, though it be often tried and adjudged for either party.[172]

Coke warned litigation would 'never' come to a 'final end' through the use of personal actions, such as trespass, for freehold. A wise litigant should choose the real actions instead and this opinion seemed to stand with logic: real actions were meant for land, while personal actions addressed people and their conduct. The consequence of the use of personal actions for land was profound: 'great oppression might be done under colour and pretence of law; for if there should not be an end of suits, then a rich and malicious man would infinitely vex him who hath right by suits and actions'.[173] As early as 1592 in his reading on uses he had warned of the problems that these devices posed to security of property: 'And forasmuch as noe one thinge tended soe much to the subversion of the auncient comon lawes of this realme, as feoffments and other [e]states made to secreate and subtell uses.'[174] Uses, Coke claimed, might hide true

---

[169] 4 Co. *Rep.*, pp. xviii–xix.   [170] 3 Co. *Rep.*, pp. xxii–xxiii.
[171] 4 Co. *Inst.*, 'Proeme'.
[172] 8 Co. *Rep.*, p. xxv; *Ferrers Case* (1598), 6 Co. *Rep.* 9a, 77 ER 266.
[173] *Ferrer's Case* (1598), 6 Co. *Rep.* 9a, 77 ER 266.
[174] BL Hargrave MS 33, f. 136v.

ownership, and the complexity of their arrangements was cause for litigation and the locking up of land. He stridently condemned uses which
were 'never known the ancient sages of the law … [and] fettered freeholds
and inheritances'.[175]

If the law was uncertain it was owing to such innovations and the
ignorance of its principles. Tinkering with the law by inventive lawyers
and the novelties introduced by 'long and ill penned statutes' had debili-
tated the law.[176] Coke's principal example of these 'ill penned statutes' was
De Donis, 'shaking a main pillar of the law, that made all estates of inheritance fee-simple, no wisdom could foresee such and so many mischiefs
as upon those fettered inheritances followed'.[177] Coke provided details of
its many mischiefs: 'purchasers defeated, leases evicted, other estates and
grants made upon just and good consideration were avoided, creditors
defrauded of their just and due debts, offenders emboldened to commit
capital offences'.[178] Poor drafting of other statutes led judges into interpretative contortions that confused the case law.[179] Coke declared that the
troubles grew because 'the right institution of the Law is not observed, to
the unjust slander of the common law, and to the intolerable hindrance
of the commonwealth'.[180] If James had complained about the wavering
decisions of the judges, Coke responded that statutes and innovations had
forced the judges to make opaque pronouncements. The 'right institution'
of the law might require 'strictness' in order 'to take away the multiplicity and infiniteness of suits, trials, recoveries, and judgment in one and
the same case', a determination that would later spark conflict with the
Chancery.[181]

What was to be done? The king, Egerton and Coke agreed that the
common law was uncertain, but had different perspectives on the solutions. Charles Reid, for instance, persuasively points to the contrasting
approaches of Coke and Bacon to uses: Bacon tended to embrace and
seek to rationalize the new learning, whereas Coke adopted a more rigid,
conservative view of change.[182] Traditionalists such as Coke and Egerton
could not hope to have their true programmes realized: the shrinking of

---

[175] 10 Co. *Rep.*, p. x.   [176] 4 Co. *Rep.*, p. xvii.

[177] 9 Co. *Rep.*, p. xxxvii, and 3 Co. *Rep.*, p. xxxiii; also the statute of 34 Edward III, of non-
claim, 4 Co. *Rep.*, p. vi. Egerton also complained about the statute; W. H. Bryson (ed.),
Cases Concerning Equity and the Courts of Equity 1550–1660 (London, 2001), vol. I,
p. 306.

[178] 4 Co. *Rep.*, p. vi.   [179] 10 Co. *Rep.*, p. xiii.

[180] 8 Co. *Rep.*, p. xxvi; 4 Co. *Rep.*, p. xvii.

[181] *Ferrer's Case*, 6 Co. *Rep.* 9a, 77 ER 266.

[182] Reid, 'Revolution in the English Land Law', 281–91.

the Bar and the ancient actions returned to pre-eminence. Coke might write wistfully that eventually the 'corruptions' of the present law would be rejected and haven sought in the older learning 'with great applause, for avoiding of many inconveniences restored again'.[183] But competition, the clamour of litigant-customers and the superiority of the new actions mitigated against such a restoration.

Instead Egerton and Coke worked as consolidators and rationalizers in different ways. Egerton developed the Chancery as a forum of ultimate justice, by working to reform the system as whole.[184] In 1585 a pair of documents circulated that suggested lawyers' fees should be limited, the author proposing that the courts be required to report their fees and any change from the first year of the reign.[185] The idea of such a general investigation into the fees of the central royal courts was not new and ultimately developed into the Commissions on Fees.[186] The mandate of the commissions, however, was broader than merely the inspection of fees, and included the investigation of corruption and the improvement of procedure across the royal courts.[187] Whereas criticism had led to the shelving of an earlier proposal for special commissions to investigate local corruption and informers, the Commissions on Fees met with approval.[188] The first of these commissions ran from 1594 to 1598, and later generations remembered it as Egerton's project.[189] The investigation was thorough: the

---

[183] 3 Co. *Rep.*, p. xxxiii.

[184] His work of 'procedural clarification' in the Chancery is discussed by Jones, *Elizabethan Court of Chancery*, pp. 79, 82–3.

[185] BL Lansdowne MS 44, f. 28r. See also Alford's complaints in 1571, BL Lansdowne MS 44, ff. 2r–v and those of Thomas Lichfield concerning corruption in the Exchequer: BL Lansdowne MS 28, nos. 1, 2; Lansdowne MS 35, esp. ff. 23r, 31r; Lansdowne MS 40, no. 40; Lansdowne MS 37, no. 50; Lansdowne MS 44, f. 17v.

[186] See Brooks, *Pettyfoggers*, p. 146; Jones, *Elizabethan Court of Chancery*, pp. 86–7; Aylmer, 'Charles I's Commission on Fees, 1627–40', 58–67; Wilson, 'Sir Henry Spelman and the Royal Commission on Fees, 1622–40', pp. 456–70. See also the proposal sent to James I for a general visitation complaining of abuses in the courts, BL Hargrave MS 395, ff. 1r–8v.

[187] The Elizabethan instructions are found in Lambeth Palace Library, Fairhurst MS 2002, ff. 84r–92v.

[188] Nicholas Bacon had proposed these commissions as early as 1563 and Burghley launched investigations into informers in 1574–5; PRO SP 12/110/25, ff. 60–5. Bacon also 'proposed a major official consolidation in 1575' of the statutes; J. H. Baker, 'English Law Books and Legal Publishing' in John Barnard and D. F. McKenzie (eds.), *The Cambridge History of the Book in Britain* (Cambridge, 2010), vol. IV, pp. 474–503, at p. 493.

[189] The *teste* of the Commission being 10 June, 36 Elizabeth I (1594); Bodl. Tanner MS 101, f. 90r (probably from 1627); Barnes, 'Slow Process', 318; Huntington Library Ellesmere MS 2749.

presentment from March 1598 of the Chancery and several other courts provided a list of fees, revealed any changes, their causes and whether they were accepted or rejected by the commissioners.[190] Later commissions used the fees recorded in this survey as the benchmarks by which they calculated increases in their own times.[191] As the new Master of the Rolls, Egerton used the commissions as a vehicle for the review of the royal courts alongside the recording of their charges.[192] The commissioners in the Star Chamber, for example, were instructed to investigate extortions and to record the court's ordinances.[193] The instructions for the Chancery also directed the commissioners to look into abuses.[194] The commissions' effects were varied. They seem to have inspired the setting down of ordinances in several courts and the consideration of defects that allowed for vexation.[195] But as Egerton discovered, limiting vexatious litigation and the expense of the law was difficult: entrenched interests, the dynamics of the system and economic forces militated against change.[196]

Alongside their judicial and administrative efforts, Coke and Egerton also attempted to use parliament to reform the law. The root of certain problems, especially the repeal of the penal laws, could only be tackled by legislation. Both lawyers and laymen joined their work, often motivated by personal experience. In one debate over law reform Thomas Digges reported that 'I had my self a cause which after long sute I lost by non suit by reason my counsell had pleaded amysse. I told and complynd to the iudge; he answered I had right but he could not help me.'[197] William Fleetwood added that he 'knewe a C[li] land once lost by cunninge pleading of 2 lawyers ... I sawe it and sighed at it when I sawe it and could not help it'.[198] Signalling perhaps the disagreement within the profession over

---

[190] PRO 30/26/119; for the Exchequer see PRO E 407/71.

[191] Later commissioners believed that Egerton had set the fees back to their levels before 1587. A list of all legal fees in the Court of Westminster from 1597 may be a result of the 1594 commission, see BL Harley MS 6808, f. 116ff; Bodl. Tanner MS 101, 90r.

[192] A sample of the articles used in the commission is Bodl. Tanner MS 280, f. 472r. For Egerton's continuing concern over legal costs, see Egerton, 'Memorialles for Iudicature, Pro Bono Publico', in Knalfa, *Law and Politics*, pp. 274–81; PRO C 66/1414 [5623]; *CSPD, James I, 1603–1610*, p. 637; A. P. Newton (ed.), *Calendar of the Manuscripts of Major-General Lord Sackville* (London, 1940), vol. I, pp. 221–2.

[193] BL Cotton MS Vespasian C XIV, vol. II, f. 15r.

[194] PRO 30/26/119, p. 1.

[195] BL Harley MS 2310 and Bodl. Tanner MS 101, ff. 71v–77.

[196] Barnes, 'Slow Process', 316; Brooks is more optimistic that concern over fees limited their rise; Brooks, *Pettyfoggers*, pp. 149–50.

[197] Hartley (ed.), *Proceedings in the Parliaments of Elizabeth I*, vol. II, p. 115.

[198] *Ibid.*, p. 116. See also, for example, the case of *Snigg* v. *Shereston* (1605) in which Baron Snigg purchased land that he discovered was encumbered with a reversion. The case led

the law's transformation, Digges recounted that parliament had previously considered a reform bill that the 'elder lawyers' had approved, but the younger had not. Legislative reform was made difficult by the limited duration of parliamentary sittings and competition from more immediate issues, such as the war with Spain, the Union project and Crown finance. Yet law reform was, nonetheless, a preoccupation of these parliaments: David Dean, expanding the work of Geoffrey Elton, has recorded a sharp jump in the volume of legislation and attempted legislation dealing with law reform during the last six sessions of the reign of Elizabeth I.[199] Dean has also provides a thorough survey of this legislation in the Elizabethan parliaments, revealing that parliamentarians concerned themselves with problems in legal process, including corruption, *latitats*, vexatious litigation and especially fees.[200]

Coke was among those common lawyers advocating reform by statute, a labour that was most apparent in the 1620s. Stephen White has described in detail Coke's efforts in 1621 and 1624 to restrain abuses related to court proceedings. His priorities, White argues, were to stem judicial corruption, the manipulation of procedures to extort or oppress individuals, reduce costs and delays in law, and prevent the 'illegal delegation of judicial and quasi-judicial powers'.[201] Coke was 'highly critical of the English legal system', though White acknowledges that the parliamentary records capture only a portion of his reform agenda and reveal little of his underlying motivations. Coke's interest in reform was a 'basically moralistic critique' and 'did not imply the need for fundamental institutional change'.[202] A longer perspective suggests that Coke's interest in reform was programmatic and more fundamental than the parliamentary records of the 1620s reveal. Reform was the crucial influence on his legal thinking and led him to claim that the common law functioned as the guardian of royal authority and the use of its delegation. Moreover, Coke's advocacy of extensive common law oversight was a recognition that the problems in the law extended beyond the actions of a few bad individuals, and into the very dynamics that incentivized behaviours in the system.[203] His work in the 1620s was the outgrowth of those experiences that preoccupied him earlier in his career.

---

to a warning that soliciting to 'stirre upp old tytles uppon noe ground' was contrary to the law. HLS MS 149, f. 7v and STAC 8 267/20.

[199] David Dean, *Law-Making and Society in Late Elizabethan England: The Parliament of England, 1584–1601* (Cambridge, 1996), p. 188.

[200] *Ibid.*, pp. 188–216.   [201] White, *Sir Edward Coke*, pp. 46–85, 49.

[202] *Ibid.*, p. 84.   [203] *Pace* White, *Sir Edward Coke*, pp. 48, 51.

Coke's use of legislation to pursue law reform stretched back to the 1590s. In 1597–8 he brought down a bill from the Lords that attempted to prevent the alteration of fines by searchers in the archives.[204] The final concord was of special interest to Coke, and when he lectured on the Statute of Fines in 1579 he declared that it was 'first instituted for the quiet establishing and sure setting of men[']s inheritances'.[205] Anticipating his work in the 1620s that would restrict the multiplication of suits, Coke also achieved some legislative success in 1601 by introducing a bill 'to avoid triflinge and frivolous suits', which imposed a penalty on sheriffs and 'procurers' who summoned or attached persons without writ or process.[206]

Though parliament was a means of reform, it also contributed to the problem of uncertainty in the law through the creation of statutes. James acknowledged as much when he described the 'divers crosse and cuffing Statutes' and urged their reconciliation.[207] By the middle of the reign of James I there were 115 penal statutes in force, their number having grown rapidly.[208] One member of the Commons in 1601 recalled that, at the beginning of the queen's reign, 'we had nothinge neere soe manye penall and entrappinge lawes as we nowe have'.[209] Professional informers undertook most of the enforcement of penal laws, and their low reputation reflected their conduct. It was frequently claimed that they received protection money in exchange for not informing against individuals, by reaching unofficial settlements by which the Crown was cheated of its share, and falsely informing against parties to compel them to settle suits in order to avoid the expense of defending themselves.[210] As early as 1566,

---

[204] Dean, *Law-Making and Society*, p. 197; Simonds D'Ewes, *A Compleat Journal of the Votes, Speeches and Debates, both of the House of Lords and House of Commons throughout the Whole Reign of Queen Elizabeth* (London, 1693), Wing D1247, p. 569. Coke was concerned about abuses in fines; see Edward Coke, 'Reading on Fines', in *Three Law Tracts* (Abingdon, 1982), p. 250.

[205] Coke, 'Reading on Fines', p. 222.

[206] 43 Elizabeth I, c. 6; *SR*, vol. IV, pt. 2, p. 971. Hartley (ed.), *Proceedings in the Parliaments of Elizabeth I*, vol. III, p. 340. Dean, *Law-Making and Society*, pp. 214–15; White, *Sir Edward Coke*, pp. 66–70.

[207] James I, *Political Writings*, p. 187.

[208] Maurice Beresford, 'The Common Informer, the Penal Statutes and Economic Regulation', *Economic History Review*, 2nd series, 10:2 (1957), 221–37, at 222.

[209] Hartley (ed.), *Proceedings in the Parliaments of Elizabeth I*, vol. III, p. 436.

[210] Lidington reports that only seventeen per cent of the penal actions between 1558 and 1576 reached a judgment. D. R. Lidington, 'Parliament and the Enforcement of the Penal Statutes: The History of the Act "In Restraint of Common Promoters" (18 Elizabeth I, c. 5)', *Parliamentary History*, 8:2 (1989), 309–28, at 327n2; and also his 'Mesne Process in Penal Actions at the Elizabethan Exchequer' in A. Kiralfy, M. Slatter and R. Virgoe

after riots in Whitehall and attacks on notorious informers, Nicholas Bacon and Burghley created administrative commissions to investigate informers and royal corruption.[211] Coke was well aware of these shifts and supported penal law reform, disdainfully referring to informers as 'viperous Vermin ... the Vexatious Informer ... who under the reverend Mantle of Law and Justice instituted for protection of the innocent ... did ver [sic; 'vex'] and depauperize the Subject ... for malice or private ends, and never for love of Justice'.[212] In the parliament of 1621 Coke strongly supported the bill against informers that was enacted in 1624.[213]

George Alkynton's reports to the Elizabethan government add detail to complaints about the administration of the penal laws. Alkynton had been a professional informant himself and charged that informers colluded with clerks to cheat subjects through fraudulently drawn or forged writs or informations, and private compositions.[214] These allegations of corruption might be turned to profit by ambitious projectors whose petitions suggest that abuses continued into the next reign.[215] The government's reluctance to act on these proposals signalled the political difficulties sometimes inherent in reform. In response to Stephen Lesieur's proposal (1604), Popham acknowledged the accuracy of the charges, but admitted the following: 'although we finde the abuses by him alleadged in his Peticion to be true, and that his Majestie is much defrauded of his due by the Corruption of such comon Informers, yet considering the present estate of tymes, we cannot thinke it convenient that any such office be raised'.[216]

When the government did erect such an office for Stephen Procter, who also provided similar accounts of abuses, the patentee was condemned in 1610 on charges of corruption himself.[217]

(eds.), *Custom, Court and Counsel* (London, 1985), pp. 33–8. William Lambarde's brief tract against private informations is HLS MS 5116, f. 20r. White also discusses the abusive behaviours of informers in *Sir Edward Coke*, p. 65. For an earlier period, see G. R. Elton, 'Informing for Profit: A Sidelight on Tudor Methods of Law-Enforcement', *Cambridge Law Journal*, 11:2 (1954), 149–67.

[211] There had been other bills proposed; see Lidington, 'Enforcement', 311–12, 315.

[212] 3 Co. *Inst.*, p. 194 and Coke's promotion of the bill against informers in 1621 in Wallace Notestein (ed.), *Commons Debates 1621* (New Haven, CT, 1935), vol. II, p. 43. See also 4 Co. *Rep.*, p. xi; BL Hargrave MS 395, f. 8r; Folger Shakespeare Library MS v. b. 303, p. 347.

[213] White, *Sir Edward Coke*, pp. 67–9.

[214] PRO SP 46/15/193–208.

[215] BL Additional MS 10038, f. 201r; BL Lansdowne MS 172, f. 242r.

[216] BL Lansdowne MS 172, f. 244r.

[217] University of Kansas MS D 114 ff. 595r–653v; BL Additional MS 22591, f. 62r.

Common lawyers led the attempt to reform penal statutes and restrain informers, tacitly admitting that the law had become a potential snare to innocent subjects. In 1571 a parliamentary committee of seven members drew up a bill to check abuses of informers. Its membership included Popham, Fleetwood and the civilian Francis Alford, all of whom would promote law reform throughout this period. They produced a bill that passed both Houses, but seems to have been vetoed.[218] The determined efforts of Sir Nicholas Bacon and Lord Burghley eventually bore fruit in the statute of 18 Elizabeth I, c. 5, providing punitive sanctions against abusive informers and introducing several procedural remedies.[219]

Other reformers sought a more comprehensive remedy by striking at the root: the review and amendment of the penal laws themselves. Unnecessary laws would be removed and the activities of informers curtailed.[220] An early call for a recodification and rationalization of statutes came from Ferdinando Pulton of Lincoln's Inn, who had made it his business to organize the penal statutes in handbooks. His *Abstract of All the Penall Statutes which be Generall* was published in 1577 and had gone through eight editions by 1603, testimony to both the rapid development of penal statutes and the popularity of the work.[221] Pulton dedicated the *Abstract* to Sir William Cordell, who had only three years previously reformed the Chancery with a collection of ordinances (1574) and would in the following year reorganize the office of the six clerks (1578).[222] The dedication closed with a plea to Cordell to continue his support so that he might reduce 'into some perfect Method the confused number of our Lawes provided in severall ages'.[223]

---

[218] Lidington, 'Enforcement', 316.

[219] A detailed set of ordinances circulated soon after the statute, PRO E 163/15/32.

[220] An attempt occasionally linked to previous interest in codifying English law; Shapiro, 'Codification', 433; cf. Holdsworth, *HEL*, vol. V, p. 222; Whitney Jones, *The Tudor Commonwealth, 1529–59* (London, 1970), p. 211; Charles Ogilvie, *The King's Government*, p. 77. Baker, *OHLE*, vol. VI, pp. 248–50.

[221] Ferdinando Pulton, *An Abstract of All the Penall Statutes which be Generall in Force and Vse* (London, 1577), STC 9526.7. Pulton capitalized on this success by publishing other related texts, *A Kalender* (London 1606), STC 9547; *A Collection of Sundry Statutes Frequent in Use* (1618), STC 9328. *The Statutes at Large* (1618), STC 9305.7 is also ascribed to him. See *DNB*, 'Ferdinando Pulton'. J. H. Baker discusses Pulton's project and the support provided by Ellesmere in 'English Law Books and Legal Publishing', pp. 493–5.

[222] *DNB*, s.v. 'William Cordell'.

[223] Pulton, *An Abstract of All the Penall Statutes*, sig. Aiiii v. The work of Justinian was often cited as the precedent; see Spedding *et al.* (eds.), *Works*, vol. VII, p. 316.

The parliament of 1584 opened up a wider debate on the penal laws.[224] Upon Egerton's motion a committee was formed to investigate and, reflecting the continuity of reform, he and Fleetwood were named, both having served on the committee of 1571.[225] The period also saw the beginning of Francis Bacon's dedication to reform – his father Nicholas Bacon had been been involved in reform in the 1560s and into the 1570s. When the project to abrogate some of the penal laws was taken up again in the parliament of 1592, Bacon was one of its staunchest proponents.[226] He recited the words of the Lord Keeper John Puckering from the opening of the session who had complained that the number of statutes was so great that 'neither Common People can practise them, nor the Lawyer sufficiently understand them'.[227] Bacon also began a campaign outside of parliament to rouse support for a thorough review of the penal laws and the broader reform of the common law system. He wrote that the multiplication of laws led to their misuse, that, 'all the indirect and sinister courses and practises to abuse law and justice should have been much attempted' and warned about 'the uncertainty of the law, which is the most principal and just challenge that is made to the laws of our nation at this time'.[228] He took up these themes at the Christmas revels at Gray's Inn in 1594 and in his *Maxims* connected his project for a review of the penal statutes as well as a digest of cases at the common law so that 'the great hollowness and unsafety in assurance of lands and goods may be strengthened'.[229]

Attempts to further statutory reform continued with Egerton urging the assembled parliament in 1597 'to enter into a due consideration of the Laws, and where you find superfluity, to prune and cut off, where defect, to supply, and where ambiguity, to explain'.[230] He took up the theme again in 1601 in another parliament distracted by the press for war against Spain.[231] In the new reign after the Treaty of London (1604) the Crown's attention to law reform and codification increased with the approval of the king and without the distraction of war. A remark by Coke reveals

---

[224] D'Ewes, *Compleat Journal*, p. 345.

[225] In 1588 the Privy Council instructed James Morice along with fifteen other common lawyers to begin to draft bills on reform and statutory revision. *DNB*, 'James Morice'.

[226] Bacon thought the statute of 18 Elizabeth had been ineffective. Spedding *et al.* (eds.), *Works*, vol. VIII, pp. 121, 130.

[227] D'Ewes, *Compleat Journal*, p. 473.

[228] Spedding *et al.* (eds.), *Works*, vol. VII, pp. 315, 319.

[229] *Ibid.*, vol. IV, p. 316; vol. I, p. 339 and vol. VII, p. 192; BL Lansdowne MS 486, f. 16r.

[230] D'Ewes, *Compleat Journal*, p. 524.

[231] *Ibid.*, p. 599.

that as early as 1604 James was urging the review of the penal laws and Egerton had prepared proposals for the reform of statutes.[232] The common law judges wrote to the Privy Council in 1604, identifying regulations to control the enforcement of the laws and their administration.[233] That year they also warned that the grant of forefeitures before they had been collected 'maketh the more violent and undewe proceeding against the subject to the scandal of justice and the offence of many'.[234] Adding to the momentum, the king urged statutory reform explicitly in 1607 and 1610 and a thorough review of the statute book.[235]

With the king's support and Bacon's diligence there had been some preparatory work prior to the parliament of 1610. Bacon's notes include a series of memoranda from June 1608 including, 'The recompiling of the laws of England' as a service 'on foot'.[236] Bacon's efforts and those of his fellow reformers were further formalized in the parliament. A document titled 'Statutes Obsolete and Fit to be Repealed' was delivered on 14 November 1610 by Henry Finch, who was later named by Bacon as one of his co-reformers.[237] On 14 February Sir Thomas Foster JCP and Edward Bromley BEx carried a message to the Commons requesting that they should confer with the Lords about penal law reform.[238] The next day in the Lords, Egerton moved in a speech that the parliament needed to amend contrary statutes and in this he was seconded by Salisbury.[239] That afternoon at the conference between the Houses, Salisbury declared that 'we have had something in contemplation concerning statute laws, which we have divided into three classes, some are utterly unpossible, some more fit when they were made than now ... some very fit to be observed and of those many that are defective in their direction and rigorous in their execution'.[240]

The eventual bill in which obsolete laws were to be repealed, however, was tied with a provision that there should be no 'proclamation law' and

---

[232] 4 Co. *Rep.*, p. x. James complained in 1609 about the 'oppression' of the penal statutes. HMC, *Salisbury*, vol. II, p. 23; Knafla, *Law and Politics*, p. 105.

[233] PRO SP 9/209, f. 170r.

[234] BL Harley MS 6686B, f. 602r.

[235] *PP 1610*, vol. I., p. 47; Knafla, *Law and Politics*, p. 105.

[236] Spedding (ed.), *Letters and Life*, vol. VI, p. 59.

[237] BL Lansdowne MS 160, pp. 338–49; Notestein (ed.), *Commons Debates 1621*, vol. II, p. 73n37; *DNB*, s.v. 'Heneage Finch'. Another copy, with slight variations, of this document was in the possession of Edward Coke, Holkham MS 677, ff. 77r, having similarities with the list in his 3 Co. *Inst.*, p. 191.

[238] *PP 1610*, vol. I, p. 9.   [239] *Ibid.*, pp. 8–9.   [240] *Ibid.*, vol. II, p. 27.

that parliaments were to be every seven years.[241] Loaded in this way, the bill had little chance of surviving. It was not until July that Edward Alford made a motion for the 'reviving of penal laws and also for the reconciling of contrary judgments in the year books' and this was followed a few days later by a motion of Edwin Sandys that the king be petitioned for a survey of all penal statutes.[242] Comprehensive law reform again failed, buried by the other demands of the session, a cycle of events that repeated itself in the parliament of 1614.[243] These failures did not deter Bacon, who suggested that the king should approve a commission and have it prepare bills for the next parliament. A committee was formed to begin work on this project whose membership included Bacon, Henry Hobart, Henry Finch, Heneage Finch, William Noy and William Hakewill.[244] The parliament of 1621 built on their efforts: Hakewill raised the work of the previous 'commission' and asked that Heneage Finch and Noy be joined with him on the committee for law reform.[245] A committee was then appointed composed of several members of the commission, including Noy, Henry Finch and Hakewill, together with Coke.[246] Though the session failed to pass a bill for comprehensive penal law reform, the general support for law reform was manifest in the acts that passed in 1621 and 1624, relating to penal laws, vexatious lawsuits, corruption and abuse of office.[247]

While these legislative attempts were proceeding, Coke's principal instrument of law reform was his *Reports*. These were published explicitly, 'for the common good, (for that is my chiefe purpose,) in quieting and establishing of the possessions of many in these general cases, wherein there hath been such variety of opinions'.[248] He addressed two audiences: practitioners and those who criticized the common law as confused. Lawyers, through their ignorance, had contributed to the corruption of the law, and Coke wrote that 'the Law is not incertain in abstracto, but

---

[241] *Ibid.*, p. 71.   [242] *Ibid.*, p. 384; vol. I, p. 155. *LJ*, vol. I, p. 661.

[243] Spedding (ed.), *Letters and Life*, vol. V, pp. 15, 41.

[244] *Ibid.*, vol. VI, p. 61.

[245] *Ibid.*, p. 72. For a complete list of the members of the committee, see Bodl. Tanner MS 276, f. 163.

[246] 4 Co. *Rep.*, pp. x–xi.

[247] White, *Sir Edward Coke*, pp. 56–75; Robert Zaller, *The Parliament of 1621: A Study in Constitutional Conflict* (Berkeley, 1971), pp. 116–40, esp. pp. 128–9. See, in particular, 21 James I, c. 3 (grants of monopoly), 4 (informations on penal statutes), 12 (vexatious lawsuits against certain royal officers), 13 (reformation of jeofails), 16 (limitation of formedon and other actions), and 23 (against the removal of actions from inferior courts); *SR*, vol. IV, pt. 2, pp. 1,212–14; 1,220–2, 1,232.

[248] 1 Co. *Rep.*, p. xxix.

in concreto, and that the incertainty thereof is hominis vitium and not professionis: and to speak plainly there be two causes of the uncertainty thereof ... preposterous[249] reading and oversoon practice'.[250] His *Reports* were demonstrative, while being didactic, and attempted to remedy the epistemological problem of poor law reporting and practice:

> for I have often observed, that for want of a true and certain Report the Case that hath been adjudged standing upon the rack of many running Reports (especially of such as understood not the state of the question) hath been so diversely drawn out, as many times the true parts of the Case have been disordered and disjointed, and most commonly the right reason and rule of the judges utterly mistaken.[251]

Coke explained that in the past there had been professional reporters, but since their work had ceased there was now much need for credible and accurate reporting.[252] The purpose of a good report, Coke commented, was to 'reconcile the doubts in former reports, rising either upon diversity of opinions or questions moved and left undecided'. The *Reports* hushed the babble of many arguments in different cases and supplanted them with models of the harmonious application of legal reason.[253] As even Bacon conceded of his rival, 'had it not been for Sir Edward Coke's Reports ... the law by this time had been almost like a ship without ballast'.[254]

Ignorance among lawyers had led to dangerous innovations that attracted doubts about the law. Coke's conservatism was apparent when he made the following warning: 'either when an ancient pillar of the Common Law is taken out of it, or when new remedies are added to it. By the first arise dangers and difficulties; and by the second the common law rightly understood is not bettered, but in many cases so fettered, that it is thereby very much weakened.'[255]

Even as his *Reports* identified a framework of rules and principles to restrain his fellow lawyers, Coke articulated a professional self-identity built on his ultimate confidence in the common law. The claim that the common law was 'the most equall and most certain, of greatest antiquitie, and least delay, and most beneficiall and easie to be observed' responded to criticisms of the law's uncertainty. In pursuing these goals,

---

[249] 'Absurd' or 'roundabout'.
[250] 9 Co. *Rep.*, p. xxxvii; for similar comments see also 2 Co. *Rep.*, p. ix.
[251] 1 Co. *Rep.*, pp. xxvi–xxvii.   [252] 3 Co. *Rep.*, p. xxix.
[253] 3 Co. *Rep.*, p. xxx, and iv–v.
[254] Spedding (ed.), *Letters and Life*, vol. VI, p. 65.
[255] 9 Co. *Rep.*, p. xxxvi.

as subsequent chapters will show, Coke did not distance the common law from the king. Tactfully he had positioned his reforming activities as a response to James's demands. But more significantly, Coke argued that when the common law was threatened so too was royal authority. He warned of the ulterior motives of those who criticized the common law upon which the frame of state and royal power depended: 'wofull experience hath often taught ... that many of those men that have strayned their wits, and stretched their tongues to scandalize or calumniate these Lawes, had either practised or plotted some hainous crime'.[256] The admonition took aim at Robert Parsons and other Catholic apologists who threatened the queen's title and criticized the common law itself. This commitment to royal power, moreover, would justify common law interference to limit the 'swelling' of other jurisdictions. This interference marked the culmination of Coke and the common law judges' campaign to establish greater coherency in the legal system – an attempt to reform its excesses.

If Coke could seem both like a man on the defensive and one whose assertiveness has often been interpreted as arrogance, this was because he perceived the common law's vulnerability to criticism and the danger this posed to confidence in the legal system. But his response was characteristically fierce. The common law could look within itself to its own wisdom to reform its present-day practices. The common law would also serve as an instrument of reform to control practitioners and others who used legal authority: the King's Bench was the court of the king and therefore the superintendent of all regular courts in the kingdom. If James I was to interpret this claim as an example of common lawyers overreaching, it was because he too had heard the criticisms of the common law – and believed them.

[256] 4 Co. *Rep.*, pp. xxi–xxii.

2

'The most dangerous oppressor'

The misuse of the law

When Coke was appointed as her attorney-general in 1594, Elizabeth I charged him 'to carrye thie selfe in my service as no suspicion may be had of the[e], of any respect or inclination'.[1] Coke's subsequent prosecutions were a mixture of supererogation and viciousness: his rude conduct towards the Earl of Essex is remembered as out of place with social decorum. The words he used in Raleigh's trial were 'shameful, unworthy, never to be forgotten'.[2] Perhaps such disapproval was a necessary evil of an office that combined great power with a duty to protect royal interests.[3] However, the efforts of Edward Herbert, whom one historian described as the king's 'lickspittle', have not helped improve assessments of the attorney-generals of the period.[4] It was, perhaps, Coke's good fortune to reclaim his reputation among historians, after he passed from office, with his principled campaign to protect the rights of his fellow subjects.

The queen had also reminded Coke of this balance, commanding him, 'that my subjects receive at thie hands that which to them apperteyneth according to lawe and Justice'.[5] These duties of the conscientious attorney-general paralleled the implicit tension at the heart of the common law: a responsibility to protect individual rights while preserving royal interests. The decisions of the judges to uphold royal policies in *Bates's Case* (1606), the *Five Knights' Case* (1627) and the *Case of Ship Money* (1637) suggested to some at the time and many since a failure of judicial independence.[6] But the common law had many biases in favour of the king,

---

[1] BL Harley MS 6686A, ff. 86r–v.
[2] Bowen, *Lion and the Throne*, pp. 148, 195–6.
[3] J. L. J. Edwards, *The Law Officers of the Crown* (London, 1964), pp. 58–60; BL Stowe MS 159, f. 28; Hawarde, *Les Reportes*, p. 293.
[4] Edwards, *The Law Officers of the Crown*, p. 56.
[5] BL Harley MS 6686A, f. 86v; *Harris v. Austin* (1615), 3 Bulstrode 43, 81 ER 37.
[6] Braddick, *State Formation*, pp. 60–1; W. J. Jones, *Politics and the Bench* (London, 1971), pp. 39–40; J. S. Cockburn, *A History of English Assizes, 1558–1714* (Cambridge, 1972), pp. 219–237; Roger Wilbraham, *Journal of Sir Roger Wilbraham*, ed. Harold Scott (London, 1902), pp. 86–7.

as James himself perceptively observed.[7] These prerogatives, whether the king's claims to wrecks or the maxim that time did not run against him, explicitly recognized the monarch's pre-eminence over his subjects and the importance of the needs of his government. When the judges declared the return good in the *Five Knights' Case*, their decision accorded with precedents that prioritized reason of state. Even Coke in *Henry Ruswell's Case* (1615), at the height of the dispute with the Chancery, admitted as much.[8] If some increasingly found a repository of rights in the common law, it was also a resource for royal authority.

Coke's service as attorney-general reflected the search for this balance. Two contexts shaped this pursuit and his experience of the office: law reform and the security priorities of the Elizabethan war-state. The first involved Coke's duty to protect the integrity of the law. Coke declared that justice was the 'most beutyfull thinge in the world', while frequently warning against those who 'under couller of justice doe breake and wrest the lawe[;] they observe the law but only in words'.[9] While those who misused the law did not pose the same threat to the government as dangers arising from war, they eroded confidence in legal institutions and interfered with the duty of the monarch to give justice to her subjects. Such abuses brought the monarch and her courts into disrepute, as aggrieved subjects projected fault for corruption onto them.[10] Early in his career Coke responded, in part, by elaborating restrictions on the use of legal power in the Star Chamber and at the common law. His arguments articulated elements of public law or rules and principles intended to control the behaviours of those making use of royal power in legal or official forms.[11]

The question of the relationship between the individual and the monarch is also discernible in Coke's work to maintain public order – the second context this chapter touches upon. The most significant threat came from England's struggle with Spain and the forces of the Counter-Reformation. For most of Coke's time in office, England was a war-state responding to the threats of conspirators who worked to undermine the

---

[7] James I, *Political Writings*, pp. 184–5.

[8] John Rylands Library, French MS 118, f. 282r.

[9] Society of Antiquaries MS 291, ff. 11v–12r.

[10] Similarly, Coke reasoned, a scandal affecting a peer reflected as a scandal on the monarch since they were 'partners in government'; J. P. Cooper (ed.), *Wentworth Papers, 1597–1628* (London, 1973), p. 60.

[11] The issue also preoccupied Bacon, see Spedding *et al.* (eds.), *Works*, vol. VII, p. 732; Martin Loughlin, *Foundations of Public Law* (Oxford, 2012), pp. 3–12; B. H. G. Wormald, *Francis Bacon: History, Politics and Science, 1561–1626* (Cambridge, 1993), pp. 130–2. Cf. Burgess, *Absolute Monarchy*, p. 170.

government. Against the danger of social and political disorder, Coke urged a rigorous interpretation of the law of treason, a development that provided an opportunity for his discussion of the relationship between the sovereign and the subject. Whereas the corruption of inferior officers demanded redress from the monarch, Coke thought of treason in terms of the obligations imposed by a subject's allegiance. Coke identified among these obligations an imperative neither to harm nor lessen the majesty of the sovereign. It was this latter concept, which Ian Williams argues was borrowed from the Roman law through *Bracton*, that to detract from the 'greaterness' of the sovereign was itself constitutive of treason.[12] To undermine majesty contradicted the logic of power that supported both the frame of law and administration: the monarch must have supreme power to protect and lead her people. Coke's understanding of the treason law, which he maintained even as a judge, assumed that the monarch's authority was ultimately irresistible and that sovereignty reposed in the person of the monarch alone. The mere thought of harm to the monarch, Coke reasoned, was treason.

In 1592 the judges, led by Sir Edmund Anderson, warned the lord chancellor that 'some order may be taken that her highnes subjects may not be committed nor deteyned in prison by Comandement of any noble man or Councellors against the lawes of the Realme'.[13] In the past, the judges went on to relate, 'diverse have been imprisoned for sueing ordinarie actions and suits at the Comon lawe, untill they have been constrained to leave the same against their wills and putt the same to order'. While many had been delivered and then freed upon writs of habeas corpus, some of those were again committed 'in secrett places' so that it was not possible to learn to whom the writs for their release should be directed.[14] Their letter demonstrated the judges' concern over the misuse of legal authority, especially if it denied litigants their rights at the common law. Similarly when they wrote to the Privy Council in 1604 identifying the penal laws that they most thought fit to be 'put in execution', the list was led by forgery, but then followed by perjury, champerty, maintenance, embracery and extortion – crimes related to abuses in legal proceedings.[15] Misuse of the law by officers and patentees might affect the reputation of the entire system

---

[12] Ian Williams, 'A Medieval Law Book and Early-Modern Law: *Bracton's* Authority and Application in the Common Law c. 1550–1640', *The Legal History Review*, 79:1 (2011), 47–80, at 71–7.

[13] PRO SP 12/261, pp. 175–6, and reported as 1 Anderson 297–8, 123 ER 482.

[14] *Ibid.*, p. 177.

[15] PRO SP 9/209, ff. 169v–170r.

and those with greater authority. For example, a report of the activities in local vice-admiralty courts in September 1591 exposed the collaboration of court officers in corrupt dealings.[16] The simmering anger of those affected was directed beyond the inferior officers and to the Lord Admiral. It was recorded that the people held: 'An inward and secrett hatred of your Lordship ... by rayson of the knowen and felt oppressions and wronges offered to the people by your officers.'[17] Contemporaries perceived that the manipulation of legal power might ultimately reflect on the queen, warning of: 'a greate scourage to the people and a dishonor to the Crowne ... that the prerogative roiall allowed by the ordinary lawes to the Crowne, and noe other, is for private gaine of some Subjectes and servantes, made an instrument of oppression'.[18]

In 1609 Coke identified two groups who should be punished: those who used their legal power to oppress and so turned 'publike authoritye for his private purposes' and those who 'will plague his neyghbour by suits'.[19] When he had served as attorney-general these abuses were evident to him at first hand, and his efforts to restrain both groups were of a piece with his later work as a judge. In Coke's prosecution of Thomas Ashe,[20] while he was attorney-general, the information explained what was at stake:

> That whereas amongeste all other offences and misdemeanors which by lewde and evill disposed persons are usually done ... there are none greater or more greevious nor indeed so great or greevious as those whereby your highnes lovinge subjects ... are by wicked and malicious persons (to satisfie their owne humors of rancor and malice) vexed and disquieted without just cause ... in a pretended course and proceedinge of law and with a dissembled and counterfeite shewe of Justice.[21]

Coke pursued many of these early attempts to limit the misuse of the law in the Star Chamber.[22] This was a natural forum to curb the corruptions arising from legal authority, since its proceedings were meant to overawe even the powerful.[23] Knafla, in his recent study of Kent, has

---

[16] The delegated structure of royal power is touched on by Braddick, *State Formation*, pp. 33–43.

[17] BL Additional MS 12505, f. 360r–v.

[18] BL Additional MS 41613, f. 90r; A similar case in 1612 was *Queen* v. *Empringham* et al., STAC 8 16/11; *Empringham's Case*, 12 Co. Rep. 84, 77 ER 1361; HLS MS 149, f. 23r.

[19] Folger Shakespeare Library MS v. b. 303, p. 350.

[20] This was not Thomas Ashe of Gray's Inn, but rather of Tuttington, Norfolk.

[21] *Iveson* v. *Ashe* (1606), PRO STAC 8 5/20.

[22] Cf. the assessment of the court in Boyer, *Sir Edward Coke*, p. 253.

[23] Complainants in the Star Chamber could expose themselves to retaliatory litigation if their case was somehow deemed unfit for the court; *Memorandum* (1577), Rylands

noted that Coke was very active in pursuing cases in the Star Chamber. In Kent alone Coke prosecuted seventeen cases during his decade in office, while Egerton pursued six cases throughout the entire country over two years.[24]

Coke's informations in the Star Chamber unfold the myriad frauds practised using legal process by clever or desperate individuals, especially those made possible by the strict proceedings of the common law. In two cases, for example, Coke attacked the practice of convincing young men to enter into bonds, statutes, recognizances and confessions of action by attorney. By binding them they could not avoid the obligation once of age. A comment by Egerton suggests that this was not an isolated incident, but rather 'this is a great and common offence' that was probably aimed at young men at the Inns.[25] The binding power of legal devices at the common law was well known, and drew others into trouble, especially over the failure to void a bond or recognizance once the amount was fully paid. The common law would enforce the undefeased bond, even though payment had been made. Coke prosecuted Sir Robert Jermyn for unjustly pursuing a penalty on a recognizance (whose principal had been paid) made by his father forty years earlier, and the information declared that the case was an evil example to others.[26]

Coke also pursued officials who undermined legal process by ignorance or partiality. When a justice of the peace failed to pursue a case of rape, remarking that the misconduct was but 'a trick of yought',[27] Coke successfully intervened against him and the accused. The failure to punish the perpetrator, Coke claimed, was a 'great evill example' and led to their 'great emboldninge ... to continewe in sundry other owtrages'.[28] Another case raised issues of malfeasance when Coke brought a suit

---

Library, French MS 118, f. 81v. Coke urged that action on the case would lie if a cause was brought in the court that was not punishable there; *Nota* (1599), IT Petyt MS 511/13, f. 127v.

[24] *Kent at Law 1602*, vol. III, ed. Louis Knafla (Surrey, 2013), p. xii.

[25] *Attorney-General* v. *Howe and East* (1596), Hawarde, *Les Reportes*, p. 48. Another case prosecuted by Coke involved an uncancelled (but repayed) bond. The creditor dying, his son combined with other persons to begin suit on the bond; *Attorney-General* v. *Pepis* (1605), STAC 8 5/14.

[26] For other examples prosecuted privately, see *Bigge* v. *Bono* (1611), PRO STAC 8 71/23; *Clutterbooke* v. *Askwith* (1606), STAC 8 88/21.

[27] 'Youth'.

[28] Knafla (ed.), *Kent at Law*, pp. xxiv, vol. III, 237. Coke also brought an information against justices of the peace who had come to blows at the Quarter Sessions in Yorkshire, *Attorney-General* v. *Wentworth* et al. (1601), IT Petyt MS 511/13, f. 142r.

against a bailiff in Norfolk for jury tampering, extortion and breaking his oath.[29] He also brought several prosecutions for corruption by under-sheriffs and against those exercising their jurisdiction beyond their legal warrant.[30] In another case the information against Gilbert Jones asserted that no 'maintayners of evill nor barraters in the Contrey should be assigned Justices of the Peace'.[31] Jones had a legal practice before the Council in the Marches, but he was also a justice of the peace and developed other sidelines that made use of his position. Coke accused Jones of concealing fines, accepting bribes and extortion, and claimed that he sought 'revenge towards any ... in anywayse crossinge or contradictinge him'. He confederated himself with Charles Lloyd to bind those to the peace who opposed or displeased them. Out of spirit of revenge they imprisoned another man surmising that he had stolen a ladder, when in truth he had been sent by its owner to fetch it. Soon after the accession of James I, Lloyd was appointed High Sheriff and in that capacity submitted false returns of writs for bribes, and wrongfully arrested and extorted individuals. This last may have been the cause of the duo's downfall when two individuals who were 'of farre better carriadge' than Lloyd were bound to the peace and complained.[32]

Coke prosecuted officers and common informers who used the law to enrich themselves through the use of shifts.[33] He brought a case of corruption in the collection of the subsidy when three commissioners colluded to defraud the Exchequer.[34] In *Attorney-General v. Nixen* et al. (1596) Coke informed against several individuals for counterfeiting warrants 'for the apprehending of papists, seminaries, *agnes* [sic] *dei* and crucifixes'.[35] Through these means the accused were able to collect money through extortion: 'The other three, wearing on their breasts a box with the Queen's arms as pursuivant ... did threaten a priest that he had burnt a

---

[29] *Attorney-General v. Worsley* (1605), PRO STAC 8 7/1. See also the case against Robert Pie, a 'late barrister', for maliciously procuring an indictment, *Attorney-General v. Pie* (1602), IT Petyt 511/13, f. 150r.

[30] *Attorney-General v. Barter* (1602), PRO STAC 8 8/7; *Regina v. Hickman* (1601), BL Additional MS 25203, f. 364v; *Attorney-General v. Evans* (1601), IT Petyt MS 511/13, f. 149r.

[31] *Attorney-General v. Jones* (1606), PRO STAC 8 5/9, and a similar case *Barbor v. Cutler* (1616), Folger Shakespeare Library MS v. a. 133, f. 61r.

[32] See also a similar, though later, case under Bacon involving official corruption on the Isle of Wight, PRO STAC 8 20/18.

[33] *Attorney-General v. Gerrard and Parsons* (1605), PRO STAC 8 5/19.

[34] *Attorney-General v. Vaughan* et al. (1605), PRO STAC 8 5/17.

[35] Hawarde, *Les Reportes*, p. 36.

child in an oven, and for this he agreed with them and gave them £5'.[36] The court declared that this was a 'great and "heynous" offence, and worthy to be punished with death' and that the offence was 'the most dangerous mischief that can be', since legal authority was perverted. Coke and the rest of the court had to settle for mutilation, pillory and galley service – the lord treasurer still carped that the punishments were insufficient.[37]

The disputes over parliamentary supply, of which much has been written, and the structural problems of royal finance were compounded by the fact that individuals used their legal authority to cheat the government.[38] Coke prosecuted justices of the peace and others who took money for discharging soldiers pressed for service.[39] In another case of embezzlement in the military, Coke worried that the strength of the realm depended on the faithfulness and upright dealings of her Majesty's officers.[40] Perhaps most disturbing was the behaviour of some of those who had their authority by patent and were the frequent subject of parliamentary grievances, culminating in the 1620s.[41] In 1597 Coke charged several 'saltpeter men', who were commissioned to make gunpowder. They had used their commission to force 'divers Hundreds in Suffolke with the carriage of wood and liquor' at inconvenient times. Having demanded bribes from the Hundreds to avoid the service, they were punished with fines and the pillory.[42] In 1600 Coke began the 'great case' against Sir Thomas Jones, a deputy lieutenant of the Earl of Pembroke in Wales, and an unstated number of captains, mustermasters and constables. The attorney-general alleged the 'extortion of great sums by colour of his office, and taxing and levying [the same] to find soldiers when there was a "Countermaunde" of this, and for taxing great sums'. The other officers colluded, 'extorting fees for the discharge of pressed men, and other offences'.[43] Coke chose this moment to repeat the aphorism 'Leges silent arma' – war provided opportunities for illegal profiteering.

The case of Arthur Duckett further exposed how royal patentees could misuse their authority. Duckett was the patentee of saltpetre and exercised

---

[36] *Ibid.*, p. 37.   [37] *Ibid.*, p. 38.

[38] A complaint noted in the collection of subsidies, BL Additional MS 22587, f. 24r.

[39] Buckhurst commended Coke for this prosecution, *Attorney-General* v. *Gresham* et al. (1596): Hawarde, *Les Reportes*, p. 33; and a similar case in Nottingham, *Attorney-General* v. *Willoughby* et al. (1600), IT Petyt 511/13, ff. 136v–137v.

[40] *Attorney-General* v. *Wescott* (n.d.), PRO STAC 5 A6/1.

[41] In 1621, for example, Coke attacked patents for concealed lands, perceiving that they offered opportunity for extortions. White, *Sir Edward Coke*, pp. 72–5.

[42] *Attorney-General* v. *Parker* et al. (1597); Hawarde, *Les Reportes*, pp. 78–9.

[43] *Attorney-General* v. *Jones* (1600); *ibid.*, pp. 115–16; IT Petyt MS 511/13, ff. 134v–135r.

some ingenuity in his racket. The information alleges that, under pretence of searching for materials for saltpetre, Duckett had 'offered to digge the kytchens parlers bedchambers workehouses and most necessary roomes of divers your said subjects ... of purpose to drawe ... great somes of money ... to have their houses spared'.[44] The owner had refused and not only were the floorboards of his pigeon-house dug up, but so were several rooms in his house. Duckett's servants added insult by leaving piles of dirt and broken floorboards behind. These abuses led to a judicial conference in 1606 to establish rules for the patentees' conduct.[45]

Aware of the corruptions in the legal system, Coke pursued his reforming agenda at the common law by helping to advance the development of barratry. Offences to punish abuses of the law had long been available, such as champerty, conspiracy and maintenance, and Coke may also have helped to expand these offences.[46] But another, barratry, was more closely defined as a specifically legal crime in the sixteenth century, suggesting that the offence was shaped to address concerns about the vexatious behaviour of litigants and their lawyers. Coke defined the 'barrettor' as: 'a common mover and exciter, or maintainer of suits, quarrels, or parts, either in courts, or elsewhere in the countrey'.[47] Coke also went on to describe a 'Barretor' as 'not only a wrangling suit, but also such brawles and quarrels in the country ... '.[48] This double meaning reflected the word's etymology: barratry derived partly from the Old French 'barat' for 'deceit, fraud, confusion, trouble, embarrassment' and the Old Norse 'barátta', meaning 'fight, contest, strife'.[49] On the Germanic side 'barratry' thus referred to physical violence, while its Romanic etymology was probably rooted in mercantile transactions, and sharp or fraudulent practice. By the end of the sixteenth century, barratry signified a specific form of legal malfeasance.[50]

Until the sixteenth century lawyers and judges used the word generally to denote quarrelling and extortion that was often related to maintenance.

---

[44] *Attorney-General* v. *Duckett* (1606), PRO STAC 8 5/11.

[45] *The Case of the King's Prerogative in Saltpetre*, 12 Co. *Rep.* 13, 77 ER 1295, and see the cases reported there at 1297.

[46] Percy Winfield, 'The History of Maintenance and Champerty', *The Law Quarterly Review*, 35 (1919), 58–9.

[47] Co. *Litt.* f. 368a; 3 Co. *Inst.*, p. 175.

[48] Co. *Litt.*, f. 368b.   [49] *OED*, s.v. 'barrat'.

[50] Examples of barratry referring to physical violence include, *Sir Gawain and the Green Knight*, trans. William Vantuono (New York, 1991), l. 21; Mary Braswell (ed.), *Sir Perceval of Galles* (Kalamazoo, MI, 1995), l. 263; Richard Arnold, *The Customs of London, Otherwise Called Arnold's Chronicle* (London, 1811), p. 90; Fuller, *Worthies*, p. 199.

Britton used the word at the end of the thirteenth century: 'Par extorsioun ... par barat et par contek'.[51] Holinshed's usage in 1577 similarly suggested that barrators were extorters.[52] The Statute of Westminster I (1275) declared that 'no Sheriff shall suffer any Barretors [or Maintainers of] Quarrels in their Shires, neither Stewards of great Lords, nor other unless he be Attorney for his Lord, to make Suit [nor] to give judgements in the counties'.[53] In this act 'barrat' referred to a quarreller and maintainer of suits. The Statute of Conspiracy (1305) similarly referred to maintenance and those who upheld other people's legal quarrels ('baretz').[54] The drafters of 34 Edward III, c. 1 (1361) used 'barators' as a broad, descriptive term that included rioters.[55] A Year Book case from 1366 uses the word in the sense of one who raised quarrels, though it did not refer to a distinct offence of barratry.[56] In a case from around 1501 barratry referred to those who stirred up physical fights.[57] Similarly in 1581 William Lambarde described a barrator as a 'common quarrellour' or 'deceiver' who might come within the statutes of maintenance or embracery.[58] This language was tightened in 1591 when Lambarde drew upon the language of 34 Edward III, c. 1, and used the word to refer to those who raised contention in the courts.[59] It was no coincidence that Lambarde emphasized the legal dimension of barratry when he did: the judges had begun to sharpen the common law offence of barratry as an abuse of the law. Coke reported how the judges defined this offence in 1588: 'A common barretor is a common mover or stirrer up or maintainer of suits, quarrels, or parties, either in Courts, or in the country, in Courts of Record and in the County, Hundred, and other Inferior Courts.'[60]

---

[51] *Britton*, vol. II, trans. F. M. Nichols (Holmes Beach, FL, 1983), p. 176. William Caxton, *Thystorye and Lyf of the Noble and Crysten Prynce Charles the Grete Kynge of Frauuce* [sic] (London, 1485), STC 5013, p. 231.

[52] Raphael Holinshed, *Chronicles*, vol. II (London, 1807), p. 538.

[53] 3 Edward I, c. 33, *SR*, vol. I, p. 35.

[54] 33 Edward I, *SR*, vol. I, p. 145. Conversely 33 Edward I clearly defined a 'champertor'.

[55] 34 Edward III, c. 1, *SR*, vol. I, p. 364.

[56] YB Trin. 40 Edward III, pl. 16, ff. 33b–34a.

[57] J. H. Baker (ed.), *The Reports of Cases by John Caryll: 1501–1522* (London, 2000), vol. II, p. 388.

[58] William Lambarde, *Eirenarcha* (London, 1581), STC 15163, p. 342. John Cowell followed this definition in *The Interpreter* (London, 1607), STC 5900, s.v. 'Barrator', though that same year Thomas Ridley noticed the stricter definition of common barrator in his *A View of the Ciuile and Ecclesiastical Law* (London, 1607), STC 21054, p. 4. See also HLS MS 2079c, f. 158r and Richard Montagu, *A Gagg for the New Gospell? No: A New Gagg for an Old Goose* (London, 1624), STC 18038, p. 146.

[59] William Lambarde, *Archeion* (London, 1635), STC 15144, p. 188.

[60] *The Case of Barratry* (1588), 8 Co. *Rep.* 36b–37a, 77 ER 528–9.

Their interpretation applied barratry to the contemporary problem of vexatious litigation. In doing so they signalled that those who encouraged lawsuits were disturbers of the peace. Though their contention was verbal and legal, the barrator nonetheless undermined the charity that bound the community together.

The common law judges' read their interpretation back onto the sources with the purpose of punishing individuals who generated legal conflict, leading to an idiosyncratic reading of Littleton's mention of 'barrettors' in his *Tenures* (1481).[61] There were few precedents specifically on point, and when Coke reported the judges' definition of barratry he could only vaguely refer to 'many other authorities which might be cited' without actually citing any authorities.[62] Confusion over the precise authority upon which the offence was founded soon followed. In *Burton's Case* (1589) Burton was 'indicted as a common barretor *contra formam statuti*'. However, Coke as counsel excepted and declared 'that there is no statute that makes this an offence; but it was at common law; and that 34 Edward III c. 1 doth not make this, an offence … But it was held good, for so are many precedents'.[63] These precedents were not cited, and the judges may have been involved in some expansive statutory interpretation. Coke was correct in his interpretation of 34 Edward III, c. 1 – there was a punishment assigned for violent behaviour identified as barratry, but by 1588 barratry was a specific offence concerning legal abuse.[64] Barratry as a legal offence continued its development so that in 1598 a countersuit in the form of an action on the case could be attempted for those who claimed they had been wrongfully accused.[65] In the case of *Andrewes* v. *Wilson* (1611), a pun on barrister and barrator was the basis for an accusation of defamation.[66] In 1616 Coke prevented Richard Allen from continuing his vexatious lawsuits *in forma pauperis* after he was indicted as a common barrator.[67]

---

61 Thomas Littleton, *Tenures* (London, 1825), §701, p. 313.

62 *The Case of Barratry*, 8 Co. *Rep.* 37a, 77 ER 529.

63 *Burton's Case*, Cro. Eliz. 148, 78 ER 405.

64 As suggested to me by J. H. Baker, the development of barratry may also have been part of the effort to restrain solicitors. See Baker, 'Solicitors and the Law of Maintenance 1590–1640', in *The Legal Profession and the Common Law*, pp. 125–50.

65 *Constantine* v. *Bell* (1599), BL Additional MS 25203, f. 11r; Oxford Exeter College MS 152, f. 102v.

66 HLS MS 1192, f. 187r; though compare an earlier case *Hacke* v. *Molton* (1606), BL Additional MS 25213, f. 69r, and also *Poole* v. *Benbrigg* (1596), BL Additional MS 25232, f. 17v.

67 PRO C38/24 'Richard Allen'; Other cases include: *Hodson's Case* (1603), BL Lansdowne MS 1096, f. 38v; *Constantine* v. *Bell* (1599), BL Additional MS 25203, f. 11r, *Couper's Case*

Coke advanced the connection of barratry with vexatious litigation in his *Reports* and *Institutes*. He relied partly on precedent, but also on his own etymology of the word. Asserting biblical authority, Coke condemned those who sought to stir up discord between neighbours and pursue quarrels in the courts. Feuding through litigation undermined the morality and justice of the law:

> under colour of law, as by multiplicity of unjust and feigned suits, or by information on penal laws ... to enforce the poor party *ad redimendam vexationem*, to give him money, or to make other composition; and this is the most dangerous oppressor, for he oppresses the innocent by colour and countenance of the law, which was instituted to protect the innocent from all oppression and wrong.[68]

The barrators was 'the most dangerous oppressor' because their use of the law against innocent parties was a crime committed 'by collour of justice'. Yet it was symptomatic of the complexity of the problem that it was soon alleged that accusations of barratry were also used vexatiously.[69] Coke himself warned in 1615 that he had seen diverse 'honest men' indicted in the counties, revealing the challenge of assessing how the law was used.[70]

Alongside these efforts to restrain vexatious litigation, Coke pursued another group, whom he perceived were misusing legal authority, namely, purveyors. Parliamentary complaints about their activities intensified in the reign of James I, who issued as many as 200 commissions a year for purveyance.[71] Complaints over purveyance were long-standing, 'genuinely a popular grievance', stretching back to the medieval period.[72] A letter from Christopher Wray to Anderson in 1586 described the 'generall offences as have beene comitted by the Purveyors in abusing her Majesties Comissions under the color of their offices' and hints of a recent inquiry into their activities.[73] Unhappy suppliers accused purveyors of

---

(1600), f. 171v; *Paxton's Case* (1601), f. 318v; *Tunstall's Case* (1601), f. 370r; *Roy* v. *Wells* (1616), 1 Rolle 296, 81 ER 496.

[68] *The Case of Barratry*, 8 Co. *Rep.* 37b, 77 ER 529.

[69] *Bell* v. *Anonymous* (1609), BL Additional MS 25213, f. 101v.

[70] BL Additional MS 35957, f. 2v.

[71] Eric Lindquist, 'The King, the People and the House of Commons: The Problem of Early Jacobean Purveyance', *Historical Journal*, 31:3 (1988), 549–70, at 556. For an analysis of purveyance as a more straightforward struggle between parliament and prerogative, see Pauline Croft, 'Parliament, Purveyance and the City of London, 1589–1608', *Parliamentary History*, 4 (1985), 9–34.

[72] Lindquist, 'Purveyance', 550, and touched on by Magna Carta, c. 19, 21.

[73] BL Lansdowne MS 43, f. 193r.

wrongfully seizing property, underpayment and defalcation, and these cases appear in the common law courts as well as the Star Chamber. These charges may not always have been justified: in one case a commissioner pursued a defamation suit because of the accusations against him.[74]

Parliamentary clamour over purveyance provides the backdrop and possibly the explanation for a series of prosecutions of purveyors at the beginning of James's reign. Several bills in parliament had failed to pass that would have addressed abuses by purveyors, and so orders were made in the household to restrain them. James also issued a proclamation declaring that he had punished some of his officers and sought to discipline other offenders.[75] Taken together these measures promised rules by which purveyors might be held accountable. But it was in the courts that this form of public law would be enforced, as James himself admitted in his proclamation of 1606.[76] Eric Lindquist has suggested that the subsequent trials were aimed at demonstrating the government's seriousness in pursuing prosecutions and demonstrating the lawfulness of purveyance.[77] It suited the courts to oblige and examine the legal issues at stake: the misuse of legal authority and the expectation that judicial forums would provide redress. As early as 1598 it was declared in the Star Chamber: 'that if any Judge, Justice, officer or subject of the realm shall go beyond his bounds and limits, and misdemean himself in any manner, this Court has power and authority to examine and punish this'.[78] Coke, while attorney-general, had already attempted an unsuccessful suit against purveyors in 1600.[79] In pursuing these cases at the government's behest Coke exercised his calling to redress legal abuses while protecting the king's rights.

With the support of the government, Coke informed against purveyors in the Star Chamber in 1605, some of them having allegedly taken advantage of James I's progress south to extract monies.[80] In the King's Bench, *Citizens of Bristol* v. *Jacob* (1605), he demonstrated his commitment to upholding royal authority. The suit was brought against Jacob, a purveyor. Aldworth had denied Jacob a composition payment, and the purveyor

---

[74] *Sir Robert Stroud's Case* (1609), BL Additional MS 25213, f. 106v.

[75] James Larkin and Paul Hughes (eds.), *Stuart Royal Proclamations of James I, 1603–1625*, vol. I (Oxford, 1973), p. 139. For the orders see PRO LS 13/168, ff. 75–82, 100 and 102.

[76] Larkin and Hughes (eds.), *Stuart Royal Proclamations*, vol. I, p. 139.

[77] Lindquist, 'Purveyance', 563; the trials are discussed briefly at 562–3.

[78] Hawarde, *Les Reportes*, p. 98.

[79] Knafla (ed.), *Kent at Law*, vol. III, p. 4.

[80] Larkin and Hughes (eds.), *Stuart Royal Proclamations*, vol. I, p. 137.

demanded goods in kind at the king's rate. In response, Aldworth asked for a ready-money payment, which the purveyors were unable to provide, and refused either composition or supply. For his contempt the Greencloth ordered him to be imprisoned, and Aldworth prayed habeas corpus. But Coke, who was attorney-general, dutifully insisted that the imprisonment was valid. He defended the authority of the Greencloth to imprison – though the judges would also insist that the board's proceedings were reviewable on habeas corpus.[81] Yet Coke was certainly aware of the reputation of purveyors and made what might have been a wry joke when he said, 'The ancient name of purveyor was a cheater.'[82] Moreover, conscious of the need to control the legal power delegated to purveyors, Coke disagreed with parts of the patent granted to Jacob. He argued that subjects could not be bound to pay composition without their free assent and that Jacob should not have deputized another to take these payments.[83] He also affirmed that the king's prerogative of purveyance arose at the common law and denied that it was a statutory grant, a point that seems aimed at protecting purveyance from its curtailment 'without recompense' by parliament.[84]

Another case concerning carters that same year occasioned a speech from Coke in which he proposed a clearer regulatory framework.[85] He declared seven rules aimed at accountability, including the requirement that purveyors should be persons of sufficient ability to answer to the king and the subject. They should perform the service in their own person and not by deputy since they held an office of confidence. They must have labels annexed to their patents and whatever they took must be inserted in the label, and they ought never to take more than sufficed.[86] Perhaps most importantly as a means to limit corruption, they should take things in kind and never in money.[87] Coke's rules implied his awareness that the

---

[81] HLS MS 118(c), f. 56r, though Popham suggests that this authority arose by an uncited statute (f. 57r); Wilbraham, *Journal*, p. 86. Letters from the town are in PRO LS 13/280, pp. 166–8.

[82] HLS MS 118(c), f. 57v.

[83] *Ibid.*, f. 56v; Wilbraham, *Journal*, p. 83.

[84] Confirmed by Popham, Fleming and Gawdy in another case, *Richards Case* (1605), Moore 764, 72 ER 890, and by Popham in BL Harley MS 6686B, f. 597r.

[85] The case, *Attorney-General* v. *Browne and Stevenson* was brought alongside *Attorney-General* v. *Richards* discussed below. The carters were able to account for the funds and they were not punished 'at this time'; *Attorney-General* v. *Clerke* (1605), Folger Shakespeare Library MS v. a. 133, f. 16v.

[86] Hawarde, *Les Reportes*, p. 249.

[87] *Attorney-General* v. *Clerke*, Folger Shakespeare Library MS v. a. 133, ff. 16v–17r.

underlying problem was not simply the immoral conduct of a few individuals, but a lack of accountability and the incentives for abuse that were built into the system. But far from being perceived as restricting royal authority, John Hawarde interpreted the case as enhancing the royal prerogative by protecting confidence in its exercise: 'The Atturnie and the Lord Chauncellor did greatly advance the Kinge's prerogative royall and the necessitie of purveyors, beinge both as auncyente as the Fundamentall lawes of the kingdome.'[88]

Another case from 1605 reveals how these prosecutions could prompt statements of rights over property or how the behaviour of local officials raised larger constitutional questions.[89] In this case a deputy purveyor, named Stoke, was described as a 'poore carpenter' and had his deputation not by the proper papers, but only by the Great Seal (which it was claimed no deputy ought to have).[90] Stoke proved quite entrepreneurial once he had a legal warrant in his hands. He went into the woods of Samuel Backhouse, who happened to be a member of parliament around the time of the prosecution, without his knowledge, and removed a large number of trees.[91] After informing Backhouse of the king's price for the trees, Stoke under-accounted for them to the Greencloth. He then sold the tops of the trees and the poles at a higher price than he had valued the trees, pocketing the difference. By this conduct the king's prerogative was 'highly abused' and that 'the abusinge thereof is dishonor to the kinge, greevance and oppressyon to the subiectes, and the kinge would not in any wyse have his prerogative rackte or strechte, but used tenderlye and with all possible Favoure'.[92] The judges punished Stoke with a fine and the pillory.[93] Coke then asked the judges for their opinion on the taking of trees, citing Magna Carta. The judges responded that 'none of the kinge's offycers Can take any trees growinge, for they are parcell of a man's enherytaunce and thereunto fyxed, nor take any thinge but suche as the owner hathe a purpose to sell and departe withall for gaine'.[94] Popham declared that trees were united with the freehold, and so purveyors were not able

---

[88] Hawarde, *Les Reportes*, p. 194.
[89] *Stockwel's Case* (1605), Moore 760, 72 ER 888; Hawarde, *Les Reportes*, p. 194; HLS MS 118(c), ff. 56v–57r and Folger Shakespeare Library MS v. a. 133, f. 17r.
[90] His name is given as 'Stockwel' in some of the reports.
[91] Lindquist, 'Purveyance', 568. The trees seem to have been willows whose placement was presumed by Egerton to 'safeguard' and ornament the house, making their removal more 'heinous'; BL Additional MS 25215, f. 26v.
[92] Hawarde, *Les Reportes*, p. 194.
[93] Folger Shakespeare Library MS v. a. 133, f. 17r.
[94] Hawarde, *Les Reportes*, pp. 194–5.

to seize them.[95] In this way the misdeeds of individuals who had obtained legal authority were stated in the language of security of property.

Later, after his elevation to the bench, Coke gave another speech in the Star Chamber on the issue of timber. He began by arguing that a purveyor might take only wood that had been felled for sale. The king should have first claim on this timber, but his officers could not demand that the subject surrender their trees:

> for there is great reason, that in such cases the kinge should be first served; but the dignetye ... of his Maiesty's prerogative royall is not used to inforce his subjects to endure wronge; but the rust beinge scowred off which abused time hath cased upon it, then will the glorye thereof shine in the perfection of an Incorrupt brightnes. If therefore anye of you doe desire to preserve your tymber growinge be not scared with a Purveyors warrant, nor doe not preserve your trees by bribing anye one of them.[96]

Coke ended by referring to purveyors who extorted money in return for not felling trees. The king needed provision, but the subject needed protection. Accountability through judicial oversight would ensure the fair operation of the royal prerogative so that 'the glorye thereof shine in the perfection of an Incorrupt brightnes'.

The problems arising from deputation were evident in Coke's prosecution of Richard Richards, also in 1605, for granting acquittances on penal laws and pocketing the money.[97] Of greater interest to Coke was Richards's activities as deputy-purveyor, where he had developed more inventive schemes to enrich himself: 'he had charged the counties ... with such great amount of beans and peas for the purpose of taking money as composition. He shared this money amongst himself, the chief purveyor and the other deputies, all of whom numbered 12.' He also confessed to a range of misdemeanours that he and his confederates, including some of the high constables, had committed during the king's progress, as well as other embezzlement schemes in the household. Coke believed Richards's crimes merited death and he seemed increasingly alarmed about the activities of purveyors, declaring: 'For purveyors they are grown to such great insolency, that sometimes they take trees that are growing on franktenements, sometimes fruit trees out of orchards for transplanting into the King's orchards, sometimes glass in houses and similar such things.'[98]

---

[95] *Stockwel's Case*, Moore 760, 72 ER 888.
[96] BL Harley MS 1578, ff. 221v–222r. The text refers to Coke as the 'Lord Chief Justice'.
[97] *Richard's Case* (1605), Moore 762, 72 ER 890; BL Harley MS 1330, f. 5v.
[98] *Ibid.*, 890–1. He was punished with mutilation, pillory, fine and imprisonment.

The case gave the judges the opportunity to state several rules that suggested Coke's influence, including the requirement that purveyors should not obtain goods without informing those they took from or without showing their commissions. The judges were especially concerned about the activities of deputies, declaring that purveyors could not delegate their powers to others, and established that the purveyor would be liable to provide compensation for a deputy's misdeeds. Finally, and perhaps most importantly, the judges claimed it was a felony to sell those things taken as purveyance for private gain. By making such corruption felonious the judges substantially raised the legal risks for dishonest purveyors.

Contemporaries perceived Coke's attempts to articulate rules controlling the conduct of officers and purveyors as enhancing the prerogative – as a means to protect royal authority from coming into disrepute. During the same years Coke's development of the treason law further exposed his complex attitude to the prerogative, as confessional differences and England's war with Spain weighed on the government. Superficially Coke contributed his energy to treason prosecutions, but he also worked to strengthen the substantive law itself in favour of the queen.[99] Beneath his advocacy of a harsher law was Coke's belief that ultimate authority rested in the prince. His ideas were traditional and he understood the subject's duty to obey as a consequence of the primordial duty of allegiance.[100] Treason lay bare that bond and, in Coke's view up to 1616, revealed the irresistible force of royal authority.

Treason is the most serious offence known to English law.[101] Conviction brought the corruption of the blood, a gruesome execution and forfeiture of property.[102] Treason had originated at English law as a broad class of wrongs, including both petty and high treason, until the statute of 1352 defined it more closely.[103] The statute identified high treason as a cluster of offences, especially the compassing or imagining of the death of the

---

[99] John Bellamy, *The Tudor Law of Treason: An Introduction* (London, 1979), p. 48.

[100] D. M. Jones, 'Sir Edward Coke and the Interpretation of Lawful Allegiance in Seventeenth-Century England', *History of Political Thought*, 7:2 (1986), 321–40, at 330.

[101] James Stephen, *A History of the Criminal Law of England* (London, 1883), vol. II, p. 242.

[102] The fear that it would be used for political purposes led to restraints on its application; BL Lansdowne MS 486, f. 17r. For a longer-term perspective, see James Willard Hurst, 'Historic Background of the Treason Clause', *Federal Bar Journal*, 6 (1945), 305–13, at 307.

[103] 3 Co. *Inst.*, p. 2. *Bracton* in the thirteenth century assimilated treason to lese-majesty; see *Bracton*, vol. II, p. 334. Treason could be broadly construed; Matthew Hale, *History of Pleas of the Crown* (Philadelphia, PA, 1847), vol. I, p. 80.

monarch, or the levying of war against him.[104] Coke believed that betrayal was the unifying theme in the offences and insisted that the 'betraying itself' was the crime.[105] Though the drafters had warned against the expansion of treason without legislative approval they did not provide clear definitions for each form of high treason.[106] This omission gave the judiciary considerable scope in their interpretation of the law. While it was clear what it meant to violate the king's unmarried eldest daughter, to 'compass or imagine the Death, of our Lord, the King' was less certain. What actions, for instance, signalled that a subject was levying war against the king or compassing his death? By Coke's time it was certain that adhering to the king's enemies, imagining the king's death and levying war required some 'overt act'.[107] But was the overt act either simply evidence of the criminal intent or the crime itself? Coke wrote that levying war against the king was only treason upon the overt act: 'A compassing or conspiracy to levy war, is no Treason, for there must be a levying of war *in facto*.'[108] In the case of imagining the death of the king, the function of the overt act prompted greater debate. Some common lawyers, including Coke, believed that the bare thought of 'compassing or imagining the death of the king' was treason, and therefore the overt act merely revealed or proved that treason. This line of reasoning potentially criminalized thought. But to delve into the minds of the accused was fraught with problems of proof as the well-known medieval dictum of Thomas Bryan CJCP ran, 'the intent of a man shall not be tried, for the Devil does not know a man's intent'.[109]

For these reasons and to preserve the loyalty of Catholic subjects, the policy of the late Tudor state was supposedly not to 'make windows into men[']s hearts and secret thoughts'.[110] Coke, however, asserted the maxim that the 'will should be considered by the deed' and pursued the overt act as evidence of a corrupted, treasonous heart.[111] It remained to

---

[104] 3 Co. *Inst.*, pp. 3–4.   [105] *Ibid.*, p. 4.

[106] *SR*, vol. I, p. 320.   [107] 3 Co. *Inst.*, p. 5.

[108] *Ibid.*, p. 9. Under 13 Elizabeth, c. 1, the intent to levy war had been made a crime, but this statute was only for the lifetime of the queen.

[109] YB Pasch. 17 Edward IV, f. 2, pl. 2 (trans. J. H. Baker). The dictum was proverbial in Coke's time; see Bacon 's *Promus*, ed. Henry Pott (Boston, MA, 1883), no. 653, and William Shakespeare, *The Tempest*, Act 3, Scene 2, line 87 and *Twelfth Night*, Act 1, Scene 3, line 38; Bodl. MS Rawlinson B 410 [n.f.]; *Master and Fellows of Magdalen College* (1615), 13 Co. *Rep.* 11, 77 ER 1422, though here Coke adds the qualification 'as long as a man doth not offend neither in act nor in word any law established'.

[110] Spedding (ed.), *Letters and Life*, vol. I, p. 178.

[111] See for example, *Everard* v. *Hopkins* (1615), 2 Bulstrode 335, 80 ER 1166; *Crofts* v. *Brown* (1616), 3 Bulstrode 167, 81 ER 141; *Bagg's Case* (1615), 11 Co. *Rep.* 99a, 77 ER 1279.

define the overt act that revealed the treason: stabbing the king might
be sufficient, but what about a few words spoken at an alehouse?[112] Coke
wrote that in the ancient law words alone might have proved the compassing or imagining the death of the king.[113] On the bare facts, Coke
may have been correct. But the underlying reasoning of the medieval
lawyers had been different than that developed by their Tudor successors. Treasonous words, according to the medieval lawyers, had the
effect of either disrupting the love between king and subject or they
affected the king in such a way as to shorten his life.[114] Tudor lawyers,
including Coke, reoriented the treason law to the conscience of the
accused, finding the essence of the crime in the corruption of the heart
and the secret disloyalty of the subject.[115] In the most extreme formulation, words were held to be sufficient at the common law for maintaining a conviction, a position that Coke helped to advance, but rejected
later in his career.[116]

These developments capped a rapid evolution of the law in the sixteenth century. During the trial of the Duke of Buckingham in 1521, it
was asserted by Fyneux that words alone were sufficient proof to reveal
treason.[117] Henry VIII extended treason by statute in 1534 to include
certain words, such as calling the king a heretic.[118] G. R. Elton reported
that 394 cases of treason for words were prosecuted with 184 found not
to be treasonous.[119] Resistance to these prosecutions seems to have been
muted, though legislation under later Tudors mentions that the Henrician
statutes were 'verie streighte sore extreme and terrible'.[120] Reaction set

---

[112] Andy Wood, ' "A lyttull worde ys tresson": Loyalty, Denunciation, and Popular Politics
       in Tudor England', *Journal of British Studies*, 48 (2009), 837–47, at 837–8.
[113] 3 Co. *Inst.*, p. 5.
[114] Bellamy, *Tudor Law of Treason*, p. 11; Baker, *OHLE*, vol. VI, p. 527.
[115] For this reason a madman could not be convicted of treason; 3 Co. *Inst.*, p. 6. The import-
       ance of intent is also suggested by BL Harley MS 6687B, f. 45v.
[116] 3 Co. *Inst.*, p. 14.
[117] Bellamy, *Tudor Law of Treason*, pp. 27–32; J. H. Baker (ed.), *Year Books of Henry VIII,
       12–14 Henry VIII 1520–1523* (London, 2002), p. 57; Holinshed, *Chronicles*, vol. III, p. 658;
       R. v. Duke of Buckingham (1521), John Port, *The Notebook of Sir John Port*, ed. J. H. Baker
       (London, 1986), pp. 123–4.
[118] 26 Henry VIII, c. 13, *SR*, vol. III, pp. 508–9; Bellamy, *Tudor Law of Treason*, pp. 28–9;
       G. R. Elton, 'The Law of Treason in the Early Reformation', *The Historical Journal*, 11:2
       (1968), 211–36, at 227–32.
[119] Cited in Bellamy, *Tudor Law of Treason*, p. 45.
[120] 1 Edward VI, c. 12, *SR*, vol. IV, pt. I, pp. 18–20; see also 1 Mary, st. 1, c. 1, *SR*, vol. IV, pt.
       I, pp. 197–8. Bellamy did not believe that there was significant 'outcry' over the treason
       statutes; *Tudor Law of Treason*, p. 14.

in, and both Edward VI and Mary assented to legislation that softened prosecutions for words.[121]

From the time of Mary the lawyers also argued that the statute of 1352 was declaratory of the common law.[122] Common law treason was asserted in *Throckmorton's Case* (1554) when Serjeant Stanford responded to criticisms of the indictment: 'There doth remain divers other treasons at this day at the common law, which be not expressed by that statute, as the judges can declare.'[123] This assertion of common law treason is a reminder of the importance of judicial interpretation to the development of the treason law, a point central to the debates over whether two witnesses were required to prove statutory treason.[124] During his prosecution in 1603 Sir Walter Raleigh demanded to come face to face with his accusers and unsuccessfully argued for the necessity of two witnesses, which he believed were required by 25 Edward III, the statutes of 10 and 13 Elizabeth and the law of canonical proof.[125] The rejection of Raleigh's demands was justified by Popham on the grounds of reason of state: 'There must not such a gap be opened for the destruction of the king, as would be if we should grant this.'[126]

Raleigh's trial also revealed another element at work: the moral revulsion associated with treason. Treason might be reduced to an act or thought for analytical purposes, but it was understood as a corruption of the individual, and so at Raleigh's trial it was urged, 'the matter nowe to be discovered is in his nature treason'. This attitude towards treason joined with the practical necessity of suppressing it to support a lower requirement for proof: 'for that yt is of that vile and horrible nature in the sight of men and soe capitallie daungerouse to the practizers that they ever bend the spirit of theire wittes to secreate and conceale yt, and there-

---

[121] Bellamy, *Tudor Law of Treason*, p. 58; Dean, *Law-Making and Society*, pp. 70–1; 1 and 2 Phillip and Mary, c. 10, 2-III, *SR*, vol. IV, part I, pp. 255–6; though expanded again under Elizabeth, 1 Elizabeth I, c. 5, and 13 Elizabeth I, c. 1, *SR*, vol. IV, pt. I, p. 527. The act was followed by 23 Elizabeth I, c. 1, VI, *SR*, vol. IV, pt. I, p. 658, and 27 Elizabeth I, c. 2.

[122] Bellamy, *Tudor Law of Treason*, p. 56.

[123] William Cobbett (ed.), *State Trials and Proceedings for High Treason and Other Crimes and Misdemeanors* (London, 1809), vol. I, col. 889. Bellamy, *Tudor Law of Treason*, p. 56.

[124] The statutes of 5 and 6 Edward VI, c. 11, required two 'lawfull accusers', and debate followed over the meaning of this term. See Baker (ed.), *Reports of William Dalison*, pp. 105–6; Bro. *Abr.*, tit. 'Corone', pl. 219, f. 187v; and discussed in Baker, *OHLE*, vol. VI, p. 518.

[125] *ST*, vol. II, col. 15; BL Harley MS 6686B, f. 584r.

[126] *ST*, col. 19.

fore both lawe and reason aloweth vyolent concurring presumptions for concluding prooffe'.[127]

Betrayal undermined the structure of moral kingship: the guilty disobeyed God's authority, which had set up kings. At the Gunpowder Plot trial, Coke observed that the king was 'God's anointed' and that had 'his power derived from God within his territories'.[128] The corrosion of this natural order would lead to the unwinding of the state and society: the 'prodigious and unnatural' Plot had aimed at the destruction of the constitution and 'even the deletion of our whole name and nation'.[129] The Plot fitted into Coke's understanding of the popish conspiracy that misled subjects into renouncing their allegiance and inverted the order of power.[130] Having failed to subdue England through the Armada, the pope and the Spanish king turned to 'moste develish and dangerous attempts' to harm the Queen and weaken the state. The temporal ambition of the pope and king of Spain was the true cause, Coke argued, of the bull *Regnans in Excelsis* (1570).[131] From this bull, Coke claimed, the recent treasons had sprung, since English Catholics were faced with a difficult choice: 'for either they must be hanged for treason, in resisting their lawful sovereign, or cursed for yielding due obedience unto her majesty'.[132] As they had done in the medieval past, the pope and his agents unnaturally disrupted the bond of allegiance between lord and subject, leading to regicide.[133]

This inversion perverted the natural relationship of allegiance: the traitor rejected a subject's natural duty of obedience to legitimate authority.[134] Coke hyperbolically expressed outrage over such treachery and described Dr Lopez as 'a dearer Traitor then Judas himself'.[135] In the trial of the Earl of Essex Coke emphasized that treason was a perversion: 'I hold it an unnatural act for a natural subject to commit Treason against his natural sovereign … this High Treason is, and must be, both against the law of God, nature, and reason.' Treason had a diabolical quality, and during the same trial he observed that the treason 'was not only carried in their

---

[127] Bodl. MS Carte 205, f. 131r.

[128] *ST*, vol. I, col. 176.

[129] *ST*, vol. II, cols. 157, 168; PRO SP 12/249 f. 220r; *Roy* v. *Owen alias Collins*, 1 Rolle 187, 81 ER 420.

[130] *ST*, vol. II, cols. 224, 183; Holkham MS 677, ff. 115v–116r.

[131] PRO SP 12/247, f. 166r–v.   [132] *ST*, vol. II, cols. 222, 178.

[133] *Ibid.*, col. 220.

[134] Jones, 'Lawful Allegiance', 330; Bellamy, *Tudor Law of Treason*, p. 75. Coke described this relationship in *Calvin's Case* (1608), 7 Co. *Rep.* 16b, 77 ER 396; *Darcy* v. *Allen* (1602), BL Additional 25213, f. 34v.

[135] PRO SP 12/247, f. 167r; PRO SP 12/248, f. 55r.

hearts, but, for a continual remembrance, kept in a black purse, which my lord of Essex wore on his breast next to his skin'.[136] Essex's followers had rejected God or been misled: 'none but Papists, Recusants, and Atheists'.[137]

The analysis of treason as a crime of allegiance could bring even aliens into the offence's purview. Coke recorded that Egerton had described a resolution of the judges in 1571 that aliens within the realm would be liable to treason prosecutions if they were under the protection of the queen. Coke explained this application as a consequence of allegiance, since an alien, 'because he is reputed in law as a subject so long as he remains here under the protection of the queen and in subjection to her, and consequently, if any such alien himself imagines the death of the queen etc this is treason'.

Coke based this construction on a case from 1557 that should a visiting alien be prosecuted for treason the indictment should read 'against his liegeance' since 'so long as he remains here under the safe conduct and protection of the queen, he owes allegiance to the queen'.[138] Once the alien's king was at war with England, no protection could be offered and therefore no duty of obedience.[139] Using statutory sanction and allegiance the common lawyers were also able to extend the reach of the treason law of England beyond the realm, so that those subjects who committed treason beyond the seas could be prosecuted.[140]

The mental decision of the individual, in which they broke allegiance with their prince by intending harm to him or her, was treason, and the overt act merely proof of the intention.[141] Coke captured this relationship in the metaphor that he repeatedly used to describe treason's spread:

> For treason is like a tree whose root is full of poison, and lieth secret and hid within the earth, resembling the imagination of the heart of man, which is so secret as God only knoweth it. Now the wisdom of the law provideth for the blasting and nipping, both of the leaves, blossoms, and buds which proceed from this root of Treason; either by words, which are

---

[136] *ST*, vol. I, col. 1338. Coke's description of the bag is found in another account, PRO SP 12/278, f. 158v. See also Bodl. Carte MS 205, f. 131r for similar sentiments in Raleigh's trial.

[137] *ST*, vol. I, col. 1337.

[138] *Nota* (1594), BL Harley MS 6686A, f. 83r. Coke was citing *Sherley's Case* (1557), discussed in Baker, *OHLE*, vol. VI, p. 616. Bro. *Abr.*, tit. 'Treason and Traytors', pl. 32, f. 285v.

[139] Following the precedent set in *Roger Mortimer's Case* (1487), 3 Co. Inst., pp. 4–5.

[140] 35 Henry VIII, c. 2, *SR*, vol. III p. 958. See the case of O'Rourke, BL Harley MS 6686B, f. 432v, and BL Harley 4817, f. 89r, and discussed in *Calvin's Case*, 7 Co. *Rep.* 23b, 77 ER 405; *Lewis v. Coke* (1617), Croke Jac 424, 79 ER 362.

[141] Similarly, see *R. v. Duke of Buckingham* (1521), *The Notebook of Sir John Port*, p. 124.

like to leaves, or by some overt act, which may be resembled to buds or blossoms, before it cometh to such fruit and ripeness, as would bring utter destruction and desolation upon the whole state.[142]

The overt act was an eruption of the poison, a sign of the broken allegiance as Coke declared to Raleigh: 'thou hast an English face, but a Spanish heart'.[143]

This analysis suggested that treason was an inward crime and so Coke was able to record in his unpublished report of *Cobham's Case* and elsewhere that 'the thought of Treason to the prince, by the law is death'. The insistence on treason as a mental act had a real effect on the proceedings, for it was determined by the judges in the same case that, 'if one should compass or imagine [the death of the king] at one time and [commit] the overt act at another time, the forefeiture should be of all that he had at the time of compassing or imagining which then was the treason'.[144] Coke explained in his notebooks that, 'concerning the said imagination of the heart is founded on the law of God' and cited biblical justification for the premise that words alone might reveal the corrupt heart.[145]

While the mere imagining of the death of the monarch was treason, the overt act was still a necessary element to the crime of levying war. Over the next decades Coke helped to develop common law treason, arguing that the intent or actual levying of war was a constructive compassing of the king's death.[146] In doing so, Coke delved into the relationship between subject and monarch leading to some of his clearest statements on the duties of the subject and the power of the prince. This expansion of treason is evident from 1595 when the Star Chamber sentenced apprentices in London to imprisonment and the pillory for riot after they had insisted on paying three pence, rather than five, per pound of butter.[147] Heavy rains in the summer and autumn had raised the price of victuals, and tempers had frayed. Sympathetic apprentices conspired to free those imprisoned and allegedly to murder the Lord Mayor, burn his house and then seize weapons from two houses near the Tower.[148] Three hundred apprentices

---

[142] *ST*, vol. II, col. 157; *ibid.*, vol. II, col. 7; BL Harley MS 6686B, f. 567r.

[143] *ST*, vol. II, col. 7, cf. col. 20; see also PRO SP 12/249, f. 299v.

[144] *ST*, vol. I, col. 1337; BL Harley MS 6686B, f. 566r.

[145] Ecclesiastes 10:20, Exodus 21:28 and Psalm 64:8; BL Harley MS 6686B, f. 568v.

[146] 3 Co. *Inst.*, p. 12.

[147] The indictment is found in PRO SP 12/253/48. John Stow, *The Annales, or a Generall Chronicle of England* (London, 1615), STC 23338, pp. 768–9; *The Case of the Southwark Apprentices* (1595), 2 Anderson 4–5.

[148] Coke's unpublished account of the riot adds further details and differs slightly; BL Harley MS 6686A, f. 114v.

appeared near Tower Hill, but the mayor's swift response and the arrest of five protestors prevented further action.[149] The government revealed its anxiety at the situation when it appointed Sir Thomas Wilford with martial powers in London while the law officers met to consider the charge against the rioters.[150] They looked to the statute of 13 Elizabeth that made the intent to levy war treasonous and considered a precedent of 1517 when thirteen rioters were sentenced to death for treason for attacking foreigners granted safe conduct by the king under a statute of 3 Henry V.[151] Fyneux had stated at the time that the riot was treason 'as a thing practised against the regall honour of our sovereigne lord the king'. The Elizabethan judges offered a more specific analysis according to Coke: 'this intent to levy war by the freeing of prisoners or by the sacking of the city was in law to levy war against the queen, because … the queen is bound to preserve her people in peace and to administer justice to all'.[152] By threatening the city and defying the law, the apprentices had prevented the queen from fulfilling her duties as part of the compact of allegiance. Thus even the intention to levy war was treasonous, since it was 'Against the office and authority of the Queen to levy war'. This logic opened up another possibility that Popham attempted to foreclose when he denied that levying war also implied compassing the death of the monarch. This judicial opinion was to change as levying war assumed a broader interpretation that focused on the queen's sovereign power.

Soon after the rising of the London apprentices there was another riot precipitated by the high price of corn.[153] The Crown prosecuted Richard Bradshawe and Robert Burton for gathering men in Oxfordshire at Enslow Hill to tear down enclosures. It was alleged that they also intended to gather arms from Lord Norris's house 'to go from one gentleman's house to another, and so from house to house to pull down enclosures generally'.[154] Another judicial conference debated how to frame the indictment

[149] They also appeared with evidence of martial harness, including a trumpet. *The Case of the Southwark Apprentices*, 2 Anderson 5; Bellamy, *The Tudor Law of Treason*, pp. 78–9; Stow, *The Annales*, p. 769.
[150] John Walter, '"A Rising of the People"? The Oxfordshire Rising of 1596', *Past and Present*, 107 (1985), 92.
[151] BL Harley MS 6686A, f. 115r. Richard Grafton, *A Chronicle at Large and Meere History of the Affayres of Englande and Kinges of the Same* (London, 1569) STC 12147, pp. 1,021–4. *R. v. Lincoln* (1517), *The Notebook of Sir John Port*, no. 74, p. 123, and also no. 73, p. 123.
[152] BL Harley MS 6686A, f. 115r.
[153] PRO SP 12/261/10.
[154] The story of the riots is told by Walter, '"A Rising of the People"?', 90–143. *The Case of Armes*, Popham 122, 79 ER 1227; though Coke reports that it seemed to some that the

of the rioters. The question arose as to what made this enclosure riot different from others.[155] Consensus was reached on a basic premise: 'for all agreed that rebellion of subjects against the Queen hath been always high treason at the common law'.[156] While in medieval England rebellion meant disobedience, in the sixteenth century it had come to be equated with treason.[157] Popham recorded further agreement that 'rebellion is all the war which a subject can make against the King'.[158] But where the act of rebellion, the levying of war against the sovereign, began remained the key question: there was no direct evidence that Bradshawe or Burton intended harm to the queen or even the government. The Enslow Hill riot seemed an example of the common enclosure riot.

Responding to Thomas Walmesley's JCP suggestion that the indictment should be for riot, Coke presented a different opinion.[159] He argued that the offence affected the public as a whole. Coke drew on the admission that the rioters intended to continue on to other enclosures and so become a public threat. In the words of Popham, 'the case here tending to a generality makes the act if it had been executed to be high treason by the course of the common law'. Coke, in his report, added that the difference between the Enslow Hill riot and a riot that was only felonious was that one had a more general purpose that involved the wider public. Coke explained the underlying reasoning, not as a matter of safety or even order, but instead by discussing allegiance and touching on ideas of sovereignty: 'but when the intent is to make reformation of enclosures ... and by this to relieve wrongs and injuries made to others and not to themselves, this is to assume on the authority and office of the queen, because it is the office of the queen to administer justice to all her subjects ... and to preserve them in peace'.[160] Coke argued that however well meaning, the rioters had 'usurped' the authority of the queen and he recorded that the judges accepted this argument. Though Popham reported more generally that the riot was treasonous since it tended to the derogation of the royal dignity, Coke applied the same language used against popish conspirators and priests. It was agreed that if the riot had destroyed enclosures 'it

conspiracy 'had no intent to levy war'. BL Harley MS 6686A, ff. 194v–195r; Popham 121, 79 ER 1227; HMC, *Salisbury*, vol. VII, p. 236. Boyer, *Sir Edward Coke*, pp. 256–8.

[155] 1 Mary, st. 2, c. 12.

[156] *The Case of Armes*, Popham 122, 79 ER 1227. For example, see William Shakespeare, *Richard II*, Act 2, Scene 3, line 109.

[157] Bellamy, *The Tudor Law of Treason*, p. 30.

[158] *The Case of Armes*, Popham 123, 79 ER 1228. Popham indicates that this was accepted unanimously 'for all agreed'.

[159] Bellamy, *The Tudor Law of Treason*, p. 79.   [160] BL Harley MS 6686A, ff. 195r–v.

would have been treason at the common law'. It was Sir William Peryam CBEx who pointed the way of the future when he declared that: 'for all these tend against the Queen, her Crown and dignity, and therefore shall be as against the Queen herself'.[161] The connection between levying war and compassing the death of the Queen was being made explicit, and it led to robust assertions about royal authority.

This occurred in *Essex's Case* (1601) for reasons peculiar to the evidence. Though they were charged with compassing the death of the Queen, the defendants claimed that they had no intention of harming her.[162] In response Coke distilled from the precedents of treasonous riots the principle that: 'If servants should come to their masters with armed petitions, this is a shew of disobedience, and tendeth to destruction.'[163] Popham signified his agreement during the trial that any compulsion of the prince tended to treason, especially where it touched the alteration of the laws and religion. Opening the case against Sir Christopher Blount, Sir Charles Danvers and Sir John Davies, Coke stated the general principle: 'Wherever the subject rebelleth, or riseth in a forcible manner to overrule the royal will and power of the king, the wisdom and foresight of the laws of this land maketh this construction of his actions, that he intendeth to deprive the king both of crown and life.' Christopher Yelverton, queen's serjeant, then continued portentously that this was not a 'quiddity of law' but that, 'when the subject will take upon him to give law to the king, and to make the sovereign and commanding power become subject and commanded, such subject layeth hold of the crown ... The crown is so fastened upon the king's head, that it cannot be pulled of, but head and life will follow.'[164]

Levying war against the queen or rising in disobedience to her necessarily imported her death for two reasons. First, rebellion made it necessary to kill or neutralize the queen. Conspirators would not await their punishment – historical example had shown that they would remove the prince. The Lord Admiral affirmed as much during the trial of the Essex conspirators relating that the earl told him 'the queen could not live and he too'.[165] Coke himself reasoned this way in one account of his arguments at the trial: 'I beleeve she [the Queen] showld not have lived longe after

---

[161] They were found culpable under 13 Elizabeth I, c. 1; *The Case of Armes*, Popham 123, 79 ER 1228.

[162] *ST*, vol. I, col. 1411.

[163] *Ibid.*, cols. 1420–1; *ibid.*, col. 1337.   [164] *Ibid.*, col. 1410.

[165] *Ibid.*, col. 1430.

she had bene in your power. Note but the precedents of former ages, howe long lived Richard 2 after he was surprised in the same manner.[166]

Second, as Yelverton stated in the trial of Essex and the Earl of Southampton, the prince was 'head of the common wealth and his subjects as members owght to obey and stand with him'.[167] Coke wrote in his notes that 'rebellion and insurrection is overt gathering of power and strength [and] levieng of forces to doe or reforme any thing in the common wealth'.[168] Two powers, he claimed, could not exist within a commonwealth: 'the world may as well bear two suns as the state suffer two such governments'.[169] Levying of forces and gathering of power was against the 'kingly office', the very essence of which was power derived from God.[170] Yelverton explicitly linked the idea of rebellion with the Roman law offence of lese-majesty: 'for subjects to sway things at their list, is crimen *laesae majestatis*'.[171] Rebellion was, as Coke later disapprovingly remarked, to make the king 'tenant at will of his Crowne and of his land'.[172] The derogation of royal authority violated the subject's obligation of obedience implicit in allegiance.[173] Coke continued to connect common law treason with lese-majesty even in his later years, suggesting that the derogation of royal authority was a betrayal.[174]

This reasoning suggested that treason was a challenge to the prince's 'greaterness', a point that led to the consideration of sovereignty. Coke reiterated the reasoning in his manuscript account of *Cobham's Case*:

> the dignity of the king consists in his crown of sovereignty, in his sceptre of command and direction, and in his royal robe of absolute power and authority, but those who intend and conspire or make the said treasons intend to seize the crown of sovereignty ... to wreste the scepter of command from his hand and to despoil him of his royal robe of authority and power, and of their sovereign to take him in their wardship and possession by such power that he is not able to resist, and to make him a subject.[175]

[166] PRO SP 12/278, f. 172v; for similar reasoning, see SP 12/278, f. 159v; BL Harley MS 6686A, f. 246v; BL Harley MS 6686B, f. 565v.

[167] PRO SP 12/278, f. 167v.

[168] *Ibid.*, f. 159r.

[169] *ST*, vol. I, col. 1419. The same metaphor was used by Edward Forset, *A Comparative Discourse of the Bodies Naturall and Politique*' (London, 1606), STC 11188, p. 10.

[170] PRO SP 12/278 f. 259r.   [171] *ST*, vol. I, col. 1419.

[172] *Rex* v. *Griffith and Holland* (1613), 2 Bulstrode 156, 80 ER 1029.

[173] For example, *ST*, vol. II, cols. 7, 167–8.

[174] Williams, 'Bracton's Authority', 72; 3 Co. *Inst.*, p. 2.

[175] BL Harley MS 6686B, ff. 568r–v.

In this same report, Coke added 'the thought of Treason to the prince, by the law is death'.[176] Such was the authority of the prince that even thought could be treasonous.

These developments returned to the problem of whether or not words alone might overtly prove the treasonous thought. Under Henry VIII the wrong words might well be treasonous, a position fortified by statute.[177] Although these acts were repealed in 1547, the question remained controverted.[178] Subsequent debates up to 1628 suggested that the common law judges were giving greater weight to words alone as proof of treason.[179] Words, it was believed, revealed the inward corruption and breach of allegiance. But this reliance on words as proof of the treasonous thoughts of the accused had dangerous implications. In the summary of Sir John Perrot at his trial, what was feared was that 'You winne menes lyves awaye with words.'[180]

Coke's notes of a judicial conference held during *Cobham's Case* reveal the debate over whether words alone were sufficient to convict.[181] During the conference it was asked whether 'words importing the treasonable compassing or imagining etc are overt deeds within the said act of 25 Edward III'?[182] The judges responded by setting out a unanimous principle that the imagining or compassing the death of the king within one's heart was treason based on their interpretation of the Edwardian statute.[183] Whether words were sufficient proof was then debated. Some persons, unnamed, argued that the implication of the Tudor statutes, especially 13 Elizabeth, c. 1, which made words treasonous, was that words had not always been overt acts and were thus provided for by the statutes, which in any case had inflicted inferior punishments for the first offences.[184]

Coke's report then introduced the tree metaphor describing how the treasonous heart was the root that put forth its buds, leaves and fruits. He

---

[176] *ST*, vol. I, col. 1337; BL Harley MS 6686B, f. 566r.

[177] Baker, *OHLE*, vol. VI, p. 586.

[178] *Ibid.*, p. 587; Bro. *Abr.*, tit. 'Treason and Traytors', pl. 24, f. 285r.

[179] Cf. Philip Hamburger, 'The Development of the Law of Seditious Libel and the Control of the Press', *Stanford Law Review*, 37:3 (1984–5), 661–765, at 667.

[180] Roger Turvey (ed.), *The Treason and Trial of Sir John Perrot* (Cardiff, 2005), p. 159.

[181] Coke may have influenced the use of the tree metaphor in the manuscript recently used in discussions of the case, Bodl. Carte MS 205, f. 127r; Mark Nicholls, 'Sir Walter Ralegh's Treason: A Prosecution Document', *English Historical Review*, 110:438 (1995), 902–24, at 902–3.

[182] BL Harley MS 6686B, f. 566r.

[183] For example, see Turvey (ed.), *Sir John Perrot*, p. 142.

[184] BL Harley MS 6686B, ff. 566r–v. These arguments modify the account in James Stephen, *History of the Criminal Law* (London, 1883), vol. II, pp. 263–8.

then interpreted the meaning of his metaphor: 'thus when the imagination of the heart produces words as leaves ... these show the imagination of the heart[,] and the wisdom of the law is to blast and destroy treason in the leaves or buds before they are able to attain to the effect of the fruit which would be the subversion and confusion of the state'.[185] Coke also cited half a dozen precedents from the Middle Ages, the sixteenth century and the Bible in support of his contention that words could be the overt act.[186]

But other lawyers were more careful. A hypothetical case was posed in the same conference. A man had imagined the death of the king in his heart and he had fallen under suspicion. He was taken, and the council examined him. During the examination he confessed imagining the death of the king. There was no other overt act. Was this treason within the statute of 25 Edward III? This was a hard case, for it made it possible that men could be forced under the pressure of interrogation to confess to something that they had never actually done or perhaps even intended – for who could truly know the inward conscience? Coke's notes reveal the ambivalence. The answer he originally recorded was: 'and this confession is such an overt fact by which he provably is able to be attainted of an overt fact within the statute of 25 Edward III because the imagination is the treason and the confession of the party the most sure proof that is able to be'.[187] However, at some point this had been changed to 'it was not such an overt fact'. Admitting that a confession alone, with no other evidence, should be an overt act and expose the inward heart would have completed treason's transition to a crime of mere thought.

A later case continued to test the use of words as proof of common law treason. In *R. v. Owen* (1615) the defendant had been accused of intending the death of the king for the following words: 'the King being excommunicate by the Pope, may be lawfully deposed and killed by any whatsoever; which killing is not murder'. Owen supported his claim by appealing to the papal bulls of excommunication. Bacon pleaded for the Crown and having cited the treason of the Duke of Buckingham (1521), made the following conclusion: 'And it seems to me that such words in this indictment are treason by the common law.'[188] Coke and the rest of the bench concurred that the words imported treason even though no statutory

---

[185] BL Harley MS 6686B, f. 567r. See also the treason trial of Sir John Perrot (1592) for the metaphor used there by Serjeant Puckering; Turvey (ed.), *Sir John Perrot*, p. 142.
[186] BL Harley MS 6686B, ff. 568r–v.   [187] *Ibid.*, f. 567v.
[188] *Roy v. Owen alias Collins*, 1 Rolle 186, 81 ER 419; *ST*, vol. I, cols. 287, 292.

authority was cited. Coke himself hinted at a broad interpretation of treasonous words, drawing from his experience pleading the Enslow Hill riot:
'So if discontented persons with enclosures say, that they will petition
unto the King about them, and (if) he will not redress the same, that then
they will assemble together in such a place and rebell: in these cases it is
a present treason: and he said, that in point of allegiance none must serve
the King with ifs and ands.'[189]

Coke urged that their allegiance imposed on the subject an absolute
duty to obey. The judges added that Owen had denied royal authority and
aided the papal usurpation by claiming that the pope had power over the
king. The crux was again the denial of sovereign power and the breach of
allegiance, and Coke declared that Owens was condemned by the statute
of 25 Edward III, 'which is but a declaration of the common law, and this
law is originally derived from the crown and not from any other law'.[190]
Owen would die the death of a traitor accompanied by the ruthless words
of the chief justice: 'it was necessary to exterminate such locusts as the
defendant'.

Two further decisions late in Coke's tenure as chief justice tested
the limits of the treason law. *Peacham's Case* (1615) exposed how treason prosecutions could be used to attack critics of the government and
revealed misgivings among the judiciary about the wide net opened by
common law treason.[191] Peacham was a minister who drafted a sermon in
which he seems to have criticized the corruption of the government and
the ability of the king.[192] The draft indictment alleged that Peacham had
imagined and compassed the death of the king, since 'he composed and
wrote a certain detestible and venemous libel', which was written, 'For
the purpose that the liege people and true subjects of our lord king might
withdraw their love from our lord king and abandon him, and that they
might make and levy war against him.'[193] The indictment was drawn to
suggest that Peacham's criticism of the government corroded the ties of

---

[189] *Collins's Case*, Godbolt 264, 78 ER 154. The reporters explicitly stated that the indictment was at common law.

[190] *Roy* v. *Owen alias Collins*, 1 Rolle 187, 81 ER 420.

[191] The judges, e.g., agreed that the collection of thousands of names on petitions by puritans was a misdemeanour near to treason. *The Lord Chancellors Speech to Sir Henry
Mountague* (1616), Moore 756, 72 ER 885; *Memorandum*, Croke Jac 37, 79 ER 30.

[192] It is unclear what he wrote though Walter Yonge records that he identified corruption
in the Court of High Commission; Walter Yonge, *Diary of Walter Yonge*, ed. George
Roberts (London, 1848), p. 27; *ST*, vol. II, col. 870.

[193] *ST*, vol. II, col. 874.

allegiance and might lead to the raising of rebellion or disobedience. The prosecution proceeded on the basis of Peacham's words alone as proof of this intent. The judges seemed hesitant that the words amounted to evidence of treason, and it was later remembered that the judges 'held' that criticism alone could not amount to treason.[194] Nonetheless, Peacham was convicted of treason, but not executed. Interpreted within the modern context, *Peacham* had raised what amounted to an issue about the limits of public speech. But from the Tudor–Stuart perspective, the deeper problem was Peacham's interior loyalty.

That disloyal thought alone might allow a treason prosecution was reiterated the following year in *Crofts* v. *Brown* (1616). The judges contrasted felony, which required an overt act as an element of the crime, and treason, where the overt act might merely prove the crime.[195] This reasoning was again explained in *Hitcham* v. *Brooks* (1625) where Serjeant Hitcham sued Brooks in defamation for the words: 'Sir Robert Hitcham, hath spoken treason'.[196] The defence argued that the words must be construed *in mitior sensu*, and that 'the speech of treason is not treason, but when there is an intent to commit that'. This strategy assumed that words alone on their face did not prove treason. Serjeant Bawtrey responded by emphasizing that treasonous words demonstrated intent: 'it was plain, that the defendant spoke the words with a full intent to take away his life, and to speak treason is to speak *ex corde suo*'.

Hitcham v. *Brooks* revealed the dangerous implications of a broad treason law, as subjects could inform to pursue their private agenda. This possibility had already been raised in *Lovet* v. *Faulkner* (1614) when the judges considered whether an action in the nature of a conspiracy might lie for indictment for treason. Coke again articulated a rigorous interpretation of the treason law as a means to protect the commonwealth, denying that action might lie for 'procuring one to be indicted of treason'.[197] Robert Houghton JKB and Dodderidge JKB concurred, declaring that every man was bound on his oath to discover treason.

But continued concern about the misuse of treason accusations by private individuals, and not the government, eventually led to a reversal by the common law judges. In *Smith* v. *Crawshaw* et al. (1625) Smith was

---

[194] *Williams's Case* (1628), Croke Car 126, 79 ER 711.
[195] *Crofts* v. *Brown*, 3 Bulstrode 167, 81 ER 141.
[196] *Hitcham* v. *Brooks*, Winch 123, 124 ER 103.
[197] *Lovet* v. *Fawkner*, Croke Jac 357, 79 ER 306; *Lovet* v. *Faulkner*, 2 Bulstrode 270, 80 ER 1114.

indicted for speaking treasonable words in Norfolk. He was acquitted and brought an action on the case for conspiracy, winning damages of two hundred and forty pounds.[198] Arrest of judgment was sought, but this time the court was of the opinion that the action of conspiracy did lie. The defence appealed to the reasoning in *Lovet* v. *Fawkner* (1614) that should conspiracy lie then men would avoid reporting treasons to the detriment of the state.[199] But the court decided to break with precedent and policy, and accepted that cases could be brought for false indictments of treason.[200] Croke reported that this was the first time that the court accepted this reasoning.[201] Recognizing the possibilities that indictments for treason offered for private abuse, the court observed that if conspiracy would not lie, then 'for then no person would be safe, if such practices should be suffered, and the parties endangered thereby should have no remedy'. The Caroline judiciary eventually went further to protect individuals from treason prosecutions. In *Pine's Case* (1628) they moved to allow criticism of the king and declined to accept that words alone might prove treason without statutory provision.[202] In this conclusion, anxieties over the misuse of the law influenced the curtailment of decades of experimentation in the treason law.

Coke's achievements as attorney-general have rarely been thought praiseworthy. But during his time in office he worked to protect the integrity of the law and royal authority, gaining greater experience of the dangers to both. He attempted to restrict the abuse of legal power, using the Star Chamber and the common law, a goal that he would continue to advance towards on the bench. Individuals would be held to account in their use of the law lest they strain the prerogative or erode confidence in legal process. In the service of his monarch Coke also aggressively pursued those who contested royal authority, and his contributions to the law of treason intruded into individual conscience. They revealed his early commitment to monarchical power, his belief that subjects could not resist the monarch's authority. This thread of Coke's jurisprudence

---

[198] *Smith* v. *Crashaw, Ward and Ford* (1625), Croke Car 15, 79 ER 618; *Smith* v. *Crashaw*, Benloe 152, 73 ER 1019; *Smith* v. *Cranshaw*, 2 Rolle 258, 81 ER 785; *Smith* v. *Cranshaw, Spurle and Warne*, Palmer 315, 81 ER 1100; *Smith* v. *Cranshaw*, Jones, 93, 82 ER 48.

[199] *Smith* v. *Crashaw, Ward and Ford*, Croke Car 15, 79 ER 618; *Lovet* v. *Faulkner*, 2 Bulstrode 272, 80 ER 1115; *Lovet* v. *Faukner*, 1 Rolle 109, 81 ER 364.

[200] *Nota*, 2 Bulstrode 272, 80 ER 1115.

[201] *Smith* v. *Crashaw, Ward and Ford*, Croke Car 17, 79 ER 619; though Dodderidge mentioned a precedent at assizes in Cambridgeshire; *Smith* v. *Cranshaw*, 2 Rolle 261, 81 ER 787; *Smith* v. *Cranshaw*, Jones, 95, 82 ER 49.

[202] *Pine's Case*, Croke Car 117, 79 ER 703.

emerged from the demands of war, a time when even liberal democracies strain to limit the state's power. But such a position flowed logically from the belief that the queen needed such power to protect her subjects. These claims for such an overmastering royal authority were necessary to Coke's theory of sovereign power, a theory within which he would embed common law claims.

3

Confidence and corruption

The law in the Fens

'Drowned by the clouds and drained by the sea' was how a seventeenth-century contemporary described the rhythm of the English Fens, a low-land area of marsh and bog in eastern England spreading over 1,500 square miles.[1] This was an unstable landscape, with the Fens and the rivers that drained them flooding seasonally. Yet the Fens were also a rich ecosystem dotted by islands of higher ground, pastures and permanent human habitation. The most prominent of these was the town of Ely, which was the site of a major liberty and bishopric. Around Ely, and indeed throughout much of the submerged fen, lay rich soils. The soil, which now supports one of the most productive agricultural regions in England, was black gold for those investors daring and ingenious enough to tame the flood waters. The draining of the Fens by 'projectors' or 'undertakers' from the seventeenth century onwards involved the creation of elaborate systems of canals, pumps and dykes that superseded the older and more limited medieval works. The ambitions of the drainers, however, were not shared by many of the inhabitants of the Fens who struggled to preserve the landscape and a way of life that followed the rhythm of the flood waters.[2]

[1] H. C. Darby, *The Draining of the Fens* (Cambridge, 1968) and Keith Lindley, *Fenland Riots and the English Revolution* (London, 1982). Other studies include M. E. Kennedy, 'Charles I and Local Government: The Draining of the East and West Fens', *Albion*, 15:1 (1983), 19–31; M. E. Kennedy, 'Fen Drainage, the Central Government, and Local Interest: Carleton and the Gentlemen of South Holland', *Historical Journal*, 26 (1983), 15–37; L. E. Harris, 'Charles I and the Fens', *History Today*, 2:8 (1952), 564–70; Clive Holmes 'Drainers and Fenmen', in Anthony Fletcher and John Stevenson (eds.), *Order and Disorder in Early Modern England* (Cambridge, 1985), pp. 166–95.

[2] A discussion of their opposing attitudes is found throughout Lindley, *Fenland Riots*, and Clive Holmes, who argues for political and ideological consciousness in the fen riots, in 'Drainers and Fenmen'; see also Julie Bowring, 'Between the Corporation and Captain Flood: The Fens and Drainage After 1663', in Richard Hoyle (ed.), *Custom, Improvement and the Landscape*, (Farnham, 2011), pp. 237–40 and the contemporary arguments in *The Anti-Projector, or, the History of the Fen Project* (c. 1646), Wing A3504. Some of the early projectors, including John Popham, were also involved in settlements overseas; Rice, *John Popham*, pp. 193–202.

These 'fenmen' resisted the schemes of the projectors, since they were well aware that draining involved the extinguishing of their common rights. The projectors' call for 'new works' to replace the older medieval system meant the enclosure of large parts of the recovered lands to compensate and incentivize investors, and local taxation to pay for their schemes.

The resulting litigation would be among the causes of Coke's fall from the bench. In 1603 during his progress south James I knighted Coke, and in 1606 promoted him to the position of chief justice of the Common Pleas along with the dignity of serjeant-at-law. Coke's judicial tenure is remembered for its spectacular battles with other jurisdictions, including the Ecclesiastical High Commission, the Councils in the Marches and the North, the Court of Marshalsea and lesser authorities, such as the Commissions of Sewers. The king 'promoted' his troublesome judge again in 1613 to the more prestigious, but less lucrative, Court of King's Bench as its chief justice.[3] This appointment appears to have been against Coke's desire, but not his will.[4] Superficially, his judicial policy had protected the common law against other courts by preventing their expansion. But too close a focus on his championing of the common law overlooks his larger design: to bolster confidence in the legal system, a confidence that criticisms of legal proceedings had begun to shake. Coke's involvement with the dispute in the Fens illustrates this purpose. On the surface these cases brought two specific questions before Coke: how taxes should be assessed to pay for sewer works and whether the commissioners had the power to direct the creation of new works. This legal dispute culminated in the *Case of the Isle of Ely* (1609), which set out restrictions on the activities of the commissions.[5]

The case stands out as an aberration against a background of 'drainage-friendly' judicial decisions and opinions, including those by Thomas Egerton, Francis Gawdy, Edmund Anderson, Henry Hobart and John Popham.[6] These arguments were also represented in the law readings of Robert Callis in 1622 and John Herne in 1638, which both explicitly

[3] Chamberlain, *Letters*, vol. I, p. 482.

[4] *Ibid.*, p. 479. There were also rumours that he would be made treasurer; Chamberlain, *Letters*, vol. I, p. 392, and again in 1613, *ibid.*, p. 493; Bacon's 'Reasons for the Remove of Coke', in Spedding (ed.), *Letters and Life*, vol. IV, pp. 381–2.

[5] *The Case of the Isle of Ely*, 10 Co. *Rep.* 142b, 77 ER 1141. Coke's autograph manuscript version of his report of *The Case of the Isle of Ely* is found in CUL MS Ii.5.21, f. 67r.

[6] William Dugdale, *History of Imbanking and Draining* (London, 1662), Wing D2481, pp. 352–3 (Gawdy); pp. 243, 370–1 (Popham and Anderson); pp. 371–2 (Hobart); Knafla, *Law and Politics*, pp. 309–10 (Egerton).

rejected the precedent of the *Case of the Isle of Ely*.[7] Callis's reading and the extensive Caroline drainage projects that followed it suggest that Coke's fall in 1616 also represented the defeat of those judicial forces sympathetic to the fenmen. The direct involvement of the legal community in drainage projects may also explain the success of the investors in securing legal support for their projects: the judges Thomas Fleming and John Popham, and the lawyer Robert Callis, and probably also John Herne, were investors themselves.[8] The Privy Council certified Francis Bacon's opinion in November 1616 that approved the powers of the commissions to order new works and threatened those who resisted their decrees with imprisonment.[9] Finally, the personal support of James I and Charles I, who themselves became undertakers in these projects, provided unmatchable patronage.[10]

Coke, however, was among those who argued against a broad taxing power for the commissioners and their authority to order new works. Clive Holmes has interpreted Coke's decisions during this period, especially during the Ely case, as evidence of the chief justice's larger unease about discretionary power and an affirmance of the common law's authority.[11] These concerns, and Coke's desire to prevent the overturning of common law judgments, anticipated his dispute with the Chancery and explained his forceful actions in *Hetley* v. *Boyer* (1614). But the analysis shared by the cases reveals that Coke had additional motives: the commissioners exemplified the problem of the use of legal power that coloured his wider jurisprudence. Coke's decision in *Case of the Isle of Ely* was an attempt to prevent both corrupt practice and the perception that legal authority was being misused. His misgivings were astute during a time when, as earlier

---

[7] Robert Callis, *The Reading of the Famous and Learned Gentleman, Robert Callis Esq; Sergeant at Law, Upon the Statute of 23 H. 8. Cap. 5. Of Sewers* (London, 1647), Wing C304.

[8] Dugdale, *History of Imbanking*, p. 383; Samuel Wells, *The History of the Drainage of the Great Level of the Fens, Called Bedford Level* (London, 1830), vol. I, p. 88; Callis's background in Lincolnshire is discussed in Clive Holmes, *Seventeenth-Century Lincolnshire* (Lincoln, 1980), p. 48.

[9] *APC 1616–17*, pp. 57–9; *CSPD, James I, 1611–1618*, p. 403; Dugdale, *History of Imbanking*, p. 392.

[10] Dugdale, *History of Imbanking*, 'To the Reader', pp. 207–8, 408 and 412.

[11] H. C. Richardson, 'The Early History of Commissions of Sewers', *English Historical Review*, 34 (1919), 385–93; Kennedy, 'Fen Drainage', 15–37; Clive Holmes, 'Statutory Interpretation in the Early Seventeenth Century: The Courts, the Council, and the Commissioners of Sewers', in *Law and Social Change in British History: Papers Presented to the Bristol Legal History Conference* (1984), pp. 107–17.

chapters have shown, 'The volume, if not the vehemence, of criticism and satire directed at the judiciary increased exponentially.'[12]

Even as he acknowledged that the commissions were necessary to maintain existing works, Coke recognized that the projects involving new works joined the legal power of the commissioners with the private pursuits of projectors. The authority of the commissioners, though limited by statute, was a delegation of the royal responsibility to preserve and maintain the king's subjects. To use that power as a part of a speculative venture that often involved unfamiliar technologies and foreign specialists was inherently risky. Though the projectors argued that their works advanced the public good and were needed to replace the poorly functioning medieval drains, Coke instead rested his analysis on a stricter standard of imminent necessity, a standard that would have made the actions of the commissions seem less partial.

The dispute exposed another dynamic that stymied reforming efforts more generally. The charge that the law was misused was flung on both sides. Opponents of drainage complained that the projectors intended the new works as a means to relieve themselves of their burden of servicing the old drains. They had subverted the commissions to advance their private interests under the cloak of public power. The undertakers described the legal actions taken by the fenmen to prevent new works as vexatious and charged that their obstruction exposed the commonwealth to flooding and damage. As Julie Bowring has recently noted, both sides manipulated information to suit their arguments.[13] Much depended on perspective: one person's corruption was another's improvement. The charges and countercharges of abuse of the law eroded confidence in legal proceedings even at higher levels. When Coke sought to settle the matter in the *Case of the Isle of Ely,* Egerton commented on the report of the case that it was 'a great blowe to the power of that Comission and may bring much mischeife with it'. He later remonstrated in a speech in 1616 that Coke would have lawyers argue 'moote points' while the lands were flooded.[14] Coke's fall and the Privy Council's subsequent move to punish and imprison those who resisted the commissioners by suit weakened the common law as a forum for redress against legal wrongs.[15] But the

---

[12] Prest, 'Judicial Corruption', 74, 78.

[13] Bowring, 'Between the Corporation', p. 240.

[14] *The Lord Chancellors Speech to Sir Henry Mountague* (1616), Moore, King's Bench 828, 72 ER 932; BL Additional MS 34217, f. 6v and CUL MS Additional MS 335, f. 31v.

[15] Marking also a failure of the judges to assert themselves as 'impartial constitutional arbiters'; see Prest, 'Judicial Corruption', 81.

Council's intervention also demonstrated that the commissions would be effective only if buttressed with an increasingly coercive power.[16]

While Coke's attitude was conservative, he did not deny that it was possible to create new works using the law, but that such authorization should not rest on the decrees of the commissioners. He recognized that vested interests might co-opt the commissions. The use of the authority of the commissions to pursue private aims under the guise of the public interest not only suggested a corruption of legal proceedings in general, which ought to be indifferent, but might be a perversion of the royal prerogative. The arguments between Coke and those who found broader powers in the commissions revealed another division within the profession over the operation of legal power and the need to sustain confidence in legal institutions.

The perceived crossing of public and private interest in the commissions was so explosive because new works touched on those two most sensitive topics of the period: taxation and the security of property.[17] New works implied expropriation, both of lands on which the drains might be built, and more significantly, the extinguishing of common rights throughout the Fens. Projectors invariably preferred that the expropriation proceed through willing composition and agreement with commoners and landowners. But this was not always a possibility and led advocates of drainage into discussions of the underlying theory of expropriation. The arguments of common lawyers such as Robert Callis and John Herne, however self-interested, led them to insist that expropriation related to the king's duty to preserve his subjects and advance the public good.[18] These claims demonstrated that common lawyers were fully capable of embracing the prerogative for their own purposes and that even acts that many viewed as oppressive were couched in the language of the public good. Yet these expropriations were eventually the grounds of the grievance that the Grand Remonstrance (1641) stated with precision: 'Large quantities of common and several grounds hath been taken from the subject by colour of the Statute of Improvement, and by abuse of the Commission of Sewers, without their consent, and against it.'[19] Coke, as Holmes has also

---

[16] Paul Slack connects these projects to royal attempts at improvement based on ideas of absolute power in *Reformation and Improvement: Public Welfare in Early Modern England* (Oxford, 1999), pp. 68–70.

[17] David Seipp, 'The Concept of Property in the Early Common Law', *Law and History Review*, 12:29 (1994), 29–91; Reid, 'Revolution in the English Land Law', 43 (1995), 221–302.

[18] Susan Reynolds, *Before Eminent Domain* (Chapel Hill, NC, 2010), p. 41.

[19] Rushworth, *Historical Collections*, vol. IV, p. 437.

observed, had been 'prescient' of the troubles that lay ahead.[20] But perhaps one of the most important legacies of the dispute in the Fens was that the common law courts were disabled from intervening to protect the rights of fenmen who were accused of acting vexatiously. Though common lawyers defended the drainers, the consequence was the erosion of the reach of the common law itself, and perhaps crucially, the judges' claim to remedy legal wrongs throughout the kingdom.

The principal instrument of the projectors to advance fen drainage was the local commission of sewers.[21] The commissions had emerged in the medieval period to oversee the maintenance of drains, weirs and river courses.[22] Statutes in the reigns of Henry VI and Henry VIII, especially 23 Henry VIII, c. 5, placed their authority on a legislative footing.[23] The act of Henry VIII allowed broad powers in the commissions, observing that the king granted the commissions 'by reason of our dignity and prerogative royal ... to provide for the safety and preservation of our realm'.[24] The act admitted broad powers in the commissions to inspect sewers, bridges and weirs and in case of fault 'the same cause to be corrected, repaired, amended, put down, or reformed'. They were also authorized to 'taxe assesse charge distreyne and punysshe' those who held lands, tenements or commons affected by the works.[25] Another clause empowered the commissions to repair and reform 'in all places nedefull and the same as often and where nede shalbe to make newe ... '. This 'make new' clause was the focus of much later debate. Some, including Coke, interpreted the wording to mean only that the commissioners could 'make new' old works that had been destroyed or fallen into irrecoverable decay. Others, including Robert Callis, preferred a more expansive interpretation, insisting that the clause allowed the commissioners to order the construction of new works and the tax to fund them.

If the commissions had simply concerned themselves with the medieval works then their actions might not have been such a flashpoint of dispute. But rivers, coasts and marshes are landscapes in flux, and at the

---

[20] Holmes, 'Statutory Interpretation', p. 117.

[21] Though the commissions could at times object to these schemes; see Holmes, *Lincolnshire*, p. 128.

[22] Darby, *Draining of the Fens*, pp. 1–11. See also his *Medieval Fenland* (Newton Abbot, 1974).

[23] Holmes, 'Statutory Interpretation', pp. 110–12.

[24] See also Dugdale, *History of Imbanking*, p. 369.   [25] *SR*, vol. III, p. 369.

end of the sixteenth century complaints increasingly appeared that the medieval sewers were no longer adequate and that flooding had reached problematic levels.[26] At the end of the sixteenth century, some of the commissions began to face squarely this problem of change though they might not have always preferred new works to the repair of older systems.[27] In the seventeenth century, however, the commissions approved new works in partnership with projectors and foreign specialists that involved sizeable undertakings. Several of these efforts were placed on a statutory footing, although some, such as those near Ely, were not.

The earliest of these drainage acts approved the recovery of lands in Durham and East Anglia in the reign of Elizabeth, and this statute was followed by two acts in the reign of James I.[28] The drafters of the Elizabethan statute noted that most of the land that would be drained consisted of commons and wastes. They were cautious and expected that commoners and lords of the soil would bargain with projectors to drain their land. Since commoners 'in respecte of their Povertie are unable to pay the greate charges', they could provide part of their commons as payment to the undertakers. This clause signalled an unstated assumption: those who benefited from the works would also contribute along with the projectors. This opened the possibility that commoners who were unable to pay towards the projects might suffer distraint or even loss of rights in their land. Their contribution could be their rights in the commons, and the taxing power might serve as a lever to conform them through the threat of distraint. The statute 7 James I, c. 20, for example, allowed that commoners should be taxed for the improvement of commons and wastes. Commissioners were appointed with powers similar to a commission of sewers and were empowered to seize lands for failure to pay rates.[29] An earlier act of 1606 had more directly approached the problem of expropriation. The statute required that the projectors 'satisfy' owners of lands whom the new drain would affect, suggesting that compensation was required for any expropriation or flooding caused by the works. The drafters continued by vaguely denying that the statute 'g[a]ve any power

---

[26] Darby, *Draining of the Fens*, pp. 34–5. Several tracts were published in this period on the floods; see, for example, the anonymous tract, *A True Report of Certaine Wonderfull Ouerflow[ings] of Waters* (London, 1607), STC 22915.

[27] Kennedy, 'Fen Drainage', 22; Dugdale, *History of Imbanking*, p. 205.

[28] 43 Elizabeth I, c. 11; 4 James I, c. 13 and 7 James I, c. 20. *SR*, vol. IV, pt. 2, pp. 977–8, 1,152, 1,174–80. For earlier experiments in draining, see Darby, *Draining of the Fens*, pp. 11–22.

[29] *SR*, vol. IV, pp. 1,177–8.

to cutt and drayne thorowe any other grounds in any other manner then by the Lawes and Statutes of this Realme'.[30]

These statutes were accompanied by a general development of the law as cases arose due to draining. The overarching trend over the next three decades was to reinforce the powers of the commissions of sewers to fund and establish new drainage works. A case in 1602 involving Sir Edward Dymock's project in Kesteven demonstrates how the commissions and judicial opinion were used together to establish new works over the objections of the 'country'. Dymock used the local commission of sewers to order the construction of two new goats (a type of drainage engine) that the 'country' contested. The case went before Popham and Anderson who explained that 'if they were found to be profitable for the good and safety of the county, [the machines] might be erected by the power of this Statute'. Yet the judges also warned that the commissioners should proceed cautiously and carefully avoid making 'such devices at the suit, prosecution and request of private persons for their private and peculiar good'.[31]

Drainage was not always forced on an unwilling community: projectors preferred to obtain local consent and composition. Late in the reign of Elizabeth I, some in Deeping, 'being commoners in the said Fens', wrote to the Privy Council to request draining. The Council advised that the writ *ad quod damnum* should be sued and an inquisition followed. The inquisition returned that the works would be a 'great benefit', and letters were sent from the Council to the local commission of sewers to proceed with drainage works. The commissioners bargained with Thomas Lovell, who had 'been beyond the Seas much used and employed' for the draining, agreeing with him in 1602 that in return for his undertaking of the works he would receive one-third of the Fens.[32] Despite the care taken by the commissioners, unhappy commoners sabotaged Lovell's works and he was unsuccessful.[33]

Opponents, often headed by village elites, were adept at using legal process, including the commissions themselves, to deadlock projects that they rejected.[34] In 1632 in Huntingdon it was reported that, 'the commoners in Ely Fens, and the fens adjoining, that Mr. Cromwell of Ely, had undertaken, they paying him a groat for every cow they had upon the

---

[30] 4 James I, c. 13; *SR*, vol. 4, p. 1,152. The expectation seems to have been that the lords of the soil would voluntarily surrender their lands in the hope of having them drained.

[31] Callis, *Reading*, p. 73; Dugdale, *History of Imbanking*, p. 243.

[32] Dugdale, *History of Imbanking*, p. 206.

[33] Holmes, *Lincolnshire*, p. 123.

[34] Holmes, 'Drainers and Fenmen', pp. 181–2, 191–2; Kennedy, 'Fen Drainage', 17–18.

common, to hold the drainers in suit of law for 5 years, and that in the meantime they should enjoy every part of their common'.[35]

Against these tactics projectors commanded significant legal resources: they called upon the royal prerogative, the Privy Council, the local commission of sewers, the common law and statute law. An opinion of Sir John Popham CJKB, written to Sir Thomas Lambert in 1605, was among the most important of these resources. Popham, himself an investor in drainage schemes, did not doubt the legality of new works and approved the rating of towns rather than individuals. Popham believed that broad authority lay in the commissioners, and claimed that the common law courts should not review their decrees, a prescient step given the opposition that the tribunals often faced.[36] Such was the authority of the commissions that, 'where your doings shall come before the judges that [sic] will soon see the laws of sewers are like acts of Parliament and therefore not examinable by any other authority ... although your persons may be called to account if you have not proceeded as you ought to do'.

Those who sought to delay or stop the work of the commissioners were liable to additional fines, and 'if need be you sell their lands'. Again anticipating the legal manoeuvres that opponents of draining would deploy, he reminded Lambert that 'if it should be otherwise that authoritye might be defeated and derided which is the most absolute that passeth under the great seal of England'.[37]

Popham's opinion stood in for the lack of recognized decisions from the bench. Judicial opinion began to be reported, mostly by Coke, from the turn of the century. In his reports and decisions, Coke determined the extent of the commissions' powers through an analysis of the benefits of the courts' proceedings. In *Rooke's Case* (1598), where the question of those whom the commissioners might tax was addressed, it was supposedly decided that the tax should extend to all those who were in danger of harm from the non-repair of existing works, even if a single owner was bound by prescription to repair the work. This resolution was later remembered differently in *Keighley's Case* (1609). Sir Thomas Walmesley JCP, who had been on the bench during the earlier case, claimed that the commission's discretion to ignore the prescription and tax broadly was narrow and applied only in the case of a failure

---

[35] Cited in Darby, *Draining of the Fens*, pp. 55–6.

[36] Dalton also observes that officers were subject to lawsuits; Michael Dalton, *The Countrey Justice* (London, 1618), STC 6205, p. 307; and the act of 7 James I, c. 5, *SR*, vol. IV, pt. 2, p. 1,161.

[37] BL Hargarve MS 33, ff. 215v–216r.

to repair or maintain existing works by the owner of the land encumbered with the prescription. In that case, 'inevitable necessity' would require that the works be repaired and the tax would extend broadly, though those charged would have remedy by action on the case against the owner. The owner was not excused from his obligation merely by a failure to perform. But if the works, having been maintained, were destroyed by an act of God of such fury that the damage could not be prevented, then those who might have loss were also liable to the tax to repair or rebuild.[38] Walmesley's statement suggested that if the levy were not extended, then the safety of the area might depend on whether a single owner could or was willing to afford the repair of a pre-existing work. *Rooke's Case* and *Keighley's Case* seemed to consider the limited situation where a prescription to repair or maintain was already in existence, but it was the underlying benefit–harm analysis that was their legacy. *Rooke's Case* was later used to uphold the principle that the commissions might tax only those who benefited from the works: this reasoning precluded a blanket tax that might fall on an entire town with no attempt to distinguish whom flooding might harm. This reasoning, in turn, complicated the commissions' authority to tax broadly to support drainage works.

The restriction of the commissioners' discretion to tax broadly in *Keighley's Case* was of a piece with the *Case of the Isle of Ely*, which was decided that same year. The judicial opinion in the Ely case was cited for centuries afterwards, often as a contrasting authority to the pro-drainage reading of Callis. This case and another involving a causeway in Chester suggested that Coke had a very narrow conceptualization of the commissions' function and authority.[39] In an address to a jury of sewers in 1613, Coke repeated the reasoning from these cases. He urged that the commissions were a means for the prevention of danger and that their tasks involved compelling those responsible to repair their works, making assessments on others in case of overflow, and punishing individuals who were negligent. He closed with a warning that no one involved in the proceedings of the commissions should 'intermeddle for their private profit'.[40] Similarly, Coke warned elsewhere that the exercise of their

---

[38] *Keighley's Case* (1609), 10 Co. *Rep.* 139a, 77 ER 1136; Dalton, *Countrey Justice*, pp. 106–7. The manuscript report of *Keighley* is found in CUL MS Ii.5.21, f. 42.

[39] See also the limit on altering an ancient causey, *Chester Mill upon the River of Dee* (1609), 13 Co. *Rep.* 35, 77 ER 1447; CUL MS Ll.5.21 ff.

[40] BL Additional MS 25213, ff. 156v–157v.

discretion should be bound with the 'rule, of reason and law' and 'not to do according to their wills and private affections'.[41]

Coke returned repeatedly to this theme of private interest operating under legal cover, perhaps most vigorously in response to the imprisonment of William Hetley by a commission in Northampton. The commissioners had levied a fine on the village, and distrained Hetley's cattle. The judges deemed this broad levying of the fine illegal, citing *Rooke's Case*, and insisted that the fine be assessed on each inhabitant. Presumably for this reason, Hetley obtained a judgment at the common law against the commissioners. When summoned before them, he refused to release the judgment and was ordered to be imprisoned, 'till he should hear further from them'.[42] In 1614 Coke and the other judges called the commissioners before them for punishment – in the case of Sir Anthony Mildmay with praemunire.[43] The commissioners had attempted to frustrate the common law judgment and tested the relative authority of the courts.[44] As Robert Houghton JKB remarked, 'The warrant by them made, is a direct opposition, unto the order, and judgement of this Court.' The commissioners' actions were easy to represent as self-interested rather than an indifferent punishment for Hetley's disobedience, as Coke observed: 'for they do pretend the good of the common wealth, but do intend their own proper good'.[45] Dodderidge also implied that the commission's administration of the fine was itself tainted. He queried why, though the fine was assessed on the township, yet 'for malice, the cattell of this party, onely taken, and of no others; this appears to be malice apparent, the whole town amerced, and one man to be onely punished'.

Coke's preoccupation with the influence of private interest on public power erupted in the *Case of the Isle of Ely* in 1609.[46] The case's background exposed the interaction of charges of corrupt dealing and claims for improvement, and the difficulty of disentangling them. The Ely case

---

[41] *Rooke's Case* (1598), 5 Co. *Rep.* 100a, 77 ER 210; also found in his MS report, BL Harley MS 6686A, f. 250v and repeated in his charge at Lincoln, Society of Antiquaries MS 291, ff. 11v–12r.

[42] *Hetley* v. *Boyer and Mildmay*, Croke Jac 336, 79 ER 287; *Hetley* v. *Boyer*, 2 Bulstrode 197, 80 ER 1064.

[43] *Rex* v. *Mildmaye* (1615), 2 Bulstrode 299, 80 ER 1137; *Roy* v. *Sir Anthony Mildmay*, 1 Rolle 190, 81 ER 423; BL Additional MS 35957, f. 7v; Rylands Library French MS 118, f. 282r.

[44] Though they did not readjudicate the same matter in violation of the principle of *res judicata*; cf. Holmes, 'Statutory Interpretation', pp. 115–16.

[45] *Hetley* v. *Boyer*, 2 Bulstrode 198, 80 ER 1065.

[46] *The Case of Isle of Ely*, 10 Co. *Rep.* 141a, 77 ER 1139.

was also a reminder of the large investments of leading common lawyers in these projects, especially by Popham and Sir Thomas Fleming CBEx, who had led schemes in 1605.[47] At that time, the undertakers argued that the old drains were inadequate because of siltation at the outfall of Wisbech, and argued that their new works would protect the country against flooding and increase the productivity of the land.[48] The plan, in its conception, was grandiose. The drainers proposed to dry 307,242 acres of land in return for 130,000 acres to be held by them.[49] The centrepiece of the work was a new cut, later named 'Popham's Eau', that would run 40 feet wide for 3 miles.[50]

The drainers could expect both local support and resistance. Sir John Peyton, a local landowner, and his son complained in 1605 that the 'unwillingness of the people to the bettering of their estates' had obstructed previous improvement.[51] In 1605 the king ordered that the commission of sewers 'take special care to suppress the spreading of all false rumours ... and to punish the Offenders'.[52] Yet Peyton also reported that some landowners were interested in voluntarily surrendering in return for having dried lands returned to them by the undertakers.[53]

The legal authority of the project was established at the commission of sewers held at Wisbech in July 1605. The contents of the decrees indicate that landowners were expected to join with the undertakers by providing them with lands to drain. Those who would receive benefit from the works, yet did not contribute in lands, should instead be levied 'such summes of money as shalbe sett down and decreed, at any Sessions of the Commissioners of Sewers ... by vertue of the said commission'.[54] Commoners were also liable to this tax.[55] More direct expropriation was expected and so it was also decreed that,

> if any newe Rivers, sewers or draynes shalbe made throughe any mans severall grounds not subject to inundation, composition be first made with the owners of such grounds by the undertakers. And if they cannot agree that then it be ordered by the Commissioners of Sewars. And that

[47] BL Harley MS 5011, f. 14v; Dugdale, *History of Imbanking*, p. 383.
[48] CUL MS EDR A8, pp. 113–18.
[49] Dugdale, *History of Imbanking*, p. 384; the figures range widely in different sources.
[50] Darby, *Draining of the Fens*, pp. 31–4.
[51] *Calendar of the Manuscripts of the Marquis of Salisbury*, vol. XVII, p. 452.
[52] Dugdale, *History of Imbanking*, p. 384.
[53] The inquiry is briefly described in *CSPD, James I, 1603–1610*, p. 132.
[54] CUL MS EDR A8, p. 99; Dugdale, *History of Imbanking*, p. 385.
[55] BL Harley MS 5011, f. 15r.

any man that shall receive losse by the work shall have recompence by the undertakers at the iudgment of the Commissioners.[56]

Although the decree carried the force of law, the commissioners requested that the orders be confirmed by an act of parliament. In the parliamentary session of 1606–7, however, the bill for draining was defeated.[57] If the undertakers argued that drainage would protect the land and increase its abundance, those opposed to the schemes countered that depopulation was the consequence of enclosure.[58]

Popham's death in 1607 did not end attempts to drain the Ely Fens. They were continued under Sir Miles Sandys of Wilberton.[59] Sandys was the brother of Sir Edwin Sandys, a leading parliamentarian and investor in the Virginia Company and Bermuda, and a staunch promoter of drainage works.[60] Suspicion gathered that the drainers, led by Sandys, had used their power and influence to pack the commission of sewers: the charge was that the commissioners were not 'indifferent'.[61] Instead, they were 'great owners and ought to scoure and mayntaine many sewers and draines at their proper costs'. Their failure to maintain the ancient drains had resulted in flooding, and now they 'seeke utterly to putt of[f] those charges from themselves and to lay them upon Commons and other inferior persons'. The new works would benefit only a 'few private persons' and the commissioners themselves, while the taxes to fund them lay heavily on the towns. The towns' refusal to pay the taxes led to distraint.[62] By 1609 complaints were also being made that new works were being built through private lands: 'no satisfaction provided by the Statute on Commission of Sewers for those that have their ground cutt … therefore it is not intended such an Act should be done. The kings grounds (now the bishops) are cutt through without recompence. There hath been much cruell dealing, threatening, imprisonings, and sale of distresses taken.'[63]

Those towns resisting the decrees claimed that they had not been charged for such works in the past, and that the works were new and

[56] CUL MS EDR A8, p. 101.
[57] CJ, vol. I, pp. 270, 340, 364; for a bill in 1609 see ibid., p. 411. Peyton spoke against the bill.
[58] CUL MS EDR A8, p. 104; also pp. 102, 103; Dugdale, History of Imbanking, p. 391.
[59] CUL MS EDR A8, pp. 143, 145. On Sandys and his activities post-1630, see Darby, Draining of the Fens, p. 58n6, and the citation there; M. A. E. Green (ed.), Calendar of the Proceedings of the Committee for Advance of Money, 1642–56 (London, 1888), p. 525.
[60] DNB, s.v. 'Edwin Sandys'.
[61] BL Harley MS 5011, ff. 12r–v; CUL MS EDR A8, pp. 148, 185–6.
[62] CUL MS EDR A8, pp. 119, 122–3, and similar sentiment p. 127; SP 13/G 15 and 18.
[63] CUL MS EDR A8, p. 141.

beyond the authority of the commissioners to establish.[64] Resistance prompted consternation among many of the officials involved, including the sheriff of Cambridgeshire, who refused to tax for the new drain 'without the personal security of the commissioners' against lawsuits. The fear of lawsuits was reasonable, and he 'Hope[d] their public duties may not involve their private estates'.[65] The Council responded by certifying the legality of the commission's proceedings.[66]

Coke was personally familiar with the dispute in Ely, and at Cambridge Assizes he had spoken with some of the commissioners involved. He was informed of the situation in at least one letter from John Cuttes, John Cotton and Francis Brackin in 1609. These three were commissioners of sewers themselves, and Coke had instructed them at Cambridge to view the new works and report to him. They complained that the new works were of 'greater charge than of any assured benefitt' and that the undertakers were confused as to their own plans, debating where bridges might be placed and which rivers would be navigable after the draining. They observed that the 'new works' would be 'ledd through the middest of the Commons and fens' and would disrupt the movement of herds of cattle. These warnings may have informed Coke's statements in *The Case of the Isle of Ely* that new inventions were inherently risky. The authors of the letter pointedly described how they could not in conscience agree to the taxes to fund these new works. They had consulted with the local towns, whose answer was 'resolute' that the works would provide no benefit to them and 'therefore they will not pay one penny to those new works unlesse extremetie of law will enforce them'. The townsmen claimed that they would contest the levies through the law 'if it shall please your lordship [Coke] so to consider or allow it'. Both the townsmen and the authors described how the old drains, if maintained, were sufficient to drain and protect the Fens 'though it prove a great charge to some private men ... will shortly prove an inestimable benefit to the whole Isle'. Here Coke's informants touched on their belief of the ultimate reason behind the new works, that 'these be but new devises layd upon the Countries charge only to ease the private charge of some of the Commissioners and others for making and keeping their old draynes'.[67]

The dispute was referred to Coke, Sir William Daniel JCP and Sir Thomas Foster JCP in 1609 by the Privy Council.[68] The judges were asked to

---

[64] BL Harley MS 5011, ff. 12r–v.   [65] SP 14/48 f. 144.
[66] CUL MS EDR A8, pp. 124 (October 1609), 130 (August 1609).
[67] *Ibid.*, pp. 133–7.   [68] *Ibid.*, p. 147.

determine whether the 'new kind of draining decreed by the Commissions of Sewers were for the generall good of the Common Weale'.[69] The commissioners had ordered that a new river should be cut for seven miles, presumably as part of drainage works. Fifteen towns were assessed in order to fund the construction. The towns objected that the commissions could not levy such a general tax nor could they decree new works.[70] Ultimately the judges sided with the towns and expounded the 'new works' clause of 23 Henry VIII to mean that the commissioners could only renovate pre-existing works.[71] This resolution alone did not foreclose the possibility of new projects, only that the commission should limit themselves to repair or reconstruction. In his manuscript report of the case, Coke had described a means by which new works could be ordered under the king's licence by commission in cases of 'inevitable necessity'. The removal of this explicit statement has led Holmes to conclude that Coke 'doctored' his manuscript for publication by adding the stipulation that 'only parliamentary legislation could warrant any "new attempt"', thereby 'undercutting' his original report.[72] Coke's reference to parliamentary legislation was for broader purposes, however, than he had intended for the use of the king's licence in his manuscript report. Whereas the creation of works by the king's licence was in cases of inevitable necessity, those new works constructed under statute were intended for wider benefit. The addition of a description of new works erected by parliamentary legislation clarified how these latter projects could be lawfully undertaken.

Several explanations have been adduced to explain why Coke believed only parliament could allow for these new works. W. B. Stoebuck believed statutory sanction was essential for expropriation because the consent of landowners through their representatives was implicitly given in parliament. Moreover, takings by the prerogative and by legislation were fundamentally different, the latter requiring compensation and the former unable to 'acquire estates in land'.[73] Holmes has noted that those drainage projects with statutory approval encountered significantly less resistance from the fenmen.[74] He concluded that because of the 'theory of parliamentary sovereignty', legislation 'endowed their operations with a legitimacy superior to that of Council directives or decrees of Commissioners

[69] *Ibid.*, p. 175.   [70] BL Harley MS 5011, f. 12r ff.

[71] *The Case of the Isle of Ely,* 10 Co. *Rep.* 142b, 77 ER 1141.

[72] Holmes, 'Statutory Interpretation', p. 115.

[73] W. B. Stoebuck, 'A General Theory of Eminent Domain', *Washington Law Review*, 47 (1972), 553–608, at 565; compare Reynolds, *Before Eminent Domain*, p. 41.

[74] Holmes, 'Drainers and Fenmen', pp. 172–8.

of Sewers'.[75] Statute certainly appears to have conferred a greater legitimacy on drainage works. But Coke implied a different reasoning for the
need to turn to parliament in his report, one related to the benefit analysis
that was controlling in these cases and that ultimately related to protecting confidence in legal proceedings.

The printed report of *The Case of the Isle of Ely* provided three means by
which works might be managed. The first allowed for a type of new works.
This method followed an entry in the *Register* that explained how a 'new
trench' might be made that would be used by boats if the old had become
stopped: the petitioner should 'sue to the King to have leave to make a new
trench ... he ought first to sue *ad quod damnum,* to know what damage
it will be to the King or others'. Afterwards he might receive the 'King's
licence to make it'.[76] The example from the *Register* involved a new work
whose benefit was already known, the access of small boats, and a clear
process to determine who might be affected.[77] Why should this project be
allowed while other 'new inventions' should be referred to Parliament?

The answer is in the second manner in which new works might be
erected, presumably on private lands. The discussion of the means to erect
new works included an alteration of the report from Coke's manuscript
that new works could be created by licence of the king. The manuscript
statement had read: 'And it was resolved by all three justices that in urgent
necessity the king is able to grant a commission to make new walls to
defend the land from the sea, and this by the common law, but in such
a case it ought to be for inevitable necessity.' This statement was transformed in the printed report to an example of an old wall being broken
by the sea, and so 'to preserve the lands ... another wall, in case of inevitable necessity for the public good of that part, may be made to defend
the people, and their lands'.[78] The example of the walls served as a contrast with those projects that needed parliamentary approval. Walls were
'no new invention', and tellingly their rebuilding over the ruins of the old
confirmed their 'inevitable necessity' – both the manuscript and printed
report asserted this standard.

The emphasis on an established benefit and necessity contrasted with
those 'new inventions' proposed by the drainers. Coke represents them
in nearly the opposite manner, for they were 'new inventions', such as an

[75] *Ibid.* p. 179.
[76] Anthony Fitzherbert, *La Novel Natura Brevium* (London, 1598), STC 10964, f. 225v;
William Rastell, *Registrum Omnium Brevium* (London, 1553), STC 20837, f. 252r.
[77] Dalton, *Countrey Justice*, p. 106.
[78] CUL MS Li.5.21, f. 68r; 10 Co. *Rep.* 142b, 77 ER 1141.

'artificial mill'. Coke reasoned that if the benefit from these innovations was certain or even likely, 'no owner of the land there will deny to make a contribution for his advantage'. Coke cautioned that the commissions should not be the instruments 'to try new inventions at the charge of the country, which perhaps will never take good effect'. Instead he reasoned that 'the beaten path is the safest'. Though drainage projects promised improvement they might also be the means of harm to the countryside, worsening flooding and damaging property. Moreover, should the commissioners proceed on their own authority to order such new inventions they might be instruments of private gain while causing 'public damages' through their experiments. Coke warned that 'sometime when the public good is pretended, a private benefit is intended'. This was the context for Coke's insistence that new works be referred to parliament, since where 'no consent can be obtained for the making of [such new invention], then there is no remedy but to complain in Parliament'.[79] If benefit and necessity could not be determined at a local level by the consent of those with rights in the land then parliament was the wiser body to determine whether the projects would be 'good for the commonwealth'. The risk of allowing a commission to make this determination on its own authority, overriding local objections, would be the erosion of confidence in their proceedings: precisely what had happened around Ely. The use of the commissions as the vehicles of drainage projects led to the complaint of the Grand Remonstrance. Coke elsewhere chastised the commissioners about the disquiet that was raised through these projects and which had brought legal authority into question, writing, 'hadd yow followed such advice and directions as I left yow at Cambridge Assises this trouble hadd not bene'.[80]

Coke's admonitory reasoning in the Ely case about new works was soon disregarded. In 1616 Sir Francis Bacon, then attorney-general, prepared an opinion certified before James and the Privy Council on the legality of the commissioners' proceedings in East Anglia. Bacon described how he had reviewed the ancient records, considered Popham's opinion and noted that vexatious persons had slowed the proceedings of the commissioners. The ensuing Privy Council order in November 1616 declared that the law could not, 'be void of Providence, to restrain the Commissioners in making new works, aswell to stop the fury of the waters ... whereas upon the performance of [their orders], the preservation of thousands of his Majesties subjects, their lives, goods and lands doth depend'.[81]

But the order also acknowledged the resolution in the Ely case and *Hetley's Case* that the commissions could not tax towns or hundreds generally, suggesting that one of Coke's points should be adopted. Significantly, the Council also restrained the commissions' capacity to imprison, taking on the responsibility, presumably as a means to buttress the tribunal's authority. The order added that those who had been imprisoned by the Privy Council for vexing the commissioners at law should 'stand committed, until they release or discharge such their actions etc'.[82] This was the outcome that Coke had feared in *Hetley's Case*: the use of coercion to compel subjects to release their proceedings at the common law.

Soon after this order, a letter was sent from the Privy Council to the commissioners in East Anglia, explaining that Sir Francis Fane would 'acquaint them with the course taken with those disobedient persons who resisted their decrees'. The letter went on to reassure them to proceed 'without dread of law'.[83] By granting this protection the Privy Council confirmed Popham's earlier warning that legal process could be used to constrain the work of the projectors. From both perspectives legal power was being abused: opponents viewed the commissions as partial, while those supporting drainage interpreted lawsuits as vexatious. In 1616 the commissioners at Huntington denounced those who proceeded from their 'perverse dispositions, noe lesse dangerously threatening the iminent ruyne of those parts … by undue and enlawfull [*sic*] practices, under pretext or collour of law, to question and discourage the Comissioners'. The Privy Council had punished those malefactors and 'gave incouragement unto the Comissioners [*sic*]'.[84] These tactics continued into the 1630s, perhaps more energetically, and involved both the Privy Council and the Star Chamber to prosecute opponents of drainage for riot. Holmes has described the imprisonment of Nehemiah Rawson by the Privy Council and the government's intervention to stay his successful judgment at the common law.[85]

---

[81] Dugdale, *History of Imbanking*, p. 392.   [82] *Ibid.*, pp. 392–3.

[83] SP 14/89 f. 139; *CSPD, James I, 1611–1618*, p. 403; but the Council was also willing to review the activities of the commissions, for example, the tax for Clowse Cross drain, *CSPD, James I, 1611–1618*, p. 413, and penalties in Ely, *ibid.*, p. 552.

[84] Wells, *Great Level*, vol. II, appendix, p. 43.

[85] Holmes, *Lincolnshire*, pp. 124–5, 129.

The issue that fired emotions was expropriation. Though projectors strove for agreement and consent, the commissions were means either to encourage conformity among the parties or to impose compliance directly. Expropriation could take a number of legal forms from forced conformity to direct seizure. The early modern paradigm was complicated by the fact that contemporaries seldom discussed expropriation at either the level of theory or as a recognized process in law.[86] Lacking methodical tests for public use and benefit, early expropriation nonetheless anticipated the kinds of takings for private development that have caused controversy in modern cases such as *Kelo v. New London* (2005).[87] Expropriation led advocates of drainage into a consideration of principles that would later be associated with eminent domain. Eminent domain arguments in this period have generally been interpreted as relying on either legislative consent or the assertion of an underlying feudal interest.[88] Though the feudal theory has been discounted, the theory of legislative consent explains eighteenth-century takings, especially those related to enclosures that were approved by private bill in parliament.

Susan Reynolds has recently suggested that ideas of royal governance and communal property conditioned the justification of some early modern expropriations.[89] Contemporaries might explain takings as a process inhering in the king's prerogative and his duty to protect his people.[90] In insisting that expropriation reflected the king's responsibility to protect his subjects, common lawyers screened the drainers' actions behind the language of public necessity.

Though both Holmes and Reynolds have written that expropriation was taking place in the Fens, direct evidence is sparse. Projectors and their lawyers shied away from such discussion in their proposals.[91] Often expropriation took indirect forms. For example, the commissions might

---

[86] *Ibid.*, p. 9.

[87] Reynolds, *Eminent Domain*, p. 10; *City of New London v. Kelo* 545 US 469 (2005).

[88] Reynolds notes that literature on the history of expropriation is 'surprisingly rare' and provides a survey; Reynolds, *Eminent Domain*, pp. 7–8; See also Stoebuck, 'A General Theory', 553–608; Arthur Lenhoff, 'Development of the Concept of Eminent Domain', *Columbia Law Review*, 42 (1942), 596–638; J. A. C. Grant, 'The "Higher Law" Background of the Law of Eminent Domain', 6 *Wisconsin Law Review*, 67 (1931), 71–81.

[89] Reynolds, *Eminent Domain*, pp. 34–46 and pp. 112–30 on the underlying theory and importance of collectivist ideas pre-Grotius.

[90] Land might also be claimed if it were flooded for such a time that the bounds of the property had been obliterated and 'grown out of knowledge'; Callis, *Reading*, pp. 27–8, and 'Of Islands Arising in the Sea ...', BL Additional MS 25206, f. 17r.

[91] Holmes, *Lincolnshire*, pp. 124–30.

be used to bring pressure to bear to surrender rights in land. When commoners in Lincolnshire refused to allow drainage, commissioners were ordered to 'treat and conclude with those Commoners, by way of composition'. Further arbitration ensued when the commoners of Epworth stood outside the agreement, and they were permitted to retain part of their commons and surrender the rest to the drainers.[92] Though a Jacobean statute had allowed takings for non-payment of assessments, this procedure was more clearly adopted by the commissions under Charles I. When a tax of 30 shillings per acre was assessed near Deping in the 1630s 'forasmuch as the same was not paid, they might therefore lawfully proceed to make a Decree, for the further and perfect drayning thereof '.[93] In Lincolnshire in the 1636 the local commission decreed that 'those Fens should be forthwith taken in hand' after the adjoining townships refused to pay a tax for their draining. These fens were then offered to 'Forein Undertakers' for drainage, and then upon their refusal to Sir John Munson, a leading member of the county gentry, who was promised a tax from the locality to offset his expenses.[94]

Callis and Herne, who both read on the statute of 23 Henry VIII, c. 5, provide the reasoning behind expropriation. Callis, himself an investor, gave his reading in 1622 and ranged widely on the powers of the commission. Though most law readings of the period have disappeared into obscurity, Callis's was destined for minor fame: it circulated widely in manuscript and was printed three times in the seventeenth century (1647, 1685 and 1686), twice in the nineteenth century and was cited by Victorian judges.[95] John Herne gave another reading in 1638, deriving his arguments from Callis.[96] Both Callis and Herne directly contested the decision in *The Case of the Isle of Ely,* and Herne implied that the ruling in the case was ignored. Callis approved the commission's broad taxing

---

[92] Dugdale, *History of Imbanking,* pp. 145–7, though they later destroyed the works; BL Harley MS 5011, p. 77.

[93] Dugdale, *History of Imbanking,* p. 207.

[94] Dugdale, *History of Imbanking,* p. 152; Holmes, *Lincolnshire,* p. 126.

[95] Callis was generally not cited favourably in the nineteenth century; see, for example, *Mayor and Burgesses of Lyme Regis v. Henley* (1834).

[96] The text was printed in an abbreviated version in 1659. J. H. Baker noticed that a manuscript at the Harvard Law School library bore a resemblance, and it is a much more complete version of the reading. Baker, *Readers and Readings in the Inns of Court and Chancery,* pp. 385, 490. The manuscript is HLS MS 1165(b), John Herne, *The Learned Reading of John Herne ... Upon the Statute of 23 H. 8 cap 3. Concerning Commissions of Sewers* (London, 1659), Wing H1572.

powers and Herne went further, arguing that the commission might even tax generally.[97]

When he came to consider new works, Callis construed the statute to allow for their creation by the commission, even though he observed 'That a new River, drain or cut, cannot be made but through some man's private Inheritance'.[98] The commissioners could also affect private property by removing private banks, walls and bridges in those cases where they were 'impediments to the commonwealth'.[99] Herne followed Callis by acknowledging wide powers in the commissioners, allowed to them by the Henrician statute, to 'make lawes and decrees thereby to grant and decree away other men[']s inheritances and estates'. He reiterated that the commission might 'decree from him his estate and inheritance'.[100]

Callis and Herne assumed that takings in general were expressions of the king's responsibility to his people. Expropriation was connected to this underlying duty by two principal arguments. Claims of public utility, of an improvement that would benefit the commonwealth, were often asserted by proponents of draining. William Dugdale explained how draining would advance the public good by claiming how many 'had lived upon Almes ... and such poor means out of the Common Fens, while they lay drowned, were since come to good and supportable Estates'.[101] He continued as follows: 'That the Strength of a King is in the Multitude of his Subjects ... the most civilized Nations have by so much Art and Industry endeavoured to make the best improvement of their Wasts, Commons, and all sorts of barren Land.'[102] These claims of public utility were connected to economic ideas about population, improvement and national rivalry, and to an active monarch who patronized drainage.[103] When he described his involvement as the leading undertaker in draining, James made use of this argument in reference to his own obligations to the kingdom: 'that for the honour of his Kingdome, he would not any longer suffer these Countries to be abandoned to the will of the waters, nor let them lye waste and unprofitable'.[104] The countries were 'waste' and subject to the

---

[97] HLS MS 1165(b), f. 18v.   [98] Callis, *Reading*, p. 69.

[99] *Ibid.*, p. 64.   [100] HLS MS 1165(b), ff. 3r, 14r.

[101] Dugdale, *History of Imbanking*, p. 385. Hugo Grotius made a similar claim for public utility, cited in Ellen Frankel Paul, *Property Rights and Eminent Domain* (New Brunswick, NJ, 1987), p. 75.

[102] Dugdale, *History of Imbanking*, sig. A2.

[103] Paul Warde, 'The Idea of Improvement, c. 1520–1700', in Hoyle (ed.), *Custom, Improvement and Landscape*, pp. 127–48.

[104] Dugdale, *History of Imbanking*, p. 408.

'will of the waters'. Drainage would create a productive landscape, while implicitly protecting it: the land would be made subject to human will rather than to the whims of nature.

However, the king was also responsible for keeping his people safe. The foundation of the sewer laws and the commissions had long been connected with this responsibility. Contemporaries, including Coke, assumed that the authority of the commissions, though limited or enlarged by statute, rested 'solely' on the king's prerogative.[105] In the Ely case it was noted that before the earliest statute related to the commissions, 6 Henry VI, c. 5, 'the King ought of right to save and defend his realm, as well against the sea, as against the enemies'. The king's responsibility to protect his people was based on the conception of the royal office. As Callis wrote, 'the King by the Tenure and Prerogative of his Crown, was bound to see and foresee the safety of this realm; and so this law is Prerogative Law'.[106] Callis echoed the language of statutes such as 23 Henry VIII, which had explained by using the voice of the king, 'we be bounde to provyde for the safetie and preservacion of our Realme of England'. This claim of preservation was repeated in contemporary statutes, and so in 7 James I, c. 20, the need to preserve subjects from drowning was used to justify extensive works.

Public necessity was preferred to arguments for public utility as a basis for expropriation.[107] Coke's report of the *Case of Saltpeter* (1606), often identified as the earliest leading case of expropriation, reveals the operation of the necessity analysis.[108] The question before the judges was whether delegates of the king might dig in private lands and take saltpetre for the making of gunpowder. This prerogative, it was deemed, 'concerns the necessary defense of the realm', and so the saltpetre could only be used to make gunpowder. Against this necessity of defending from harm was weighed the problem of the harm done by those who dug in the property of the subject. This led to an extended discussion of the limits on the activities of the delegates to prevent oppressions.[109] Similarly, though in time of war trenches and bulwarks could be built on private land, for the

---

[105] *Le Case del Royale Piscarie de le Banne* (1610), Davis 57, 80 ER 542; HLS MS 1165(b), f. 112v; 10 Co. *Rep.* 142a, 77 ER 1140; See also Dugdale, *History of Imbanking*, p. 369.

[106] Callis, *Reading*, p. 5.

[107] Herne refers to the 'pubic interest'; HLS MS 1165(b), ff. 112r, 113v, 115r.

[108] *The Case of Saltpeter* (1606), 12 Co. *Rep.* 14, 77 ER 1296; another report of the case is found in BL Harley MS 4817, f. 213v.

[109] The activities of these patentees were raised as a complaint in parliament in 1606–7. See James's response at BL Additional MS 41613, f. 210v.

benefit of these defences extended to all, they should be removed once the danger had passed.

Sewers were necessary to preserve people from the destruction of flooding. Callis warned his listeners, 'what greater enemy can there be then the Sea, who threatens with his merciless waves to swallow up all before it'. From this hazard it followed that the laws of sewers were themselves 'most necessary' for the preservation of the people, and they were 'of great and urgent necessity and use for the good of the whole Commonwealth'.[110] Similar language was used in the Privy Council certification of 1616. Herne's discussion was even more telling when he argued that the powers granted to the commissions by statute were needed to erect one tyrant to protect against another.

Callis insisted that these encroachments on private property should not be pursued except upon careful reflection and clear need. However, he observed that the value of new works as protections against flooding overrode the rights of individuals, opining, 'That these new works are not to be undertaken but upon urgent necessity in defence of the countrey, or for the safety thereof, so that the Commonwealth be therein deeply interessed and ingaged; and things which concern the Comonweal are of greater accompt in the Law, then the interests of private persons.'[111]

Throughout his reading Callis returned to the necessity of new works as the justification for the extinguishing of private interests: 'The Commonwealth shall be preferred before the private Estate, and for the good of the Commonwealth a private person shall receive damage.' He likened the creation of new drainage works to the pulling down of a house on fire to preserve other men's property. Yet the expropriated individual was not without compensation, and the statutes of 27 Elizabeth I, c. 22, and 3 James I, c. 18, provided 'good Rules'.[112]

Comparisons of Callis and Coke's arguments about the commissions have stressed their disagreements. Similarly, Coke's rejection of Popham's opinion on the extent of the commissioners' authority also bespeaks dispute within the profession. Both Callis and Coke, however, stressed necessity as the basis for the commissions' actions, yet from a shared framework they had reached very different conclusions. Self-interest, including Callis's investments in draining and Coke's in the supremacy of the common law, no doubt informed their interpretations. But

---

[110] Callis, *Reading*, pp. 7–8, 71, 78.   [111] *Ibid.*, pp. 78, 71.

[112] *Ibid.*, p. 79. These statutes related to the cutting of new channels for Chichester and London; *SR*, vol. IV, pt. 1, pp. 729–32, and vol. IV, pt. 2, pp. 1,092–3.

their divergence also reflected differing attitudes about the operation of legal power. Callis viewed that power as a broad, instrumental means to improve the commonwealth, and so a group of common lawyers was willing to remove the property rights of others. Coke's interpretation recognized more cautiously the problems inherent in the exercise of legal power: the need to maintain its integrity and the confidence among those it impacted. Coke's emphasis on 'extreme necessity' as the standard by which new works should be ordered outside of parliament strictly bound the commissions. This was, of course, a difficult standard to define, and those who advanced drainage claimed that their projects countered the urgent dangers from the sea. But it was their innovation in machines and works that met with Coke's conservatism: the 'beaten path is the safest'. Coke's restriction of the commissions' freedom of action was intended to prevent precisely what occurred: criticisms of the tribunal's partiality and the erosion of confidence in its proceedings. The Privy Council's intervention to shore up the commissions' authority led it to force opponents to release their suits at common law or face imprisonment.[113] More subtly, the commissions represented the danger that the delegated authority of the sovereign might be used in experiments in the countryside, experiments that might have untoward and disastrous effects. How this misuse of legal power should be constrained, the law made more certain and confidence in its proceedings secure, was Coke's reforming enterprise.

[113] Callis, *Reading*, pp. 75–6.

4

Identity and the narratives of the past

Give me leave I pray you ... to defende our lawes against many malitious adversaries accusing them of late invention, and that the same [the laws of England] be grounded rather uppon the absolute and powerfull will of a Conqueror for his owne private pleasure and comoditie, than uppon the settled reason of a Lawgiver for the preservation and increase of the common weale.[1]

Commencing his reading on the Statute of Uses in 1592, Coke paused to clarify why he digressed into a history of the common law. He explained that his historical excursus was an 'apology' against those writers, 'malicious adversaries both domesticall and forreigne', who had argued that William the Conqueror had invented or imported the common law and many of its institutions. They had wrongly claimed that the jury, sherrifs, justices of the peace, and the courts of the Chancery and Exchequer were created by the Conqueror who 'abrogated in manner all the ancient lawes'. These introductory comments to his reading would inform the texts of his prefaces to the *Third*, *Eighth* and *Ninth Reports*, among the most important sources for reconstructing Coke's views on the ancient constitution. In these prefaces, however, Coke omitted to explain the specific reasons why he explored the history of the common law in such detail.

Writers before and after J. G. A. Pocock assumed that the answer lay in the development of common law constitutionalism and the deployment of

---

[1] Coke's reading on the Statute of Uses (1592), BL Hargrave 33, f. 134r. Coke makes reference to the reading in BL Harley MS 6687A, ff. 13r–v, and Francis Bacon also alluded to it in his reading on the Statute of Uses, printed as *The Learned Reading of Sir Francis Bacon* (London, 1642), Wing B301. Only one full manuscript of the reading has been recovered, BL Hargrave 33, ff. 134r–161r. A fragmentary copy is in the possession of John Baker. Material associated with the reading (consisting mostly of the cases used in the reading) is found in Holkham MS 725. Baker, *Readers and Readings in the Inns of Court and Chancery*, pp. 90–1.

the medieval idea of the ancient constitution as a defence against absolutist claims by Stuart monarchs.[2] The common law could have no lawgiver, since if it was accepted that a king had imposed the common law, then his descendants might change it at will.[3] Ancient constitutionalism was a strategy to uncouple the common law's authority from the monarch. However, as J. P. Sommerville has shown, Coke and other common lawyers admitted not just one conquest, but many; not just one break in the continuity of the law, but several.[4] Moreover, it has been argued that, in this period, the theory of divine right was the preferred basis for absolutist claims and only later did royalists make the argument from conquest.[5] The audience for common law claims to immemoriality, William Klein has argued, may have been the civilians whose criticisms of the law were particulary biting.[6] Charles Gray suggested that the 'Prefaces' projected an idealized, medieval past from which Coke could draw his ideas for law reform.[7]

A clue to the reception and aims of Coke's reading in 1592 is found in one contemporary's explicit response. The author doubted Coke's conclusions, since he judged that 'our lawe savoreth somwhate of a Conqueror'.[8] Coke himself had described the motivation behind his historical research in 1592: the 'defence of the most excellent government of this Realme in

---

[2] The idea, as Greenberg has demonstrated, was medieval in origin. Greenberg, *The Radical Face of the Ancient Constitution*, pp. 28–9; Pocock, *Ancient Constitution*, p. 37; Paul Raffield, *Images and Cultures of Law in Early Modern England* (Cambridge, 2004), p. 3.

[3] Pocock, *Ancient Constitution*, pp. 42–55, at p. 53.

[4] J. P. Sommerville, 'History and Theory: The Norman Conquest in Early Stuart Political Thought', *Political Studies,* 34 (1986), 249–61, esp. 252–4; J. M. Wallace, *Destiny His Choice: The Loyalism of Andrew Marvell* (Cambridge, 1968), pp. 23–43, though focused mostly on the period of the Civil War.

[5] Pocock, *Ancient Constitution*, pp. 54–5, 149–51; Sommerville, *Royalists and Patriots*, pp. 9–54; Quentin Skinner, 'History and Ideology' in the English Revolution, *Historical Journal*, 8 (1965), 151–78, pp. 154, 168, though he perceives Coke's history as forestalling debate, p. 175; Janelle Greenberg and Laura Marin, 'The Role of the Norman Conquest in Stuart Political Thought', in *Politics and the Political Imagination in Later Stuart Britain* (Rochester, NY, 1997), pp. 121–42, 122–6; but see Hill, *Intellectual Origins*, p. 363.

[6] William Klein, 'The Ancient Constitution Revisited', in Nicholas Phillipson and Quentin Skinner (eds.), *Political Discourse in Early Modern Britain* (Cambridge, 1993), 23–44, pp. 41–2. Though compare more positive aspects of the relationships discussed in Brian Levack, *The Civil Lawyers in England, 1603–4: A Political Study* (Oxford, 1973), pp. 140–1 and R. H. Helmholtz, *Roman Canon Law in Reformation England* (Cambridge, 1990), pp. 188–91.

[7] Charles Gray, 'Introduction', in Matthew Hale, *History of the Common Law of England* (Chicago, IL, 1971), p. xxv. Though Gray suggested Coke believed the process of legal evolution was self-balancing, an interpretation also preferred by Garnett, 'The Prefaces to Sir Edward Coke's Reports', 266.

[8] BL Harley MS 5265, f. 176v.

speaking of the antiquitie of the lawes of the Realme to aunsweare the reprochefull slaunders proclaimed and imprinted against our lawes'.[9] Coke had begun his reading by contesting the idea that the common law had its origin in William's 'absolute and powerful will' for his 'private pleasure and commoditie' rather than the 'settled reason of a Lawgiver'.[10] In 1592 his 'many malitious adversaries' who charged the common law with such a 'late invention' included François Hotman, and Coke also singled out Polydore Vergil, who had suggested that the Conqueror had introduced the law, and Raphael Holinshed who had criticized the common law.[11] Much later Robert Parsons, who made the connection between the Conquest and the law's condition explicit, would be among these adversaries. These criticisms may not have posed a serious threat to overthrowing the common law, but they provided a historical explanation for those deficiencies in the law that upset contemporaries.[12] Eventually the Levellers exploited this vein of history and the 'Norman bondage' it exposed, in order to criticize the procedures of the common law and advocate for reform.[13] Coke's writings anticipated this problem, even as he provided two histories in his *Reports* that dressed the common law with a heroic identity as the ally of kings and the protector of subjects. Coke's history of the origins of the common law has attracted the most attention, but this chapter also explicates another: the history of the common law's resistance to popery.[14] These histories assured his audience of lawyers of a common law identity that was certain and approved, responded to criticisms of the law's present condition, and served as an inspiration

---

[9] BL Hargrave MS 33, f. 134v.

[10] Coke later asserted that the wisdom of the common law was such that no man 'could ever have effected or attained unto'; *Calvin's Case*, 7 Co. *Rep.* 4a, 77 ER 381.

[11] François Hotman, 'De Verbis Feudalibus Commentarius', in *Opera*, vol. II (Lyons, 1599), p. 913; 10 Co. *Rep.*, p. xxix; Cowell, *The Interpreter*, s.v. 'Litleton' [*sic*]; Vergil was often criticized: BL MS Egerton 3376, ff. 47r, 51v; Davies, *Le Primer Report*, sig. *3r.

[12] Though an earlier generation of historians considered the possibility of a reception; Charles McIlwain, 'Introduction', in *The Political Works of James I* (Cambridge, 1918), pp. xl–xli; Brian Levack, *The Civil Lawyers*, p. 126; though compare Daniel Coquillette, 'Legal Ideology and Incorporation I: the English Civilian Writers, 1523–1607', *Boston University Law Review*, 61:1 (1981), 1–89 at 10.

[13] R. B. Seaberg, 'The Norman Conquest and the Common Law: The Levellers and the Argument from Continuity', *The Historical Journal*, 24:4 (1981), 791–806, at 794–6. Christopher Hill, 'The Norman Yoke', in *Democracy and the Labour Movement: Essays in Honour of Donna Torr*, ed. J. Saville (London, 1954), 11–66, pp. 28–30.

[14] Parts of this chapter have been reprinted from my article, 'Remembering Usurpation: The Common Lawyers, Reformation Narratives and the Prerogative, 1578–1616', *Historical Research*, 86:234 (2013), 619–37.

for reform. They also illuminated the connection between the common law and the monarch, revealing that the common law had defended the prince, who had favoured and contributed to the development of the law.

Other common lawyers joined Coke in writing these histories and addressing contemporary problems. George Saltern, who acknowledged his debt to Coke, reminded his readers of the ongoing argument with both the living and the dead when he wrote to support the Union project and attacked Polydore Vergil: 'Such a labour it is to overthrowe these Italian opinions, of which our nation is too fondly credulous.'[15] Sir Roger Owen, himself a 'notable parliamentarian' and common lawyer, was also among those who formulated extended answers to the critiques of civilians and others.[16] His unpublished treatise on the common law (1611–13) was preoccupied with a sustained attack on those who detracted from the law. Owen was explicit about naming those whom he sought to refute, including thirty-four medieval historians and contemporary foreigners.[17] Like Coke's writings, Owen's history had another purpose: demonstrating how the common law had inhibited the clergy from usurping jurisdiction in the pre-Reformation past. This history had a special resonance among his contemporaries, as they sought to resist the Counter-Reformation and looked askance at the spiritual courts. Owen warned against the clergy and the civilians who 'would transforme us into another politique nature'.[18] Like similar writings by other common lawyers, Owen drew on Protestant polemicists such as William Tyndale and John Foxe to describe the common law's resistance against popery. This understanding of the past insisted on the common law's vigilance against usurpation, a problem that continued into Owen's day in disputes over the Church courts and Catholic criticisms of the legitimacy of the government. The profession did not speak with one voice on any of these issues, and it is

---

[15] George Saltern, *Of the Antient Lawes of Great Britaine* (London, 1605) STC 21635, sig. I2r, F2v. Greenberg, *The Radical Face of the Ancient Constitution*, pp. 128–9; Galloway, *The Union*, p. 40. Saltern also relied on the civilian Sir John Prise whose *Historiae Brytannicae Defensio*, published in 1573, attacked Vergil and defended the British origins of the common law; *DNB*, s.v. 'John Prise'; Greenberg, *The Radical Face of the Ancient Constitution*, pp. 128–9.

[16] *DNB*, s.v. 'Thomas Owen' (containing the biography of his son Sir Roger).

[17] BL Harley MS 6604, ff. 5r, 141r. The best study of this work is William Klein's unpublished dissertation, 'Ruling Thoughts: The World of Sir Roger Owen of Condover', Ph.D., The Johns Hopkins University, 1987. The text is broken up among many manuscripts, identified in Klein, 'Ruling Thoughts', pp. 265–7. For the dating I rely on his reference to Coke's 'eight Reports'. The foreigners were Jean Bodin, François Hotman, Charles Loiseau, Paulus Jovius, Paulus Aemilius, Josiah Berault and René Choppin.

[18] BL Harley MS 6604, f. 141v.

notable that even though many agreed with the same general assumptions, they reached very different conclusions. Diversity of opinion and interpretative originality characterized common law culture, as befitted a profession that relied on historical research in their own arguments at the Bar.[19]

Coke and others recognized that the claim that the Conqueror had introduced the common law had a dangerous implication. If the common law had been flawed ab initio by its invention or introduction by an individual, then this origin explained its contemporary imperfections.[20] History could thereby be the basis of a critique of the common law: William, some wrote, had given the English 'newe ordes and newe lawes: whiche kepte them prostrate under an intollerable yoke'.[21] This attitude towards the common law was informed by historical accounts, especially Polydore Vergil's *English History* (1534), which suggested that the 'common law' was an amalgam of customs compiled by King Edward and augmented or replaced by Norman innovations.[22] Vergil's insistence that the Normans had altered the law and his condemnation of the jury made him a target of common law apologists. But his writings remained influential in Coke's time. Samuel Daniel, John Speed, Raphael Holinshed and William Martyn described a complex and unjust law imposed on a subject people by the Normans. Daniel's description of the effects of the imposition of their customs by 'contentious' Normans had contemporary resonance: 'And herewithal, New termes, new Constitutions, new Formes of Pleas, new Offices, and Courts, are now introduced by the Normans, a people more inured to litigation, and of spirits more impatient, and contentious, than were the English.'[23]

John Speed also described the obscurity, lengthy delays and vexation that accompanied the introduction of new laws by William. Self-interested lawyers took advantage of the law's complexity and language so that innocent subjects, 'partly by ignorance in mis-construction, and often also by the sleights of Pleaders and Iudges, who might pretend for law what they list, were ... generally so intangled with their unknowne interpretation, and tortured with their delayes, turmoils and traverses,

---

[19] An example of Coke's own historical research while litigating is Longleat House TH/VOL/VII no. 17.

[20] Hill, *Intellectual Origins*, p. 362.

[21] BL Harley MS 6850, f. 5v; Hill, *Intellectual Origins*, pp. 361–5.

[22] Polydore Vergil, *Three Books of Polydore Vergil's English History*, ed. Henry Ellis (New York, 1968), p. 292 and also p. 72.

[23] Samuel Daniel, *The Complete Works*, ed. A. B. Grosart (New York, 1963), p. 167.

they they rather chose to give over their suits, then to follow them with their endlesse vexations.'[24]

Raphael Holinshed, in particular, drew Coke's attention with his claim that William, 'abrogating in maner all the ancient lawes used in times past ... made new, nothing so equall or easie to be kept'. Holinshed also wrote that the Conqueror instituted sheriffs, the jury, the law terms and the common law courts, and that the judges sat 'in manner as is used unto this day'.[25]

Evidence for the connection between the Norman customs and the common law was found in the continued use of Law French, a symbol of the obscurity of the law.[26] Holinshed described how the foreign language of the law rendered it mysterious to laymen and ensnared them in litigation in a passage that inspired Speed to claim: 'so that even at the beginning you should have great numbers, partlie by the iniquitie of the lawes, and partlie by ignorance in misconstruing the same, to be wrongfullie condemned ... others were so intangled in sutes and causes ... that in their minds they cursed the time that ever these unequall lawes were made'.[27] More pointed still was John Hayward, a civilian, who described how William introduced laws 'to be written in the Norman language, which was a barbarous and broken French ... The residue were not written at all, but left almost arbitrarie, to be determined by reason and discretion at large'.[28] Hayward then queried why the English had come to praise such a law, explaining that the passage of time had seen the restoration of the laws of King Edward and smoothed the roughness of the Norman law. Long usage had rendered the common laws 'not onely tolerable, but easie and sweete, and happily not fit to bee changed'. But Hayward made this approval ambiguous by following with a discussion of the example of 'certaine Christians, who by long conversing with the Turkes, had defiled themselves with Turkish fashions'. This, alongside other examples of habitual obedience, suggested that custom produced

---

[24] John Speed, *The History of Great Britaine* (London, 1650), Wing S4880, p. 428.

[25] Raphael Holinshed, *The Third Volume of Chronicles, Beginning at Duke William the Norman* (London, 1586), STC 13569, p. 8.

[26] William Martyn, *The Historie, and Lives of Twentie Kings of England* (London, 1615), STC 17527, p. 4; Davies, *Le Primer Report*, sig. 3v.

[27] Holinshed, *The Third Volume of Chronicles*, p. 2.

[28] John Hayward, *The Lives of the III Norman Kings* (London, 1613), STC 13000, p. 100. For commentary on Hayward's motivations and the disapproval of his histories by the government, see Levack, *The Civil Lawyers*, pp. 89–101 and *DNB*, s.v. 'Sir John Hayward'. Greenberg discusses Hayward's assertion of a break in 1066 in his polemical exchange with Robert Parsons, in *The Radical Face of the Ancient Constitution*, pp. 124–5.

a familiarity that inhibited objective reflection: 'whatsoever law a people hath lived, they doe esteeme the same most excellent and divine'.[29]

Writers such as Coke responded with their own histories. These views of the past were characterized by debate and shifting positions: there was no orthodox narrative of the common law's historical development.[30] John Lewis, for example, reflected on the contrasting accounts by George Saltern and John Selden, and sought to reconcile them with his own exploration of the Welsh laws.[31] Positions changed as ongoing research and reading influenced individuals. William Lambarde was one of the earliest common lawyers to write on the history of the common law and a member of the historical circle around Archbishop Parker.[32] In his *Perambulation of Kent* he noted that though other writers believed that Edward the Confessor had been the compiler of the common law, Lambarde instead preferred William, who also added to them: 'by advice of his counsel allowed some, altered others, and quite abrogated a great many, in place of whiche he established the lawes of Normandie his owne countrey'.[33] By 1591, however, Lambarde had shifted his position and claimed instead that: 'And truly, the Normans (that invaded the posteritie of the same Saxons here) did not so much alter the substance, as the name of the Saxons order, which they found at their coming hither'.[34] William I retained the local courts of the shire and hundred that King Alfred had

---

[29] Hayward, *Norman Kings*, p. 102. Greenberg argues that Hayward held a more restricted view of William's long-term influence after the Conquest; *The Radical Face of the Ancient Constitution*, pp. 153–5.

[30] It has often been assumed that these debates were related to the union project. Greenberg and Marin, 'The Role of the Norman Conquest', p. 122; Greenberg, *The Radical Face of the Ancient Constitution*, pp. 119–24. Garnett has also recently argued for the 'threat of [the common law's] imminent termination' as the motivation for Coke's historical discussions in 'The Prefaces to Sir Edward Coke's Reports', 248–50. The debates over the common law's continuity, as Coke's account in 1592 demonstrates, were already underway by the time of the Union project. Debates over the union drew upon long-standing ideas about the common law's immemoriality; Galloway, *The Union*, p. 39; Levack, *Formation of the British State*, p. 88.

[31] Lewis's tract was dedicated to Coke, who possessed an early draft. Holkham MS 277, no pagination. Robert Snagg, *The Antiquity & Original of the Court of Chancery and Authority of the Lord Chancellor of England* (London, 1654), Wing S4381A, p. 4.

[32] *DNB*, s.v. 'William Lambarde'; W. Dunkel, *William Lambarde, Elizabethan Jurist, 1536–1601* (New Brunswick, NJ, 1965); R. M. Warnicke, *William Lambarde, Elizabethan Antiquary, 1536–1601* (London, 1973); Wilfrid Prest, 'William Lambarde, Elizabethan Law Reform, and Early Stuart Politics', *Journal of British Studies*, 34 (1995), 464–80; P. L. Ward, 'William Lambarde's Collections on Chancery', *Harvard Library Bulletin*, 7 (1953), 271–98.

[33] William Lambarde, *A Perambulation of Kent: Conteining the Description, Hystorie, and Customes of That Shyre* (London, 1576), STC 15175, p. 5.

[34] Lambarde, *Archeion*, p. 8.

erected, and the King's Bench had existed 'as it was before his coming ther'.[35]

Arguments about the Norman contribution to the evolution of English law inflected the debate.[36] William Martyn believed that William had replaced the Saxon customs with the Norman. His *Historie* was faithful to the cataclysmic reading of the reign of the first two Norman kings. Without giving specifics, Martyn declared that William I founded new courts and caused suits to flow to them and 'tyred out the English Nation with extraordinarie troubles, and excessive charges in the prosecution of their Suites in Law'.[37] Moreover, it was William I who introduced tenures, including knight service, 'Which tenures are continued at this day'.[38] Implying that aspects of this law remained in force, Martyn wrote that later kings, including Henry II, 'reformed the common Lawes; making them to be more tolerable'.[39]

Edmund Plowden joined Martyn in accepting that William had interrupted and altered the development of English law. Plowden was one of the most respected of sixteenth-century common lawyers – Edward Coke referred to him as 'a grave man, and singularly well learned'.[40] In 1583, while arguing a case, Plowden recounted:

> for at the first when William the Conqueror had conquered this realm, he by this conquest took from each inhabitant … all their property in franchises, liberties, goods and chattels which they had, and deprived them also of all their laws by which the people were able to hold lands or goods so that all things were by his disposition and depended on his judgment and will.[41]

Plowden explained that contemporary tenurial arrangements, including tenancy-in-chief, developed from the Norman Conquest. He also seemed to suggest that William had intruded Norman customs into the common law.

---

[35] *Ibid.*, pp. 18, 24–5.
[36] Hearn (ed.), *Curious Discourses*, vol. I, p. 8. Some common lawyers late in the fifteenth century had already argued for William's contribution to the common law. Baker, *OHLE*, vol. VI, pp. 18–19.
[37] Martyn, *The Historie*, pp. 4, 5.   [38] *Ibid.*, p. 6.
[39] *Ibid.*, pp. 18, 34. These statements may have led to his summoning by the Privy Council; *APC*, 1615–16, pp. 62, 67, 73, 100.
[40] 3 Co. *Rep.*, p. viii and 10 Co. *Rep.*, p. xxxiv. Plowden was one of Coke's informants, see *Westby's Case* (1597), 3 Co. *Rep.* 79a, 76 ER 807.
[41] *Tresham's Case* (1583), BL Additional MS 25206, f. 2v.

Coke records in his notebook in 1598 that Popham had told him that when a conqueror should attain another realm then he might appoint any law that he wished for its good government, 'and he said that the Duke of Normandy ... when he conquered this realm of England, he made an oath to observe the laws of St. Edward the Confessor except certain chapters and articles, but he added as many of the laws and customs of Normandy as he pleased'. Coke, perhaps rejecting the opinion of his mentor, crossed out, in a different ink, the statement that William I had changed the laws and substituted: 'and in truth [this was so much] the opposite of changing any of the laws of England that he translated many of [them?] to Normandy'.[42] Even at the other end of Coke's career, the judge Sir Richard Hutton JCP noted that the 'common law was introduced with the Conqueror'.[43]

Others acknowledged that William had altered the laws, but examined this intervention as part of a tumultuous process of nation building, as new migrants arrived in England and added their customs to those of their predecessors. The result was a fusion of an 'English Brittish Law'.[44] Writers might minimize the effect of the Normans or indicate that their influence had been reversed – George Saltern referred to William's 'some smal addition'. Francis Ashley in his reading on Magna Carta in 1616 explained that William ruled arbitrarily until the old laws were restored by Henry III's time.[45] The assertion that another king, often Henry I, had restored the old law and corrected the legal excesses of William I diminished whatever changes there might have been.[46] Moreover, as Coke and Owen had argued, even if William had introduced Norman customs, these in turn had once been borrowed from the laws of King Edward.[47]

[42] BL Harley MS 6686A, f. 274r (translation mine).
[43] Though he also included Catesby's dictum on the antiquity of the common law, but this probably referred only to the reason of the law. Sir Richard Hutton, *The Diary of Sir Richard Hutton*, ed. W. R. Prest (London, 1991), p. 119; cf. BL Lansdowne MS 174, f. 207v.
[44] John Selden, 'Jani Anglorum Facies Altera' in *Tracts* (London, 1683), Wing S2441A, 'Preface to the Reader'; Hutton, *Diary*, p. 121; Pulton, *Kalender*, sig. Aiii(v); William Fulbecke, *Parallele Conference of the Ciuill Law, the Canon Law, and the Common Law of this Realme of England* (London, 1601), STC 11415, 'To the Courteous Reader', sig. 9r; Hearn (ed.), *Curious Discourses*, vol. I, p. 2; Tubbs, 'Custom, Time and Reason', 381–2.
[45] Saltern, *Of the Antient Lawes of Great Britaine*, sig. O4r; Davies, *Le Primer Report*, sig. 3r; BL Harley MS 4841, f. 2v.
[46] Selden, 'Jani Anglorum', p. 60; Snagg, *Antiquity & Original*, pp. 7–8, 13, 18; William Hakewill in Hearn (ed.), *Curious Discourses*, vol. I, p. 7.
[47] Selden was relying on the account of William le Rouille; Selden, 'Jani Anglorum', p. 49; BL Lansdowne MS 646, f. 230r. See also Spelman, 'Of the Ancient Government of England', in *Reliquiae Spelmannianae*, p. 49, and his 'Original of the Terms of Law', in *Reliquiae Spelmannianae*, p. 80.

In his own *Reports*, published by him over fifteen years, Coke similarly minimized the interruption caused by the Norman Conquest.[48] In this claim he was not original, but elaborated long-standing ideas among common lawyers.[49] He answered those who 'slandered' the common law with a paraphrase of Holinshed that the common laws 'are the most equal and most certain, of greatest antiquity, and least delay, and most beneficial and easy to be observed'.[50] Coke warned his readers that ignorance made critics, and urged them, 'meddle not with any point or secret of any art or science, especially with the laws of this realm, before they confer with some learned in that profession'.[51] But Coke conceded that the law was flawed in practice, a problem that gave critics their opening: 'the right institution of the law is not observed, to the unjust slander of the common law, and to the intolerable hindrance of the commonwealth'.[52] Parliament had further confused the law, and Coke warned that legislative action might be dangerous, 'either when an ancient pillar of the common law is taken out of it, or when new remedies are added to it: by the first arise dangers and difficulties; and by the second the common law rightly understood is not bettered, but in many cases so fettered, that it is thereby very much weakened'.[53]

The ignorance of practitioners and legislators had corrupted the law, so 'that divers doubts and questions of law remained undetermined, the same rising partly upon long and ill penned statutes lately made, partly by reason of late and new devises and inventions in assurances'.[54] Coke's principal example of these 'ill penned Statuts' was De Donis, but he also singled out the Statute of Nonclaime, 'enacted against a main point of the common law, whereby ensued the universal trouble of the King's subjects'.[55] Poor drafting of statutes led judges into interpretative contortions that then confused the case law. Coke suggested that experts should be closely involved in the creation of statutes to neutralize the influence of those who had 'very little judgment in law'.[56]

---

[48] For other opinions similar to Coke's, see Saltern, *Of the Antient Lawes*, sig. G3r, B2r; Davies, *Le Primer Report*, sig. 3r; Baker, *The Reports of Sir John Spelman*, vol. II, pp. 32–3; Snagg, *Antiquity & Original*, pp. 17–18; Bodl. Rawlinson MS B 410, f. 1r; and James Morice's account in BL Egerton MS 3376, f. 47r. The sources of Coke's prefaces and his historical methods are discussed by Garnett, 'The Prefaces to Sir Edward Coke's Reports', 257–61.

[49] Baker, *OHLE*, vol. VI, pp. 20–2.

[50] 2 Co. *Rep.*, p. v; cf. Holinshed, *The Third Volume of Chronicles*, p. 8.

[51] 3 Co. *Rep.*, p. xxiii; 10 Co. *Rep.*, pp. xxix–xxx.

[52] 8 Co. *Rep.*, p. xxvi.   [53] 9 Co. *Rep.*, p. xxxvi.

[54] 4 Co. *Rep.*, pp. xvii–xviii.   [55] 4 Co. *Rep.*, p. vi.

[56] 2 Co. *Rep.*, pp. ix–x.

If parliament had created problematic law, from the 1580s to 1616 Coke's attitude towards the monarch was more deferential. Kings and queens played an important role both in the development and preservation of good law. In autograph notes to his historical readings that were probably written between 1579 and 1588, Coke laid out his interpretation of the law in the pre-Conquest period, suggesting that Dunwallo Malmucius 'first made laws in Britain'. Later Martia Proba 'made a lawe full of wit and reason'.[57] Gildas translated these laws from British to Latin, and they were later translated again into the Saxon language. Alongside this British law was a law from Alfred called 'west saxon law'. The Danes during their conquest introduced a third law: 'Dane law'. St Edward the Confessor amalgamated the three laws of the different peoples in England and 'made one common lawe'.[58] Three peoples had carried their laws into England, and their kings had modified or compiled them. Edward the Confessor had himself united them into a common law: the law was a collective enterprise stewarded by the monarch. Coke continued his description of the ancient relationship between the monarch and the law in his reading in 1592 on the Statute of Uses. He declared that Brutus was the first king of England and 'for the safe and peaceable government of his people wrote a booke in the greeke tongue calling it the lawes of the Britons, and collected the same out of the laws of the Trojans'.[59] Though Brutus was not the lawmaker he was its compiler and lawgiver. As a king he was obliged to provide his people, newly arrived from Troy, with a municipal law, since the period in which kings might simply speak law and appeal to equity had passed. Later Dunwallo wrote two books of laws, whose titles, Coke believed, translated 'as much to say the statute lawe and the common lawe'. Martia Proba, Sigebert and Alfred were also authors of books of laws. Finally Coke recorded how King Edward compiled the laws into one, 'which he wished to call the common law'.

The kings of England preserved the laws that they had compiled or received from many sources. When he turned to the Conquest itself, Coke

[57] Baker provides the dating for this manuscript; J. H. Baker, 'Coke's Note-books and the Sources of his Reports', *Cambridge Law Journal*, 30:1 (1972), 59–86, p. 61. Coke continued to update the notebook into the time of James I.

[58] BL Harley MS 6687A, f. 1r; 8 Co. *Rep.*, pp. ix–x. Attributing the blending of the laws to St Edward followed another established line of common law thought, for example John Hales's reading in 1514, cited in Baker, *OHLE*, vol. VI, p. 21. Greenberg discusses the influence (and radical potential) of the *Leges Edwardi Confessoris*, in *The Radical Face of the Ancient Constitution*, pp. 59–62. Coke elsewhere rejected the claim that the 'fragments' published as the *Leges Edwardi Confessoris* contained 'the very body of the common laws before the Conquest'; 8 Co. *Rep.* p. xi.

[59] BL Hargrave MS 33, f. 135r.

stayed true to the theory of conquest that he would later put forward in *Calvin's Case*. William had the choice either to replace the laws of England or continue the old laws in force. Coke cited Gervase of Canterbury here and again in the preface to his *Third Reports* to describe William's effect on the laws of England: 'it appeareth that some of the English laws he allowed, and such of his own as he added were efficacissimae ad regni pacem tuendam; and therefore if such laws as he added of his own had continued (as in troth they did not) they were not so shamelessly and falsely to be slandered'. [60]

Coke did not condemn William I for augmenting the English law, since he had done so for the peace and safety of the realm. Coke suggested that had these additions survived, he would defend them against those who 'maliciously and ignorantly' slandered them. He continued by referring to the critics who scorned William's additions, with a citation referring to the Trojan horse.[61] This was a telling reference: a greater danger would follow if these criticisms against William were admitted – presumably the denigration of the common law. Nonetheless, these changes were not continued because Henry I removed them from the common law. Coke then claimed that Henry II 'wrote a booke of the common laws and statutes of England', though there was now no trace of any of those (ten) books. The framework of this story was printed with only minor modifications in the *Eighth Report*.

Coke's history achieved a number of goals. First, its assertion of the common law's antiquity deflected the imputation that the law arose as either an instrument of oppression or through the imperfect will of an individual. Coke's history offered an alternative explanation for the law's uncertain condition: ignorance and meddling in the medieval law. The common law developed over time in sympathy with its people and through the wisdom of their rulers. Edward, like a master distiller, had carefully mixed the different customs of the people together. His participation in the development of the law was of a piece with his predecessors and successors.[62] At the outset of his *Sixth Report*, Coke quoted Fortescue

---

[60] 3 Co. *Rep.*, p. xxi, probably adapting the account of the *Dialogus de Scaccario*; E. Amt and S. D. Church (eds.), *Dialogus de Scaccario* (Oxford, 2007), p. 63. Garnett discusses Coke's use of the *Dialogus* in 'The Prefaces to Coke's Reports', 262–4. Coke had earlier stated (citing Fitzherbert) that the common law was not 'altered or changed by the Conqueror'; 3 Co. *Rep.*, p. xii.

[61] 'Either this machine was built [to be used] against our walls, or some deception is concealed: Trojans, give no credit to the horse'; 3 Co. *Rep.*, p. xxi from Virgil, *Aeneid*, Book II.

[62] In his account, Pocock minimized or rejected this involvement; *Ancient Constitution*, p. 44.

to claim that the wisdom of the kings of England had permitted the continuance of the common law, which they might have extinguished if they had chosen: 'if they had not been right good, some of these Kings, moved either with justice, or with reason or affection, would have changed them, or else altogether abolished them'.[63] The repeated conquests of the island had given the victorious kings numerous opportunities to do so. In his printed reports Coke repeated the points that he had made in 1592: Brutus had collected the laws, Dunwallo had written two books of the laws of the Britons and Mercia Proba, Alfred and Sigebert were also compilers of their national laws. St Edward the Confessor had brought them together into a single, unified body of law, and Coke quoted from 1592: 'From the immense accumulation, which the British, Romans, Angles, and Danes had established, he selected the best, and formed them into one body, which he wished to be called the common law'.[64] Coke's history rejected criticisms of the law, identified the true source of uncertainty, and asserted the relationship between the law and the king. Time and England's monarchs had approved the common law, owing to its underlying rationality and the vital protection the law offered for subject and monarch alike.

Coke narrated another history throughout his prefaces that was also freighted with meaning for the present. This history, most accessible in the preface to the *Fifth Reports*, narrated the common law's resistance to popish usurpation throughout the Middle Ages. This history was directly involved in current problems by grounding Coke's response to Catholic arguments against the Elizabethan religious settlement. But this history's narrative of clerical usurpation was also admonitory and could justify the common law's authority to police the Church courts. The past demonstrated that the common law protected the monarch's prerogative from encroachment by the clergy and from challenges to their title by Catholics.[65] As with debates over the common law's temporal history, these narratives also revealed a diversity of opinion among common lawyers about the significance of the pre-Reformation past, revealing once again how they might reach radically different conclusions from shared propositions.

---

[63] 6 Co. *Rep.*, p. v.   [64] 3 Co. *Rep.*, pp. xiv, xx.

[65] 'The Apology to the Bishop of Ross', in Bodl. English History MS B 117. Coke owned a copy of Ross's arguments in manuscript; Hassall, *The Library of Sir Edward Coke*, no. 280.

The history of the common law's relationship to the Church and the Reformation drew upon the writings of those Protestant polemicists, especially William Tyndale, Robert Barnes, John Bale and John Foxe, who had described the spreading corruption of the bishop of Rome.[66] Their narratives reconstructed a vast effort by the papacy to make temporal governments subservient.[67] This remembrance of usurpation and persecution, memorably and exhaustively described in *Acts and Monuments*, explained even to illiterate audiences the dangers of popery. At the heart of many of these narratives was the observation that jurisdictional creep often furthered the expansion of clerical power at the expense of the rights of princes and laymen. From an initial assertion of primacy among bishops, the pope had expanded his legal claims into the temporal sphere, 'challenging to himself both the swords'.[68] Foxe argued that spiritual men should pray and minister instead, and avoid the lucrative temptations that came from temporal authority.[69] Temporal jurisdiction, in particular, waylaid the clergy from their spiritual mission, and Foxe urged the recovery of all jurisdiction back to the secular arm as a means of reversing the popish usurpation and to prevent future corruption.[70]

Common lawyers examined the role of their law in this narrative as a means to respond to Catholic writers who contested the authority of the English government, and to assess the claims of the Church of England and its courts.[71] The common law disputes with the spiritual courts have traditionally been interpreted as 'part of the general confrontation

---

[66] A. G. Dickens and John Tonkin, *The Reformation in Historical Thought* (Cambridge, 1985), p. 60; Helmholz, *OHLE*, vol. I, pp. 240–3; Cromartie, *Constitutionalist Revolution*, pp. 59–79.

[67] Historical reconstruction was an important aspect in the character of English Protestantism; Rainer Pineas, 'William Tyndale's Use of History as a Weapon of Religious Controversy', *Harvard Theological Review*, 55 (1962), 121; Dickens and Tonkin, *The Reformation in Historical Thought*, p. 63; F. J. Levy, *Tudor Historical Thought* (San Marino, CA, 1967), p. 79.

[68] John Foxe, *The Acts and Monuments of John Foxe; with a Life of the Martyrologist, and Vindication of the Work* (New York, 1965), vol. I, pp. 12–13, 6, 18.

[69] *Ibid.*, vol. I, p. 26.

[70] The idea was also found in Presbyterian circles; see William Stoughton, *An Assertion for True and Christian Church-Policie* (Middleburg, 1604), STC 23318.

[71] These narratives are an important point where legal and religious thought intersect, *pace* J. S. Morrill, 'The Religious Context of the English Civil War', *Transactions of the Royal Historical Society*, 5th series, 34 (1984), 155–78, at 157. Similarly, see Ethan Shagan, 'The English Inquisition: Constitutional Conflict and Ecclesiastical Law in the 1590s', *Historical Journal*, 47:3 (2004), 541–65, at 542.

between the common law judges and the Stuarts'.[72] Yet the example of past usurpations informed the judges' motives and their anxiety over the jurisdiction of the modern Church. Disputes such as the *jure divino* controversy fed suspicion, and advanced Protestants urged a continuing reformation.[73] Concerns were raised, for instance, about process issuing from the ecclesiastical courts in the name of the bishop rather than the king.[74] While some urged the abolition of the spiritual jurisdiction altogether, more moderate critics complained that popish canons continued to corrupt ecclesiastical law and demanded more limited reform.[75] At stake was the fear of renewed tyranny: in 1610 Nicholas Fuller urged in parliament that the Church canons might be used to seize the property and body of the subject.[76] These misgivings became an increasingly dominant theme in political life, culminating in the accusations against Laud of reintroducing popery into the Church.[77]

The shrill concern of Fuller and others that reform needed to continue contrasted with the more placid, official version of the Reformation. Laid out in the Henrician statutes that accomplished the break with Rome, their legal magic reunited the ecclesiastical jurisdiction with the Crown and depicted a harmonious relationship between the temporal and ecclesiastical jurisdictions. As Conrad Russell has discussed, however, these statutes were also equivocal about the future relationship between the ecclesiastical and temporal jurisdictions.[78] The Statute in Restraint of Appeals (1532) suggested that the process of legal reformation would be straightforward, and the temporal and spiritual jurisdictions would

---

[72] Robert Rodes, *Lay Authority and Reformation in the English Church: Edward I to the Civil War* (Notre Dame, IN, 1982), pp. 110, 193–243.

[73] IT Petyt MS 516/11, p. 20; Peter Lake, *Anglicans and Puritans?: Presbyterianism and English Conformist Thought from Whitgift to Hooker* (London, 1988), pp. 97–101, 117–19; Richard Bancroft, *A Sermon Preached at Paules Crosse* (London, 1589), STC 1347.

[74] PRO SP 9/209/15.

[75] These criticisms was recorded by Richard Cosin, *An Apologie: of, and for, Sundrie Proceedings by Iurisdiction Ecclesiasticall* (London, 1593), STC 5822, sig. Cv; cf. the reproduction of 'An Abstract', in Richard Cosin, *An Answer to the Two First and Principall Treatises of a Certeine Factious Libell ...* (London, 1584), STC 5819.5, sig. Bv. For reform of the canon law, see Helmholz, *OHLE*, vol. I, pp. 168–9; Leo Solt, *Church and State in Early Modern England, 1509–1640* (New York, 1990), pp. 23, 54; Baker, *OHLE*, vol. VI, pp. 248–9.

[76] *PP 1610*, vol. II, p. 408.

[77] Peter Lake, 'Anti-Popery: The Structure of a Prejudice', in Richard Cust and Ann Hughes (eds.), *Conflict in Early Stuart England* (Harlow, 1989), pp. 72–106; Scott, *England's Troubles*, pp. 27–31, 122–40.

[78] Conrad Russell, 'Parliament, the Royal Supremacy and the Church', *Parliamentary History*, 19 (2000), 27–37, at 28.

hear clearly defined causes and support one another.[79] This vision was both organic and functional, implying a scheme that proved much more difficult to achieve in practice and was soon undermined.[80] The repugnancy clause in the Act for the Submission of the Clergy (1533) undercut the assumption of equality between the jurisdictions, disallowing those canons and ordinances that were 'contrariant or repugnant to the King's prerogative royal, or the customs, laws or statutes of this realm'.[81] By conforming the ecclesiastical canons to the temporal law the clause anticipated the threat of future clerical usurpation.[82]

Russell has written that these two statutes seemed contradictory: insisting first on an equality that was then undermined. The driver of conflict, however, was that the neat boundary between temporal and spiritual was poorly defined. The boundary was crucial: Tyndale and others used its limit to mark where clerical overstep became corruption.[83] Efforts to identify this divide made common lawyers into historians. The reasoning was put succinctly in one case: 'what the Pope alone used lawfullye to doe, that the kinge by the statute of 26 Henry 8 might lykewyse doe'.[84] But what had the pope 'lawfully' done? Where was the boundary between temporal and spiritual? Common lawyers traced precedents back to the pristine Church to discover how the ecclesiastical courts had lawfully proceeded. The past provided both examples of repugnancy and the Church's legitimate jurisdiction. But as opaque as the past was, so too were the markers between the spiritual and temporal jurisdiction.[85]

The repugnancy clause also held another powerful assumption that informed many of the proceedings against the Church courts: the idea that the ecclesiastical jurisdiction existed only at 'sufferance'.[86] In contrast to arguments that the authority of Church courts arose from the

---

[79] 24 Henry VIII, c. 12, *SR*, vol. III, p. 427.
[80] The description of the two jurisdictions supplementing each other was a commonplace; Baker, *The Reports of Sir John Spelman*, vol. II, p. 64. Writers such as Ridley assumed the equality of the jurisdictions; Ridley, *A View*, p. 134.
[81] 25 Henry VIII, c. 19, *SR*, vol. III, p. 461.
[82] See, for example, *Gaudyes Case* (1610), 2 Brownlow and Goldesborough 38, 123 ER 802.
[83] The distinction at the common law preceded the Reformation; see YB Trin. 15 Henry VII, pl. 8, f. 9a.
[84] *The Case of the Dean and Chapter of Norwich* (1596), BL Additional MS 25206, f. 98v; *Colt and Glover* v. *Bishop of Coventry and Lichfield* (1612), Hobart 147, 80 ER 296.
[85] For one method of determining spiritual and temporal, see Ridley, *A View*, p. 139.
[86] The term entered case law to describe whether the common law might permit a proceeding of the spiritual court, see *R.* v. *The Bishop of Coventry* (1602), 2 Anderson 184, 123 ER 612; *Prohibition*, Hobart 188, 231, 80 ER 335; *Pitt* v. *Webly* (1614), 2 Bulstrode 72, 80 ER 968.

pope, directly from God, or that they had existed among Christians from the religion's earliest days, many Elizabethan common lawyers, including Coke, believed that Church courts were a recent invention and held plea by the sufferance of the monarch.[87] Their jurisdiction being suffered, it followed that it might be limited or extinguished altogether. It also implied that these courts were not, at root, the 'the king's courts', but rather an allowance of a foreign law.[88] Spiritual jurisdiction was permissible, but not necessary.[89] Finally, the violation of the boundary between temporal and spiritual held the potential, as it had in the past, to mark a renewed encroachment that needed to be resisted.[90]

These three characteristics – the divide between spiritual and temporal, the sufferance of Church jurisdiction, and resistance – shaped common law histories. They were present in common law writing from the earliest period of the English Reformation in the works of Christopher St German.[91] Yet even within this shared framework the interpretative possibilities were broad, and individual common lawyers came to radically different conclusions about the allowance of the ecclesiastical jurisdiction. Writers such as Roger Owen might argue that testaments, matrimony and tithes, which he believed had originally been heard at the common law, should be returned from the spiritual courts.[92] Henry Finch also demanded that jurisdiction over testaments and marriage be returned, since marriage was a 'mere civill contract', or a temporal procedure.[93] Among Coke's papers, with annotations and corrections in a hand resembling his own, was a treatise defending the royal supremacy that offered a more radical possibility.[94] The author of the manuscript described the history of Roman usurpation and contended that the

---

[87]   Though Ridley admitted that the authority of the Church courts derived from the grant of the prince; Ridley, *A View*, p. 105.

[88]   Thomas Smith captures the ambiguity in *De Republica Anglorum* (London, 1583), STC 22857, pp. 117–18.

[89]   Foxe, *Acts and Monuments*, vol. I, p. 26.

[90]   Christopher St German, *The Addicions of Salem and Byzance* (London, 1534), STC 21585, f. 30v; HLS MS 1006, f. 193r.

[91]   For example, St German, *Addicions*, ff. 14r–15v, 23r–v, 30v, 36r; St German, *A Treatise Concerning the Division betwene the Spirytualtie and Temporaltie* (London, 1532), STC 21587, ff. 28r, 35v.

[92]   BL Lansdowne MS 646, f. 184r.

[93]   Henry Finch, *A Conference and Reformation of the Comon Law by the Law of God*, Bodl. Rawlinson C 43, p. 14; see also BL Cotton MS Cleopatra F I, 6r–44v, at 13r.

[94]   This treatise is found in Yale University Law School MS G R 24, ff. 55r–70v.

ecclesiastical jurisdiction existed at sufferance.[95] The claim that the common law had protected the king was reiterated throughout. The author used the example of the bull of excommunication published in the reign of Edward I, the same example that Coke gave in his notes and in 'De Iure', and it was affirmed that the bull 'was treason by the common lawes of this Realme, to affirme any forrein power to take place here'.[96] The author continued into the heart of the dispute, arguing that the distinction between temporal and spiritual was a false one and asserting that anyone who offended the laws of the realm also offended against God.[97] The very act of adjudication distracted clergy from their spiritual calling, and so the Church courts should be abolished. This was the radical conclusion that some readings of common law history could reach.

Coke himself was more moderate. He was conscious of the visible and supernatural dimensions of the religious struggle of his time. At the trial of Anne Turner in 1615, he worried that the reading of some her 'conjurations' might summon the Devil and ordered their recital stopped.[98] Folded into a collection of his notes is the 'Christian Knight Map', a world map by Jodocus Hondius.[99] The map's titular allegory was a reading on the sixth chapter of Ephesians, itself a gloss on Isaiah. Protestants such as Tyndale had given this exegesis a distinctive function.[100] The knight resisted the confusion between worldly and spiritual things, a confusion that was central to criticisms of popery. Coke's history writing made him a participant in this ongoing struggle as he wrote to address Catholic antagonists and those who sought to enlarge the jurisdiction of the English Church courts. Yet recognizing the practical demands of the times, he reconciled his arguments with the needs of the regime to maintain its religious settlement. His history of the Reformation therefore defended the Elizabethan settlement against its critics while limiting the actions of the Church jurisdiction.

The foundation of Coke's thinking about the ecclesiastical jurisdiction was the Henrician statutes. His notes recorded from '24 Henry VIII, c. 12'

---

[95] *Ibid.*, ff. 59r, 60v.   [96] *Ibid.*, ff. 56v, 65r.   [97] *Ibid.*, f. 59v.

[98] Harvard University, Houghton Library MS Eng 622, f. 3r. Boyer has traced Coke's religious beliefs, arguing that he was a 'puritan' or had 'puritan' tendencies; *Sir Edward Coke*, pp. 156–75; Bowen, *Lion and the Throne*, p. 533.

[99] Holkham MS 677, ff. 260r–261v.

[100] William Tyndale, *The Obedie[n]ce of a Christen Man* (Antwerp, 1528), STC 24446, f. 148. For the use of the metaphor, see also Lancelot Ridley, *A Commentary in Englyshe vpon Sayncte Paules Epystle to the Ephesyans for the Instruccyon of them that be Vnlearned in Tonges* (London, 1540), STC 21038, sig. P1r; William Perkins, 'Epistle Dedicatorie', [n.f.]; Thomas Taylor, *Christs Combate and Conquest* (Cambridge, 1618), STC 23822, p. 41.

reveal his observance of the royal supremacy and the organological division of the king into private and public capacities.[101] The latter was further
divided into two bodies: the temporal and the spiritual that aided each
other 'in the due administration of Justice'.[102] The 'head of government' or
the king, 'is instituted and furnished with plenary and full power, prerogative, and jurisdiction to give justice to each of his subjects'.[103] Coke noted
that the English kings should order and protect the Church: 'the kinge
beinge the vicar of Christe etc'.[104] Though the 'king did not have any superior except God', his power was still limited in two ways. Historically, Coke
recognized that the king's power had been undermined by Rome: 'the
pope had usurped spiritual jurisdiction of this realm in derogation of the
imperial crown of the king'. Though restored by the Henrician and then
the Elizabethan acts, the king's power over the Church was still restrained:
'the king is not subject to any law but to the law of the land '.[105]

Coke later affirmed the royal supremacy in his extensive report on
Caudrey's Case, 'De Iure Regis Ecclesiastico' (1607). This text was a lengthy
response to Catholic challenges to the royal supremacy, which prompted
an extensive rebuttal from the Jesuit Robert Parsons.[106] In a letter to Cecil
in 1605 Coke discussed the disputes and his intention to respond, emphasizing that danger came from both Catholics and sectaries: 'the papist
setteth the supreme jursidiction ecclesiasticall upon the popes triple
crowne, And the sectarie upon the presbiterie'.[107] In defending the king,
Coke laid out in 'De Iure' the history of the common law's defence and
preservation of royal authority in the face of papal subversion. The common law had operated for centuries to protect the king's right over the
Church, so that the Reformation statutes of Henry VIII were merely 'for
the most part declaratorie of the old'.[108] In an undated charge to Lincoln
Assizes, Coke declared that 'Neither did this law ever yield to any Pope
authority compulsive in this land, our common laws of the kingdom did
withal their force abjure his power and that which he had was but by usurpation'.[109] In 'De Iure' Coke described the slow, historical creep of popish
usurpation, culminating in the capitulation of John, under pressure of

---

[101] *SR*, vol. III, pp. 427–9.
[102] Edward Coke, 'De Iure Regis Ecclesiastico', in *Quinta pars relationum Edwardi Coke Equitis aurati, Regii Atturnati Generalis* (London, 1607), STC 5505, f. 12r.
[103] BL Harley MS 6687C, f. 183v.   [104] Holkham MS 677, f. 430r.
[105] BL Harley MS 6687C, f. 183v.   [106] Coke, 'De Iure', f. 8v.
[107] PRO SP 14/13/61.
[108] PRO SP 14/13/61; *CSPD, James I, 1603–1610*, p. 61.
[109] Society of Antiquaries MS 291, f. 12r.

excommunication, 'to make his kingdom tributarie to [the pope] and to be his vassal'. English resistance followed, and the papal bull of excommunication was 'expressly withstood and overthrown'.[110] This resistance ostensibly took the form of the statutes of praemunire and provisors, but such legislation was declarative of the common law and enforced by it.[111] Coke suggested that praemunire was merely a restatement of the common law.[112] Nor did the need for the common law to defend the king and his subjects abate with the Reformation. The Catholic threat continued, and Coke ruminated extensively in 'De Iure' on the ongoing struggle with the papacy and especially the bull *regnans in excelsis*.[113] The intrusion of Jesuits and Catholic priests into the realm poisoned people against their lawful queen and influenced them to withdraw their allegiance in conformity with the bull.[114]

In his *Answere* the Jesuit Robert Parsons rejected Coke's claims and demonstrated how history could inspire criticism of the common law.[115] He complained that the jury was composed of 'unlearned men'. Treason prosecutions attracted much of his condemnation: the defendant's lack of counsel unfairly deprived him of the aid that would be given to one who sought to protect a mere five pounds' worth of land.[116] Parsons argued that the Norman Conquest had introduced an alien and oppressive law into the land – precisely the claim Coke had sought to reject in his reading of 1592. This argument buttressed his contention that the Roman ecclesiastical law was the true ancient law of the English, having been given to them by the pope.[117] It was, he wrote, their true 'inheritance'.[118] Parsons declared bluntly of the common law: 'I, for my part, finde noe memory of any of them extant, before the Conquest and no written statute law before the raigne of King Henry the third.'[119] He went on to explicitly suggest that the Norman introduction of the law placed a stigma on the law itself:

> remember that, which all our writers do commonly note, that they were brought in principally by Conquest, and Conquerour, and such a one as intended to bridle the English ... and yet not by use, and tract of tyme,

[110]   Holkham MS 677, f. 225r.   [111]   Coke, 'De Iure', f. 12r.
[112]   *Ibid.*, f. 15v.   [113]   *Ibid.*, ff. 34v–35v.   [114]   *Ibid.*, f. 36v.
[115]   Robert Parsons, *An Answere to the Fifth Part of Reportes Lately Set Forth by Syr Edward Cooke Knight* (Saint-Omer, 1606), STC 897; see also Robert Parsons, *Treatise of the Three Conversions of England* (Saint-Omer, 1603). Garnett has surveyed Coke's use of historical sources to refute Parsons; see 'The Prefaces to Sir Edward Coke's Reports', 269–82.
[116]   Robert Parsons, *An Answere*, p. 15, sig. Ee2 *et passim*.   [117]   *Ibid.*, pp. 167–8.
[118]   *Ibid.*, p. 16.   [119]   *Ibid.*, p. 13.

the mislike being asswaged, and wee taught to be still, yea and to kisse the rodde, wherwith then we were beaten.[120]

Parsons dismissed Coke as an innovator who wrote to 'impugne the said Catholicke religion, by the antiquity of his Common-lawes'.[121] Coke responded to Parsons by insisting that the Jesuit had engaged only in an ad hominem attack and declared himself the winner in the debate.[122]

While these interactions between lawyers and Catholic writers such as Parsons remain largely unstudied, the other struggle against the usurpation of the prince's authority by clerics is better known. Though Coke accepted that the ecclesiastical and temporal jurisdictions were conjoined, in keeping with the language of the Reformation statutes, he remained watchful over the Church courts. In *Bird* v. *Smith* (1606) in which Coke was a judge, he declared that

> the temporal law and the ecclesiastical law they are joined together in matrimony such that they are not able to consist the one without the other … and yet nevertheless he also said that the ecclesiastical law is as to a sweet river within the fine meadow, which if it should go beyond [its] bounds … It ought to be corrected and reduced.[123]

By warning about the creep of clerical jurisdiction, Coke captured the basic logic of the Henrician statutes: an eirenic vision of united jurisdictions enforced by surveillance: 'for the temporall courtes must always have an eye that the ecclesiastical iurisdiction usurp not upon the temporall'.[124]

Coke gave greater details of his suspicion of clerical intentions in the treatise, 'On the Power of the Church to Make Canons', that was probably related to the canons of 1604.[125] In this document Coke revealed his mistrust of the clergy and affirmed their dependence on the prince and the common law for their authority.[126] The common law courts faced the

---

[120] *Ibid.*, p. 13.   [121] *Ibid.*, sig A2v.

[122] 6 Co. *Rep.*, p. xvi.

[123] *Bird* v. *Smith* (1606), Moore King's Bench 782, 72 ER 903.

[124] Holkham MS 677, f. 347v. See also in the same, 'Concerning Ecclesiastical Jurisdiction as well out of the Lawes and Ordinances of Spaine', ff. 209r–221v.

[125] The Convocation of Canterbury passed the canons in 1603, but the king's letters patent authorizing them was not granted until 1604. Parliamentary approval was 'technically' provided by the Act for the Submission of Clergy (25 Henry VIII, c. 19). *DNB*, s.v. 'Richard Bancroft'; Solt, *Church and State*, pp. 139–43; Helmholz, *OHLE*, vol. I, pp. 264–5. The canons are printed in J. V. Bullard, *Constitutions and Canons Ecclesiastical 1604* (London, 1934).

[126] The attribution of the treatise is based on an inscription: 'That this was by Dr. Baylie D of Sarum (sole executor of that Archbishop) found in Archbishop Lauds study, with

question of whether the canons, without the assent of parliament, bound the laity as well as the clergy, a point that seems to have been granted in *Bird* v. *Smith* (1606).[127] In the 'Treatise on Canons', Coke denied that Convocation alone could make laws for the 'outward government' of the Church.[128] Instead he agreed that the clergy might make canons 'for and concerning things properly belonging to doctrine and divine knowledge for the Institution of the soul and reformation of conscience'.[129] Coke's concern lay with the possibility that the Church could use its power to make laws to bind laymen and to enlarge its power over temporal things. The past provided numerous cautionary examples where the clergy pretended authority that they did not have. The creep of such claims was dangerous to the prerogative: 'But the Clergy by such sufferance … have taken upon them to order such things, as by their own authoritie and it hath caused much people to dread them, and their lawes, more then their Princes, Whereby the Power of Princes to them given by god have greatly decayed, and been but little regarded.'[130]

The clergy, once having obtained the power to make laws for the government of the Church, would also threaten the subject, since using the ecclesiastical laws, they might 'put the subjects out of their freeholds by colour of the same'.[131] It was necessary to avoid repeating the mistakes of the past, and to limit the tendency of the clergy to extend their power over temporal things by curbing their law-making capacity. Coke urged the clergy to limit their jurisdiction to spiritual matters: 'to govern in things properly belonging to doctrine and divine knowledge for the institution of the soule, and reformation of conscience'.[132]

The theory of sufferance was central to Coke's understanding of how the king and his courts controlled the ecclesiastical jurisdiction. The canons, he claimed, were largely a foreign importation, and their binding force was dependent on royal approval and general consent.[133] Coke

this inscription signed with my Lords owne hand Sir Ed Cooke about the power of the Church to make Canons the 25 Hen 8 cap 19'; Oxford University, Queen's College MS 215, f. 17r. Other common lawyers were concerned about the canons; see James Morice, *A Briefe Treatise of Oathes Exacted by Ordinaries and Ecclesiasticall Judges* (Middelburg, 1590), pp. 53–4.

127 Richard Helmholz, 'The Canons of 1603', in Norman Doe, Mark Hill and Robert Ombres (eds.), *English Canon Law: Essays in Honour of Bishop Eric Kemp* (Cardiff, 1998); *Bird* v. *Smith*, Moore King's Bench 783, 72 ER 903; overturned in *Middleton* v. *Crofts* (1736), 2 Atk. ER 650, 26 ER 788.

128 Compare the more hostile account in BL Cotton MS Cleopatra F II, f. 187r ff.

129 Oxford University, Queens College MS 215, f. 23v. Coke may have felt that the canons of 1603–4 did require parliamentary assent, a position he also suggests in 'De Iure', f. 32v.

130 Oxford University, Queens College MS 215, f. 24v.   131 *Ibid.*, f. 18v.   132 *Ibid.*, f. 26r.

133 Coke, 'De Iure', f. 9v.

in his notes and in 'De Iure' reiterated that the kings had 'allowed' the ecclesiastical jurisdiction.[134] In Coke's case, however, his commitment to the idea of sufferance did not lead him to advocate the abolition of the Church courts. He acknowledged a real division between temporal and spiritual matters.[135] Certain causes had been granted to the spiritual jurisdiction depending on their 'natures, conditions, and qualities of the cases and matters'.[136] Elsewhere Coke listed the specific causes that the spiritual courts might hear and which had led kings 'by publike authoritie [to] authorise Ecclesiasticall Courts under them'.[137] Yet he also wrote against those who claimed an absolute equality of jurisdictions. The spiritual jurisdiction, so they argued, did not derive from a grant by the prince, but instead was necessary to adjudicate spiritual causes in any Christian polity. Thomas Ridley in his *A View of the Ciuile and Ecclesiastical Law* (1607) agreed with Coke that there was a clear division between temporal and spiritual matters, but he viewed the common law review of the Church courts as undue interference: 'as Temporall Lawyers are to deale in Temporall Customes and spirituall men are not to intermedle therin, so also Ecclesiasticall Lawyers are to deale in Ecclesiastical causes and that temporal Lawyers are not to busie themselves thereabout'.[138]

Coke justified this interference by an insistence on sufferance. This line of argument appears most clearly in Coke's promotion of praemunire as a remedy against the growth of the ecclesiastical jurisdiction. The continued use of praemunire was justified, so Coke argued, because it was the temporal law that protected the monarch and his or her subjects. It was in a sense 'nearer' to the throne, as it safeguarded the inheritance of the prince, defended them against any treasons, and was the instrument through which the monarch gave justice to his or her subjects. Therefore to usurp on the common law was against the very 'crown and dignity' of the king: 'although both jurisdictions belong to the Crown, yet inasmuch as the Crown itself is directed and descendible by the common law, and all treason against the Crown punished by this law; for this cause, when the Ecclesiastical Judge usurps upon the common law, it is said contra coronam et dignitatem, &c.' [139]

The common law protected the king, and so to infringe upon it was to assault the royal power. This very nearness to the king gave the common

---

[134] *Ibid.*, f. 16v, and also ff. 13v–14r; BL Harley MS 6687C, f. 183r; Coke, 'De Iure', f. 40r.

[135] *Fuller's Case*, 12 Co. *Rep.* 45, 77 ER 1325.   [136] Coke, 'De Iure', f. 30v.

[137] Coke, 'De Iure', ff. 30v, 40r; *Fuller's Case*, 12 Co. *Rep.* 45, 77 ER 1325.

[138] Ridley, *A View*, p. 134.

[139] *Praemunire*, 12 Co. *Rep.* 37, 77 ER 1319–20.

law authority over the ecclesiastical courts, which were inferior by their distance from the king. To deny the subject the king's justice by drawing a cause to 'another examination' was to usurp upon his power. This argument, following the wording of the statutes of praemunire, explicitly accepted that the ecclesiastical courts were still somehow 'foreign'. This idea was not Coke's alone.[140] Influenced by their histories of resistance to clerical encroachment, Coke and other common lawyers responded by asserting the inferiority of the Church courts and the sufferance of their legal power. The pre-eminence of the common law was clearly asserted in *Murrey* v. *Anonymous* (1614) by Croke JKB: 'If [the spiritual court] will encroach upon the jurisdiction of other Courts, and so will by this draw the matter, *ad aliud examen*; we are here to correct this, for that this Court here corrects all errors, and proceedings, in other Inferior Courts.'[141]

This pre-eminence was based not on separating the common law from royal power, but by aligning them together. Temporal and ecclesiastical history illustrated this relationship and proved that the common law was instrumental in protecting against the unlawful exercise of legal authority. When Sir Francis Ashley in his reading on Magna Carta (1616) referred to the writ of prohibition, he explained its use was 'to restryne the swelling and exorbitant power of the Ecclesiastiques or of any other jurisdiction which by way of encroachment seekes to impeach the vigor of our municipall Law'.[142] Supported by histories shaped by the contexts of reform and confessional strife, Coke would move to reform his own jurisdiction, and those of the Chancery and the High Commission. While history had demonstrated the vitality and necessity of the common law, the next chapter will demonstrate that it was the law's reason that made it so authoritative.

---

[140] Thomas Smith, *De Republica Anglorum*, p. 117.
[141] *Murrey* v. *Anonymous*, 2 Bulstrode 206, 80 ER 1071.
[142] BL Harley MS 4841, f. 4r.

5

Reason and reform

Although some have concluded that Coke's jurisprudence was limited and his writings ultimately case based and atomistic, Knafla's description of Coke's thinking about the common law is more apt: 'a proper attention to method and reason could reveal the richness and relevancy of this ancient institution'.[1] That richness had been clouded, in Coke's view, by the ignorance of its practitioners and the tinkerings of legislators. His response was to identify insistently the foundation of the common law as 'the irremovable rock of reason'.[2] This connection was both a means of responding to criticisms of the common law's uncertainty, since that uncertainty emerged from an erroneous understanding of the workings of the law, and a justification for the common law's authority over other jurisdictions.[3] But Coke's claims, this chapter argues, were not made superficially: he was conscious of the difficulty of interpreting the law. This awareness led him to take up the central problem of recovering the law's reason through method and logic. In so doing, Coke confronted the problem of legal interpretation – of reasoning from the memory of the common law. Surprisingly, this approach, which grappled with the challenge of knowing the law, also explained why the common law was superior to other forms of law. Through these means Coke tapped into an old theme in common law thought – the law as reason – and developed it to address the contemporary perception of the law's uncertainty. The application of this line of thinking also shaped the jurisdiction's relationship with other forms of law, and this chapter considers how the judges used their ideas of 'reason' to control customary practices. In developing his claims, Coke's jurisprudence was in concert with others in his own

---

[1] Knafla, *Law and Politics*, p. 107; Boyer, *Sir Edward Coke*, pp. 58–9; Tubbs, *Common Law Mind*, p. 151.

[2] Coke, 'Reading on Fines', pp. 224–5.

[3] Burgess, *Ancient Constitution*, p. 120; Tubbs, *Common Law Mind*, pp. 173, 175; Allen Boyer, '"Understanding, Authority, And Will": Sir Edward Coke and the Elizabethan Origins of Judicial Review', *Boston College Law Review*, 39 (1997–8), 42–93.

profession and even continental jurists who were addressing many of the same practical problems. In these ways – as a guide to practice, an answer to criticism and as a means of restructuring the legal system around the common law – Coke's developing jurisprudence engaged with the central problems of reform.

Coke's *Reports* and his *Institutes* were the principal instruments of this reform, demonstrating the practice of his jurisprudential ideas rather than setting forth a comprehensive theory. Superficially they were statements of the law as Coke understood it, an understanding that was criticized in his day and since for the manner in which his arguments spilled over their pages. Richard Helgerson has influentially argued that in these texts Coke was 'writing the law' or recording its oral and customary traditions into a more respectable form. The *Institutes,* for example, responded to criticism from civilians about the common law's lack of systematization. Daniel Coquillette has suggested in this vein that Cowell's *Institutes* 'spurred Coke forward' to write his own work of the same name to follow in the civilian genre.[4] Lurking behind Coke's project of inscription was, of course, the need to confront expansive royal claims. Helgerson explained that, 'Only the sense of a severe menace directed at the common law, a menace associated with both the civil law and the monarch, could explain the production of a book like this.'[5]

The timing of Coke's *Institutes,* appearing twenty-three years after Cowell, suggests a more indirect relationship. Their connection can be seen from a wider perspective as part of a growth in introductory texts to the common law at the beginning of the seventeenth century.[6] The antecedent was an anonymous *Institutions* frequently printed from 1538 and offering a very basic introduction to the English law of real property.[7] These texts educated students, while often reflecting on abstract jurisprudential problems, such as the nature of law and the causes of its force and moral sanction. Prior to the publication of Coke's *First Institutes,* Thomas Powell's *The Attourney's Academy* (1623) had appeared, and soon similar writings by Henry Finch, John Dodderidge and William Noy were printed posthumously.[8] Few treatises had taken up these theoretical questions in

---

[4] Coquillette, 'English Civilian Writers', 76.

[5] Richard Helgerson, *Forms of Nationhood: The Elizabethan Writing of England* (Chicago, 1992), p. 103. Garnett, 'The Prefaces to Sir Edward Coke's Reports', 255.

[6] Baker identifies a number of manuscript introductions to practice in the central courts for the later sixteenth century in 'English Law Books and Legal Publishing', p. 477n.23.

[7] Ascribed to Richard Taverner, *Institutions in the Lawes of Englande* (London, 1538), STC 9290.

[8] Powell, *The Attourney's Academy*; Henry Finch, *Law, or, a Discourse Thereof* (London, 1627), STC 10871; John Dodderidge, *The Lawyer's Light* (London, 1629), STC 6983, and

a sustained form in the common law tradition, and so it is perhaps notable that *Bracton* was reprinted in 1569.[9] In casting about for intellectual resources the common lawyers, including Coke, relied on classical sources for the basis of much of their thinking about the law. The preface of the *Institutions*, for example, was almost entirely drawn from the Roman law, and the revised preface only made the connection more explicit.[10] This borrowing suggests that the common law remained indebted to classical learning, especially through *Bracton* and its reliance on Azo.[11] Coke's notes, for example, reveal his reading of Aristotle and the *Metaphysics*, whose emphasis on inductive reasoning can be discerned in his method.[12]

Continental jurists and common lawyers drew from similar jurisprudential resources as they confronted a diversity of legal forms, including custom and the learned law, and sought to integrate them within the developing nation-state. European writers used comparative analyses to probe the similarities among custom, the learned law and different municipal laws. They argued for an underlying rationality that was taken to sanction all good law. In this way it was possible to conceive that though local customs might diverge from central law, their shared affinity to the law of reason bound them together and revealed an underlying, universal order.[13] In England J. W. Tubbs has argued that common lawyers similarly

corrected as *The English Lawyer* (London, 1631), STC 6981; William Noy, *A Treatise of the Principall Grounds and Maximes of the Lawes of this Kingdome* (London, 1641), Wing 1451 and his *The Compleat Lawyer* (London, 1651), Wing N1442. The *Institutes* were, of course, not the easiest reading for the student whatever Coke's intention; see Baker, 'English Law Books and Legal Publishing', p. 502.

[9] Tubbs, *Common Law Mind*, p. 115. The small number of 'treatises or monographs' in the medieval law is noted by J. H. Baker, 'The Books of the Common Law', in Lotte Hellinga and J. B. Trapp (eds.), *The Cambridge History of the Book in Britain* (Cambridge, 2008), vol. III, pp. 411–32, at p. 412.

[10] Including references to *The Digest of Justinian*, trans. Alan Watson (Philadelphia, 1998) 1.1.1, 1.1.10 and *The Institutes of Justinian*, trans. Thomas Sandars (London, 1922), 1.1.1. *Institutions in the Lawes of England* (London, 1538), STC 9290 sig. Aii. Later editions draw on *Digest* 1.3.17, 1.3.2. *Institutions, or Principall Groundes of the Lawes, [and] Statut[es] of Engla[n]de* (London, 1543), STC 9292, ff. 2r–3r.

[11] There has been debate over the influence of the civil law on English law, most notably in Ibbetson, *Common Law and 'Ius Commune'*, and H. S. Pawlisch, 'Sir John Davies, the Ancient Constitution and Civil Law', *Historical Journal*, 23 (1980), 689–702. See also Luigi Moccia, 'English Law Attitudes to the "Civil Law"', *Journal of Legal History*, 2 (1981), 157–68; Knafla, 'Britain's Solomon', p. 243.

[12] BL Harley MS 6687A, f. 7r–7v. See also his entry of rules from the civil law, BL Harley MS 6687D, f. 218v.

[13] *Digest* 1.1.9. Peter Stein, *Roman Law in European History* (New York, 1999), pp. 79–85, 94–6; Manlio Bellomo, *The Common Legal Past of Europe 1000–1800*, trans. Lydia Cochrane (Washington, DC, 1995), p. 222. This interest in reconciliation was shared by

emphasized the affinity of their law with reason.[14] In doing so, common lawyers made a related assertion: that the common law was a science subject to methodical analysis through reasoning. This stress on the common law's rationality served as a means to counter criticisms that it was largely customary and therefore lacked sophistication. Instead, as Coke claimed, it was a law 'apt and profitable for the honourable, peaceable, and prosperous government of this kingdom'.[15] But the claim was also more far-reaching. Coke and his judicial colleagues asserted the superior rationality of the common law to support their review of inferior jurisdictions. They appealed not only to the common law's reason, but their own professional capacity for reasoning to apply this wisdom properly. These contentions were especially applicable to the supervision of the hinterland of courts and legal authorities that are often lost to historical view: municipalities, local customs and official power that individuals were most likely to encounter in their daily lives. Where legal power was deemed to be used unreasonably, the common law would protect the rights of the subject and void or remedy that usage. Amidst the diversity of law, the common law would ensure rationality – or at least the judges' idea of it.

This emphasis on reason during Coke's time exploited a long-standing assumption that had been used to counter charges of uncertainty by the common lawyers. When Sir Roger Hillary JCP was challenged by a suitor and observed that the law was the will of the judges in 1345, Sir John de Stonor CJCP corrected him, 'No, law is what is right ["resoun"]'.[16] Similarly, in the parliament of 1610, Thomas Hedley had echoed Stonor's words when he described the reasonableness of the law in response to those who had criticized the law as 'nothing else but what the judges will'. The common

civilians in England; see Richard Terrill, 'The Application of the Comparative Method by English Civilians: The Case of William Fulbecke and Thomas Ridley', *The Journal of Legal History*, 2 (1981), 169–85; Coquillette, 'English Civilian Writers', 32–3. For specific examples, see Levack, *The Civil Lawyers*, pp. 135–40; Coquillette, 'English Civilian Writers', 66, 75; Thomas Smith, *The Commonwealth of England* (London, 1589) STC 22859, p. 147; Lodowick Lloyd, *A Briefe Conference of Divers Lawes* (London, 1602), STC 16616; John Hayward, *An Answer to the First Part of a Certaine Conference* (London, 1603), STC 12988, A3v–A4; Cowell, *The Interpreter*, 'To the Reader'.

[14] Tubbs, 'Custom, Time and Reason', 382–4; *Common Law Mind*, pp. 110–195; Burgess, *Ancient Constitution*, p. 46; Terrill, 'The Application of the Comparative Method', 176. Cf. Pocock, *Ancient Constitution*, p. 37; W. J. Bouwsma, 'Lawyers in Early Modern Culture', *American Historical Review*, 78 (1973), 303–27, at 321; C. P. Rodgers, 'Humanism, History and the Common Law', *The Journal of Legal History*, 6 (1985), 129.

[15] 8 Co. *Rep.*, p. xviii.

[16] YB Hil. 19 Edward III, pl. 3, ff. RS 378; YB Hil. 35 Henry VI, pl. 17, ff. 52a–53b (Fortescue's CJKB discussion of 'common reason' and the law).

lawyers of Coke's time were increasingly pointed in this association. While the common law might be defined as the 'custome of the Realme', it differed from local custom partly by its 'common use' throughout the kingdom, and partly owing to the very substance of the law itself.[17] As Hedley observed: custom, unlike the common law, was not reducible through formal study, since it 'admits small discourse of art or wit'.[18] The common law was distinguished as a superior reflection of reason, for it was 'nothing els but common reason: but what reason? Not that which everie one doth frame unto himselfe: but refined reason'.[19] Only decades earlier St German had observed that reason was merely one ground of law, but Coke and other common lawyers increasingly understood reason as the very essence of the common law.[20]

For these writers, usage and argument had distilled and proven the law's reason.[21] As Hedley had argued, no part of the law that failed to 'abide the touchstone of reason and trial of time' would endure. Moreover, this reason was not an abstraction. Rational laws, as Fortescue had explained, were subject to inductive analysis and reducible to their underlying universals, such as maxims.[22] Methodical study could reveal these principles and axioms, reducing the seeming complexity of the common law to those 'primitive maxim[s]' that were indisputable.[23] Sir Richard Morgan SL explained in 1550 that: 'maxims are the foundations of the law, and the conclusions of reason, and therefore they ought not to be impugned, but always to be admitted'.[24] Coke and his contemporaries frequently referred to these maxims as principles that underlay the common law, as Tubbs

---

[17] *Wrotesley* v. *Adams* (1560), 1 Plowden 195, 75 ER 299, drawing on *Bracton*, vol. II, p. 19; *Bracton* was in turn probably echoing *Institutes* 1.2.9; *Reniger* v. *Fogossa* (1550), 1 Plowden 1, 75 ER 1; Co. *Litt.*, f. 110b, and compare HLS MS 114, f. 69v; Co. *Litt.*, f. 10b, where 'Communis lex Angliae' and 'Consuetudines' are defined separately. Some, such as Arthur Turnour, also thought the common law included statutes; HLS MS 132, f. 139r. See also Dodderidge, *The English Lawyer*, p. 101; Finch, *Law*, p. 77; Bodl. Carte MS 105, f. 27v.

[18] *PP 1610*, vol. II, p. 176.

[19] Finch, *Law*, p. 75; Bodl. MS Rawlinson B 410 f. 1r; Noy, *A Treatise*, p. 20; W. Lambarde, 'Ephemeris', in *William Lambarde and Local Government*, ed. Conyers Read (Ithaca, NY, 1962), p. 104; YB Mich. 19 Henry VI, pl. 10, ff. 4b–5b.

[20] Christopher St German, *Saint German's Doctor and Student*, eds. T. F. T. Plucknett and J. L. Barton (London, 1974), pp. 27, 31–9; *Colthirst* v. *Bejushin*, 1 Plowden 27, 75 ER 44.

[21] Noy, *A Treatise*, p. 1. Pocock, *Ancient Constitution*, p. 35.

[22] John Fortescue, *De Laudibus Legum Anglie*, ed. S. B. Chrimes (Cambridge, 1942), pp. 9, 21; borrowed from the *Digest*, 1.1.1. Tubbs, *Common Law Mind*, pp. 173–5.

[23] *PP 1610*, vol. II, pp. 173, 176, 178.

[24] *Colthirst* v. *Bejushin*, 1 Plowden 27, 33, 75 ER 44, 54; Tubbs, *Common Law Mind*, p. 177; BL Harley MS 5265, f. 179v.

has demonstrated.[25] But Coke recognized that this reason was not a transparent resource to be grasped with ease by the practitioner. This recognition of the problem of interpretation or reasoning stamps the *Reports* and *Institutes* as models of right reading. The glossing of *Coke on Littleton* most explicitly demonstrates this lesson, but the *Reports* also provided assertive statements of the rules and principles to guide the interpretation of the law. The student is cajoled and warned to read properly and methodically in order to engage with and understand the reason of the law contained within its written memory.

The emphasis on method and reason functioned to organize the law's complex culture of information that had contributed to its uncertainty. At the beginning of the sixteenth century, a lawyer's library was small and its owner often dependent upon access to circulating manuscripts.[26] By the end, an increasing volume of legal information had appeared in the form of published analyses, case reports, legal records and treatises on the law. During this period, Ibbetson has argued that the common law moved from a predominantly oral to a written culture.[27] From commonplace books to the increasing use of extensive citations in oral argument and written texts, the common lawyers found new ways to manage and take advantage of the increasing flow of information.[28] The quick adoption of the printed case reports of Edmund Plowden, Dyer and Coke speaks both to their demand after the ending of the Year Books in 1535 and to the convenience offered by the printed medium.[29] But this flow also produced problems: Coke complained about the 'farrago of citations' that muddied pleading.[30]

---

[25] Tubbs, 'Custom, Reason and Time', 400–1.

[26] W. O. Prest, *The Inns of Court under Elizabeth I and the early Stuarts, 1590–1640* (London, 1972), pp. 158–67; E. W. Ives, 'A Lawyer's Library in 1500', *Law Quarterly Review*, 85 (1969), 104–16; Tubbs, *Common Law Mind*, p. 23; Baker, 'The Books of the Common Law', pp. 413–17.

[27] Ibbetson, *Common Law and 'Ius Commune'*, p. 21.

[28] Baker, *OHLE*, vol. VI, pp. 501–6; *pace* Hill, *Intellectual Origins*, p. 232.

[29] Though, as Baker has argued, manuscript case reporting continued after the printers decided not to continue the Year Books after 1535; Baker, 'The Books of the Common Law', pp. 418, 431–2.

[30] *Preface to the Tenth Reports*, p. 336. Richard Ross, 'The Memorial Culture of Early Modern English Lawyers: Memory as Keyword, Shelter, and Identity, 1560–1640', *Yale Law School Journal of Law and the Humanities*, 10 (1998), 229–326, at 268, 296. Ross has also argued that print contributed to increasingly vocal criticisms of the law; Ross, 'The Commoning of the Common Law', 364. The growth of folio citations is discussed by Baker, 'The Books of the Common Law', pp. 412–13, 431.

These printed texts were properly read in combination with the rich oral culture of the common law. Paradoxically, as Richard Ross has argued, the growth of print culture highlighted the importance of orality and memory, creating a 'memorial culture' within the profession.[31] Memory was important as 'an individual storehouse of short to medium-term, highly particular legal authorities'.[32] Unrecorded in the lawbooks, yet informing their reading, was a vast mnemonic culture, exchanged in the Inns, moots and chambers, without which the law itself was incomplete.[33] Coke, for example, praised the learned argument and discussion that led to common law decisions.[34] On the other hand, written texts were 'dead letters', needing to be vivified by the application of orality and memory.

Contemporaries as well as subsequent writers have focused on the distinction between the 'unwritten' common law and the 'written' civil law.[35] At times Coke and his contemporaries blurred that distinction. Coke observed that much of the common law was written, and he described the books where it might be found.[36] Sir Matthew Hale wrote that although he termed the common law an unwritten law, this did not mean that the laws were 'only Oral … For all those Laws have their several Monuments in Writing'.[37] Together both oral and printed sources comprised the memory of the common law's learning, and so reference might be made to how a report 'remembered' a particular case.[38] The emphasis on the mixed character of the common law's legal memory responded to the criticism that the law was uncertain or unsophisticated because it was unwritten and customary. The common law's memorialization in both written and oral sources was instead represented as a source of flexibility. Novel misdeeds would elude the drafters of written laws who could not be expected to anticipate every malfeasance that might arise. Davies, for example, implied that the glosses of the civilians were a result of the inability of the fixed text of the *Corpus* to anticipate the evolving wrongs that society faced. These glosses made written laws (both civil and canon)

---

[31] Ross, 'Memorial Culture', 320.   [32] *Ibid.*, 271.

[33] *Ibid.*, 279.   [34] 9 Co. *Rep.*, p. xxxviii.

[35] John Cowell, *The Institutes of the Lawes of England Digested into the Method of the Civill or Imperiall Institutions* (London, 1651), Wing C6641, p. 4; Ross, 'Memorial Culture', 309–11; BL Harley MS 6687A, f. 7r.

[36] 10 Co. *Rep.*, pp. xxv–xxxv.

[37] Hale, *History of the Common Law*, p. 16. Hale distinguished between writing that was a memorial from the command of a legislator.

[38] *Waller* v. *Hanger* (1615), 3 Bulstrode 14, 81 ER 12.

'perplexed and confounded' and 'a sea full of waves'.[39] The common law, on the other hand, would discover a remedy from the breadth of its written and unwritten memory.

But the mixed character of the common law's memory required attention to the problem of interpretation: how to remember the law and reason to a decision. This was a process fraught with challenges. Superficially it might seem that written sources were privileged in reconstructing the law. The sanctity of records, for example, was necessary to preserve certainty at the law, 'for if the judicial matters of record should be drawn in question ... controversies will be infinite'.[40] In 1595, with the common law judges present in the Star Chamber, it was declared that more credence was extended to writing than to words.[41] Plowden declared that writing was more accurate than individual memory and that his reason for setting his cases in print was to avoid the hazards of 'slypper[y] memorye, which often deceiveth his master'.[42] In his manuscript account of *Shelley's Case*, Coke similarly suggested the preference for written over oral memory: 'Nothing is or can be so fixed in mind, or fastened in memory, but in short time is or may be loosened out of the one, and by little and little quite lost out of the other. It is therefore necessary that memorable things should be committed to writing.'[43]

Oral memory was 'written onely in the memory of man', and according to Coke 'unfaithful and slippery'.[44] Custom, in particular, was a major reservoir of such memory and for legal purposes it ordinarily resided in the jury, which was asked to remember the custom. The remembrance of the jury proved that the custom had run 'from time whereof memory of man is not to the contrary', and this claim to immemoriality, 'that no man then alive hath heard any proof of the contrary', was essential for a valid custom and generated a proof-claim.[45] But written memory might hold

---

[39] Davies, *Le Primer Report*, sig. *4v; a problem anticipated in *Digest*, Confirmation, 18 and 1.3.38.

[40] *The Case of Conspiracy*, 12 Co. *Rep.* 25, 77 ER 1306.

[41] *Attorney-General* v. *Harward* (1595–6), Hawarde, *Les Reportes*, pp. 28–9 and again on pp. 29–30; similarly, see *The Countess of Rutland's Case* (1604), 5 Co. *Rep.* 26b, 77 ER 90.

[42] Edmund Plowden, *Les Commentaries ou Reportes de Edmunde Plowden* (London, 1578), STC 20041, 'The Prologe', [n.f.].

[43] 1 Co. *Rep.*, p. xxv.

[44] Davies, *Le Primer Report*, sig. *2r. 7; Co. *Rep.*, p. iii; Co. *Litt.*, f. 115a.

[45] Littleton, *Tenures*, p. 66; Co. *Litt.*, ff. 113–15b; Greenberg, *The Radical Face of the Ancient Constitution*, pp. 21–6; P. A. Brand, '"Time Out of Mind": The Knowledge and Use of Eleventh- and Twelfth-Century Past in Thirteenth-Century Litigation', *Anglo-Norman Studies*, 16 (1994), 37–54; Simpson, *Land Law*, pp. 109–10; Baker, *IELH*, p. 145.

superior force against orally remembered custom, since 'regularly a man cannot prescribe or alledge a custome against a statute, because that is matter of record, and is the highest proofe and matter of record in law'.[46]

But the use of oral memory was crucial to the understanding of the law. Alongside customary memory in the minds of laymen was the personal memory of the practitioner that he called upon in the performance of his occupation. A reliable memory was necessary to the law student, and they might consult manuals on memory and mnemonics.[47] Discussions of memory were also included in professional treatises. John Dodderidge devoted a large portion of his introductory text on the common law to memory and memory exercises in which the young lawyer could engage. Memory, he wrote, was 'the store-house of all our understanding ... as Aristotle saith, it is the guide of our experience, and the ground-worke of all our wisedome'.[48] The practitioner's memory involved much more than the act of recollection: understanding or professional discernment was also thought to be a function of memory. Dodderidge described memory as a 'double faculty' and explained that the 'intellective' component 'followeth the use of reason and therefore is found in no other Creature then Man, which is indued with the faculty of reason'.[49] Coke elaborated this connection between memory and reason, arguing that a testator:

> was not of sane and perfect memory ... for by law it is not sufficient that the testator be of memory when he makes his will, to answer familiar and usual questions, but he ought to have a disposing memory, so that he is able to make a disposition of his lands with understanding and reason; and that is such a memory which the law calls sane and perfect memory.[50]

The idea of a 'disposing memory' encapsulated the belief that memory was not only recollection, but also involved understanding and reasoning – encompassing our idea of the 'mind'. The skilled practitioner was expected to come to even the most authoritative case report with judgment, weighing its logic and evidence in a process of reasoning.[51] But the practitioner's memory was also imperfect, and Coke warned of 'the

---

[46] Co. Litt., f. 115a.
[47] John Willis, Mnemonica (London, 1618), STC 25748; Ravennus Petrus, The Art of Memory, that Otherwyse is Called the Phenix (London, 1545), STC 24112; Guglielmo Gratarolo, The Castel of Memorie (London, 1562), STC 12191.
[48] Dodderidge, English Lawyer, pp. 12–13.   [49] Ibid., p. 15.
[50] Marquess of Winchester's Case (1599), 6 Co. Rep. 23b, 77 ER 288.
[51] John Manningham, The Diary of Sir John Manningham of the Middle Temple, 1602–1603, ed. Robert Sorlien (Hanover, NH, 1976), p. 141.

sliding and slippery memory of men'.[52] Coke himself, while attempting
to remember the details of a case from the time of Dyer, confessed to the
limitation of his own memory: 'I am well assured that the case was ruled
as I have said.'[53]

In fact, both oral and written memory were fraught with the difficulties
associated with interpretation and remembrance. Coke warned his readers
not to omit the usual ceremonies and acts in conveyances for 'they imprint
a better remembrance of the thing which is done, because they are subject
to sight, than words alone, which are only heard, and which easily and
usually slip out of memory'.[54] Oral and written memory might supplement
each other to accommodate their deficiencies, as Davies observed more
generally: 'For indeede those Reports are but Comments or interpretations uppon the Text of the Common lawe: which Text was never originally written, but hath ever bin preserved in the memory of men.'[55] In fact,
written records were also problematic as Coke observed in his discussion
of poor reporting: 'for I have often observed, that for want of a true and
certain Report, the case that hath been adjudged standing upon the rack
of many running Reports ... hath been so diversely drawn out, as many
times the true parts of the Case have been disordered'.[56] Reporting the law
involved more than remembering past deeds or judgments.[57] Coke wrote
that reporting added a gloss of understanding; it was 'the most perspicu-
ous course of teaching the right rule and reason of the law'.[58] An authoritative report instructed the Reader 'only in the right rule and reason of
the case in question'.[59] Excavating deeper than the particulars of the case
to the order and rule that the details represented, the report 'openeth the
understanding of the reader and hearer'.[60] At stake in this process was the
certainty of the law itself. Coke claimed that the 'greatest questions' arose
upon the practice of the law, not upon its basic rules.[61] His own task as a
reporter was to identify those rules so that 'all the Judges and Justices ...
might, as it were with one mouth in all men's cases, pronounce one and the
same sentence'.[62]

---

[52] *Dowman's Case* (1586), 9 Co. *Rep.* 9a, 77 ER 745; see similar language in *Countess of Rutland's Case*, 5 Co. *Rep.* 26b, 77 ER 90.

[53] *Bristow and Bristowe's Case* (1610), Godbolt 161, 78 ER 98.

[54] *Thoroughgood's Case* (1612), 9 Co. *Rep.* 138a, 77 ER 928.

[55] Davies, *Le Primer Report*, sig. *1v–2r.

[56] 1 Co. *Rep.*, pp. xxvi–xxvii.   [57] 7 Co. *Rep.*, p. iv.

[58] 6 Co. *Rep.*, p. xvii; repeated elsewhere as 'the right reason of the rule (the beauty of the law) ...', 9 Co. *Rep.*, p. xxxviii.

[59] 7 Co. *Rep.*, p. iv.   [60] 9 Co. *Rep.*, pp. xxxvii–xxxviii.

[61] 2 Co. *Rep.*, p. ix.   [62] 3 Co. *Rep.*, pp. iii–iv.

This purpose introduced the central epistemological problem, not only for the reader, but also for the reporter himself, who dutifully sought to uncoil the reason of the case. The challenge was semiotic, as Anderson CJCP once bluntly remarked: 'words are as we shall construe them'.[63] Both the reporter and the reader might err in their interpretation and misconstrue the reasoning of the case. Coke was well aware of this problem and for that reason recognized the limitations of writing. When discussing the Catholic books in the *Seventh Part of the Reports*, Coke makes an observation to bring this problem of reading to light: 'These Books have glorious and goodly titles, which promise directions for the conscience, and remedies for the soul. But there is *mors in olla*:[64] They are like to apothecaries' boxes, *quorum tituli pollicentur remedia, sed pixides ipsae venena continent*, whose titles promise remedies, but the boxes themselves contain poison.'[65]

The poisoned jar, *mors in olla*, was an image drawn from the story of Elisha's ministry.[66] A servant was gathering food for dinner and returned with herbs and a 'wild vine' that was placed into the pot. Elisha's followers were unable to eat since 'there is death in the pot'. Elisha then performed a miracle, transforming the food so that it was harmless. Catholic writings similarly attracted men seeking 'directions for the Conscience and remedies for the Soul'. Yet Coke punned by likening them to 'Pharmacopolarum vasculis'. On the surface Coke was referring to the likelihood of an apothecary's 'medicine' killing someone instead of helping them.[67] But in Latin the word was a Greek adoption related to *pharmakon*, which could mean either a remedy or a poison, something that might give life or kill.[68] Writing, if not interpreted carefully, could lead the reader into error.

Even though the *Seventh Part* had begun by urging the necessity of recording *Calvin's Case* to calm anxieties, it continued from the discussion

---

[63] *Anonymous* (1583), Godbolt 17, 78 ER 11.

[64] 'Death in a jar'.

[65] 7 Co. *Rep.*, p. vi. Coke made the same analogy between writing and apothecaries' boxes in a different context in *Edwards* v. *Woolten* (1607), BL Additional MS 25215, f. 39v.

[66] 2 Kings 4:44.

[67] See, for example, *Gore's Case* (1611), 9 Co. *Rep.* 81a, 77 ER 853.

[68] Coke may have been able to read Greek – he owned several works in Greek, including Aristotle (nos. 729, 730 in Hassall), and his early schooling in Norwich probably included Greek. There is also a line of Greek in his notebooks at Harley MS 6687 D, f. 207r; Boyer, *Sir Edward Coke*, pp. 12–16. Plato used this same pun in the *Phaedrus*, a dialogue that discussed oral and written memory, and debated which provided greater access to knowledge (logos); Jacques Derrida, *Dissemination*, trans. Barbara Johnson (Chicago, IL, 1981), pp. 63–171. Coke owned several works by Aristotle, including the *Politics*,

of the poisoned jar to another account of dangerous writing.[69] Coke denied the accuracy of a pamphlet that purported to be a record of what he had said in his charge at the assizes in Norwich on 4 August 1606.[70] Coke contrasted his oral statements with its misrecording by Robert Prickett in writing, and again writing appeared not only as an imperfect record but a dangerous one, since its errors were detectable only by readers 'discreet and indifferent'.

Writing implicated the recorder and reader in a series of problems of meaning. Throughout the process of transmission from hearing to recording to the reader's interpretation, the reason of the law could be distorted. Those who had been present in court accused even Coke of misrecording cases.[71] His response revealed his thinking about the character of both writing and orality:

> And let not those that heard the arguments themselves uttered *viva voce* ... fear that when they shall read them privately in a dead letter, it will want much of the former grace: for though I confess that *habet nescio quam energiam viva vox*,[72] yet when they shall read the effect of all that was spoken ... it will ease them of much labour, and conduce much to the settling of their judgment.[73]

Uttered words were living, in contrast to the 'dead letter'. Though their reproduction into writing was an act that failed to reproduce their full force, it might still communicate their 'effect'. Such a translation was a hermeneutic act fraught with many possibilities for error, as Coke's detractors had observed. Plowden, too, noted the dangers associated with writing by those who were ignorant, who did not possess the appropriate knowledge to transcribe the law accurately. He described how he had lent out his case books to his friends whose clerks had copied them. These copies had come into the hands of printers, but 'because the cases were written by Clearks and other ignorant person, that perfectly did not understande the matter, the copies were very corrupt'.[74] Writing, despite

---

Ethics and *Metaphysics*, but there is no mention of the *Phaedrus*. Mention of the work is made in Dodderidge, *Lawyers Light*, p. 106. For another pun made by Coke, see Boyer, '"Understanding, Authority" and Will', 60.

[69] 7 Co. *Rep.*, pp. vii–ix.

[70] 7 Co. *Rep.*, pp. viii–ix. Robert Prickett, *The Lord Coke His Speech and Charge with a Discouerie of the Abuses and Corruption of Officers* (London, 1607), STC 5491.

[71] Egerton, 'The Lord Chancellor Egertons Observacions upon Ye Lord Cookes Reportes', in Knafla, *Law and Politics*, pp. 297–318. More exhaustive criticisms came from William Prynne, *Brief Animadversions, passim.*

[72] 'I do not know what force the living voice has.'   [73] 10 Co. *Rep.*, p. xxiii.

[74] Plowden, *Les Commentaries*, 'The Prologe', [n.f.].

its fixing of words and memory, might still be 'death in a jar', misleading through the errors of reporters, printers or readers. Writing the law was not enough, therefore, to allay criticisms of an unwritten tradition that might simply be 'what the judges will'.[75] A law based purely on the authority of writing was perilous, for writing was dead and its silent letters open to interpretation.[76]

Law could not speak for itself – it had to be spoken for, and that speaking animated it. The idea of the speaking law was Hellenistic in origin, and it influenced common law jurisprudence through the classical sources, Cicero in particular.[77] In his manuscript notes on *De Legibus*, Coke noted Cicero's discussion of *lex loquens*.[78] The identity of the speaking law changed depending on context and author.[79] The history of the law suggested that the speaker of the law had in fact changed over time. Society had begun when one man had authority to quell disagreements and protect his people, and 'so long as they found this at his hand, they tooke for Law whatsoever hee pronounced, and they obeyed (as an Oracle) whatsoever was commanded by him'.[80] The speaking of the law had an oracular quality, a mystical moment when transcendent reason was applied to the muddy disagreements of humans. It was the exercise of reason through interpretation, as Davies described, 'it must bee a worke of singular Iudgement, to apply the groundes and rules of the lawe which are fixt and certeine, to all humaine acts and accidents which are in perpetuall motion and mutation'.[81]

---

[75] St German, *Doctor and Student*, p. 15.

[76] The dead law was a commonplace; see a sermon by William Est, *Two Sermons Preached before the Judges and Juries at Assize* (London, 1614), STC 10539, p. 2; Davies, *Le Primer Report*, sig. *4v.

[77] Cicero, *De Legibus*, trans. Clinton Keyes (London, 1970), 3.1.2; Andrew Dyck, *A Commentary on Cicero De Legibus* (Ann Arbor, MI, 2004), pp. 432–3. For discussions of *lex loquens* see Baker, *OHLE*, vol. VI, p. 119; E. Kantorowicz, 'Kingship under the Impact of Scientific Jurisprudence', in M. Clagett, Gaines Post and R. Reynolds (eds.), *Twelfth-Century Europe and the Foundations of Modern Society* (Madison, NJ, 1966), pp. 89–111, at p. 104; Judson, *Crisis of the Constitution*, pp. 98, 137; Lester Born, 'Animate Law in the Republic and the Laws of Cicero', *Transactions of the American Philological Society*, 64 (1933), 128–37.

[78] BL Harley MS 6687A, f. 7v.

[79] Oxford University, Queen's College MS 215, f. 21r. See also, George Buchanan, *A Dialogue on the Law of Kingship among the Scots* (Aldershot, 2004), p. 20 (as a means of restraining kings); *CSPD, James I, 1611–18*, p. 381; Francis Hargrave (ed.), *Collectanea Juridica* (London, 1791), vol. II, p. 8; Co. *Litt.*, f. 130a; and also BL Harley MS 6899, f. 78v; *Marmyon* v. *Baldwyn* (1527); J. H. Baker (ed.), *Reports of Cases from the Time of King Henry VIII* (London, 2003), p. 69.

[80] Lambarde, *Archeion*, p. 10; BL Cotton MS Vespasian C XIV, vol. II, f. 52r.

[81] Davies, *Le Primer Report*, sig. *4v.

Over time as society grew this authority had moved from the individual ruler. Sir John Port recorded in his notebook, possibly from a reading by Richard Littleton in 1493, that the king was at first the sole judge who (having found himself incapable of hearing the numerous causes before him) delegated this responsibility to judges and inferior officers.[82] Alongside the practical problem of the press of suitors, speaking the law held another challenge. As Coke liked to observe, 'no man is wiser than the law'. The law needed to be spoken properly and so it needed to be discovered and learned. William Est summarized this process as follows: 'The Magistrate lendeth a mouth to the law to speake and the law teacheth him a rule to speak aright.'[83] The oracular moment of speaking the law in a command or decision was not a transparent uttering of the law, but a recovery of the law and its rules from the collective achievement of legal memory.

This unlocking of reason from the 'hieroglyphs' of writing required discipline, training and often discussion: 'through frequent argument and exchange the hidden truth is uncovered, since multiple meanings often lie under the very same words'.[84] Those who sought to understand the common law without the appropriate training or guidance led themselves into error – or so Coke charged the civilians who criticized the common law: 'who by their sole and superficial reading of them cannot understand the depth of them'.[85] He similarly advised historians, before they commented on an aspect of the common laws, to 'confer with some learned in that profession'.[86]

Coke believed that it was the obligation of both writer and reader to follow a method, to write and read in a particular way that made plain the memory of the law in the text and so exposed the 'right reason and rule of the law'. Revealing this rule, the rule that would allow the law to be properly spoken, was one of the functions of reporting, which 'openeth the understanding of the reader and hearer'.[87] But the reader must be cautious and give proper sense to words, whose 'fair outsides of enamelled words and sentences do sometimes so bedazzle the eye of the reader's mind with their glittering shew'.[88] Coke cautioned the reader to read slowly and

---

[82] *The Notebook of Sir John Port*, p. 119; Anthony Fitzherbert, *Diversite de courtes* (London, 1535), STC 1895, sig. A2; Smith, *De Republica Anglorum*, pp. 58–64; BL Cotton MS Vespasian C XIV, vol. II, f. 52r.

[83] Est, *Two Sermons*, p. 2.

[84] 7 Co. *Rep.*, sig. A.   [85] 10 Co. *Rep.*, p. xxx.

[86] 3 Co. *Rep.*, p. xxiii.   [87] 9 Co. *Rep.*, pp. xxxvii–xxxviii.

[88] 3 Co. *Rep.*, p. xlii; 7 Co. *Rep.*, pp. ix–x.

carefully, because reading was essential to understanding: 'A cursory and tumultuary reading doth ever make a confused memory, a troubled utterance, and an incertain judgment.'[89] Coke summarized his method at the very beginning of his reports:

> reading, hearing, conference, meditation and recordation ... an orderly observation in writing is most requisite of them all; for reading without hearing is dark and irksome, and hearing without reading is slippery and uncertain, neither of them truly yield seasonable fruit without conference, nor both of them with conference, without meditation and recordation, nor all of them together without due and orderly observation.[90]

Coke's method combined speech and text to produce understanding: neither was sufficient in itself. Private study was reinforced by 'conference' with others in the profession. Not only did discussion enrich the understanding of the practitioners, but also provided for the 'great instruction and direction to the attentive and studious hearers'.[91]

The idea of artificial reason encapsulated Coke's understanding of the problem of reason and its recovery from memory. He related the functioning of artificial reason to the reason of the common law, 'which is to be understood of an artificiall perfection of reason, gotten by long study, observation, and experience, and not of every man's naturall reason ... This legall reason *est summa ratio* ... no man out of his private reason ought to be wiser than the law, which is the perfection of reason.'[92]

Coke's idea of artificial meaning has prompted much debate. Glenn Burgess explained that the law was artificial reason refined over time, though Dodderidge's use of the concept pointed to the 'reason possessed by trained lawyers'.[93] Boyer argued that artificial reason was a concept informed by the artificial logic of rhetoric, and involving the training and 'legal imagination' of lawyers, not abstract but 'law in action'.[94] Charles Gray sought a broader definition, arguing that Coke meant that the law is the 'artifice' as well as 'the natural faculty improved by cultivation'.[95] Gray and Burgess agreed that Coke 'slid[e] from one sense to the other',

[89] 6 Co. *Rep.*, p. xviii.   [90] 1 Co. *Rep.*, pp. xxvii–xxviii.
[91] 9 Co. *Rep.*, p. xxxix.   [92] Co. *Litt.*, f. 97b.
[93] Burgess, *Ancient Constitution*, p. 46, and also Sommerville, *Royalists and Patriots*, p. 89; see BL Additional MS 32092, f. 185v.
[94] Boyer, '"Understanding, Authority, and Will"', 55, 62; Tubbs, 'Custom, Time and Reason', 394.
[95] Charles Gray, 'Reason, Authority and Imagination: the Jurisprudence of Sir Edward Coke', in Perez Zagorin (ed.), *Culture and Politics From Puritanism to the Enlightenment* (Berkeley, CA, 1980), p. 31.

suggesting that both the law and the practitioner were or possessed artificial reason.[96] Similarly Tubbs has argued that Coke perceived as artificial both the reason of the practitioner and that of the law itself.[97]

Coke's concept of artificial reason responded to the frailty of memory and human reason, and the hermeneutic challenge the lawyer faced. The individual reader connected with the immensity of the law that was a memory of centuries of experience distilled into the 'perfection of reason'. These laws were greater than any single practitioner: 'by longe experience and practice of many successions of grave learnyd and wise menne have growne to perfection are grounded uppon greater and more absolute reason then the singular and private opinion of the wisest manne that liveth in the worlde ... therfor the lawe shall stand for reason'.[98] The challenge to the practitioner was to bridge the divide between the 'perfection of reason' and a human's natural reason. Coke's 'artifical perfection of reason' was the process of understanding and reasoning involving method: 'long study, observation, and experience'. Elsewhere Coke declared that cases touching the life or inheritance of subjects should 'not be decided by natural reason, but by the artificial reason and judgement of law, which law is an art that requires long study and experience before one is able to attain to the knowledge of it'.[99] 'Artificial reason' enabled the practitioner to decrypt or illuminate the common law and its reason, and to continue the process of remembering the law correctly amidst a diversity of sources.

This definition of artificial reason was a reading of Cicero's *De Legibus*: 'Law is the highest reason [*lex est ratio summa*], implanted in Nature, which commands what ought to be done and forbids the opposite. This reason, when firmly fixed and fully developed in the human mind, is Law.'[100] The highest reason was a moral imperative, and as it was 'perfected' and fixed in the mind it developed into law.[101] Law in this sense

---

[96] Gray, 'Reason, Authority and Imagination', p. 51n15; Burgess, *Ancient Constitution*, p. 243n77; John Underwood Lewis, 'Sir Edward Coke (1552–1633): His Theory of "Artificial Reason" as a Context for Modern Basic Legal Theory', *Law Quarterly Review*, 84 (1968), 330–42, at 334–5; Tubbs, *Common Law Mind*, pp. 165–6. See also D. E. C. Yale, 'Hobbes and Hale on Law, Legislation and the Soveriegn', *Cambridge Law Journal*, 31 (1972), 125–6. See also Pocock, *Ancient Constitution*, p. 35.

[97] Tubbs, 'Custom, Time and Reason', 392–3.

[98] PRO SP 12/278, f. 159r; possibly the notes for the more refined passage at Co. *Litt.*, f. 97b.

[99] *Prohibitions Del Roy*, 12 Co. Rep. 65, 77 ER 1343. My translation from the manuscripts differs from the standard printed version and relies on the text in IT Miscellaneous MS 21, f. 134r.

[100] Cicero, *De Legibus*, I.18.

[101] St German, *Doctor and Student*, p. 13.

was the apprehension in the mind of the highest reason, and its apprehension was a process of mental development. Through 'long and continual study', the practitioner acquired 'discretion'.[102] When Coke wrote that 'This legall reason est summa ratio', he modified Cicero's statement that 'lex' was the highest reason.[103] This suggests that he distinguished between legal reason and the law itself. Coke explained elsewhere that 'summa ratio' was 'law well established', or the reasonable part of the body politic.[104] 'Ratio legis' was, however, the 'soul of the law' or what animated the law.[105] In *Calvin's Case* Coke further defined 'legal reason' as the acquired skill of the practitioner: 'the legal and profound reason of such as by diligent study and long experience and observation are so learned in the laws of this realm, as out of the reason of the same they can rule the case in question'.[106] Legal reason was the apprehension of the *summa ratio* or law that study and method had developed in the mind. This distinction between the legal reason cultivated in the mind and the perfection of reason that was the law was crucial to Coke's idea of method and understanding: 'And by reasoning and debating of grave and learned men the darkness of ignorance is expelled, and by the light of legall reason the right is discerned, and thereupon judgment is given according to law, which is the perfection of reason.'[107] Artificial reason, the process of training and reasoning, guided the judges to the oracular moment, to a judgment that spoke the law, 'which is the perfection of reason'. While time had perfected the law, the artifice of the individual's study recovered and interpreted the law's reason from the collective memory and retained it there: 'This reason, when firmly fixed and fully developed in the human mind, is Law.'[108]

Reasoning led to the oracular moment when the trained understanding of the judge interrogated the memory of the law, and recovered and understood the right rule. Coke described this as a process of ecstatic union and appropriation:

---

[102] Coke, 'Treatise of Bail and Mainprize', in *Three Tracts*, p. 302.
[103] Co. *Litt.*, f. 97b.
[104] IT Petyt MS 538/51, f. 134r.
[105] *Milborn's Case* (1587), 7 Co. *Rep.* 7a, 77 ER 421.
[106] *Calvin's Case*, 7 Co. *Rep.* 20a, 77 ER 400.
[107] Co. *Litt.*, f. 232b; Tubbs, *Common Law Mind*, p. 166.
[108] Coke, citing *Bracton*, refers to 'perfected reason' in his discussion of the application of common law equity, a 'construction made by the judges'. This suggests that judicial discretion and judgment applied a perfected reason; Co. *Litt.*, f. 24b.

> for then are we said to know the law, when we apprehend the reason of the law; that is, when we bring the reason of the law so to our owne reason, that wee perfectly understand it as our owne: and then, and never before, we have such an excellent and inseperable propertie and ownership therein, as wee can neither lose it, nor any man take it from us, and will direct us (the learning of the law is so chained together) in many other cases.

Once apprehended the rule of the law would guide further study and reasoning. It would be placed fast in the mind of the practitioner, though if not properly understood, 'it is not possible for you long to retaine it in your memorie'.[109]

Through this process of understanding the practitioner's memory became part of the larger matrix of legal memory that resided in the minds of learned individuals as much as in writing.[110] By speaking the rule, the practitioner animated the law, was for that moment *lex loquens*, the law itself speaking. Coke wrote of this appropriation of the law as a strenuous labour rendered 'delightful' by experience and growing wisdom, the law 'like a deepe well, out of which each man draweth according to the strength of his understanding'.[111] Interpretation and understanding mediated between the memory of the law and the memory of the individual, the 'gladsome light, whereby the right reason of the rule (the beauty of the law) may be clearly discerned'.[112] This speaking of the law, its recovery from legal memory through interpretation, held a mystical charge. As they connected the law of reason to their natural reason in the process of understanding and adjudication, the lawyers' work had an underlay of divinity: as Coke often declared, 'summa ratio est quae pro religione facit'.[113]

The emphasis on method and hermeneutics was critical to Coke's larger reforming project: he sought to impose order through his pen by establishing that the basic rules of the common law were 'certaine and sure'. Contention over the common law, concerning the meaning of its doctrines or the clarity of its rules, could itself be traced back to ignorance. Misunderstanding or poor training caused disputes to arise with

---

[109] Co. *Litt.*, ff. 394b–395a; similarly Dodderidge's comments in BL Additional MS 32092, f. 192r.

[110] See also St German, *Dialogue*, p. 11.

[111] Co. *Litt.*, f. 71a; Dodderidge, *English Lawyer*, pp. 19–20.

[112] 9 Co. *Rep.*, p. xxxviii; for the 'light' metaphor, see also St German, *Dialogue*, p. 11.

[113] 'The highest reason is that which makes for religion.' *Case of Ecclesiastical Persons* (1601), 5 Co. *Rep.* 14b, 77 ER 70; repeated in *The Case of the University of Oxford* (1613), 10 Co. *Rep.* 55a, 77 ER 1008; *The Case of the Master and Fellows of Magdalen College* (1615), 11 Co. *Rep.* 70b, 77 ER 1241; and also *Creswick* v. *Rooksby* (1613), 2 Bulstrode 53, 80 ER 953; *Address to the Serjeants*, Popham 43, 79 ER 1161.

the common law, for example, when conveyances were made 'intricately, absurdly and repugnant[ly]'.[114] The lack of a 'certain report', in another example, had resulted in the distortion of the 'right rule' of the law. Among Coke's purposes in writing the *Reports* was to remind the profession of its own method and to discipline his fellow practitioners with rules. Later in his career he urged the student should be prepared to approach the law trained in logic and 'to use a good method in his studie'.[115]

Coke's jurisprudence was not atomistic or 'case-by-case', though neither was it an academic system.[116] His legal thinking was practical: the *Reports* were published 'for the better understanding of the true sense and reason of the Judgements and resolutions formerly reported, or for resolution of such doubts as therein remain undecided'.[117] In an age of uncertainty Coke looked to the past and sought to refound the common law on its basic rules and maxims: 'justice is ever best administered when laws be executed according to their true and genuine institution'.[118] Elsewhere he defined these maxims as, 'a sure foundation or ground of art, and a conclusion of reason … so sure and uncontrollable as that they ought not to be questioned'.[119] In his report of *Walker* v. *Harris* (1587) Coke digressed to address the importance of principles as the basis of the science of law: 'in every art and science there are *principia et postulata* … nothing can be more high and supreme than the principles themselves'.[120]

Recovering these principles involved a lifelong project of 'right reading' that was eventually exhibited in the *Institutes*. The first volume exemplified the same reading practices that Coke had honed as a student and practitioner – his earlier gloss on Littleton still survives among his notes.[121] He believed that his *Institutes* would 'open the true sense of every of [Littleton's] particular cases'.[122] When he wrote that his work would aid those 'wrestling with … difficult termes and matter', he may have recollected the challenges of his own law student days. Coke again moved his readers to bear in mind the joys of the struggle that understanding involved, wishfully writing that his *Institutes* would help students proceed 'chearfully and with delight'.[123]

---

[114] 2 Co. *Rep.*, p. ix.   [115] Co. *Litt.*, f. 235a.
[116] Boyer, "'Understanding, Authority, and Will'", 58, 61; Tubbs, 'Custom, Time and Reason', 390.
[117] 3 Co. *Rep.*, p. xxxi.   [118] 8 Co. *Rep.*, p. xxvi.
[119] Co. *Litt.*, f. 11a and also 152b.
[120] *Walker* v. *Harris*, 3 Co. *Rep.* 40b, 76 ER 726. For further references to law as a science, see *Tooker's Case* (1601), 2 Co. *Rep.* 67a, 76 ER 569.
[121] His notes are interwoven throughout BL Harley MS 6687 A–D.
[122] Co. *Litt.*, p. xxxvii.   [123] *Ibid.*, p. xxxviii.

Coke's description of the common law as reason and 'un arte que require longe study et experience' was of a piece with the development of the profession's intellectual culture in his time.[124] Humanism and the influence of continental ideas about legal education provided the language within which lawyers might sharpen the common law's identification as a science. Knafla has argued that shifts in the educational curriculum from 1540 to the 1570s, including the teaching of the New Logic of Peter Ramus, were central to the emphasis on method and reason in the Elizabethan Inns.[125] Their orientation is also revealed by the author's choice of language. Anthony Fitzherbert, writing in the early sixteenth century, represented one stream of common law thought when he described writs as the 'rules and fundamentals in the science of the common law of the land'.[126] Similarly, in the reports of Dyer and even Plowden, concentrated in the middle of the sixteenth century, an appeal to 'rule' usually refers to either the *Register*, as in Fitzherbert, or the 'rule of the court'.[127] Occasionally, however, reference will be made to the 'common rule' or infrequently the 'rule of the common law'.[128] However, the printed reports of cases spanning the years 1580–1616, the more abstract phrases 'general rule' or 'infalliable rule' are frequently used, most often by Coke.

A literature emerged to assure practitioners that they could manage the abundance of information and that despite the seeming confusion of the law there was a placid core of reason underneath.[129] Abraham Fraunce's *Lawiers Logike* (1588) exemplified proposals to order the common law

---

[124] Tubbs, *Common Law Mind*, pp. 164–73; Wilfrid Prest, 'The Dialectical Origins of Finch's Law', *Cambridge Law Journal*, 36:2 (1977), 326–52; Sommerville, *Royalists and Patriots*, pp. 88–9. Compare Thomas Hobbes and his discussion of Coke and the law as an art, *The Art of Rhetoric, with A Discourse of the Laws of England* (London, 1683), Wing 106, p. 4.

[125] Louis Knafla, 'The Influence of Continental Humanists and Jurists on English Common Law in the Renaissance', in R. J. Schoeck (ed.), *Acta Conventus Neo-Latini Bononiensis: Proceedings of the Fourth International Congress of Neo-Latin Studies* (Binghamton, NY, 1985), pp. 64–7; Terrill, 'The Application of the Comparative Method', 169–70.

[126] Fitzherbert, *La Novel Natura Brevium*, preface.

[127] *Crown Matters Happening at Salop* (1553), 1 Plowden 101, 75 ER 159; *Throckmerton v. Tracy* (1555), 1 Plowden 150, 75 ER 229; *Hill v. Grange* (1556), 1 Plowden 169, 75 ER 261. In two instances it referred to a 'rule' established by *Bracton* or Littleton. *Willion v. Berkley* (1562), 1 Plowden 223, 75 ER 339; *Throckmerton v. Tracy*, 1 Plowden 163, 75 ER 251.

[128] *Basset's Case* (1557), 2 Dyer 137a, 73 ER 298; *Reniger v. Fogossa*; 'by the rule of the common law', *Norwood v. Norwood and Read* (1558), 1 Plowden 182, 75 ER 280.

[129] Peter Stein, *Regulae Iuris: From Juristic Rules to Legal Maxims* (Edinburgh, 1966), p. 159; Tubbs, 'Custom, Time and Reason', 399–404; Cromartie, *Constitutionalist Revolution*, pp. 182–5; Mark Walters, 'Legal Humanism and Law-As-Integrity', *Cambridge Law Journal*, 67:2 (2008), 352–75, at 357.

using logical methods, and in doing so revealed an emphasis on abstract rules as the basis of the common law.[130] Anticipating Coke's complaints, Fraunce referred to 'those vast heapes of scattered discourses, throwne into every corner of our yeare bookes', and that 'the Law is in vaste volumes confusedly scattered and utterly undigested … yet herein blame not the Law, if it bee datke [*sic:* dark], but Lawyers themselves that had no light: blame not the Lawe, I say, which was out of order, but Lawyers themselves that never knew Methode'. Fraunce proposed that 'the whole body of our law to be rather logically ordered', so that there might be 'a Methodical coherence of the whole common law'. The end result would be 'that the confusion of writers may bee removed, the maner reformed, the matter better ordered'.[131] Lastly, Fraunce implicitly rejected criticisms of the common law that it was too incoherent to be an art or science: 'It is not my purpose, at this time to dispute, whether the law of England … consisting of so many particularities, being subiect to such continuall change and alteration, can be made an art.'[132]

Fraunce's successors were not reluctant to declare the common law an art or a science, a point advanced by Bacon in his *Maxims of the Law* (1597). He offered his work as a collection of 'many of the grounds of the common laws, the better to establish and settle a certain sense of law which doth now too much waver in incertainty'.[133] Bacon's ideas paralleled with those of Fraunce. His purpose was to add to the 'science' of the common law 'by collecting the rules and grounds dispersed throughout the body of the same laws … so that the uncertainty of law, which is the principal and most just challenge that is made to the laws of our nation at this time, will by this new strength laid to the foundation somewhat the more settle and be corrected'. Bacon offered these maxims and rules without systematizing them, so that they might be applied to any number of situations.[134]

This emphasis on maxims and rules as a means to unfold the reason of the law was continued by other writers, often as an explicit response to criticisms of the law. Fulbecke observed that some complained the law was 'covered with cloudes, and wrapped in darknes'. His response was

---

[130] Fraunce, *The lawiers logike*, sig. 1v.
[131] *Ibid.*, sig. 3v, f. 119v.
[132] *Ibid.*, sig. 3v, f. 119v. The terms 'art' and 'science' might be used interchangeable in the literature. See, for example, John Rastell, *The Expositions of the Termes of the Lawes of Englande* (London, 1572), 'The Prologue'.
[133] Spedding *et al.* (eds.), *Works*, vol. VII, p. 316.
[134] *Ibid.*, vol. III, pp. 319, 322.

that 'it is very expedient, that there should be a certaine art and science of the Law, general rules and precepts, and convenient discourses'.[135] Dodderidge acknowledged that the consequence of 'confusions' in the law was that 'coherency, constancye and conformitye thereof is almost utterly lost and not without some blemish and reproach of our nation'. Method would bring order to the law.[136] Henry Finch proudly declared to the reader of *Nomotechnia*: 'this onely of al the Bookes of Law (as concerning the Method) is without President'.[137] He asserted that the law carried with it a 'golden chain' of all good learning, implying that positive law was linked eventually to the eternal laws of nature and reason, from which 'all the other Lawes receive their Light'. Method and the 'discourse of sound reason' opened the law of reason and its maxims to the practitioner. Maxims and 'rules of reason' were the grounds of the common law, and these 'undoubted Oracles' would guide the practitioner as 'so many starres and shining lights, to direct our course in the arguing of any case'.[138] Finch then provided one hundred rules of reason with their explanations.

John Dodderidge in his *English Lawyer* followed Finch's emphasis on the importance of method, and laid out some of his ideas in manuscript form.[139] Dodderidge was an associate of Coke's on the bench, and his work was a practical guide for the training of the practitioner, exhorting the reader as follows: 'Reason is naturall, but yet it is polished by Art, and therefore best by the Art of Reason, which is Logicke.'[140] Dodderidge insisted that it was necessary for the student to proceed by method and logic, and he urged practitioners to prepare for disputation by 'collect[ing] the Axiomes, principles, grounds and rules observed in that Art which he studieth'. Dodderidge explained that though lawyers dealt with individual cases, their debates in court led to them to 'more generall theses and propositions' and offered an extensive illustration of the application of logic and the rules of the art that relied on Cicero and Aristotle.[141]

---

[135] Fulbecke, *A Direction*, f. 4v.
[136] BL Additional MS 32092, f. 189v.
[137] Finch, *Law*, sig. A3; Pulton, *A Kalender*, sig. A3v.
[138] Finch, *Law.*, pp. 5, 74.
[139] Ibbetson remarks that it was 'a creditable attempt to impose some order on the depressingly haphazard common law of his day'. *DNB*, s.v. 'Sir John Dodderidge'.
[140] Dodderidge, *English Lawyer*, p. 65, and also pp. 29, 34–5, 56.
[141] Aristotle's influence on this generation is assessed by Tubbs, *Common Law Mind*, p. 170 and 'Custom, Time and Reason', 397–400; and the analysis of *epieikeia* in Cromartie, *Constitutionalist Revolution*, pp. 7–8. Dodderidge explicitly discusses Aristotle in his study of method; BL Additional MS 32092, ff. 161r–162v.

Towards the conclusion of his work Dodderidge faced the question that his analysis of method had raised: if method and logic were so important to the art of the common law, why had no one previously discussed them extensively?[142] The answer was that many, including the authors of *Glanvill*, *Bracton*, *Britton*, as well as St German, had indeed tried.[143] He offered three other answers, one of which brought the problem of memory to the reader's attention. Dodderidge claimed that 'our Ancestors thought it more convenient, to be rather governed by an unwritten law, not left in any other monument, than in the mind of man; and thence to be deduced by deception [*sic*] and discourse of reason'.[144] The past had left the discourse of reason scattered in the books of law, sometimes clouded by obscurity. This obscurity had worsened, so that the present desperately sought a method, 'to purge the English Lawes, from the great Confusions, tedious and superflous iterations, with which the Reports are infested ... so that the Coherencie, constancie, and conformitie thereof, is almost utterly lost, and not without some blemish and reproach of our Nation'.

Using method, 'men may view a perfect plot of the coherence of things'.[145] The practitioners discovered this order through their rigorous interpretation of the law and, as John Davies explained, 'the lawe is nothing else but a Rule, that is made to measure the actions of men. But a Rule is dead and measures nothing, unlesse the hand of the Architect doe apply it.'[146]

The identification of the common law with reason responded to criticisms of the law's uncertainty, while guiding lawyers to resolve that uncertainty.[147] Appeals to reason also shaped the judges' adjudication on issues arising from the exercise of legal authority – this was again more a development of an old practice than an innovation. For example, litigation over customs and corporate bylaws confronted the judges with the question of whether a custom or practice was valid despite its settled usage or other legal sanction.[148] These local usages often represented exceptions to the common law: prescriptions, for instance, were taken to

---

[142] Dodderidge, *English Lawyer*, p. 240.

[143] *Ibid.*, p. 262.   [144] *Ibid.*, p. 241.

[145] *Ibid.*, pp. 243–5, 258; Fulbecke, *A Direction*, f. 5r.

[146] Davies, *Le Primer Report*, f. 8r and sig. *4r.

[147] For the increasing willingness of judges to explain the underlying reasoning of a case, see Baker, 'The Inns of Court and Legal Doctrine', in *The Common Law Tradition: Lawyers, Books and the Law*, p. 51; Baker, *OHLE*, vol. VI, p. 489.

[148] Boyer, '"Understanding, Authority, and Will"', 81.

be 'against common right'. Davies explained that merely because a custom was contrary to a rule of the common law 'this does not prove the custom to be unreasonable'.[149] This exceptionalism and the grievances of litigants invited judicial scrutiny of the question, as Davies implied, of whether these customs were reasonable. By establishing which customs were reasonable, and which were not, the judges asserted basic standards to which legal rules should adhere. Through their intervention in these cases, the judges affirmed the superiority of the common law and its reasoning to control legal power.

The integration of copyhold litigation into the common law illustrates the process. In 1589 Walmesley SL and Sir Richard Shuttleworth SL debated before the bench whether a copyhold custom was good. Walmesley argued that the custom was 'repugnant to reason' and hence 'void'. He also stated the older view that from the perspective of the common law the copyholder was merely a tenant at will. But Shuttleworth, while admitting the novelty of the copyhold estate at common law, nonetheless argued that the custom 'seems to be grounded upon the reason of the common law' and should be held valid.[150] Shuttleworth was well aware that a conservative interpretation of the case might 'overthrow all copy-hold estates', or set back the creep of common law adjudication. The exchange touched on a thorny problem. Common lawyers acknowledged that valid local customs varied from common law rules and 'common right', for example, in customs of borough English or gavelkind.[151] How then to determine whether they might be recognized as valid? In some cases it was urged that the custom not only violated a rule of the common law, but this rule represented an underlying reasonableness that could not be violated. Hence Anderson CJCP explained that a custom that an infant could make a feoffment was invalid because they had not attained the age of discretion.[152] This approach tested whether a local practice was a 'reasonable custom', or whether it could be construed as valid by the common law judges.[153] Given the complexity of some local customs, debate over the reasonableness of a custom often proceeded cautiously, as when the bench considered a case over the validity of a custom whereby a

---

[149] *Case of Tanistry* (1608), Davis 30, 80 ER 518; *Case of the City of London* (1610), 8 Co. *Rep.* 126a, 77 ER 664. Coke suggested that if the rationale underlying a law or rule ceased, so too would the law; Co. *Litt.*, f. 70b.

[150] *Anonymous* (1589), Godbolt 140, 78 ER 85–6.

[151] For example, *Davenant* v. *Hurdis* (1599), Moore King's Bench 588, 72 ER 776.

[152] *Shipwith and Sheffield's Case* (1591), Godbolt 143, 78 ER 87.

[153] *Crabbe* v. *Bale* (1605), BL Additional MS 25213, ff. 60r, 63v, 71r.

copyholder indicted (but not convicted) for felony forfeited their land.[154] Determining whether a custom was reasonable could be difficult, and so the barristers and judges in these cases attempted to reason from accepted propositions and maxims.

What could not be tolerated was an unreasonable custom or one that created a repugnancy.[155] How to define these conditions was a difficult exercise. At points the reports are silent on the details: when an action of defamation arising from a custom of London was brought to the common law on habeas corpus, the judges were reluctant to return it to the lower court because 'their custom is against the law'.[156] Sometimes the explanation was that the custom was simply 'against common reason'.[157] In other examples we can detect appeals to established principles. Walmesley gave the example from the Year Books of a custom that a commoner should not be held back from using a common before the lord had put his cattle there, for it was 'not reasonable to be restrained at the pleasure of another'. Tanfield, who was of counsel in another case, also appealed to principles of consent when he argued that bylaws should be made by the 'greater number of tenants'.[158] In other cases such underlying principles were made explicit, allowing their insertion into customary practices at the local level.[159] In one case this insertion was explicit: 'copyhold wanting custom should be directed by the common law', and so the judges went on to 'void' a grant.[160]

The invocation of reason, however, often seemed to reflect a sense that the practice was somehow unfair or may, as Tubbs suggested, reflect 'common erudition'.[161] This opacity is in evidence in a case where it was alleged that a custom allowed all copyholders on a manor to fell trees at their discretion during their lifetime. The 'greater part' of the judges thought the custom unreasonable since a copyholder might remove all the trees on the land and prevent their use by succeeding copyholders for shelter and repairs. When the case raised a technicality that suggested that even those who held at will or for a month might exercise the custom, this was

---

[154] *Gittin* v. *Cooper* (1608), BL Additional MS 25213, ff. 91v, 95r, 106r.
[155] *Salforde's Case* (1577), 3 Dyer 357b, 73 ER 802; BL Harley MS 5265, f. 186r.
[156] *Oxford* v. *Cross* (1599), BL Additional MS 25203, f. 60r.
[157] BL Additional MS 25213, f. 104r, a citation of *Salforde's Case*, 3 Dyer 357b, 73 ER 802.
[158] *Anonymous* (1586), Godbolt 50, 78 ER 31.
[159] *Shipwith and Sheffield's Case* (1591), Godbolt 143, 78 ER 87; see also *Skipwith's Case* (1583), Godbolt 14, 78 ER 9.
[160] *Brian and Elsworth's Case* (1604), BL Additional MS 25206, f. 70r.
[161] Tubbs, *Common Law Mind*, p. 111.

'held to be too large and unreasonable'.[162] No fundamental principle was stated here, but the outcome suggests that it was deemed wrong that even the most transient copyholder might remove all the timber by the custom and so deprive future copyholders of its benefit.[163]

The common law judges' regulation of these customs and bylaws raised many of the same issues that would later be addressed by them in cases of much greater constitutional import. These issues included economic regulation, the limits of judicial power, taxation and impositions, and the relationship between clergy and laymen, especially in cases of tithes and church repair.[164] The case of *Daymonde* v. *Greenwood* (1602), for example, resulted from a custom in Devonshire by which the inhabitants of the town might pull down houses that were on fire 'according to their sensible ('sanas') discretion' for the preservation of other buildings in the town and the 'public good'. On an action of trespass, the question arose whether the custom was good. The court initially compared the custom with the rule of the common law that allowed for the pulling down of houses next to a burning house. But under the custom, houses might be demolished even if they were only near to those that were burning. Concern followed that the custom was unreasonable, since it permitted 'men to pull down any house at their discretion although it was not next to the house that was afire'.[165]

The case presented the problem that also arose in the conflict over the Fens: balancing claims for the public good with the discretionary or judicial powers of local individuals. Throughout his career Coke had worked to prevent the misuse of local law. In the unpublished *Case of Butter* (1595) Coke challenged London for a custom that allowed its officers to search, seize and destroy rancid butter.[166] The custom was open to abuses: officers of the city might seize butter that was never intended for sale or search homes in their pursuit. The custom, he declared, was 'illegal and against reason'. The home was a man's 'castle' and searches should be restricted to the open shop or market, and not private warehouses or cellars because 'this is against reason and full of inconvenience'. At the other end of his

---

[162] *Powel* v. *Peacock* (1604), Croke Jac 30, 79 ER 23–4.

[163] Compare the similar case, *Huckworst* v. *Pill* (1600), BL Additional MS 25203, f. 245r.

[164] For example, *Jucks and Sir Charles Cavendish's Case* (1613), Godbolt 234, 78 ER 135; *Nicholls* v. *Small* (1601), BL Additional MS 25203, f. 265v; *Griffin* v. *Dimble* (1607), BL Additional MS 25206, f. 45r; *Sir Walter Heale's Case* (1607), BL Additional MS 25206, f. 68v.

[165] *Daymonde* v. *Greenwood* (1602), BL Additional MS 25203, ff. 600v–601r; BL Additional MS 25213, ff. 36r–v.

[166] BL Harley MS 6686A, ff. 140r–142v.

career, in *Bullen* v. *Godfrey* (1614), an issue arose when the steward of a court-leet sought a customary payment from twelve presenting jurors. When they refused to pay they were fined. It was argued that the custom was not good because such a charge should fall on all those who bene-fited from the court. The custom was 'unreasonable' because it was ill-defined: the steward might swear and fine any as he pleased, even infants and madmen. Coke declared that he did not 'like this custom', worrying that the steward would have power to charge the same twelve persons year after year.[167] The judges shared Coke's concern over the discretion of local authorities. When in 1587 a case arose on a custom in London that the mayor might remove causes after verdict in the Sheriffs' Court and mod-erate them in equity, it was asked whether this was a 'reasonable custom'. Anticipating the later conflict with the Chancery, Thomas Gawdy JQB replied that such a review should be before judgment, citing the statute of 4 Henry IV, c. 23.[168]

Cases arising from local custom or bylaws also raised the question of the scope of economic regulation by local authorities.[169] These less prom-inent cases suggest that the judges' underlying concern was the oper-ation of legal power in general, rather than the extent of royal authority in particular. In *Gobye* v. *Knight* (1602) the city of Canterbury claimed a use 'time beyond memory' by which a candlemaker was appointed and could obtain tallow at a set rate from the local butchers. Should the butch-ers not agree to sell at the price, a custom allowed for their committal. When Gobye, a butcher, was imprisoned for refusal he sued a writ of false imprisonment. Gobye argued that the custom was unreasonable because it compelled the butchers to sell their tallow to the chandler against their consent, tended towards a monopoly, and the committal itself was against Magna Carta. The defence raised the point that acts of parliament allowed for such regulation of prices and wages, and so the custom was thought reasonable 'for acts of parliament they ought not to be condemned as a thing against reason'. However, the judges spoke strongly against this cus-tom, Gawdy declaring that it was 'an unreasonable prescription to compel a man to sell his tallow willingly or not willingly ... it is against reason

---

[167] *Bullen* v. *Godfrey*, 1 Rolle 32, 81 ER 306, and BL Additional MS 25213, ff. 161r, 165v–166r; BL Additional MS 25209, f. 103r.

[168] *Anonymous* (1587), Godbolt 127, 78 ER 77.

[169] These cases may also suggest the judges' underlying economic attitude. For the debate, see Donald Wagner, 'Coke and the Rise of Economic Liberalism', *Economic History Review*, 6:1 (1935), pp. 30–44; Barbara Malament, 'The "Economic Liberalism" of Sir Edward Coke', *Yale Law Journal*, 76:7 (1967), pp. 1,321–58, 1,322nn.6–8.

to imprison a man for this cause who refused to obey their ordinances'. Judgment was entered for the plaintiff.[170] When an act of London's common council prevented freemen from employing any foreigner using a manual trade it was similarly claimed that the bylaw was 'an unreasonable act'.[171]

Behind the judges' attitude was a suspicion that local authority would be misused to protect private interests.[172] In a case in Newcastle upon Tyne in 1599, a merchant who was transporting lead from Durham to London through the port was stopped. It was claimed that a custom from time immemorial had given a monopoly to a group of merchant adventurers for transporting through the port of Newcastle. In words that would be echoed in *Bates's Case*, it was argued that every port was the 'high street of the king', and it was 'unreasonable and thus void' to restrain merchants who were non-resident in the town.[173] The plaintiff succeeded against the custom, and Popham CJQB frowned on the custom for restraining trade too generally, while Fenner JQB 'urged that such restraints of merchants such as this are illegal'.

In 1599 Popham had warned that ordinances made to regulate tailors tended towards a monopoly that was 'against the public good and against reason'.[174] He was referring to the case then underway, *Davenant v. Hurdis* (1599), where the authority of the company of merchant tailors to enforce their bylaws had come into question.[175] The particular ordinance was a requirement (certified by Sir Christopher Wray and Dyer) that a member of the company would put out at least half his cloths to be dressed

---

[170] *Gobye v. Knight* (1602), BL Additional MS 25203, ff. 619r–621v. Other cases concerning imprisonments by local courts include *Clark's Case* (1598), 5 Co. *Rep.* 64a, 77 ER 152; *Lambe v. Hurlebert* (1600), BL Additional MS 25203, ff. 422v, 506r; *Willes v. Portman* (1602), f. 604r; *Anonymous* (1605), BL Lansdowne MS 1096, f. 51v and BL Additional MS 25213, f. 66r.

[171] *Porter's Case* (1606), BL Additional MS 25213, f. 67v.

[172] Coke and the judges may have also been animated by concerns over policies that restricted (as opposed to regulated) trade, see Malament, 'Economic Liberalism', pp. 1,354–5.

[173] *Tonge v. Tempest* (1600), BL Additional MS 25203, f. 263v.

[174] These remarks were made during another London case touching trade regulation, *Payne v. Haughton* (1599), BL Additional MS 25203, f. 203r. Similar issues were also discussed in *Le Maior et Communality de London* (1609), HLS MS 1192, f. 174r.

[175] *Davenant v. Hurdis* (1599), Moore 576, 72 ER 769; Coke's notes are BL Harley 6686B, f. 381v. The case, like others involving guilds and societies, was probably related to increased competition over control of the trades, see William Letwin, *Law and Economic Policy in America: The Evolution of the Sherman Antitrust Act* (Chicago, IL, 1981), p. 23; Charles Clode, *The Early History of the Guild of Merchant Taylors of Fraternity of St. John the Baptist, London*, (London, 1888) vol. I, pp. 199–203; George Unwin, *The Gilds and Companies of London* (London, 1938), p. 262.

by brothers of the society. Davenant violated the bylaw and he was fined ten pounds and so sought relief at the common law. Coke argued on his behalf, claiming that the ordinance 'was against law and the liberty of the subject' and was 'unreasonable'. Francis Moore, speaking for the Merchant Taylors, explained that the grounds of customs and bylaws were 'reasonable cause' and that those bylaws with reasonable grounds were good, and 'those against reason bad'.[176] The case, alongside others, opened up consideration of the law-making power of regulated corporations.[177] This led Coke to repeat principles that had already been identified in the *Chamberlain of London's Case* (1590), where it was stated that bylaws that were repugnant to the 'laws and statutes of the realm are void and of no effect'.[178] The tailors' case probed the extent to which corporations might operate as judicial entities. Coke identified the underlying concern: if they were able to make a bylaw requiring the employment of members in the dressing of half the cloths, then they could make another law requiring that their members dress all such cloths, 'and thus by degrees are able to appropriate clothdressing to those only of their company'.[179] At issue was whether bylaws might be used to advance the private interest at the public expense, 'because the by-law makes a monopoly and a prescription of such nature to induce sole trade ... to one company or one person'.[180]

The argument developed in *Davenant* was revisited in the case of the Ipswich tailors (1614), which again considered the scope and reach of corporate bylaws. According to the bylaw no one in the city might tailor without first presenting themselves before the society with proof of apprenticeship. William Sheninge had practised as a tailor in the city before presenting himself, but he had done so privately.[181] In his report Coke explained the consequence of this restriction on economic freedom: it was 'a means of extortion in drawing money from them ... or of oppression of young tradesmen, by the old and rich of the same trade, not permitting them to work in their trade freely'.[182] Another report suggested

---

[176] *Davenant v. Hurdis*, BL Additional MS 25206, f. 113v.

[177] *Ibid.*, f. 110r.

[178] *Chamberlain of London's Case* (1590), BL Additional MS 25203, f. 93r; the case runs 92r–94v, 104v–108v, 203r; compare *Chamberlain of London*, 5 Co. Rep. 63a, 77 ER 151. Also reported as *Chamberlain of London Case*, 3 Leonard 264, 74 ER 674.

[179] *Chamberlain of London's Case*, BL Additional MS 25206, f. 110v.

[180] *Per curiam, Davenant v. Hurdis*, BL Additional MS 25206, f. 115r, and BL Additional MS 25203, f. 203r.

[181] *The Wardens and Community of Ipswich* (1614), BL Additional MS 25213, f. 160r.

[182] *Ipswich Tailors Case*, 11 Co. Rep. 53a, 77 ER 1218.

that such quasi-judicial power was problematic, for it made the society judges in their own cause.[183]

These attempts to regulate local legal authority explain aspects of *Bonham's Case* (1610). The case has usually been interpreted within two frames: the story of judicial review and common law 'imperialism'. The first follows from Coke's claim that 'the common law will controul Acts of Parliament, and sometimes adjudge them to be utterly void: for when an Act of Parliament is against common right and reason, or repugnant, or impossible to be performed, the common law will controul it, and adjudge such Act to be void'.[184] Great powers of subtlety have been applied to this passage to determine whether Coke meant that the common law would void legislation as an act of judicial power or whether the judges would simply interpret the act in such a way as to render its repugnancy harmless.[185] Debate has also continued over the meaning of 'void' and whether Coke meant the act was void ab initio or simply that the clause or statute would have no effect. The second interpretative frame has placed *Bonham* as part of a larger effort by the judges to assert the common law as the supreme legal authority in the kingdom.[186] The authority of the College of Physicians has occasionally been viewed as a stand-in for the prerogative (despite its confirmation by parliament).[187]

The College's authority over the regulation of medicine in London was well fortified by precedent, judicial opinion, patent and especially statute. These statutes confirmed the College's charter, which contained two key clauses: first, it approved the College's power to license practitioners,

---

[183] *The Clothworkers of Ipswich*, Godbolt 252, 78 ER 147.

[184] *Bonham's Case*, 8 Co. *Rep.* 118b, 77 ER 652.

[185] The argument for a broad reading that the case invoked a judicial power to strike down statutes was made by Theodore Plucknett, '*Bonham's Case* and Judicial Review', in Allen Boyer (ed.), *Law, Liberty, and Parliament: Selected Essays on the Writings of Sir Edward Coke* (Indianapolis, 2004), pp. 150–85, and Raoul Berger, '*Doctor Bonham's Case:* Statutory Interpretation or Constitutional Theory?' *University of Pennsylvania Law Review*, 117 (1969), 521–45. Others have argued that the case represents instead an interpretative strategy; Samuel Thorne, 'The Constitution and the Courts: A Re-examination of the Famous Case of Dr. Bonham', *Law Quarterly Review*, 54 (1938), 543–52, and 'Introduction', in *A Discourse upon the Exposicion and Understanding of Statutes*, pp. 85–90; Charles Gray, 'Bonham's Case Reviewed', *Proceedings of the American Philosophical Society*, n.s. 116 (1972), 35–58; Williams, 'Dr Bonham's Case and "Void" Statutes', 111–28.

[186] Burgess, *Absolute Monarchy*, pp. 181–92; note the criticism by Tubbs at *Common Law Mind*, pp. 159–60.

[187] Harold Cook, 'Against Common Right and Reason', in Boyer (ed.), *Law, Liberty, and Parliament*, pp. 127–49, at p. 148.

since no one, 'nemo', might practise medicine in London or seven miles around without the admission of the College. The penalty, which was to be obtained through judicial process, of five pounds for each month of unlicensed practice was given in the patent and split between the College and the king.[188] The second key clause allowed the College to punish malpractice by fine or imprisonment. The statute of Mary suggested that the College might also imprison for contempts, a point relied on by counsel in the case.[189]

The College actively used its powers to regulate the practice of medicine in London by imprisoning or fining unlicensed practitioners. Harold Cook has described the prosecutions, in the late 1590s, of several surgeons practising internal medicine. Thomas Bonham was also associated with the Surgeon and Barbers Company, eventually becoming a member, and probably part of a larger attempt by the surgeons to expand into internal medicine.[190] The dispute thus involved economic competition between two groups of specialists, one of which was attempting to protect their monopoly. The College examined Bonham for membership in 1605, but he was denied and fined for practising without a licence.[191] Bonham appears to have continued to practise in defiance of the College, and in 1606 he was again fined and brought before the College, where he claimed that the society did not have authority over graduates from Oxford or Cambridge. The College ordered Bonham imprisoned for contempt, and he sued habeas corpus to the Common Pleas where Coke was chief justice.[192] After the court had freed Bonham, the College obtained a resolution from Egerton and several of the common law judges, including Popham and Fleming in 1607. This opinion affirmed the College's authority over graduates and to imprison for contempt and 'for not well doeing using or practising the facultie or arte of physike'.[193] The College proceeded to sue Bonham at the common law for practising without a licence for twelve months, seeking

[188] 14 and 15 Henry VIII, c. 5, *SR*, vol. III, p. 213; 1 Mary, st. 2, ch 9, *SR*, vol. IV, p. 207. One hundred shillings was the penalty given in the superseded statute of 3 Henry VIII, c. 11, *SR*, vol. III, p. 32.

[189] *Bonham's Case*, 8 Co. Rep. 116b, 77 ER 650.

[190] Cook, 'Against Common Right', pp. 131–3, 139; *Historical Account of Proceedings Between the College of Physicians and Surgeons* (London, 1690), p. 4.

[191] The reconstruction of Bonham's relationship with the College relies on Cook, 'Against Common Right', pp. 133–6, and is also told in *The College of Physician's Case*, 2 Brownlow and Goldesborough 263, 123 ER 932.

[192] BL Additional MS 25215, ff. 43v, 54r, 61r.

[193] Christopher Merrett, *A Collection of Acts of Parliament ... Concerning those Grants to the Colledge of Physicians London* (London, 1660), Wing M1836.

the statutory penalty of sixty pounds, and Bonham responded with his suit for trespass in the Common Pleas. Issue was joined and though Bonham lost in the King's Bench, he prevailed in the Common Pleas.

The judges had scrutinized many other customs and bylaws leading up to *Bonham*. Their use of reasonableness as a means to impose consistency and order had led them either to confirm, favourably construe or void local practices. *Bonham* was significant because it brought under scrutiny the relationship between statute and local law. In this way the review of the judicial actions of a local authority assumed constitutional import- ance. The decision in *Bonham's Case* has generally been ascribed to Coke's influence or the desire among the common judges for increased author- ity. In fact, *Bonham's Case* was part of a pattern of cases in which local authority was regulated. The common law judges, though often siding with the College prior to *Bonham's Case*, demanded greater transparency and precision in its proceedings. Elizabeth Clarke sued habeas corpus in 1603 when the College imprisoned her for the 'evil and unlawful practice of physick'. When the return failed to cite the location of these practices or their specifics, the court discharged her, finding the return too gen- eral.[194] Yet, in 1614, the College again made a general return on habeas corpus to the judges' exasperation, and Dodderidge petulantly remarked that *Bonham's Case* had explained how the return should be made.[195] In fact, Coke had concluded his decision in *Bonham* with seven rules for the College to inject greater clarity into their proceedings.[196]

Coke agreed that the College might imprison for malpractice, but asserted that they could only fine according to the statute and at law for practising without a licence. This distinction was key to his interpretation of the case and allowed him to limit the College's authority through con- strual rather than voiding.[197] Coke drew a distinction in the statute and patent between two offences: practising without a licence and malprac- tice. The former was punishable by the statutory fine of five pounds, and Coke insisted that this must be brought by information in the common law courts – exactly as the College had done in the concurrent suit against Bonham.[198] The College might imprison and fine only for malpractice.[199]

[194]   *Clarke* v. *College of Physicians* (1603), BL Additional MS 25203, f. 688r.
[195]   *Alphonso and the Colledge of Physitians in London*, 2 Bulstrode 259, 80 ER 1105.
[196]   8 Co. *Rep.* 121a, 77 ER 657.   [197]   Cook, 'Against Common Right', p. 142.
[198]   *The College of Physician's Case*, 2 Brownlow and Goldesborough 265, 123 ER 933; BL Additional MS 25213, f. 89r.
[199]   8 Co. *Rep.* 117a, 77 ER 651; compare 117b. This issue seems to have been the focus of the reporter of BL Additional MS 25213, ff. 107r–v.

The College had proceeded against Bonham for practising without a licence and contempt, and not for malpractice. On Coke's reading of the statute, it was therefore possible to conclude that the College could not imprison Bonham unless he had committed malpractice. The College justified their imprisonment for contempt with an expansive clause in the statute of Mary I. But the statute added that the College might only imprison 'for his or their offences or disobedience, contrary to any article or clause contained in the aforesaid grant, or act'. If Bonham had been accused of malpractice, the College might have imprisoned for contempt, but since practising without a licence should have been pursued at the common law, the College had no authority to imprison him for contempts in response to that charge.[200]

His line of reasoning was not original.[201] During a judicial conference in 1607 the judges had unanimously resolved that the College could commit for malpractice, 'but for the committing to prison of such as practise (not being admitted by the Colledge) they held it doubtful, for that the Charter and Statute do in that case inflict a punishment of £5 a moneth against such practiser'.[202] The judges recommended that the College create a bylaw that by prohibiting such practice would allow them to commit for violation of the ordinance.

Coke applied these arguments in *Bonham's Case*. This interpretation avoided an unreasonable construction of the statute: if the College could fine unlicensed practitioners and benefit from half the amount then they were judges in their own cause. The observation of this conflict of interest occasioned Coke's famous dictum, which is also found elsewhere in his notes: 'when an act of parliament is against common right and reason or repugnant or impossible to be performed, the common law will control this act and adjudge [it] void'.[203] Charles Gray, however, has argued influentially that it was an addition to the edited case report, since it was not included among other reports.[204] Ian Williams has recently developed

---

[200] 8 Co. *Rep.* 120a, 77 ER 656.

[201] Though it has been assumed Coke's argument was novel; Cook, 'Against Common Right', p. 142.

[202] Merrett, *A Collection*, pp. 119–20; and noted in *Maunsell and Onon's Case* (1607), BL Additional MS 25206, f. 56r. Coke may have attempted to foreclose this self-legislation in *The College of Physician's Case*, 2 Brownlow and Goldesborough 266, 123 ER 934.

[203] Yale University Law School MS G R 24, f. 157v; CUL Ii.2.21 (2), f. 93v; 8 Co. *Rep.* 118b, 77 ER 652.

[204] Coke's dictum appears in another manuscript report of the case though it is stated differently; BL Additional MS 25206, f. 244r. This report was an addition to a much larger

this line of reasoning and discovered Coke applying rules of construction for assessing grants of jurisdiction: 'Coke's report does not suggest Coke to have considered the case as one concerning any important question of legal theory or principle.'[205] Conversely, Boyer has placed the decision within the context of copyhold cases and the interpretation of the statute De Donis, concluding that the 'Coke acted in the belief that courts could strike down statutes.'[206]

Perhaps the most important objection to a restrictive reading of Coke's dictum is that some at the time seem to have thought that he was making a claim to limit parliamentary statute.[207] Such a claim was within contemporary imagination. In one example, the judges had debated a hypothetical statute that would eliminate purveyance and had resolved that 'an Act of Parliament against that [purveyance] is void, because it is a necessary prerogative'.[208] Coke also recorded that Popham had made a similar assertion about a statute that removed purveyance without recompense.[209] Moreover, Sir Henry Hobart's dictum in *Savadge* v. *Day* (1614) alluded to *Bonham* when he suggested that: 'even an Act of Parliament, made against natural equity, as to make a man Judge in his own case, is void in it self'.[210] Gray also brought to light a case in Chancery where Serjeant Crewe relied on *Bonham* to make a comparable claim in argument.[211] However, such claims might be delicately reasoned. For example, if parliament confirmed the customs of a town that were against law or reason, then the effect of the statute was void, because no valid custom could be against law or reason and therefore the act had confirmed nothing: 'for evil use makes no custom'.[212]

The most prominent criticism of *Bonham* came from Egerton who took umbrage both at the construal of the statute and the claim to void parliamentary acts, writing that 'acts of parliament ought to be reversed by Parliament and not otherwise'. Challenging the judges' use of reason as

---

book of reports and may be derived from Coke's account of the case. The report was dismissed by Gray, 'Bonham's Case', 43n.13.

[205] Williams, 'Dr Bonham's Case', 128, 122. Williams argues that appeals to reasonableness implicated only common law rules, 'not something external to it'.

[206] Boyer, '"Understanding, Authority, and Will"', 85; Raffield, 'Contract, Classicism, and the Common-Weal', 88.

[207] *PP 1610*, vol. II, p. 153.   [208] Wilbraham, *Journal*, p. 83.

[209] BL Harley MS 6686B, f. 597r.   [210] Hobart 88, 80 ER 237.

[211] *Rouswell* v. *Ivory*, cited in Gray, 'Bonham's Case', 51–4.

[212] *The Earl of Leicester's Case*, 1 Plowden 400, 75 ER 605; BL Harley MS 5265, f. 186r.

a framework to guide their review, Egerton wrote that '3 judges on the bench [shall] destroy and frustrate all their points because the Act agreeth not in their particular sense with common right and reason, whereby [Coke] advances the reason of a particular Court above the judgement of the realm'.[213] In making these criticisms, Egerton signalled that he disapproved of the judges' use of their ideas of reason to regulate statute.[214] This practice, and the assertion that the common law was a superior body of reason, positioned the common law judges as arbiters of the validity of the exercise of legal power. Ellesmere's concern that the judges were making expansive claims for their discretion led to his opposition, even as he conceded that statutes might under some circumstances be voided: 'I speak not of impossibilities or direct repugnancies.'[215]

The principles that informed Coke's dictum can be discovered in *Rolles v. Mason* (1612). This case, soon after *Bonham*, is the only known case where Coke cited *Bonham* from the bench. The case was an adjudication of copyhold custom, and in his decision Coke made the following claim:

> the law consists of three parts. First, common law. Secondly, statute law, which corrects, abridges, and explains the common law: the third custom which takes away the common law: but the common law corrects, allows, and disallows, both statute law, and custom, for if there be repugnancy in statute; or unreasonableness in custom, the common law disallows and rejects it, as it appears by Doctor Bonham's case.[216]

Coke acknowledged that statute law might alter and 'correct' the common law. Second, he explained that custom 'takes away' the common law insofar as its operation might abate the exercise of a common law rule. A custom may only do so, however, if it is reasonable. Similarly, the common law 'disallows and rejects' statute 'if there be repugnancy'. The term is generally taken to mean an outright contradiction. The passage can be read as distinguishing the common law approach to custom and statute: custom is assessed on rationality, while statute on whether the drafting permits intelligibility and execution.[217]

---

[213] BL Hargrave 254, ff. 40r–v.   [214] See also Thorne, 'Introduction', p. 90n.191.

[215] *The Lord Chancellor's Speech*, Moore 828, 72 ER 932. Ellesmere may have feared 'legislative sovereignty'; see Sommerville, *Royalists and Patriots*, p. 92.

[216] *Rolles v. Mason*, 2 Brownlow and Goldesborough 198, 123 ER 895; though Coke did not always think positively of legislative interference; Yale University Law School G R 24, f. 158v.

[217] Williams, 'Dr Bonham's Case', 125.

A manuscript report of the same case, however, suggests that Coke believed reasonableness was crucial to the validity of both custom and statute. The report relates that Coke,

> said that the law of this realm had three main pillars[:] 1. The common law[,] 2 the statute law[,] which in some cases alters, abridges, explains and enlarges the common law[,] 3. Custom, what [is called] a private common law [;] which having reason and ground[ed] with them the common law gives way to them but where they do not have reason for their support the common law judges them merely void[,] as acts of parliament in which there is some repugnancy or inconvenience of reason in it[,] the common law disallows them also.[218]

The report adds further detail to Coke's remarks. First, statute law has a more significant role developing the common law. Second, Coke refers to both custom and statute when he admits that if they have reason the law will 'give way', but they will be voided if they 'do not have reason'. This is the case for statutes with 'some repugnancy or inconvenience of reason'. Statutes that are contradictory would be voided, but the term 'inconvenience of reason' is more difficult to discern. Coke associated 'inconvenience' with statutes of whose effects he did not approve, such as De Donis, but legal inconveniences involved the 'infringing' of a maxim of the law such that 'in the end a publike incertainty and confusion to all would follow'.[219] The comments in *Rolles* v. *Mason* suggest that Coke was thinking in terms of the inherent reasonableness of a statute rather than only how they were read. Statutes that remained unreasonable despite their careful construal might be voided – that is, they would have no effect. These claims were not constitutional in the sense that they elevated the common law above statute. Coke did not mean in *Bonham's Case* that the common law courts would 'strike down' a statute. Rather, the judges would construe a statute's meaning and make it consistent with their ideas of reason.

Coke's statement in *Rolles* v. *Mason* was the extreme expression of an analysis that the judges had used for decades to adjudicate local customs and bylaws. Their vision of law was an integrative one and they used their idea of reason to shape the relationship among laws through their underlying rationality. The claim of the common law's intrinsic rationality was a powerful tool: it responded to claims against the common law, provided a means to conceive of the law's underlying coherency, and bolstered the

---

[218] HLS MS 114, f. 69v.
[219] 4 Co. *Rep.*, pp. iii–iv; 3 Co. *Rep.*, p. xxxiii; Co. *Litt.*, 152b.

common law's authority over the diversity of customs and jurisdictions in England. Appeals to the law of reason might buttress confidence in the common law's proceedings and justify its interventions. But driven by the demands of reform these interventions increasingly tested the authority of the common law and raised the question of whether others would have the same confidence that the judges should impose their ideas of reason onto the system.

6

Pragmatism and the High Commission

The common law protecteth the king, quoth the L. Cooke. Which the King said was a traiterous speech: for the King protecteth the lawe and not the lawe the King. The King maketh Judges and Bishops. If the Judges interprete the lawes themselves and suffer none else to interprete, then they may easily make of the laws shipmen[']s hose.[1]

It was recorded that this exchange aroused the king's fury to such a degree that Coke fell to his knees in submission. Memorable and dramatic, the incident in November 1608 has come to symbolize the disagreement over the king's relationship to the law. As with many such stories, however, the altercation is more opaque than the retelling suggests. R. G. Usher noticed long ago that the four surviving accounts varied in important details: Coke's account is in many ways the least trustworthy, having been published posthumously during a time of upheaval and partisanship in 1656. Edward Bulstrode wrote soon after that the reports were poorly edited and 'not fit for publike view'.[2] Despite their differences, however, the claim that the common law 'protected' or 'defended' the king appears in three of the accounts as the spark for James's wrath. Involved in the statement may have been a constitutional commitment: either the king was under the law or above it. But though James perceived the statement to pose such a constitutional challenge to his authority, Coke's claim was instead grounded in historical experience and related to his ideas for reform.[3]

[1] BL Lansdowne MS 160, f. 424v. R. G. Usher, 'James I and Sir Edward Coke', *English Historical Review*, 18:72 (1903), 664–75, at 670. Garnett has most recently retold the story in 'The Prefaces to Sir Edward Coke's Reports', 245–6; Brooks has considered prohibitions to the Church courts in *Law, Politics and Society*, pp. 109–18.

[2] Usher, 'James I and Sir Edward Coke', 665–7; published as Edward Coke, *The Twelfth Part ...* (London, 1656), Wing C4969; Bulstrode, *The Reports*, sig. b2v.

[3] According to Coke's account, James believed that the claim that the law defended the king placed him under the law, prompting the chief justice to cite *Bracton*'s dictum; *Prohibitions Del Roy*, 12 Co. *Rep.* 65, 77 ER 1343.

Coke believed that the common law protected the king in two ways. The first is found in his own report of the exchange when he asserted that the king should not judge in his own person because his judgment was of a special kind: 'for that if it be a wrong to the party grieved, he can have no remedy'. The king could act as a judge in his proper court, the House of Lords, 'in which he with his lords is the supreme judge'. Coke perceived that the king could err and that owing to his position there might be no correction of that wrong, save by petition. The law was technically complex and Coke had already argued that ignorance of its rules had confused it. The fear that the untrained king might err explains Coke's extended discussion of artificial reason in his report.[4] Should the king commit such an injustice he would fail in his moral duty to protect his subjects.

The second reason, which this chapter takes up, was subtler. As Coke makes clear in his own report, a disagreement over statutory interpretation had preceded the tempestuous exchange. Bancroft had claimed that the king could settle the differences between the common law and the Church courts in his own person by interpreting the relevant statutes. Sir Rafe Boswell's account, however, records that Coke had explained to the king that the Church courts were foreign.[5] This assertion, as Chapter 4 has shown, was a reminder that the ecclesiastical law was assumed to have been an alien introduction into England and that the jurisdiction existed at sufferance. The warning was clear: history had taught that the Church courts had aided an external power, the pope, in the usurpation of authority from the king and the law. It was this historical example that animated Coke's self-described 'zeale' in the claims that he made before James. Among the issues that the conference considered was the conduct of the High Commission and common law prohibitions against its proceedings. Reflecting the judicial entrepreneurship of the period, the commissioners had expanded their hearing of causes. Coke and other common law judges interpreted this expansion within a familiar history, finding in the Commission's activities the threat of a renewed encroachment on the royal prerogative and the rights of the subject. Coke meant what he said: the law protected and defended the king.

The framework of the Reformation settlement offered the judges the intellectual and legal tools for asserting themselves over the ecclesiastical

---

[4] *Prohibitions Del Roy*, 12 Co. *Rep.* 65, 77 ER 1343.
[5] Usher, 'James I', 669–70.

jurisdiction. Their principal aim was the control over the interpretation of those statutes that restrained the Church courts, such as 2 Edward VI, c. 13, on tithes, and 1 Elizabeth I, c. 1. Statutes, the judges argued, were temporal and so beyond the authority of the Church courts, which should deal only in spiritual matters. The common law's histories of the Reformation made these claims self-validating. Once statutes were assumed to be temporal objects, the clergy's demand that they should have a share in their interpretation was further evidence of their overreaching.

These arguments made with earnestness by the judges smelled of jurisdictional imperialism to those who disagreed with the common law interpretation of the past and its role in the present.[6] James was the most important among those who needed to accept the peculiar history that provided the context for the judges' actions, so the tilt of the debate demonstrated the crucial role that confidence in the common law played. However, the exchange between Coke and James in 1608 revealed that the king did not have confidence in the common law as an instrument of reform or to restrain the Church courts. The king, instead, had thrown back Coke's anxieties about usurpation and levelled a similar charge: 'The Judges are like the papistes. They alleadge scriptures and will interpret the same.'[7] Anticipating Ellesmere's critique of the judges' use of their own reason to interpret customs and statutes, James warned, 'If the Judges interprete the lawes themselves and suffer none else to interprete, then they may easily make of the laws shipmen[']s hose.' Although the judges supported their claims with reference to 'artificial reason' and partisan readings of history, the complaints against the common law were more straightforward and had already been admitted by Coke among others. The pull of those criticisms of the common law had convinced the king that there were other ways to reform the legal system than to trust the common law judges. In fact the judges themselves, practising their mysteries and exercising their discretion, might also become an arbitrary power.

Coke's conduct towards the High Commission was complicated by his commitment to protecting religious reform. Even as he opposed many of its actions, Coke acted to steady the Commission as an instrument to preserve the settlement against both Catholic and Protestant non-conformists. He and the other judges exercised care in circumscribing the Commission's powers clearly but in such a way that it could perform its

---

[6] R. H. Helmholz provides an overview of the key issues and the civilian response in *Roman Canon Law in Reformation England* (Cambridge, 1990), pp. 172–180.

[7] BL Lansdowne MS 160, f. 424.

original function of detecting and punishing non-conformity. Their campaign reveals how Coke reconciled the imperatives to police usurpation while maintaining a device for disciplining non-conformists. Two perspectives on reform therefore met in the famous exchange in November 1608. Whereas Coke's outlook was more moderate than the historiography has allowed and his desire to protect the royal prerogative more sincere, the king's lack of confidence in the common law proved decisive in subsequent events.

Of the many Church courts, the High Commission for Causes Ecclesiastical most concentrated the common law judges' anxiety and their commitment to protecting the government's religious settlement. The statute of 1 Elizabeth I formally authorized the Elizabethan commissions, and letters patent created them as early as July 1559.[8] The task of the laymen and clerics who staffed these commissions was to assist in the reformation of the ecclesiastical state and to advance the larger work of securing the settlement.[9] The recognition that purely spiritual penalties would have little effect against recalcitrant Catholics led to the granting of an authority to punish by fine and imprisonment.[10] From these beginnings the court grew to entertain jurisdiction over a number of ecclesiastical offences, including slander, perjury, adultery, divorce and even the stealing of metal from church bells.[11] Though Roland Usher, the conflict's historian, believed that the judges of the commissions conducted themselves with 'moderation' and 'conservatism', their actions nonetheless increasingly attracted the ire of the common lawyers. The expansion of the commissions to hear private causes, Usher argued, was needed to shore up the waning jurisdiction of the Church courts and

[8] J. E. Neale, 'The Elizabethan Acts of Supremacy and Uniformity', *English Historical Review*, 65:256 (1950), 304–32, at 330–1, and *pace* Elliot Rose, *Cases of Conscience* (Cambridge, 1975), p. 134. R. G. Usher discusses the Commission's early Tudor antecedents in *The Rise and Fall of the High Commission* (Oxford, 1968), pp. 21–2; see also Tyler, 'Introduction', pp. xii–xxiv. A list of the surviving records is found in Philip Tyler, 'Introduction', pp. xxxv–xxxviii, and is supplemented by the list in Helmholz, *Roman Canon Law*, pp. 46–7. Tyler continued the work of Usher in his dissertation (Oxford University, 1965), and some of his findings were distilled into 'The Significance of the Ecclesiastical Commission of York', *Northern History*, 2 (1967), 27–44.

[9] *SR*, vol. IV, pt. 1, p. 352, 1 Elizabeth I, c. 1, § 8; Claire Cross, *The Royal Supremacy in the Elizabethan Church* (London, 1969), pp. 21–7, 82–5; N. L. Jones, 'Religion in Parliament', in D. M. Dean and N. L. Jones (eds.), *The Parliaments of Elizabethan England* (Oxford, 1990), pp. 117–38.

[10] Bodl. Rawlinson MS B 202, f. 128v.

[11] Usher, *High Commission*, p. 102; *Sturgeon and Frost's Case* (1603), BL Additional MS 25203, f. 678r.

their limited battery of penalties. On the other side, ambition mostly animated the judges, for 'If the common law courts were to become supreme in England, the Commission must be overwhelmed and abolished for all time.'[12] Usher, however, noted that the judges were initially circumspect, cautiously supporting the Commission despite intermittent conflict.[13] *Fuller's Case* (1607), however, marked the turning point and the beginnings of Coke's offensive, even though he had previously helped to soothe tensions between the jurisdictions.[14]

The struggle quickly developed into a constitutional conflict, according to Usher and subsequent historiography: the High Commission rested its case on the royal prerogative and the letters patent, and the common lawyers on 'the Law' and the statute of 1 Elizabeth I. The effect of the statute focused contemporary attention: the common lawyers were committed to the belief that the statute represented a parliamentary grant of ecclesiastical jurisdiction to the queen. The commissioners argued instead that the statute was a 'concession by the Crown to the nation'. Behind the statute was a 'residual authority' held by the Crown, a judicial power that might be delegated as the queen saw fit through letters patent.[15]

The narrative, as established by Usher, has remained largely unchallenged, and it maps easily onto the larger story of constitutional conflict. Philip Tyler, who continued Usher's researches, acknowledges that the Commission's zealous prosecution of moral offences, such as adultery, worried the judges. But principle was the lesser influence on their opposition: Tyler insists that much of the antagonism of the common lawyers was based on the desire for 'financial advantage' through the taking of cases from the Church courts and suggests, with little evidence, that the Commission had become a 'popular court for private litigation'.[16]

Richard Helmholz has demonstrated, however, that far from a waning jurisdiction, the Church courts in this period benefited from strong demand.[17] The common law courts were not, in this period, short of

---

[12] Usher, *High Commission*, pp. 157, 155.

[13] Usher, *High Commission*, p. 157. Usher notes that prohibitions were observed in the 1580s in some testamentary cases; *ibid.*, p. 161.

[14] *Ibid.*, p. 169.

[15] Usher, *High Commission*, pp. 223, 225–7; followed by Sommerville, *Royalists and Patriots*, p. 200; M. H. Maguire, 'Attack of the Common Lawyers on the Oath Ex Officio as Administered in the Ecclesiastical Courts in England', in *Essays in History and Political Theory in Honour of Charles Howard McIlwain* (Cambridge, MA, 1936), p. 218; Hart, *Rule of Law*, pp. 39, 43; *DNB*, s.v. 'Richard Bancroft'.

[16] Tyler, 'Introduction', p. xxxii; Hart, *Rule of Law*, p. 35.

[17] Excommunication may also have been a more effective sanction than Usher appreciated; Helmholz, *OHLE*, vol. I, pp. 283, 288–9; 'Excommunication as a Legal Sanction: The

business either, and so James increased the number of judges in the courts of Common Pleas and King's Bench.[18] Christopher Brooks, who has studied lawyer's earnings, has suggested that they peaked around 1600, though inflation and the increasing size of the profession slowly reduced the 'average' lawyer's earnings afterwards.[19] The most telling evidence that the judges were not solely animated by pursuit of additional business can be found in defamation, an area where they had taken causes from the Church courts. In slander cases especially, the judges appeared resistant and even peevish at the number of cases they were hearing, confirmed that the spiritual courts had concurrent jurisdiction, and developed the *mitior sensus* rule to limit these cases.[20] Nor were they quick to grant and insist on prohibition. From the bench, Coke warned counsel that the judges would not 'grant prohibition on every trifling matter', and Gray has written that the evidence supports his restraint.[21] Coke's private papers do not suggest that the desire for business drove his campaign against the Commission. Instead they imply a principled opposition, as when he wrote in the margins of his account of the York House Conference, 'great is truth and it has prevailed'.[22]

The truth that Coke sought was a boundary: the historical limits of the ecclesiastical law that had been returned to the Crown. Usher's argument that the struggle pitted the power of statute against the royal prerogative is a neat division that continues to endure. Yet the reality was more complex. Contemporaries on both sides of the dispute viewed the statute as controlling, because it was the gateway to historical practice. The statute had restored what was the queen's by right and had been usurped by the popish clergy. Salisbury, when writing to James I, informed him that although the commissioners acted by letters patent, these were 'grounded upon an Act of Parliament' not on any residual authority.[23] Hobart, writing in defence of the High Commission in 1609, explicitly declared, 'the

---

Attitudes of the Medieval Canonists', in Richard Helmholz (ed.), *Canon Law and the Law of England* (London, 1987), pp. 101–18.

[18] 4 Co. *Rep.*, p. xvii; John Sainty, *The Judges of England, 1272–1990* (London, 1993), pp. 19, 43.

[19] Brooks, *Pettyfoggers*, pp. 227–62, at p. 252.

[20] Baker, 'Introduction', in *The Lost Notebooks of Sir James Dyer*, pp. 441–2.

[21] *Blackden's Case* (1610), HLS MS 1192, f. 202v and BL Additional 25209, f. 208r; Charles Gray, 'Self-Incrimination in Interjurisdictional Law: The Sixteenth and Seventeenth Centuries,' in R. H. Helmholz, et al. (eds.), *The Privilege Against Self-Incrimination*: Its Origins and Development (Chicago, 1997), p. 59; similarly, Jones, *Elizabethan Court of Chancery*, p. 465.

[22] Found in Coke's hand on two texts related to the ecclesiastical disputes; Holkham MS 677 ff. 334r, 352r.

[23] HMC, *Salisbury*, vol. 19, pp. 344–5.

proceedings of the High Commissioners [are] grounded upon the statute of 1 Elizabeth c. 1'.[24] Richard Cosin, who wrote the most extensive
defence of the Commission, certainly emphasized the patents, but he did
not believe that they might override statute or even the common law.[25]
In his argument for the administration of the oath ex officio, he went
to great lengths to prove that it was warranted by statute and the common law.[26] When discussing the High Commission's power to fine and
imprison, Cosin attributed this capacity directly 'out of the words of the
very Acte'. As Cosin explained, since ecclesiastical courts before the statute of 1 Elizabeth, c. 1, had authority to attach and imprison, the statute
had operated to reannex this power. Cosin thereby pointed to the real
source of the debate: what the Church courts had been able to do lawfully
before the Reformation.[27]

The difficulty lay with the wording of the statute of 1 Elizabeth, c. 1,
which was agreed by both sides to be declaratory of the nebulous 'ecclesiastical law' that was 'restored' to the Crown.[28] This jurisdiction, Hobart
argued, had been usurped by the pope, but returned to the queen 'as large
as that was'.[29] And some claimed that it had been large, including both
instance and criminal jurisdiction, and authority to fine and imprison.
If the statutes restored the ancient law, the letters patent relied on the
statute and the historical law to instruct the commissioners. The High
Commission, Hobart declared, 'is not created by the statute of 1 Elizabeth
nor by any other statute, but stands by the auncient fundamentall and
common lawe of the land'.[30]

The common law judges also looked to history to discern the ecclesiastical law, conceding that the statute of 1 Elizabeth I, c. 1, was not the sole
authority for the High Commission.[31] Coke observed in 1607 that even
without the statute Elizabeth might have created the Commission 'by the

---

[24] Bodl. Rawlinson MS B 202, f. 116r; see also f. 125r. This was acknowledged by Usher, *High Commission*, pp. 193–7.

[25] Cosin, *An Apologie*, pt. I, pp. 106, 110.

[26] *Ibid.*, pt. III, pp. 98–104, esp. 104; pt. II, pp. 111–12.

[27] *Ibid.*, pt. I, pp. 102–4, 111.

[28] *SR*, vol. IV, pt. I, p. 350; *Whette* v. *Southcote* (1599), UCL Ogden MS 29, f. 99v; *Bird* v. *Smith*, Moore King's Bench 782, 72 ER 903; BL Lansdowne MS 27, f. 46r.

[29] Bodl. Rawlinson MS B 202, f. 126r.

[30] *Ibid.*, f. 127v; 128r–v, 129v; see also the comments of Finch in *Maunsell and Onon's Case* (1607), BL Additional MS 25206, f. 60r.

[31] *Bird* v. *Smith*, Moore King's Bench 782, 72 ER 903; *Maunsell and Onon's Case*, BL Additional MS 25206, f. 55r–56v. Conrad Russell, 'Parliament, the Royal Supremacy and the Church', *Parliamentary History*, 19 (2000), 27–37. See also Gray, *Writ of Prohibition*, vol. II, p. 363.

ancient prerogative and law of England'.[32] Historical recovery posed the problem of separating the ecclesiastical law from its corruptions, and on that point interpretations differed. The author of an Elizabethan treatise described this task: 'that ancient jurisdiction is now united to the Crowne againe notwithstanding any former usurpation or encroachment of the treytor Clergie, it is to be considered what they heretofore mighte and may now lawfully doe, and not what they might have done in time of usurpation'.[33]

Interpretations of the ancient jurisdiction could bolster any number of arguments. In 1607 Nicholas Fuller moved in defence of his clients whom the Commission had imprisoned that the ancient jurisdiction did not warrant imprisonment and the Church courts should proceed only by ecclesiastical censure.[34] Popham accepted that 'in ancient times' the ecclesiastical authority only had power to excommunicate, but the power to fine and imprison had arisen from the writ *capiendo* and the statutes 2 Henry IV and 1 Elizabeth I, c. 1.[35] While those advocating a wide jurisdiction for the Commission had only to find examples from the past, those who sought to constrain the courts had to argue that some of these practices were corruptions and should no longer be practised.

The second problem for those trying to understand the limits of the Commission's powers was the broad wording of the statute and the patent. The act specifically authorized the queen to delegate her ecclesiastical powers to commissioners in order that they might 'visit refourme redres order correcte and amende all such Erroures Heresies Scismes Abuses Offences Contemptes and Enormitiees [sic]'.[36] The text of the statute (including language such as 'any maner', 'all such' and 'whatsoever') supported wide interpretations of the scope of the commissioners' jurisdiction. The patent was drawn with a similar language, granting 'full power and authority' to the commissioners to correct 'all such errors'.[37]

---

[32] *Cawdrey's Case*, 5 Co. Rep. 8b, 77 ER 10.

[33] IT Petyt MS 511/16, f. 11r.

[34] *Maunsell and Onon's Case* (1607), BL Additional MS 25206, ff. 59v–60r.

[35] Coke took a similar position; see BL Cotton MS Faustina D VI, f. 5v.

[36] *SR*, vol. IV, pt. I, p. 352.

[37] G. W. Prothero, *Select Statutes and Other Constitutional Documents Illustrative of the Reigns of Elizabeth and James I* (Oxford, 1913), pp. 228–9; Usher, *High Commission*, pp. 24, 26, 29; John Guy, 'The Establishment and the Ecclesiastical Polity', in John Guy (ed.), *The Reign of Elizabeth I: Court and Culture in the Last Decade* (Cambridge, 1995), pp. 126–49, at p. 139.

Proceedings might be initiated in a number of ways, including witnesses, but also 'all other ways and means ye can devise for all offences, misdoers and misdemeanors done'. The commissioners were given the broad authority to fine and imprison. Popham observed that this wording was 'too general and very liberal'.[38] In response to concerns about the capacious language, the patent of 1611 provided greater specificity, requiring that witness or presentment should begin proceedings and requiring a 'reasonable' fine or imprisonment.[39] In their attempt to control the interpretation of these words, especially the definition of 'enormities', and the looseness of the drafting, the common law judges asserted their authority over the judicial interpretation of statutes.[40]

The common law judges were also mindful of the necessity of the Commission, and this pragmatism balanced their apprehension. The Elizabethan commissions were born in a moment of political precariousness – in the years just before their passage Protestants had burned for their beliefs. After the instability of Mary's reign, the Commission was remembered as being created for fear of 'what tumult might arise upon the change of Religion'.[41] Importantly, the tribunal was also recalled in 1611 to have been of a 'temporary nature'.[42] Whatever its origins as a temporary measure to protect the transition to Protestantism and deprive the popish clergy, the Commission's usefulness ensured its survival, as separatists emerged alongside Catholics to contest the Crown's religious policies. John Whitgift wrote to the queen that the Commission 'ys the onlie meanes we have to punish and restraine sectaries and contentious persons which refuse to observe Lawes and to keep order'.[43] From its earliest years the common law judges not only supported many of the Commission's activities that protected the government, but they were actively involved in its work. Even Usher conceded that the judges' decision in 1591 in *Cawdrey's Case* suggested that they were 'reconciled to the Commission's existence'.[44] Those who later debated with Coke reminded him of the

---

[38] *Maunsell and Onon's Case*, BL Additional MS 25206, f. 55v.

[39] Prothero, *Select Statutes*, pp. 430, 425–6, 429.

[40] *Needham's Case* (1607), HLS MS 118(c), f. 99r.

[41] Huntington Library Ellesmere MS 2013; *Maunsell and Onon's Case*, BL Additional MS 25206, f. 60r; Bodl. Rawlinson MS B 202, f. 128v; Cosin, *Apologie*, pt. I, p. 111; Nicholas Fuller, *The Argument of Master Nicholas Fuller, in the Case of Thomas Lad, and Richard Maunsell, His Clients* (London, 1607), STC 11460, p. 30.

[42] Prothero, *Select Statutes*, p. 425; *Needham's Case* (1607), HLS MS 118(c), f. 99r.

[43] BL Additional MS 28571, f. 172.

[44] Usher, *High Commission*, pp. 162, 146, 157. The judges, for example, allowed the Commission to fine recusants; BL Lansdowne MS 27, f. 46r.

common lawyers' involvement with the commissions. They recalled, for example, John Southcote's committal of a preacher who refused to christen a child in 1559, and William Fleetwood and Sir Thomas Bromley's imprisonment of another for disturbing an incumbency in 1572.[45] Roger Manwood JCP was said to have committed John Hynde and so produced one of the earliest conflicts with the Commission. It was even reported that Coke, while he was attorney-general, ordered the arrest of a man 'who had layd violent hands upon his Chaplaines Curate: and he caused the Attachment to be sent before letters missive'.[46]

This support was mitigated when the common law judges suspected that the Commission was encroaching beyond its lawful jurisdiction, especially when the matter was temporal. The common law, Popham declared, was ready both to protect the subject and preserve the king.[47] The first flashpoint of the dispute was over the administration of the oath ex officio, which echoed a practice of pre-Reformation courts that Protestant reformers had condemned. As defenders of the Commission argued repeatedly, the procedure was not unique to the tribunal, but sanctioned by canonical law. The court would summon a deponent who would know neither the questions nor the accusations against them. A general question, such as 'Have you recently committed a wrong?', could reveal a hidden transgression or lead the deponent into perjury. The oath raised the problem of self-incrimination, and in doing so it seemed to violate the canonical rule insisted upon by the common lawyers *quod nemo tenetur seipsum prodere*.[48] From the perspective of those who warned that the Church courts should operate solely within the spiritual sphere, offences detected by the oath might be prosecuted under temporal statutes.[49]

Ethan Shagan has argued that those objecting to the oath feared that it opened a 'window' into men's consciences.[50] This anxiety points to the historical depth in which the conflict with the Commission was entrenched. Using history as a guide some identified the oath as an

---

[45] Huntington Library Ellesmere MS 2013, f. 2v.

[46] *Ibid.*, ff. 3v–4r. For a complete list of other examples, see Huntington Library Ellesmere MS 2013.

[47] *Maunsell and Onon's Case*, BL Additional MS 25206, f. 55r.

[48] 'No one is bound to betray himself.' See R. H. Helmholz, 'The Privilege and the Ius Commune: The Middle Ages to the Seventeenth Century', in *The Privilege Against Self-Incrimination: Its Origins and Development* (Chicago, 1997), pp. 17–46, at 43–5; M. R. T. Macnair, 'The Early Development of the Privilege Against Self-Incrimination', *Oxford Journal of Legal Studies*, 10 (1990), 66–84.

[49] Gray, *Writ of Prohibition*, vol. II, pp. 293–430.

[50] Shagan, 'The English Inquisition', 541–65.

instrument of corruption: purgation had been a 'popish usage'.[51] William Tyndale had warned that it was in the nature of popery to seek access to conscience to regulate the thought of individuals, declaiming specifically against such oaths.[52] The oath had been a prop of the popish usurpation, enabling churchmen to acquire land and worldly goods.[53] James Morice, notable for his defence of Robert Cawdrey, was among the most vociferous in his opposition to the oath, believing that it was the 'trap of the devil'. Through this legal device the clergy regained the access to conscience that they had lost when auricular confession had been reformed. Morice argued that proceeding by oath ex officio tempted deponents to perjure themselves to avoid temporal penalties, while an oath itself was an act of worship that called upon God as a judge to take vengeance for any deceit.[54] The administration of the oath, it was agreed by others, created a trap for the deponent: either they would expose their body to penalties or risk their soul. Sir John Croke JKB explained that it was the invention of the devil for the destruction of men's souls, and Finch claimed it was contrary to natural law.[55] Reverence towards the act of oath-taking was shared by Coke, and in a book on the Jesuit practice of equivocation, he wrote 'the mouth which lies kills the spirit'.[56] Elsewhere Coke described an oath as sacrosanct in language similar to Morice's: 'ane othe is a taking of god to witnes, to confirme the truth of that whiche we speake ... swearing truly is a worshipping of god'.[57] Perjury called down the judgment of God who would open the secrets of the heart: 'We cannot call god to be a witnes of our sayings, but that we also wishe him to take venegeance of our perjury.'[58]

Rather than resolve contention the oath ex officio stirred new controversies, since its purpose was 'to procure some accusation'. Its administration was implicated in the spread of popery, since through the device of the oath: 'there should be erected a Court of Inquisition, more then

---

[51] *Searle's Case* (1617), BL Additional MS 25213, f. 197v.

[52] William Tyndale, *On Christian Obedience*, ed. David Daniell (London, 2000), p. 64.

[53] *Ibid.*, p. 40; HLS MS 1006, f. 295r.

[54] James Morice, *A Briefe Treatise of Oathes Exacted by Ordinaries and Ecclesiasticall Judges* (Middleburg, 1590), STC 18106, p. 10; BL Lansdowne MS 68, f. 100v; William Est, 'The Iudges and Iuries Instruction', in *Two Sermons*, p. 24. For the use of oaths in commercial transactions, see Craig Muldrew, *The Economy of Obligation: The Culture of Credit and Social Relations in Early Modern England* (New York, 1998), p. 106.

[55] *Burrowes Cox Dyton* v. *High-Commission Court*, 3 Bulstrode 54, 81 ER 46; BL Additional MS 25206, f. 56r.

[56] 'The mouth that lies kills the spirit.' Bodl. Laud MS 655, p. 1, quoting Wisdom 1:11.

[57] BL Harley MS 6687A, f. 8r.

[58] Citing 1 Samuel 14.

Spanish to sifte and ransacke by oath the most secret thoughtes and consciences of all men in generall'.[59] These unnatural proceedings were known from their historical example, such as Foxe's account of Bishop Longland, 'Which bloudie Bishop by forced and violent oathes and captious interrogatories, constrayned the children to accuse their parentes, the parentes their naturall children, the wife her husbande, the husbande his wife, one brother and sister and other ...' If prosecution by oath was a sign of popery, refusal to take the oath was in the example of the Protestant martyrs. Morice described William Thorpe the Lollard, who refused to swear before Archbishop Arundell 'that bloodie persecutor of the true Christians'.[60]

The Commission's use of the oath was raised in *John Hynde's Case* (1576).[61] The case involved the imprisonment of Hynde, who sued habeas corpus, and turned on whether the commissioners might imprison for a temporal matter. Although the circumstances are murky, Hynde was investigated on a charge of usury, which incurred a statutory penalty. It was claimed in his defence that 'he was not bound to answer by oath ... where there may be a penaltie thereby incured by statute law'.[62] The court asserted that, where a man was committed for a temporal matter by an ecclesiastical judge, he should be released, though he would not be discharged for a spiritual crime.[63] Baker notes that subsequent to this case 'returns to habeas corpus by order of the High Commission began to specify causes'.[64] The scrutiny of these committals would exercise the judges' distinction between temporal and spiritual matters, and their perception

---

[59] Morice, *A Briefe Treatise of Oathes Exacted*, pp. 10, 8.

[60] *Ibid.*, p. 11; also see pp. 17, 18 for other examples.

[61] Dyer, *Reports*, vol. II, pp. 355–6, discussed by Baker in 'Introduction', in *The Lost Notebooks of Sir James Dyer*, vol. I, pp. lxxix–lxxx; 4 Co. *Inst.*, p. 333; CUL MS Ll.4.9, f. 41v. Cosin doubted the facts of the case; *An Apologie*, part III, p. 83, and Huntington Library MS Ellesmere 2013, f. 4r. The use of the oath was also considered in *Thomas Lee's Case* (1568), when Lee, an attorney of the Common Pleas, was committed for attending mass and refused to swear. Dyer reported 'they ought not in such cases to examine him upon his oath', though Lee was released on habeas corpus due to privilege; *The Lost Notebooks of Sir James Dyer*, vol. I, pp. lxxix, 143; Huntington Library Ellesmere MS 2013, f. 3v.

[62] Huntington Library Ellesmere MS 2013, f. 4r. The statute was 37 Henry VIII, c. 9, *SR*, vol. III, pp. 996–7.

[63] The judges had debated in 1565 whether the common law could deliver those who were imprisoned by the Commission in *R. v. Mytton* (1565); *The Lost Notebooks of Sir James Dyer*, vol. I, pp. 107–8; *APC*, 1558–70, p. 177; 3 Co. *Inst.*, p. 42, and also possibly earlier in 1556 in *Leigh*, CUL MS Ii.4.9, f. 41v; *Burrowes Cox Dyton v. High-Commission Court* (1615), 3 Bulstrode 49–50, 81 ER 42; *Dighton and Holt's Case* (1615), Cro. Jac. 388, 79 ER 332; and 4 Co. *Inst.*, p. 333.

[64] Baker, 'Introduction', in *The Lost Notebooks of Sir James Dyer*, vol. I, p. lxxx.

that the Commission, despite its mixed lay and clerical personnel, was a spiritual court.

Two other developments marked the evolving relationship between the courts that same year. In *Burton's Case* the judges asserted their authority over statutory construction related to ecclesiastical proceedings and began to develop the legal framework that would limit the Commission.[65] Attempts by the tribunal to expand beyond its original purpose would be thwarted by the common law reading of the statute of 1 Elizabeth I, c. 1, and the ecclesiastical law behind it. The judges wanted a tribunal focused on its mission to protect the settlement, agreeing that individuals could be committed only in cases involving 'enormities', such as heresy.[66] Yet also in 1576, the judges conferred and agreed that the tribunal could fine recusants, thereby confirming that they would buttress the court's powers to restrain threats to the Church.[67] The Commission had its authority protected as long as it was confined to its original, narrow purpose. But the defining of 'enormities' was among those problems produced by the broad wording of the act of 1 Elizabeth I, c. 1, and so the judges' insistence on their ultimate authority to interpret statutes became decisive to their struggle.

There is further evidence from the period that the judges were mindful to restrain jurisdictional creep by the Commission. In 1581 Sir Christopher Wray CJQB, though often viewed by historians as a malleable instrument of the Crown, issued one of the earliest known prohibitions to the High Commission for testamentary disposition of temporalities.[68] Wray warned that the Commission should hold itself to matters of religion and 'be carefull and circumspect in the causes they deal [with]'. This prohibition suggests that Wray was serious about limiting the Commission to its purpose of protecting the settlement.

Protestant non-conformity prompted further ambivalence among the common law judges especially as it relit the dispute over the oath ex officio.

---

[65] Baker (ed.), *The Lost Notebooks of Sir James Dyer*, vol. II, pp. 356, 364–6; *APC*, vol. I, pp. 60, 87. *Burton* was cited as *Fox's Case* (Cro. Eliz. 41, 78 ER 305) in *Morris v. Webber* (1587), 2 Leonard 171, 74 ER 451.

[66] *Needham's Case* (1607), HLS MS 118(c), f. 99r.

[67] BL Lansdowne MS 27, ff. 46r–v; Cambridge University, Gonville and Caius College MS 103, f. 336; and see also the conference in 1585 in J. Strype, *Aylmer* (London, 1821), pp. 75–6.

[68] The verdict of both N. G. Jones in *DNB*, s.v. 'Christopher Wray', and Cockburn, *Assizes*, p. 202; Bodl. Tanner MS 79, f. 153r. Wray alludes to other prohibitions having been sent to the Commission in London, suggesting that prohibitions were more common at this time than Usher suspected; see Usher, *High Commission*, p. 180. Gray identified two Queen's Bench prohibitions obtained by Coke, in *Writ of Prohibition*, vol. II, p. 322.

The use of the oath and its popish resonance drew the Commission into conflict with the judges as they pursued advanced Protestants. Whitgift's campaign brought several non-conformists before the Commission, where they were examined under oath ex officio. Refusal to swear led to imprisonment, and accounts of the examination of Henry Barrow in 1586 revealed the presence of Wray CJQB, Edmund Anderson CJCP and one of the barons of the Exchequer. Barrow's recollection suggested that he expected no help from the common law judges though Wray intervened to advise Barrow to swear to the oath, but refuse to answer unlawful questions.[69]

Disagreement with the oath was expressed much more publicly in 1591 at an assize charge given by Francis Wyndham JCP and Francis Gawdy JQB, who were Coke's most prominent judicial patrons in Norfolk.[70] The charge included the admonition 'that ther ordynarye cowld not cyte men to appere pro salute anime to answer upon oathe'. This declaration had the effect of bringing into question not only the High Commission's procedure, but also the procedure of other ecclesiastical courts. The bishops warned that 'they dowbt how to procede in theyr courtes for that they have ever synce the Conquest used no other course'.[71] Whitgift himself urged that on account of the charge the entire ecclesiastical government would be overthrown, and complained to the Council. Elizabeth was angered and ordered that the judges be summoned before the next circuit and instructed not to issue similar instructions at their charges.[72] Despite these warnings, however, Gawdy repeated his objection to the oath ex officio in Hunt's Case (1591). The indictment against Hunt, a commissary to the archdeacon, declared that 'by the law of the land no person is to be cited into the Spiritual Court to take any oath, but in cases of matrimony and testamentary'. Though the other judges vaguely acknowledged that the spiritual court might proceed according to the civil law, Gawdy

---

[69] Henry Barrow, *The Examinations of Henry Barrowe Iohn Grenewood and Iohn Penrie, before the High Commissioners, and Lordes of the Counsel* (Dortmund[?], 1596), STC 1519, sig. A 2r–v.

[70] Coke and Gawdy served as Wyndham's executors, and Coke conducted business with both men. Coke also played cards at Gawdy's house; BL Egerton MS 2715; NRO, Walsingham/WLS (Merton) MSS, XVII / 1, 410x5; Bodl. Tanner MS 285, f. 25. Coke and Gawdy were allied also to the anti-Essex faction in Norfolk; NRO FX 25 / 1; Holkham MS 724, n.p., September 1597. The best point of entry into Norfolk politics is Smith, *County and Court*, pp. 157–342.

[71] A. Hassell Smith, Gillian Baker and Robert Kenny (eds.), *The Papers of Nathaniel Bacon of Stiffkey*, vol. III (Norwich, 1990), p. 118.

[72] Boyer, *Sir Edward Coke*, pp. 71–81, 177; *Hunt's Case* (1591), Cro. Eliz. 262, 78 ER 518.

dissented and asserted that the 'oath cannot be minstred to the party, but where the offence is presented first by two men'. This would have barred the inquisitorial use of the oath ex officio.

These tensions coincided with *Cawdrey's Case* (1591). Defenders of the ecclesiastical commission would later celebrate the case as a validation of their authority.[73] Historians have also seen in *Cawdrey* a decisive moment, John Guy describing it as a 'swing to the right', and its decision 'sweeping' and highly controversial.[74] Usher believed the case represented a sharp change in the relationship between the common law courts and the Commission, implying that the common law courts might decide of 'so undoubtedly an ecclesiastical matter as the deprivation of the clergy'.[75] Allen Boyer's evaluation suggested a triumph of 'prerogative' over 'constitutionalism', with significant consequences: 'The decision appeared to say that the queen's common-law courts would deferentially allow the queen's ecclesiastical courts to interpret the Reformation statutes, rather than serve as arbiters themselves.'[76]

The decision being so in favour of the Commission, historians have assumed that it was some sort of error on the judges' part. Usher wrote that 'Coke who reported it conveniently forgot [the opinion] in later days', while overlooking the objection that Coke published his report of *Cawdrey's Case* in 1605, 1607 and again in 1612, near the height of the dispute with the High Commission.[77] Set within the frame of a struggle between prerogative and common law, the case appears to have been a victory for prerogative. But the case instead reveals the moderation of the common law judges as they stretched between two positions: limiting the Commission and the danger of usurpation, and the practical need to enforce conformity.

The facts of the case are generally agreed upon: Robert Cawdrey held the living of South Loughnam or Luffenham in Rutland, which was in the gift of Burghley. He had long-standing sympathies with 'puritan' reform, and proceedings against him can be found as early as 1576.[78] In 1586, during a

---

[73] On Cawdrey himself see E. A. Irons, 'Sir Robert Cawdrie: Rector of South Luffenham, 1571–87', *Annual Report and Transactions of the Rutland Archaeological and Natural History Society*, 14 (1916), 23–33.

[74] Guy, 'Ecclesiastical Polity', pp. 131–5; Usher, *High Commission*, p. 140. Helmholz suggests some disagreement in civilian circles over the case in *Roman Canon Law*, p. 142.

[75] Usher, *High Commission*, p. 138.

[76] Boyer, *Sir Edward Coke*, p. 170.

[77] Documents related to Cawdrey are scattered across the Lansdowne papers, for example in BL Lansdowne MS 53, 55, 58, 61, 64, 68, 115 and 982.

[78] *DNB*, s.v. 'Robert Cawdrey'.

sermon, he said of the Book of Common Prayer that it was a 'vile book' and 'fye upon it'.[79] He was enjoined by the High Commission from December 1586 to 30 May 1587 to retract and conform, but declined to do so and was eventually deprived. The Commission, led by the Bishop of London, but also including Wray and the attorney-general, then passed sentence of deprivation against him.[80] Though initially acquiescent Cawdrey soon determined to oppose the sentence, an opposition tinged with anti-prelacy.[81] Having attempted to bring an action in the Star Chamber against the new occupant for riot, he began suit in the Queen's Bench at the beginning of 1591 for trespass.[82] The common law judges were thus drawn into the case as part of a litigation strategy, and they were more deeply involved when the jury returned a special verdict that depended on whether 'the said deprivation were not warranted by law'.[83] Thus the common law issue of trespass could only be determined by assessing the validity of the deprivation. The question was 'constitutional' insofar as it required the judges to rule on the validity of the ecclesiastical sentence.

Cawdrey's barrister was James Morice, who argued four points as to why the sentence was erroneous, the most important of which was that the Commission had not proceeded according to the Statute of Uniformity, which required several steps be taken before deprivation for offences against the Prayer Book.[84] Cawdrey and his counsel complained that the commissioners had incorrectly proceeded to the most severe censure first, and therefore the deprivation was not valid.

While the case has been interpreted as a struggle between statutory authority and the prerogative, this was not how the common law judges viewed it. Counsel for the Commission was clear that the commissioners had not proceeded by the Statute of Uniformity, but instead according to 'the law ecclesiastical, or according to their sound discretions'.[85] The interpretation of Coke and the judges who adjudicated the case was that the commissioners were 'authorised by another Act in the same Parliament'. That act was the Statute of Supremacy, and the commissioners proceeded

---

[79] Strype, *Aylmer*, p. 88, probably following BL Lansdowne MS 68, f. 108r; BL Lansdowne MS 68, f. 129r.

[80] The Commission also included William Fleetwood.

[81] Strype, *Aylmer*, p. 88.

[82] *Cawdrey v. Baillie, Mattoke* et al., PRO STAC 5/C78/3, STAC 5/C28/36, STAC 5/C80/40.

[83] *Cawdrey's Case*, 5 Co. *Rep.* 3a, 77 ER 4. The verdict is given in slightly different form elsewhere; *Cawdrey v. Atton*, Popham 59, 79 ER 1175.

[84] In his report to Burghley, the civilian Aubrey recognized the reading of 1 Elizabeth I, c. 2, § 2; as the essential point, BL; Lansdowne MS 68, f. 127r *SR*, vol. IV, part 1, p. 355.

[85] BL Lansdowne MS 68, f. 127r.

under the ecclesiastical law. The distinction comes through more clearly in Coke's manuscript report of the case. Coke notes that even if the Statute of Uniformity had not specified a process for deprivation, the commissioners would still have had the power to deprive Cawdrey for offending against the Prayer Book and the ecclesiastical law.[86] Coke noted in particular that the Act of Uniformity had not abrogated the offence at the ecclesiastical law. In fact the act included a proviso that ordinaries should continue to have full power and visitatorial authority, thereby reserving to them the power to deprive their clergy. Since this authority came historically from the ecclesiastical law, the ordinaries were not bound to follow the procedures outlined by the Act of Uniformity, and so a fortiori neither were the commissioners.[87] The other surviving report of the case confirms the reasoning outlined in Coke's report.[88] The narrow question of law that the judges ruled on in order to determine whether a trespass had been committed was whether the ecclesiastical law allowed the Commission to deprive ministers and whether this authority had in any way been limited by the procedures set forth in the Act of Uniformity. Their position was reaffirmed at a judicial conference with James I in 1604.[89] The reasoning was the same: the queen had supreme ecclesiastical power and it could be delegated to commissioners who would then have the power of deprivation 'by the canon law of the realm'. The judges continued to uphold this reasoning in *Bird v. Smith* (1606), *Parson Munfeld's Case* (1609), where the commissioners also imprisoned the offending minister, and by implication in *Candict and Plomer's Case* (1610).[90] Their decision reiterated the residual authority of the reannexed ecclesiastical law and the need to recover its past proceedings.

---

[86]   BL Harley MS 6686A, f. 111r.

[87]   *Cawdrey's Case*, 5 Co. *Rep.* 6b, 77 ER, pp. 7, 8; *SR*, vol. IV, part I, p. 357, 1 Eliz I, § 11; BL Harley MS 6686A, f. 111r. Cawdrey's counsel tried to argue that the bishop's authority to deprive was not held by the Commission, but the court rejected this argument. *Cawdrey's Case*, 5 Co. *Rep.* 4a, 77 ER 5; and affirmed in *Roper's Case* (1607), 12 Co. *Rep.* 47, 77 ER 1327. Coke had earlier argued in *Frankwell's Case* (1588), 2 Leonard 177, 74 ER 456, that the court might defer to a deprivation by the High Commission. Coke's report is BL Harley 6687D, f. 730r.

[88]   *Cawdrey* v. *Atton*, Popham 60, 79 ER 1175, and also, Yale University Law School MS G R 24, ff. 45r–51v.

[89]   *Memorandum*, Croke Jac 37, 79 ER 30; *Anonymous*, Moore 755, 72 ER 885.

[90]   *Bird* v. *Smith*, Moore King's Bench 782, 72 ER 903; *Candict and Plomer's Case*, Godbolt 163, 78 ER 99; *Parson Munfeld's Case*, HLS MS 1192, f. 140r. Baron Altham cited this reasoning in his notes to the *Case of Commendams*; see Lincoln's Inn Hale MS 80, ff. 256v–257r.

Cawdrey's Case reasserted the importance of historical knowledge and did not quell the major issues that continued to fester: the administration of the oath and the jurisdiction of the Commission over matters that were not 'enormities'. While the judicial conference of 1576 had approved the Commission's discretion to fine and imprison, the turn of the century found litigants trying to undermine their sentences by appealing to the common law courts. As two cases in 1600 reveal, their strategy included seeking release on habeas corpus with the claim that the cause of imprisonment was invalid.[91] A procedural limitation on the Commission's power to imprison was found when John Simpson was indicted for the murder of a constable sent to arrest him by the Commission. Simpson claimed self-defence, since the constable had come by night to his home with only a warrant from the Commission.[92] Coke related that upon conference the judges determined that the statute of 1 Elizabeth I, c. 1, gave no power to the commissioners to imprison except 'they ought to proceed according to ecclesiastical law, by citation; for the statute of 1 El. did not give them any such authority to arrest the body of any subject upon surmise'.[93] Without an initial citation, the attachment was against the ecclesiastical law.[94] In the similar case of *Allen Ball* (1608) this was also the thrust of the ruling, which relied upon, though it did not name, *Simpson's Case*.[95] Again the court insisted that the High Commission should proceed by citation, excommunication and then by *capias* for imprisonment. The judges in *Allen Ball's Case* claimed that to arrest a person on mere surmise was against Magna Carta.[96] In *Sir William Dethick's Case* (1611) the judges also insisted upon procedure by *capias*.[97] In neither case did the judges assert that the High Commission could not imprison, but demanded that they follow the ecclesiastical law and the traditional process of signification.

Moreover, in *Stocke's Case* (1600), the judges revealed their suspicion of the use of letters missive to attach excommunicants, and insisted upon

---

[91] There is a third case of the same year involving Edward Thicknesse who was released upon habeas corpus. Coke gives the plea roll reference as Pasch. 42 El. Rot. 1209 and mentions it in *Chancey's Case* (1611), 12 Co. *Rep.* 84, 77 ER 1361, and again in 4 Co. *Inst.*, p. 334.

[92] 4 Co. *Inst.*, p. 333. A different account of the case is found in Huntington Library Ellesmere MS 2013. The defence of the home was considered in *Semayne's Case* (1604), 5 Co. *Rep.* 91a, 77 ER 194.

[93] 4 Co. *Inst.*, pp. 333–4.   [94] Helmholz, *OHLE*, vol. I, p. 318.

[95] The description of the precedent in the report of *Allen Ball* matches the facts of *Simpson*.

[96] *High Commission*, 12 Co. *Rep.* 50, 77 ER 1329.

[97] *Dethick and Stoke's Case*, Godbolt 181, 78 ER 110.

procedural protections. Coke reported that the whole court held that the commissioners did not have authority to apprehend Anne Stocke and took issue with the manner of her attempted arrest. Their inclination reflected the concern that arrests by letters missive were dangerous because an individual would not have an ordinary means of review, and they might be placed in 'perpetual prison' at the 'pleasure of the commissioners', even before they were cited to appear.[98] In several of these cases, the judges again reiterated the crucial importance of the ecclesiastical law, explaining that the prince could not circumvent the traditional process of citation by patent.[99]

Judicial discussion in these years brought into focus the Commission's jurisdiction and proceedings. At a conference in 1601 it was agreed that the High Commission, and not the common law, could punish for heresy.[100] But Coke, who spoke as attorney-general, insisted that the Commission must follow a procedure settled historically, aware that the definition of heresy had shifted over time. He urged that examinations for heresy might proceed only 'by the authority of canonical scripture, and by the four first general councils, or by any other general council, wherein the same was declared heresy by the express and plain words of canonical scripture, or such as shall hereafter be determined to be heresy by Parliament'.[101] The emphasis on remaining within the boundaries of historical practice was repeated at a conference in 1604 involving the judges and the Council in the Star Chamber. When queried whether the Commission might deprive Puritan ministers, the judges responded affirmatively that the king's ecclesiastical power had been delegated to the commissioners. They reminded him that the statute, which had merely 'explained and declared the ancient power', had not given this power.[102]

The most prominent of the Jacobean cases involved Nicholas Fuller, who was well known as a lawyer who defended Puritans, and his arguments touched more directly on substantive issues.[103] When the Commission

---

[98] BL Harley MS 6686B, f. 377v.

[99] *Chancey's Case* (1611), 12 Co. *Rep.* 82, 77 ER 1360; BL Harley MS 6686B, f. 378r.

[100] Helmholz, *OHLE*, vol. I, pp. 639–42 has a general discussion of the offence. See also BL Additional MS 25203, f. 206v.

[101] *The Case of Heresy* (1601), 12 Co. *Rep.* 57, 77 ER 1336, 1337.

[102] BL Harley MS 1330, f. 5r.

[103] The story is told in manuscript accounts of the case contained in BL Hargrave MS 33, ff. 117r–134v, and Lansdowne MS 1172, ff. 97r–106v; Fuller, *Argument*. A Star Chamber case that emerged from the Argument's publication suggests that it was indeed gathered

imprisoned two of his clients for contempt, Fuller sought review by habeas corpus in 1607.[104] Many of the same issues were debated in the concurrent case of his clients, and Popham agreed that the Commission could only administer the oath to willing laymen.[105] In making his arguments for relief in his own case, Fuller claimed that the Commission did not have any historical authority to imprison – in fact history spoke ominously of such power. The only precedents of clergy being able to order imprisonment directly were under the statute of 2 Henry IV, c. 15, which was 'procured by popish prelates in the time of darknes'.[106] The likening of the Commission to an instrument of popery was obvious, and Fuller hit the point home by accusing the clergy of imprisoning men 'without showing any cause or matter why they did soe committ them, and that they detayned them in prison as longe as they list'.[107] The ecclesiastical law that had been reannexed by 1 Elizabeth I, Fuller claimed, did not include the power to imprison, as this had been a popish innovation.[108] He concluded that the Commission proceeded by Antichrist rather than Christ.[109]

The Commission responded to these arguments by summoning Fuller for slander and contempt. Fuller obtained a prohibition from the King's Bench, and the judges considered whether the Commission could punish him for contempt. Given that his comments were raised as part of arguments before the court, the common law judges assumed to themselves the authority to punish Fuller.[110] They reiterated that only the judges might construe the statute of 1 Elizabeth I and the letters patent, and thereby determine the Commission's authority. They added the reasoning – an allusion to the swelling of the spiritual court jurisdiction in the Middle Ages – that, 'if the Ecclesiastical Judges shall have the determination of what things they shall have cognizance ... they will make no difficulty

---

from Fuller's own notes; PRO STAC 8 19/7. See also *Fuller's Case*, 12 Co. *Rep.* 41, 77 ER 1322; HMC, *Salisbury*, vol. XIX, pp. 285–6; and R. G. Usher, *The Reconstruction of the English Church* (New York, 1910), vol. II, pp. 134–54, and *High Commission*, pp. 170–9.

[104] Fuller's clients had been committed primarily for their refusal to undergo an examination under oath ex officio; Gray, *Writ of Prohibition*, vol. II, pp. 338–69.

[105] *Maunsell and Onon's Case*, BL Additional MS 25206, ff. 55r–v.

[106] Fuller, *Argument*, p. 3; see also Morice, *A Briefe Treatise of Oathes Exacted*, p. 33. The statute was directed against the Lollards and authorized bishops to imprison those who violated the act; *SR*, vol. II, pp. 125–8.

[107] BL Lansdowne MS 1172, f. 102r.

[108] He made a similar argument in *Maunsell and Onon* and also Fuller, *Argument*, pp. 24–5, 11–13.

[109] *Fuller's Case* (1607), BL Additional MS 25213, f. 81r.

[110] *Fuller's Case*, 12 Co. *Rep.* 43, 77 ER 1324.

ampliare jurisdictionem suam'. Far from a decisive strike against the High Commission, however, the court reiterated that the Commission might punish for 'heresy, schism or erroneous opinion'. The judges suggested that the Commission proceed by arraigning Fuller for schism and heresy, where their jurisdiction was unimpeachable, and the commissioners duly proceeded to do so. Though Fuller proceeded to obtain a writ of habeas corpus, the judges decided that his committal was valid.[111] Once again the judges had plotted their course between history and policy.

By 1607 the common law judges had made two points clear: they would support the High Commission as they interpreted the statute and the ecclesiastical law to have allowed it; and they would prevent the Commission from swelling its jurisdiction.[112] This anxiety led Coke after he rose to the bench to insist that the Commission should have jurisdiction only in 'enormous' cases, as defined by the common law judges, and that persons could only be examined ex officio in very narrow circumstances in order to protect them from temporal penalties.[113]

The common law courts had also been concerned about the offences that the High Commission was hearing from late in the reign of Elizabeth I. In *Taylor's Case* (1602) the Common Pleas prohibited the Commission from hearing a case for irreverent speeches and carrying corn on holy days.[114] Prohibition and habeas corpus were granted to stop hearings involving matrimony.[115] Debate over the extent of the Commission's jurisdiction appeared in *Roper's Case* (1607) where the court ruled that the commissioners could not order the payment of a pension out of an impropriated rectory. The court determined that the actions of the commissioners interfered with the ordinary's jurisdiction over such pensions, which had been granted by statutory authority.[116] The common law judges were adamant that the Commission was to hold plea solely of crimes and not injuries between parties. The consequence otherwise, the court reasoned, would be that issues of *meum et tuum* would be determined by a body with

---

[111] Usher, *High Commission*, pp. 177–8; BL Additional MS 58218, f. 7v. Fuller eventually submitted though he was later arrested again; *DNB*, s.v. 'Nicholas Fuller'.

[112] Opponents feared that the Commission would enlarge its authority, imprison and confiscate at will, and 'burn any man for heresy …'; *If High Commissioners Have Power to Imprison*, 12 Co. *Rep.* 20, 77 ER 1302.

[113] *Edgar's Case* (1610), HLS MS 114, f. 10r.

[114] There also appears to be an earlier case, *Atmere's Case*, heard in the Exchequer; 4 Co. *Inst.*, pp. 332–3, and also mentioned in Huntington Library Ellesmere MS 2013, f. 3r.

[115] For marital cases see *Lady Throgmorton's Case* (1610), 12 Co. *Rep.* 69, 77 ER 1347; *Codd* v. *Turback* (1615), 3 Bulstrode 109, 81 ER 94.

[116] 34 Henry VIII; see also *Jones* v. *Bowen* (1611), HLS MS 1192, f. 225r.

little appeal or control and lead to the dissolution of the jurisdiction of the ordinary.[117]

Prohibitions for examinations on oath ex officio also continued, but the common law position was again nuanced. In a response to a query from the Privy Council in 1606 as to which cases the ordinary might examine upon oath ex officio, Coke and Popham responded that the ordinary could not force any man either ecclesiastical or temporal to swear generally to answer unseen interrogatories. Most importantly, a layman could only be examined on matrimonial and testamentary matters that 'do not concern the shame and infamy of the party', unless the party voluntarily assented to the administration of the oath.[118] Declaring that the oath in cases outside matrimony and testaments was the instrument of the devil, the judges looked back to *Lee's Case* (1568) and *Hind's Case* as precedents for their decision, though neither case was on point. They raised the concern that men would be entrapped to lose their liberty and possessions by 'captious interrogatories'. Historical experience exacerbated these fears, and it was recalled that in the reign of Queen Mary 'all the martyrs who were burnt were examined upon their oaths'.[119] The judges, however, left open the possibility that clergy might be examined on oath so long as they assented, had the articles before them and were not examined on mere surmise. Similarly, in *William Warrington's Case* (1609) the court stated that ecclesiastical persons could be examined on any matter related to religion, but nothing temporal.[120] For this exception the court in *Parson Munfeld's Case* (1609) permitted the High Commission to examine Munfeld on oath.[121]

Increasingly vocal discontent with the Commission, reflected in parliamentary bills to limit its jurisdiction, formed the backdrop to these cases.[122] In 1604 at the Hampton Court Conference complaints were made against the low status of many of the commissioners and their hearing

---

[117] *Roper's Case* (1607), 12 Co. *Rep.* 47, 77 ER 1327. Opinions varied, so that William Peryam JCP had stated in 1588 that the queen might hear appeals from the High Commission in person; *Frankwell's Case* (1588), 2 Leonard 177, 74 ER 456.

[118] *Of Ex Officio Oaths before an Ecclesiastical Judge*, 12 Co. *Rep.* 26, 77 ER 1308.

[119] *Ibid.*, 1310 and 1311. See Gray, *Writ of Prohibition*, vol. II, *passim*, but esp. pp. 327–32.

[120] *William Warrington's Case* (1609), HLS MS 1192, ff. 149v–150r. *Of Oath Ex Officio*, 12 Co. *Rep.* 27, 77 ER 1309; Folger Shakespeare MS v.b.303, 'The Some of My Lord Cookes Charge', [n.p.]. An example of a prohibition for an oath tendered to an ecclesiastic is *Latters* v. *Sussex* (1604?), Noy 151, 74 ER 1112.

[121] *Parson Munfeld's Case* (1609), HLS MS 1192, f. 140r.

[122] *CJ*, I, p. 307. Attempts to restrain the Commission by bill continued; *PP 1610*; vol. I, p. 280; vol. II, pp. 61, 263–5, 358, 396, 407–8; James's response, vol. II, pp. 294–5.

of causes that detracted from the ordinary's jurisdiction. An idea was floated to grant the bishops the power to fine and imprison and restrict the Commission to only the most grievous offences.[123] There was also concern about the number of commissions that had been established, especially the diocesan commissions, which even Whitgift seems to have regarded as excessive.[124] Towards the end of the conference an unnamed lord raised the issue of the oath ex officio, which he likened to the proceedings of the Spanish Inquisition. The appeal fell on deaf ears, for James, perhaps given the influence of the civil law in Scotland, approved the oath and defended it in a long speech.

Against this pressure and prohibitions to their courts the clerical leadership responded with increasing vigour. In 1598 Whitgift voiced several complaints to the Council and the bishops, presenting to the judges eleven main points of difference on the issuing of prohibitions.[125] Whitgift reasoned that if the surmises upon which the prohibition was based were frivolous or 'vain' then the judges were willingly infringing on the liberties of the Church.[126] Whitgift identified the heart of the problem, explaining that too often prohibitions were granted for exceptions or pleas that were deemed temporal. He observed that it would be possible in this manner to obtain a prohibition for any matter, suggesting that a strict distinction between temporal and spiritual was unworkable in legal practice.[127] The argument came with an important implication: the two jurisdictions were equal, so why might the ecclesiastical not restrain the temporal?[128] For all the sharpness of their proceedings, this Elizabethan conference still invited dialogue, whereas its Jacobean successors offered conclusions rather than questions, and revealed James's suspicion of the common law.

The precipitator to the increased tension was probably the elevation of the combative Richard Bancroft to Canterbury. By October 1605 he had presented the *Articuli Cleri* to James I, a list of complaints about prohibitions from the common law. The parties came together at the first of several conferences in 1608. James had already hinted at his disapproval of common law prohibitions and he had doubts about the integrity of the

---

[123] BL Stowe 164, f. 192, and Usher, *Reconstruction*, vol. 1., pp. 338–41.

[124] Usher, *High Commission*, p. 165.

[125] J. Strype, *The Life and Acts of John Whitgift* (Oxford, 1822) vol. II, p. 397. The documents are found in BL Cotton MS Cleopatra F I, ff. 109r–115v, and Bodl. MS Rawlinson B 202, ff. 108v–113r. Strype does not print the entire collection.

[126] BL Cotton MS Cleopatra F I, f. 109v.

[127] Bodl. Rawlinson MS B 202, f. 108v.   [128] *Ibid.*, ff. 111r–v.

judges, explaining that the 'matter of profit was the cause why the Judges embraced so much'.[129] These conferences would further reveal that the king lacked confidence in the judges and that he had accepted several of the criticisms of the common law that were in circulation.

At the beginning of the conference with the bishops in November, James asserted his authority as an umpire between the jurisdictions, since the king was also a judge:

> In England [in the past] the kings rode the circuite, and the Chanceller, and Chiefe Justice wayted on them.[130] The King [is] the supreme judge, inferior judges his shadowes and ministers ... the king may if he please, sit and judge in Westminster Hall in any Court there ... The king being the author of the lawe is the interpreter of the law.[131]

Coke suspected that Bancroft was behind the king's assertions and that he had urged James to decide the issue between the jurisdictions in his own person.[132] A contemporary document attributed to Bancroft explicitly supports James's capacity to judge in his own person, and its arguments closely resemble those that James himself made in his speech.[133] The conclusion that some drew was that Bancroft was convincing the king that he was an absolute monarch, an accusation noticed by the archbishop in a letter in 1609 where he also mentioned the rumour that 'by my meanes a Course is entred into which tendeth to the overthrowe of the Comon Lawe'.[134]

Both sides doubted the other's honesty, and so neither side had confidence in the other. Coke claimed, for example, that the commissioners were cheating the Crown of fines through embezzlement.[135] In 1609 Bancroft, responding to a petition from the civilians complaining of threats to their profession, accused the common lawyers of asserting a nearly uncontrollable power like the papists. The judges, he alleged, held

---

[129] Spedding (ed.), *Letters and Life*, vol. IV, p. 90.
[130] Possibly alluding to the statute of 28 Edward I, st. 3, c. 5.
[131] BL Lansdowne MS 160, f. 424v.
[132] *Prohibitions Del Roy*, 12 Co. *Rep.* 63, 77 ER 1342–3.
[133] The document survives in large numbers of manuscripts, for example, BL Cotton MS Cleopatra F II; BL Harley MS 1299; Bodl. Barlow MS 9; Bodleian Rawlinson MS B 202, ff. 193v–194r; and HLS MS 1003. Further notes to these debates can be found in PRO HCA 30/4.
[134] BL Cotton MS Cleopatra F II, f. 121r. Compare the list of 'Dangerous and absurd opinions affirmed before the King by Lord Chancellor Ellesmere', from Coke's notebook; CUL MS Ii.5.21, f. 48r, but also found in IT Miscellaneous MS 21, f. 36r–v.
[135] BL Lansdowne MS 160, f. 428r. A point that Usher disputes in *High Commission*, p. 189n.2.

'a vaine and ridiculous conceipt borrowed from the Pope, as if they had power to judge all menn but must be judged of none, except (saie some Papistes of the Pope) by a generall Counsell, except (saye some lawyers for them selves) by the upper howse of Parliament'.[136] Later Bancroft would claim that the common lawyers 'come with such an absolute and ravenous cause of power like a keyte and take and teare all Ecclesiasticall Courts'.[137] Bancroft suspected that various interests among the commons were encouraging the judges, because through juries and other means they could protect their own profits and interests, such as those involving tithe disputes.[138] He wrote that the judges believed 'in effect that they are the Ephori, betwixt the kinge and his Subjects', referring to the magistrates in Sparta who were elected to keep the power of the king in check. In doing so, they allowed the propertied gentry to extort their poor tenants, unequally distribute their subsidy requirements and advance their own interests rather than 'the good of the Comons'. Instead of looking to the judges for justice, his poor subjects should look to their king.

If both sides used the language of corruption and usurpation to attack the other, much depended on whom the king believed. Given these heated disputes, Egerton called a conference at York House in early 1609. His purpose was to settle the disputes between the ecclesiastical courts and the common law. The chancellor identified five points of contention between the common law and the High Commission: the Commission cited individuals out of their diocese, in contravention of the statute of 23 Henry VIII, c. 9; many matters that they heard could be determined before the ordinary; they dealt in matters that were not criminal or enormous; and no ecclesiastical judge could fine or imprison, according to Magna Carta and the *Articuli Cleri*.[139] Coke's account of the conference survives in his papers.[140] Even Coke acknowledged that Egerton tried to make the peace as best he could and behaved 'respectfuly' towards the judges. Egerton appears to have heard the judges' complaints, most importantly that the High Commission must not have cognizance of matters relating to

---

[136] BL Cotton MS Cleopatra F II, f. 121r.
[137] LRO MS 1953 D26/2595, f. 1v.
[138] BL Cotton MS Cleopatra F II, f. 121v, 122r; BL Lansdowne MS 160, f. 414v; and LRO MS 1953 D26/2595, f. 2.
[139] Holkham MS 677, f. 352r.
[140] The attribution is from internal evidence: '[Ellesmere] directing his speech to me, sayd when you were Attorney ...'; Holkham MS 677, f. 333v.

property, such as pensions and tithes, but rather should deal only with matters relating to heresy, schism and 'enormous offences'.[141]

The conferences continued in July 1609, though the presence of the king and Privy Council enlarged them. Caesar's minutes for these meetings have been assumed to be the only account, but there exists a second and more detailed record of the conferences in July that offers greater (referred to as 'LRO' hereafter) insight into James's attitude towards the judges.[142]

The first day opened with discussion of the *modus decimandi* and James demanding an explanation for the prohibitions. Here the records vary in their account of the sequence of the responses: LRO indicates that Fleming responded to the question with a list of nine ordinances that the common law judges had agreed to in their issuing of prohibitions. Caesar records that Coke made a vague response that he would issue no prohibitions except where warranted by law, statute or custom. Both answers were unsatisfactory to the king who realized that the judges were being evasive and not confronting the central issue: should the common law issue prohibitions for *modus decimandi*? The king seems to have thought not and felt that the *modus decimandi* was an 'accessory' to the 'right of tithes'.[143] The claim revealed the wide distance that separated the understanding of the judges and the king, and Coke entered into a discourse explaining that the *modus decimandi* eliminated the tithe and replaced it with a custom that was temporal. This, he claimed, had been received wisdom from at least the time of the statute of 2 Edward VI and that all customs might be reviewed by the common law. James had been studying his statute book and appears to have had the act of 2 Edward VI before him.[144] He dismissed the statutes that Coke cited, revealing that James was serious about his claims that he might interpret and understand the laws himself. He reinforced this contention with a speech that 'I can reasonably expound a Statute by gessinge att the minds of the makers, and that shall ever bee best knowne if the preamble bee well observed.'[145] The assertion illustrated the very fear that Coke had held about the judging king: that he would err through ignorance and sunder the delicate web of juristic learning.

---

[141] Holkham MS 677, f. 334r.

[142] An unnamed participant who was a partisan of Coke's wrote LRO and at one point refers to himself; LRO MS 1953 D26/2595, f. 3v.

[143] LRO MS 1953 D26/2595, f. 1v, and the similar list record by Caesar in BL Lansdowne MS 160, f. 416r.

[144] LRO MS 1953 D26/2595 f. 4r.   [145] *Ibid.*, f. 1v.

The discussion soon turned to the jury, which was disparaged by both James and Egerton as partial and unlearned. Coke replied that there was 'noe tryall in the world more indifferent'. The exchange revealed that the king held parts of the common law in low regard: the clerks' fees were too high, he was a better interpreter of statute than the judges, and the jury was untrustworthy. The afternoon's discussion kept the common law judges on the defensive: debate began with the question of whether the Common Pleas could even issue prohibitions. Coke claimed that the Common Pleas was 'as antient as any Courte in England' to which James sarcastically replied: 'By God I am glad to heare that for I have been often enformed that it was derived out of the King's Bench in the time of Henry III.' Coke's response concluded with a line that echoed the famous claim that the law protected the king: 'The ecclesiasticall Courts are like a river bounded and banked with the temporall Courts. Rex: Nay they are like rivers bounded by the kinge.' By this time the king had grown peevish and soon remarked to Coke and the judges – a direct criticism of the common law claim to apply method and reason – that 'yow binde your-selves to much to lawe logike but yow have noe true logike for that is dra-wene from the rule of Reason'. The next morning James declared baldly that although Coke had cited many precedents nonetheless: 'I holde the Judges noe competent Judges of their owne Jurisdicon concerninge the Judgments that have been vouched.'[146] After an exchange, James dropped all attempt at objectivity and confirmed that he had accepted many of the criticisms of the common law:

> All your contention is but to bringe water to your owne mill[;] yow knowe quirks of lawe but noe grounds of judgments and noe man pleadeth more for mony then yow doe in partiallity. I distrust your Posteriora juditia for that is the plea of the Church of Roome presidents of former times may excuse yow, but the first institution of Courts must ever leade and directe mee for I see the simple verity in puris naturalibus not decked like a harlott.[147]

The king's statement was a direct attack on the integrity of his judges. His allegation against Coke – that he issued prohibitions for money – sug-gests that he had accepted Bancroft's charge that the clerks were grossly profiting off the writs. We do not read Coke's response immediately, since the civilians then appear to have intervened to add fuel to the fire and remind the king that the common law judges had continued to grant

[146] *Ibid.*, ff. 2v, 3r, 4r.
[147] *Ibid.*, f. 4v. Caesar refers to this exchange in BL Lansdowne MS 160, f. 409r.

prohibitions despite his earlier request for them to refrain. The civilians then added that the king had personally intervened in *Bennes's Case* to ask for a consultation that was not granted. Coke replied that he could not grant either a prohibition or consultation since it had to arise from a motion by one of the parties. Coke's further responses seem to have infuriated the king, who resumed his ad hominem attack against the chief justice, declaring that 'yow my Lord Cooke are soe full of craturity[148] that yow cannot holde your selfe ad rem, but yow must out of yor witt, make comparisons and gird att the doeings of other men, which nothinge concerne yow I have often hearde this Complaint of yow (which the Chancellor hardly enforced)'.[149]

Later in the conference, during the discussion of prohibitions on treble value, Coke displayed anxiety that the judges' precedents were unavailing. Egerton observed of those cases that 'in all businesse of this nature the judges were parties'. As the exchange continued, the chancellor appealed to James's role as supreme judge: 'that kinge James might well have judged that case [*Calvin's Case*] himselfe without the aide of the judges, as alsoe affirme the stile and title of the kinge of great Brittaine without the aide of the parliament'. If Egerton's remark was provocative James did nothing to relieve what must have been the rising concern of the judges when he responded: 'if [I] had feared any difficulty in that case I would have sate in the Exchequer Chamber my selfe amongst yow'.[150]

The conversation then abruptly turned to the High Commission, which prompted another outburst from the king, again on the problem of statutory interpretation: 'I will have noe prohibitions att all to the High Commission, but if they offend it is the office of the Judges to enforme the kinge of it they shall have accesse and audience, for interpretation of statutes I thinke they doe more properly belonge to the kinge beeinge exercised in Parliaments, then to the Judges.'[151]

James then railed against the judges' clerks describing them as a 'great scandall to the lawe' and again insulted Coke when he implied that the chief justice had held one opinion as attorney-general and another when his fees no longer depended upon it.

The conference gave vent to complaints about the common law: the judges and their clerks had been accused of base self-interest in their issuing of prohibitions, and their precedents demeaned as 'lawyer's logicke'.

---

[148] Possibly meaning 'inventiveness' from the Scots 'craitur' or 'created thing', or related to 'creatureliness', having the weaknesses of created things. My thanks to Elizabeth Ewan and Theo van Heijnsbergen for these suggestions.

[149] LRO MS 1953 D26/2595, f. 5r.   [150] *Ibid.*, ff. 5r, 6r, 6v.   [151] *Ibid.*, f. 5v.

They may have taken slight comfort in James's more temperate decision that the High Commission should not deal in matters between parties, 'but only in exorbitant and enormous crimes between greate parsonages'. Balancing this decision, James commanded the judges not to issue prohibitions against the High Commission but to refer abuses to him personally 'for hee will accompt every such prohibition a contempt unto himselfe'. He again reiterated that the interpretation of statutes relating to jurisdictions belonged to him.

Though it has been thought that the conferences settled the dispute, in fact, prohibitions continued to be granted and the argument resumed in the form of treatises.[152] These treatises responded to a report written by Attorney-General Hobart, outlining the two positions, and delivered to the judges at the July 1609 conference.[153] James commanded Coke to reply in writing.[154] The treatises, which were deeply influenced by the common law history of the Reformation, also countered documents prepared by Bancroft and his party (the *Articuli Cleri*), Hobart's arguments for the jurisdiction of the High Commission and the interpretation of statutes and three tracts by Francis Bacon on the treble value, the *modus decimandi* and the issuing of prohibitions by the Court of Common Pleas. There were at least five major treatises attributed to Coke.[155]

The preface to these treatises was a public articulation by the judges of the common law narrative of the Reformation. Prohibitions were necessary, it was argued, to restrain the clergy from such misuse of their power 'to deliver over to Sathan, for the preservation of their owne liberties and jurisdictions'.[156] Coke then turned to history, declaring that such

---

[152] Usher, *Reconstruction*, vol. I, p. 246.

[153] LRO 1953 D26/2595, f. 5r. Copies of this document are numerous; Usher, *High Commission*, p. 193.

[154] BL Lansdowne MS 160, f. 409v. When this response was written is unclear. In a letter from Lake to Coke in March 1610 the secretary hints that the response had not yet been received (Holkham MS 677, f. 319r). The responses must have been drafted before November 1610, because internal evidence indicates that Bancroft was still alive (Bodl. Rawlinson MS B 202, f. 120r). BL Additional MS 58218 contains both Coke's and Hobart's holograph notes and revisions.

[155] *A Declaration of the True Grounds of the Prohibitions to the High Commission* (a response to *The Grounds of the Prohibitions to the High Commission* by Hobart), *The Second Question Propounded* (on statutory interpretation), *In What Cases the King's Court of Common Pleas May Grant Prohibitions*, *The Third Question Propounded* (tithes), and *An Answer to the Chief Points Selected Touching the Modus Decimandi* (along with auxiliary documents); Usher, *Reconstruction*, vol. II, p. 241. Some of Coke's revisions are in BL Cotton MS Cleopatra F I.

[156] Bodl. Rawlinson MS B 202, f. 120r.

opposition to the 'lawes of England' was 'very frequent and very aunt-ient'. Citing historical examples, Coke suggested the shared interest of the judges and the king. Should the ecclesiastical courts, he reasoned, be allowed to hold plea of matters pertaining to the common law courts, then both the prerogative of the king and the inheritance of the subjects would 'be drawen in aliud examen, that is to be decided by the Civill and Canon lawe before the Ecclesiastical Judge'. Despite the Statute of Supremacy, the canon law remained foreign, a law that was suffered by king and people in contrast to the native common law. The judges justified their prohib-itions by asserting that the common law protected the king as much as the subject. They did not perceive themselves as questioning the prerogative, but rather maintaining limits on ecclesiastical authority that had slowly waxed over time despite the Reformation.[157] As the clergy entangled themselves in secular causes, the vigour of their spiritual work declined.

The judges' anxiety was also directed at the discretionary power that they perceived belonged to courts such as the High Commission. Coke argued that 'their decrees and sentences be absolute and incontrolable'.[158] He contrasted them with the common law courts where sentence could be appealed and reviewed by others. The danger was twofold. The first was that the Commission might proceed for ulterior, extra-legal motives against individuals, possibly imprisoning them, yet there would be no ordinary remedy. In 1608 Thomas Edwards sought prohibition for pro-ceedings against him in the Commission. He was accused of libelling Dr John Woolton, a member of the Exeter Commission.[159] The relationship between the two was deeply acrimonious: Edwards had obtained a sen-tence against Woolton in the Star Chamber for defaming him in a let-ter.[160] Subsequently boasting of his victory, the Commission investigated Edwards for libel against Woolton and contempt for bringing a member of their court into disgrace. The prosecution seemed self-serving and for a temporal matter, and the investigation by oath ex officio suggested a fishing expedition. The common law judges asserted that the High Commission 'shall not have conusance of any scandal to themselves for that they are parties'.[161]

---

[157] *Ibid.*, ff. 120v, 121r.   [158] *Ibid.*, f. 121v–122r.

[159] Woolton was the son of John Woolton, formerly the Bishop of Exeter; *Edwards's Case* (1608), 13 Co. *Rep.* 9, 77 ER 1421.

[160] Hawarde, *Les Reportes*, pp. 344–5; *Edwards* v. *Wooton* (1607), 12 Co. *Rep.* 35, 77 ER 1316.

[161] *Edwards's Case*, 13 Co. *Rep.* 9, 77 ER 1422; for an anticipation of the case, see *Birry's Case* (1605), Godbolt 147, 78 ER 90.

Second, the finality of the Commission's decrees also suggested that the forum might be more attractive to litigants. This point would recur again in the dispute with the Chancery. Coke sounded a panicked note, reasoning that this meant 'Every man flocks soe fast to them as yf there were noe remedy in that behalfe. The Courtes of Legall and regular proceedinge should be utterly overthrown, and all causes be decided by discretion and power intended to be absolute and uncontrollable.'[162] Courts without an ordinary course of appeal offered closure, an attractive prospect to complainants who initiated suits, yet damaging to justice in cases of error.

Another treatise took up this danger of the Commission's discretionary authority and implied that the act of 1 Elizabeth I, c. 1, was too vague. The discretion allowed to the commissioners was 'without controllment'. This may have suited the early purpose of the Commission, the purge of popish clergy who could not be expected to reform the Church themselves, but circumstances had changed. Though the Commission was still necessary, it should hear causes that were particularly heinous and required expedition, and not intrude into litigation that might be heard by the ordinaries.[163]

Allowing the ecclesiastical courts to interpret statutes enabled them to enlarge their own power.[164] Since statutes were part of the laws of England, they should be interpreted by the judges of the laws of England 'not by the civilians and canonists'.[165] Central to this interpretation, which weighed the need of the Commission to proceed in extraordinary and urgent circumstances with a desire to restrain its jurisdiction, was Coke's interpretation of the statutory clause authorizing the scope of the Commission. Coke and the common law judges read 'enormities' adjectively in that clause and believed that the High Commission should only hear enormous offences and contempts.[166] This was the crucial point limiting the Commission's jurisdiction and it relied on the judges' claim to be the authoritative readers of statute.

Despite the king's command that the judges should refer jurisdictional disputes to him, they continued to issue prohibitions on a range of matters

---

[162] Bodl. Rawlinson MS B 202, f. 122r; a concern repeated by Coke, ff. 140v–141r.

[163] Bodl. Rawlinson MS B 202, ff. 138r, 136v, 141v; cf. 140r.

[164] *Ibid.*, ff. 147v–148r.

[165] *Porter and Rochester's Case* (1608), 13 Co. *Rep.* 5, 77 ER 1417. Coke also suggested that the encroachment of the Arches on the authority of the ordinaries paralleled papal usurpations at 13 Co. *Rep.* 8, 77 ER 1420.

[166] Bodl. Rawlinson MS B 202, ff. 204r–205v; 4 Co. *Inst.*, pp. 328–9.

consistent with the argument that the commissions should hear only enormities. Prohibitions were granted for incest, attacks against ministers, simony, non-residence and adultery. In *William Chancey's Case* (1611) the court, Walmesley excepted, declared that the Commission could not commit for adultery, which was not an 'enormous' crime, and bailed Chancey.[167] In 1614 the court released a prisoner whom the Commission had imprisoned for alimony.[168] Coke and the other judges did, however, uphold the Commission's power to imprison. Two Brownists, Randal and Hickins, sued habeas corpus in 1610, but were remanded, since 'the High Commissioners have power to commit for heresy'.[169]

In February 1611, probably during *Chancey*, Lake wrote to Salisbury concerning the king's displeasure at Coke's continued granting of prohibitions against the Church. Referring to the chief justice's 'perverse spirit', Lake suggested that 'the King will dismiss him and no longer be vexed with him'.[170] The granting of prohibitions in *Chancey* and *Cheekitt's Case*, where Cheekitt had refused the oath ex officio in a cause of heresy and schism, provoked the king.[171] The Bishop of London was commanded to forward details of the cases to the attorney-general, who was then to demand an explanation from Coke. Hobart received these papers on 2 March. Lake warned Salisbury that the king expected a more satisfactory answer than a 'quible of law', revealing James's continued lack of confidence in the science of the common law. Coke met the king at Newmarket on 27 February where he denied having known of the complaints against him.[172]

Coke and his fellow judges' response to the complaints was later reprinted in the *Institutes*, and it prompted another conference.[173] The document was a summary of the position that the judges had been developing since Elizabeth's reign. Its centrepiece was the interpretation of the statute of 1 Elizabeth I that sought to limit the Commission's power by stressing the word 'enormities' adjectively. A series of conferences

---

[167] *Chancey's Case*, 12 Co. *Rep.* 82, 77 ER 1360.
[168] BL Additional MS 25213, f. 162r.
[169] *Lady Throgmorton's Case* (1610), 12 Co. *Rep.* 70, 77 ER 1348.
[170] CSPD, James I, 1611–1618, p. 11.
[171] Holkham MS 677, f. 327.
[172] It it is possible that he meant that he had not yet received formal notice from Hobart of the complaint; Usher, *High Commission*, p. 210, though see CSPD, James I, 1611–1618, p. 13; Holkham MS 677, ff. 320–8.
[173] 4 Co. *Inst.*, pp. 324–35. Usher dated this document to 1611; Usher, *High Commission*, p. 212n2.

followed on 20 and 23 May and 7 June 1611 before the Privy Council. James requested that the Council hear the arguments and then digest them for his consideration.[174]

The bishops and the civilians who assisted them set forth a range of complaints.[175] Foremost was their concern that prohibitions were undermining the High Commission and referred to both *Chancey's Case* and *Cheekitt's Case* as the most recent examples.[176] They cited the precedent reported by Coke of *Cawdrey's Case* where they claimed the common law judges had upheld the Commission's authority to fine and imprison.[177] The civilians warned that the use of prohibitions to thwart the Commission's efforts had brought 'an impunitie of all vices in generall' and adultery in particular. They added seven other reasons, declaring that the 'natural expositione' of the Act of Supremacy supported their cause.[178]

Yet there was a more unpleasant undercurrent in the complaints of the ecclesiastics and civilians. They implied that Coke was an enemy of the Church, citing the decision in *R.* v. *Bishop of Bristol* that revalued tithes and the prohibitions that interfered with the jurisdiction of the Arches. Abbott 'with some passione' claimed that Coke 'did stricke at the Roote of the Archbishopes Jurisdictione Ecclesiasticall, And endevored to overthrowe thes Courts'. Coke bristled at the suggestion that he sought to derogate from the Church, declaring that he was a son of the Church, 'and not of any forraine or metaphisicall Church'.[179]

The shrill language of the civilians was balanced by the determination of the common law judges to impose limits on the Commission's jurisdiction. Coke's reply was succinct, an encapsulation of thirty years of development in common law thought. The High Commission heard crimes and not private causes under the authority of the statute of 1 Elizabeth

---

[174] BL Harley MS 37, f. 117v. The sources for this conference are Caesar's notes in Lansdowne 160, a breviate of the discussion on 23 May, 'A Conference by the Kings Speciall Appointment', and Coke's account in his *Twelfth Reports*. 'A Conference by the Kings Speciall ...' is almost certainly not by Coke, since it refers in the third person to 'my Lord Coke', *contra* Usher who ascribed it to the Chief Justice; Usher, *High Commission*, p. 213n.1.

[175] Though Coke recalls only two bishops being present. *High Commission*, 12 Co. *Rep.* 84, 77 ER 1361.

[176] BL Harley MS 37, f. 120r; BL Lansdowne MS 160, f. 256r; *High Commission*, 12 Co. *Rep.* 84, 77 ER 1361.

[177] BL Lansdowne MS 160, f. 412r. Ellesmere cited an opinion of the majority of the judges in 1588 that the Commission could 'in all causes before them fine and imprison'; BL Lansdowne MS 160, f. 256r. A similar interpretation was made about *Fuller's Case*, at Bodl. Rawlinson MS B 202, f. 129v.

[178] BL Harley MS 37, ff 118r, 122r.   [179] *Ibid.*, ff. 119v, 120r.

I, c. 1, and the reannexed ecclesiastical law.[180] Coke reiterated that the Commission should have the power to fine and imprison, but only for schism, heresy and the incontinency of priests, those matters that presumably informed its creation.[181]

According to Coke, later in the same term the judges of the Common Pleas and King's Bench were summoned before the Council separately and both times gave the same opinion: that the High Commission could only fine and imprison in cases of heresy, schism, incontinency and other enormities. Finally, all the judges of the King's Bench, Common Pleas and Exchequer were summoned before the Privy Council. Since those of the Common Pleas had 'contested with the King', they were commanded to leave, while their brethren remained before the king. The judges were questioned one by one and it appears that their opinions were not unanimous.[182] Nonetheless, Coke recorded that the king promised to reform the High Commission 'and reduce it to certain spiritual causes'. If the king had indeed promised reformation, the new letters patent did little to restrict the jurisdiction and powers of the Commission.[183] The patent did not limit the Commission to 'enormous' matters and it was still able to hear causes between parties.[184] The new patent led to the common law judges publicly disapproving of its contents, refusing to swear to the Commission at its reading in Lambeth Palace. After an exhortation by the archbishop to the commissioners on the necessity of their work, a 'most blasphemous heretic' was brought forward 'to shew to the Lords and the auditory the necessity of that commission'.[185]

But Coke already realized that the Commission was needed and support for its authority continued to balance his opposition. Coke accepted that it should be allowed to proceed by ecclesiastical censure, such as excommunication and penance. He also reasoned that since the statutes of 2 Henry IV and 1 Henry VII were still in force during the making of the Elizabethan Act of Supremacy that 'therefore in case of Haresye, schisme etc the high commissioners according to that Authority which was in esse at the making of that Act may fyne and imprison'.[186] Coke connected this

---

[180] *Ibid.*, f. 118v. [181] BL Lansdowne MS 160, f. 400v.

[182] 12 Co. *Rep.* 86, 77 ER 1362. [183] Prothero, *Select Statutes*, p. 424.

[184] The new letters patent were issued on 29 August 1611. For the documents surrounding their creation see *CSPD, James I, 1611–1618*, p. 65; Lambeth Palace MS Carta Miscellanea V, f. 3.

[185] 12 Co. *Rep.* 89, 77 ER 1365. For the dating of this document see Usher, *High Commission*, p. 221.

[186] Though the Statute of Supremacy repealed the act, it was assumed that the power to imprison had been transmitted to the Commission; *Throckmorton v. High Commission*, BL Harley MS 4817, f. 153v.

power to inflict temporal penalties in the 'enormous' case of heresy back to the intention behind the statute: the deprivation of the popish clergy.[187] The judges did not propose to abolish the Commission, rather they sought to limit its powers to fine and imprison to enormous offences in line with their interpretation of the Commission's purpose. Nor did they completely oppose the administration of the oath, but sought to prevent its administration to lay persons and under conditions in which temporal penalties would be avoided.

Cases from 1610 suggest that Coke and the judges attempted to plot a middle course while keeping to the claims made in the tracts of 1608–11. In *Lady Throgmorton's Case* the common law judges again asserted that the High Commission, being no court of record, could not imprison for contempt.[188] Yet that same term in *Randal and Hickins Case* the defendants were remanded on a habeas corpus because: 'they were vehemently suspected to be Brownists, &c. And they obtained a habeas corpus and were remanded for this, that the High Commissioners have power to commit for heresy'.[189] In an extra-judicial opinion in 1612 several of the common law judges, excluding Coke, stated that while the writ *de haeretico comburendo* lay for conviction before the ordinary, 'the most convenient and sure way was to convict the heretic before the High Commissioners'.[190]

In *Boyer* v. *High Commission* (1614), Boyer sought prohibition for an examination on oath for simony before the High Commission. On the point of jurisdiction Coke declared that 'Simony is worse than felony, it is an enormous offence'and that 'we are not to take any notice of simony, this being punishable in their Court; and if they there meddle only pro salute animae, they are not then to be prohibited'.[191] Turning to examination by oath, Coke concluded that, although *nemo tenetur seipsum prodere*, nonetheless 'they may there examine upon oath if he be a parson, or an ecclesiastical man, but not a lay person'. Coke insisted later in the report that 'in case of a penal matter' there could be no examination on oath whatsoever.

Another case involving a straightforward refusal to answer interrogatories under oath revealed the judges' continued attempt to balance policy with their apprehensions. The Commission responded by imprisoning the parties and they sued a writ of habeas corpus. Coke dryly commented:

---

[187] Bodl. Rawlinson MS B 202, ff. 139r–140v; cf. 141r, 142r.

[188] A point reaffirmed in *Codd* v. *Turback* (1615), 3 Bulstrode 110, 81 ER 94.

[189] Recorded in *Lady Throgmorton's Case* (1610), 12 Co. *Rep.* 70, 77 ER 1348.

[190] *Writ de Haeretico Comburendo* (1612), 12 Co. *Rep.* 93, 77 ER 1368.

[191] *Boyer* v. *High Commission* (1614), 2 Bulstrode 183, 80 ER 1052.

'This is a new case, but yet it is an old and a beaten case.'[192] Coke declared that examining on oath might 'draw [the parties] within the danger of a penal law ... they are therefore not to answer upon oath'.[193]

Dr Martin appeared before the court to defend the High Commission and warned that if it was not permitted to question on oath, 'this land will then overflow with blasphemous and wicked persons'.[194] By raising the practical issue, Martin reminded his audience that they were jeopardizing the security of the religious settlement. Coke and Dodderidge's response perhaps sounded ironic to Martin: 'No Judges that ever were in former times have done more for the High Commission Court than we have done', and Dodderidge echoed this sentiment: 'We de all of us agree with you in the due punishing of these sectaries; and in this we will rather strengthen than weaken you.'[195] To demonstrate his sincerity Coke once again offered the Commission an alternative method to proceed in the case. The court then adjourned, probably hoping that the Commission and the parties would resolve the matter. But the parties sued for habeas corpus, and the court was forced to consider the issue again. Coke objected: 'I will not by any ways maintain sectaries. But the subject ought to have justice from us in a Court of Justice.'[196] Deeming the return on the writ insufficient, Coke and Dodderidge raised the issue that the Commission might imprison a subject perpetually unless the court was able to review their commitments through habeas corpus.[197] However, to show his goodwill towards the Commission, Coke refused to deliver the prisoners and agreed only to bail them 'and they in the interim to make their application unto the commissioners in the High Commission Court and there to submit themselves to them'. Coke contrasted his conduct with that of Dyer, who had delivered the party in *Thomas Lee's Case* (1568), one of the early precedents that the common lawyers relied upon.[198] Croke JKB also reminded the parties of the courts restraint, 'we in this case here have proceeded *lento pede*', and urged the accused to conform themselves. Coke and Dodderidge JKB emphasized their restraint: 'We will not here do as the Judges in like cases did in Dyer's time, there they

---

[192] *Burrowes Cox Dyton v. High-Commission Court* (1615), 3 Bulstrode 50, 81 ER 43.
[193] *Ibid.*, p. 44.   [194] *Ibid.*, p. 45.
[195] *Ibid.*, p. 45; Gray, *Writ of Prohibition*, vol. II, p. 416. Gray suggests that the judges understood the necessity of the Commission and the challenges it faced enforcing conformity; Gray, *Writ of Prohibition*, vol. II, p. 417.
[196] *Burrowes Cox Dyton v. High-Commission Court*, 3 Bulstrode 53, 81 ER 45.
[197] *Ibid.*, p. 46.
[198] CUL MS Ii.4.9, f. 41v (Lee named 'Legh'); 3 Bulstrode 49–50 (1615); Croke Jac 388 (1615); and 4 Co. *Inst.*, p. 333.

did discharge them absolutely; but we here will now only bail them.' The accused returned the following term on another habeas corpus and the court asked them whether they had conformed themselves. After another remand, the court washed their hands of the matter and commanded the accused to submit themselves, declaring that the High Commission had power to imprison for heresy and that their imprisonment was lawful. It seems that the Commission had dutifully amended the return, giving the judges a way out.

While the campaign against the High Commission reveals the influence of history and principle on Coke's actions, it also illustrates how policy and his long-standing commitment to protect the government moderated his attitudes. The Commission was an instrument to defend the state, and Coke's ruthless approach is perhaps revealed by a rhyme in his notes on assize charges: 'When the inward man is not to be reformed by the word, the outward man must be reformed by the sword.'[199] From Coke's perspective the Commission's excesses were also dangerous to the prerogative and the rights of the subject. The balance that Coke sought was a consequence of both Protestant historiography and practical considerations, and it is part of the larger story of the judges' attempt to restrict the entrepreneurship of other courts. If their efforts were rebuffed, it was because their jurisdiction too was perceived to have its flaws, despite the attempts of Coke and others to rebut criticism. James's lack of confidence in the common law, his belief that they too were usurpers in an unruly legal world, exposed the limits of Coke's ambitions for his court. Nor was James's scepticism about Coke's claims for the common law undue: some of Coke's brethren also held them. In a letter written to Egerton in 1612, Archbishop Abbot reported that he had spoken with Sir David Williams JKB: 'Hee told mee also of his utter dislike of all the L. Coke his courses, and that himself and Baron Altham did once very roundly let the L. Coke knowe their minde, that hee was not suche a maister of the lawe as hee did take on him, to deliver what hee list for lawe and to despise all other.'[200] The subsequent dispute with the Chancery further revealed the rifts within the profession, as Coke sought to discipline his fellow common lawyers to resist the claims of another reforming jurisdiction.

[199] BL Harley MS 6687A, f. 8v.
[200] Huntington Library Ellesmere MS 2184.

7

Chancery, reform and the limits of cooperation

'The Court of Chancery and comon lawe Courts are all sonns of one Father' wrote Anthony Benn, a common lawyer and defender of the Chancery.[1] Despite Benn's irenicism, dysfunction has been the focus of the historiography on the Chancery and the common law, and so the conflict with Coke that contributed to his fall in 1616 has attracted particular attention. Coke's defeat in that year suggested the limits of common law ambition and has often been mapped onto the struggle with the prerogative power upon which the Chancery was said to depend.[2] The dichotomy is discernible in the personalities of those who drove the struggle: Egerton's assertive exercise of Chancery jurisdiction went alongside Coke's expansive claims for the common law.[3] Over time Coke grew increasingly critical of Egerton, believing that he was encouraging the king with 'dangerous and absurd opinions' about royal power.[4] Others shared his assessment. Timothy Tourneur, a contemporary common lawyer, recorded that Egerton was 'the bane of the lawe, yet not for any hate he bare yt but for the love he bare to his owne honor to greaten himself by the fall of others'.[5] The Chancery that Egerton developed, the 'high court of equity', contributed

[1] BL Lansdowne MS 174, f. 208v.

[2] Summarized by J. H. Baker, 'The Common Lawyers and the Chancery: 1616', in *The Legal Profession and the Common Law*, pp. 205–29, at p. 206; and most recently in Hart, *Rule of Law*, pp. 48–51; Mark Fortier, 'Equity and Ideas', *Renaissance Quarterly*, 51 (1998), 1,255–81; Knafla, *Law and Politics*, pp. 155–81; see also Gardiner, *History of England*, vol. III, p. 24; Maitland, *Constitutional History of England* (London, 1908), p. 270.

[3] J. P. Dawson, 'Coke and Ellesmere Disinterred: The Attack on Chancery in 1616', *Illinois Law Review*, 36 (1941), 128; Holdsworth, *HEL*, vol. V, p. 424; Burgess, *Absolute Monarchy*, p. 207; Baker, *IELH*, p. 108 and 'The Common Lawyers and the Chancery', p. 207. See also David Raack, 'A History of Injunctions in England Before 1700', *Indiana Law Journal*, 61 (1986), 539–592, at 576; Knafla, *Law and Politics*, pp. 60, 61, 157. Ellesmere's own tract supporting Chancery jurisdiction was published posthumously as *Privileges and Prerogative of the High Court of Chancery* (London, 1641), Wing B4099.

[4] CUL MS Ii.5.21, f. 48r; IT Miscellaneous MS 21, f. 36r.

[5] BL Additional MS 35957, f. 81v; Baker, 'The Common Lawyers', pp. 207–10; Raack, 'Injunctions', 574; Richard Hutton, *The Diary of Sir Richard Hutton*, ed. W. R. Prest (London, 1991), p. 17; Whitelocke, *Liber Famelicus*, p. 53.

to the larger story of judicial expansion through its use of injunctions and *supersedeas* to exercise a superior jurisdiction over other courts. It was also a forum for litigants to find a remedy for injustices they had suffered elsewhere. Coke's and Egerton's reforming efforts paralleled each other: both identified problems in the law and both amplified the claims and reach of their jurisdictions to solve them.[6] The judicial clash involved two incompatible solutions to the challenges of a growing and interdependent legal system. Their approaches differed insofar as each believed that their jurisdiction should subordinate the other as the ultimate forum in which litigants might receive the king's justice. Egerton, for example, remarked that he referred matters to the common law judges to 'hear their opinions and not to be concluded by them'.[7] Egerton intended that the Chancery would be available to litigants to correct injustices occurring as a consequence of process in other courts or the unavailability of remedies elsewhere. As the keeper of the king's conscience the Chancery was most qualified to function at the apex of the judicial hierarchy. In the pursuit of his reforming programme Egerton wisely found in James an ally who was already suspicious of common law ambitions.[8] If Egerton and Bacon flattered the king they did so using the same language as Coke by arguing that their court most closely represented the king and his justice.

Exacerbating the conflict was the close intertwining of the daily operations of the common law and Chancery. This 'brotherhood' of the courts, as Benn might term it, involved shared relationships, including procedure and personnel. Disagreement over *res judicata* was the flashpoint in 1616, but there was room for compromise on this issue, as John Popham and eventually Francis Bacon demonstrated.[9] But Coke was, as we have seen, anxious about the certainty of the common law and the finality of its judgments. He perceived that the underlying problems emerged from the pattern of litigation that intermeshed the business of the two courts together and the conduct of his own profession. Common lawyers, including serjeants, populated the Chancery bar. In the course of their practice they were often obliged to pursue their clients' interests to obtain writs of injunction, many of which stopped common law process or overturned judgments. In 1616 Francis Moore, a common lawyer and among the most prominent of the Chancery practitioners, was targeted with a

---

[6] Knafla, *Law and Politics*, pp. 127–8.   [7] BL Lansdowne MS 639, f. 105r.

[8] James ultimately favoured the Chancery as the highest expression of his duty to do justice; Knafla, 'Britain's Solomon', p. 249.

[9] Baker, 'The Common Lawyers', pp. 225–8.

praemunire prosecution as part of Coke's campaign against the use of the injunction after common law judgment. The attack on Moore signalled Coke's efforts to discipline his profession and exposed division among the common lawyers.

Cooperation raised problems, especially as the Chancery used the injunction to manipulate the common law process. The Chancery, for example, made use of the common law's fact-finding instruments, such as the jury, so that the injunction was used to start and stop the common law process. This procedure might be used to test for the appropriate jurisdiction, to obtain information unavailable through the ordinary fact-finding mechanisms of the Chancery and to adjudicate parts of complex litigation. But it also tended to render common law proceedings supplemental to the Chancery: litigation might be allowed to proceed up to execution and then enjoined. Injunctions that upset *res judicata* were the most egregious aspect of this relationship.

The relationship was, nonetheless, a close one: Chancery and the common law courts were linked together in numerous ways. They shared adjacent space in Westminster Hall, while administratively the common law courts were bound to the Chancery, and writs produced there initiated suits at the common law. The judicial activity of the Latin side of the Chancery was dependent on common law rules.[10] Though the Latin side could not proceed by jury, it might refer causes to the King's Bench to determine the legal facts and return the case to the Chancery for judgment. Coke himself wrote that 'for that purpose both Courts are accounted as one'.[11] The English side would eventually adopt this procedure, sending causes shuttling back and forth.

The English side and its equitable function had emerged as a response to petitions seeking relief against the ordinary process of law, a process traceable to the latter half of the fourteenth century.[12] The jurisdiction existed to 'supplement and complement the common law' by resolving wrongs that arose from the common law's strictness and inflexibility, so that it was said, 'no one shall leave from the court of Chancery without remedy'.[13] Beyond resolving these injustices, however, the Chancery also responded to the needs of litigants by developing remedies where none

[10] 4 Co. *Inst.*, p. 79.   [11] *Ibid.*, p. 80.
[12] Baker, *IELH*, p. 101; Bryson, 'Introduction', in *Cases Concerning Equity*, p. xix; 4 Co. *Inst.*, p. 82.
[13] Bryson, 'Introduction', in *Cases Concerning Equity*, p. xix; Statute of Westminster II (1285), c. 24; YB Hil. 4 Henry VII, f. 5, pl. 8.

were available. The extension of the equitable jurisdiction over uses is the most notable example of this practice. The courts of equity also continued their innovation into the reign of James I, when they were at the forefront of controversial developments in bankruptcy law.[14]

Central to the judicature of the English side was 'equity'.[15] Courts other than Chancery, such as the Court of Requests and the Exchequer, and even the common law, might be thought to apply it in a general sense.[16] Equity was described as a manifestation of the law of God or the law of reason that suffused all good laws and could prescribe an exception to the ordinary course of law to avoid injustice.[17] Equitable analysis required the examination of the particulars of the individual case, rather than the strict application of general rules.[18] When writers discussed equity they also spoke of 'conscience' and the appeal to the seed of divine reason and justice within each person. Equitable rulings might, for example, correct the 'corrupt conscience' of those who sought to manipulate the strict course of the law in order to advantage themselves.[19] Equity was also associated with the duty of the king to give justice to his subjects.[20]

Relations between the Chancery and the common law varied over the sixteenth and early seventeenth centuries. The diplomacy of Sir Thomas More (1529–33) repaired the frayed relations between the two jurisdictions

---

[14] David Smith, 'The Error of Young Cyrus: The Bill of Conformity and Jacobean Kingship, 1603–1624', *Law and History Review*, 28:2 (2010), 307–41; Baker, *IELH*, pp. 202–4.

[15] For analyses of the development of equity during this period see Jones, *Elizabethan Court of Chancery*; D. E. C. Yale, *Lord Nottingham's 'Manual of Chancery Practice' and 'Prolegomena of Chancery and Equity'* (Cambridge, 1965); Stuart Prall, 'The Development of Equity in Tudor England', *American Journal of Legal History*, 8 (1964), 1–19; George Spence, *Equitable Jurisdiction of the Court of Chancery* (Philadelphia, 1846; repr. 1981), vol. I, pp. 407–24; Dennis Klinck, *Conscience, Equity and the Court of Chancery in Early Modern England* (Farnham, 2010), pp. 141–72; Bryson, 'Introduction', in *Cases Concerning Equity*, p. xliii.

[16] Baker, *OHLE*, vol. VI, pp. 45–6. Egerton suggested that the judges exercised equity through their discretion; 'Some Notes and Observations on the Statute of Magna Carta', BL Additional MS 46410, f. 118r.

[17] *Anonymous*, Cary 11, 21 ER 6; BL Additional MS 46410, ff. 117v–118r. See also Charles Gray, 'The Boundaries of the Equitable Function', *American Journal of Legal History*, 20 (1976), 192–226, pp. 203, 218; William West, *The Faithfull Councellor* (London, 1653), Wing S3183, p. 374.

[18] St German, *Doctor and Student*, pp. 97, xlvi; Baker, *OHLE*, vol. VI, p. 47; William West, *The First Part of Symboleography* (London, 1598), STC 25269, f. 175r.

[19] *Finch's Case* (1579x1587), *Cases Concerning Equity*, vol. I, no. 22; see also the dictum in BL Lansdowne MS 1110, f. 5r; *Cases Concerning Equity*, vol. I, p. 295; Snagg, *Antiquity & Original*, p. 46.

[20] Lambarde, *Archeion*, p. 68.

after the rocky chancellorship of Wolsey (1515–29).[21] Throughout the
remainder of the century, as Chancery developed an increasingly sophisticated procedure, cooperation largely characterized their relationship.
W. J. Jones, for instance, has observed examples throughout the reign of
Elizabeth.[22] At times when the Chancery was in commission the common law judges might sit in the place of the lord chancellor.[23] The judges
were also not averse to assigning jurisdiction to the Chancery in relevant
cases.[24] At times Egerton expressed a desire to limit Chancery jurisdiction – if only the common law would reform itself. He hoped 'that we
lawyers would[,] as much as in us lay[,] advance our clients' causes into
the course of the common law and not to trouble him'.[25] Egerton refused
to relieve foolish bargains, perpetuities or leases of one thousand years
of lands held *in capite*, breaches of conditions in leases, titles of right to
common pasture, challenges to wills against the heir, broken conditions
in perpetuities, obligations made by infants where the intent was not to
defraud creditors, and want of surrenders in copyhold.[26] He preferred that
many of these matters be left 'wholly to the ordinary trials at the common law where [they are] most fit to be tried'. He had even promised in
1596 not to offer 'any relief in equity contrary to any positive ground in
law', nor hear any case where there might be remedy found in positive

[21] Baker, 'Introduction', in *The Reports of Sir John Spelman*, pp. 74–83; Baker, *OHLE*, vol.
      VI, p. 47; Spence, *Equitable Jurisdiction*, vol. I, pp. 322–66; Holdsworth, *HEL*, vol. V,
      pp. 215–338; William Roper, *The Lyfe of Sir Thomas Moore*, ed. Elsie Hitchcock (London,
      1935), pp. 44–5.
[22] Knafla, *Law and Politics*, pp. 157–8, 180; Hart, *Rule of Law*, p. 48; W. J. Jones, 'Conflict
      or Collaboration? Chancery Attitudes in the Reign of Elizabeth I', *American Journal
      of Legal History*, 5 (1961), 12–54, at 19–37; Bryson, 'Introduction', in *Cases Concerning
      Equity*, p. xliv; BL Stowe MS 415, f. 247v. Evidence of the growth of Chancery rules
      can be found in George Sanders, *Orders of the High Court of Chancery, and Statutes of
      the Realm Relating to Chancery, from the Earliest Period to the Present Time* (London,
      1845); Spence, *Equitable Jurisdiction*, vol. I, pp. 397–406. Conflict did occur with
      Wriothesley; Baker, *The Reports of Sir John Spelman*, vol. II, pp. 82–3; *CSPD, Edward
      VI, 1547–1550*; pp. 48–50; *Colston v. Carre* (1600), BL Additional MS 25203, f. 177r.
[23] Jones, *Elizabethan Court of Chancery*, pp. 45, 53, 55, 104, 146–7, 237, 269, 288, 298,
      468, 471.
[24] Anon. (1611), *Cases Concerning Equity*, vol. I, pp. 378, 380, 393.
[25] *Cases Concerning Equity*, vol. I. p. 285, no. 57.
[26] *Cases Concerning Equity*, vol. I, pp. 278–9, no. 12; p. 282, no. 35; p. 304, no. 207; p. 315
      no. 256; *Jemnis(?) etc. v. Sir John Mercer* (1603), p. 327, no. 55; p. 330, no. 73; p. 375, no. 171;
      p. 376, no. 256; p. 379, no. 407; BL Stowe 415, f. 92v; *Reynolds v. Chadwell and Bray* (1602),
      C33/103, f. 379v; *Dudley v. Sydney* (1602), C33/103, f. 380v; *Manby v. Warrison* (1615),
      C33/129, f. 250r.

law, and there is evidence to support restraint on the chancellor's part.[27] Egerton was also careful at points to restrain vexatious litigation where the party began a suit concurrently at both the common law and in the Chancery.[28]

Coke frequently made use of the equity courts. In 1605 he wrote to ask Sir Julius Caesar, a master of requests, to relieve a petitioner who had been defrauded.[29] Coke had recourse to litigation in Chancery as attorney-general and in his private practice.[30] The culmination of one of his most famous cases, *Buckhurst's Case* (1598), came when Egerton called Popham, Anderson and Gawdy to assist him in judgment.[31] Coke found himself personally involved in several lawsuits in the Chancery, some of them seeking to reclaim lost or stolen documents supporting title. He was forced, for example, to commence litigation over the purchase of the rectory and parsonage of Horeham when the seller allegedly detained the evidences and conveyed the land to 'others unknowne' with an antedate before Coke's assurances.[32] In *Coke v. Waldegrave* (1623) Coke complained that the evidences of conveyance and assignment of a tenement had 'casually gotten' into the hands of Sir George Waldegrave, who was avoiding the payment of leases.[33] The masters' report for a bill of costs in 1618 in another case reveals that Coke was not averse to suing for an injunction against adversaries in the Chancery.[34] As counsel in *Collyn v. Collyn* (1602), he successfully obtained an injunction against an action

---

[27] IT Petyt MS 561/5, f. 58v, cited in Baker, 'The Common Lawyers', p. 210n.35; *Anonymous*, Cary 12, 21 ER 7.

[28] *Cases Concerning Equity*, vol. I, p. 377, no. 261. See PRO C 33/121, f. 1115v; C33/122, f.1080. Bacon might also suggest similar restraint; *Fines and Haslewood* (1612), *Cases Concerning Equity*, vol. I, p. 380, no. 558; *ibid.*, pp. 304–5, no. 208.

[29] BL Additional MS 12506, f. 452r.

[30] Some cases where Coke served as counsel in Chancery are *Aske v. Aske* (1592), C33/84, f. 88v; *Boothe v. Kinge* (1592), C33/84, f. 232r; *Fulwood v. Shearington* (1592), C33/84, f. 283r; *Sonne v. Hare* (1592), C33/84, f. 324r; *Lord Stafford v. Thynne* (1592), C33/84, f. 362v; *Parstowe v. Payne* (1592), C33/84, f. 8v; *Boothe v. Kinge and Hegge* (1592), C33/84, f. 119v; *Coates v. Thetforde* (1592), C33/84, f. 147r; *Dudley v. Sydney* (1602), C33/103, f. 380v; *Collyn v. Collyn* (1602), C33/103, f. 686r; *Spurlinge* et al. *v. Pagott* (1602), C33/103, f. 619r; *Drywood v. Cook* (1588), C2/ELIZ/D8/59.

[31] *Buckhurst's Case*, 1 Co. Rep. 1a, 76 ER 1; Holkham MS 250.

[32] *Coke v. Shereman*, PRO C2/JASI/C15/49.

[33] *Coke v. Waldegrave* (1623), PRO C2/JASI/C14/84. Lost evidences were also a problem for Coke in *Coke v. Yelverton* (temp Eliz.), C2/ELIZ/C1/59; *Coke v. Seaman and Hase* (1610), C2/JASI/C6/24. See also litigation over leases: *Coke v. Burrell* (1607), C2/JASI/C13/1 and C2/JASI/C17/73; and 'deceitful practice': *Coke v. Baxter* (1600), C2/ELIZ/A6/5.

[34] The defendant, William Shackley, was awarded £32 in costs; PRO C38/30, 7 May 1618.

of ejectment at the common law.[35] Significantly, given his later actions, Coke in at least one case also requested from the Chancery permission to proceed to verdict and judgment at the common law despite an injunction, but agreed to avoid taking out execution. This had the effect of suspending the verdict at the common law while the outcome of the case in Chancery was being decided.[36]

While a judge Coke was also a participant in the Chancery's work through references to him for arbitration or certification. In 1611 a series of vexatious lawsuits was settled by final judgment in a collusive action at the King's Bench. The parties had litigated concurrently in the Chancery, but Coke's certificate into the court ended the cause there.[37] Another case the same year found the Chancery referring a matter to Coke for arbitration, though if the parties could not come to agreement, the chief justice's certificate would form the basis for the decree.[38] Scattered in the volumes of masters' reports are other certificates that Coke prepared for the court on matters such as the custom of a manor in a copyhold case and the validity of a conveyance.[39]

Coke's involvement in Chancery decisions reflected the endemic use of common law resources by the court, even at the height of the Jacobean dispute.[40] Cases determined by common law judges in the Chancery could later be cited as precedents.[41] In 1592, for example, there were a number of cases where common law judges were involved. The chancellor might simply ask the common law judges what the 'law' was on a particular point or they might actively adjudicate.[42] In *Gauntlet v. More* (1592), John Clench JQB was one of the commissioners who issued an injunction

---

[35] *Collyn* v. *Collyn* (1602), C33/103, f. 686r.

[36] *Boothe* v. *King* (1592), C33/84, f. 232r; see also *Coke* v. *Shackley and Miller* (1618), PRO C38/30; *Cases Concerning Equity*, vol. I, p. 306, no. 215; p. 312, no. 242. Benn later recalled that Coke had declared while practising in Chancery that: 'When the instruments are deficient, equity provides relief'; BL Lansdowne MS 174, f. 211r.

[37] *Sayre* v. *Pomerye* (1611), C33/121, ff. 832v–833r; also *Aikson? v. Turner and Barwicke*, C33/121, ff. 1,025r–1,026r.

[38] *Hendon* v. *Godsall et al.* (1611), C33/121, f. 1,045r. That same year Coke's certificate was also taken into account in *Kinge* v. *Saundersen* (1611), C33/121, ff. 1,202r–v. Coke refers to judges sitting in the Chancery in BL Harley MS 6686A, ff. 126r, 134v, 148v and 150r; Jones, *Elizabethan Court of Chancery*, p. 94.

[39] *Flatman* v. *Loveday* (1615), C38/22; *Poole* v. *Pelham* et al. (1607), C38/10.

[40] Jones, *The Elizabethan Court of Chancery*, pp. 481–3; *Anonymous*, Cary 33, 21 ER 18; *Ward* v. *Crouch* (1577–8), Cary 71, 21 ER 38.

[41] *Brett and Johnson's Case* (1605), HLS MS 118(a), f. 6v.

[42] *Smythe* v. *Knatchbull and Wattes* (1592), C33/84, f. 113v; *Page* v. *Wilford* (1592), C33/84, f. 385v; *Blythe* v. *Farrar* (1592), C33/84, f. 471r.

protecting the possession of the plaintiff.[43] Another example is revealing: in *West* v. *Mounson* (1592) Francis Gawdy JQB and Francis Wyndham JCP were asked whether the matter should be tried at the common law or in the Chancery. As Wyndham was ill at the time, Gawdy replied that an indifferent jury should try the validity of the offence, but that the matters of equity should be reserved to the Chancery.[44] Gawdy had encouraged the Chancery to make use of common law procedures. In another case an error in common law proceedings over a century earlier was retained by the Chancery upon agreement by the judges of the Queen's Bench. The Chancery enjoined the parties to cease prosecuting the writ of error and determined the matter in equity.[45] The two courts might even work together to settle abuses of the law. In 1602 the Chancery asked the judges whether and how the solicitors of a defendant involved in the perpetration of a fraud to undermine a conveyance might be 'weeded out as not worthie to be any more practisers of the Lawe'.[46]

That same year the common law judges were again active participants in Chancery. The case of *Spurlinge* v. *Pigalt* over a lease, with Coke as counsel, was referred to the consideration of Sir Peter Warburton JCP and Gawdy JQB as to whether the lease was good or not and whether the injunction for possession should be dissolved.[47] In a similar case, the *Countess of Shrewsbury* v. *Clifford* et al. (1602), there already existed several verdicts and judgments at the common law. The chancellor invited John Savile BEx to aid the court and urged that he might 'also have the opinion of the Judges'. Meanwhile the parties were to avoid all further suits and 'all verdicts and recoveryes may be sett aside'.[48] In *Thompson* v. *Woodward* (1602), where no money had ever been provided for a debt secured by a bond, 'the Lord Chief Justice in his dyscretion stayd the proceedings', and the matter was then taken up in the Chancery by the defendant.[49]

In 1610 Sir David Williams JQB was sitting as a commissioner in the case of *Stokes* v. *Mason*, where the defendant had obtained a verdict and a judgment at the common law on a bond with a very high penalty. Williams determined that the plaintiff should be liable only

---

[43] *Gauntlet* v. *More* (1592), C33/84, f. 217v.

[44] Wyndham died that year. *West* v. *Mounson* (1592), C33/84, f. 689r; see also *Baske* v. *Stadder* (1602), C33/103, f. 143v.

[45] *Chapter* v. *Jobson* (1592), C33/84, ff. 297r, 374r.

[46] *Kynnersley* v. *Calmet* (1602), C33/103, ff. 208r–209r.

[47] *Spurlinge* v. *Pigalt* (1602), C33/103, ff. 474v–475r.

[48] *Countess of Shrewsbury* v. *Clifford* et al. (1602), C33/103, ff. 617v–618r.

[49] *Thompson* v. *Woodward* (1602), C33/103 f. 153r; see also *Bennett* v. *Heron* (1602), C33/102, f. 262v; *Wigmore* v. *Vavasor* (1611), C33/121, f. 167r.

for the original amount of the bond and mitigated the penalty, in effect limiting the common law judgment.[50] In *Leighe* v. *Gattacre* (1611) both Warburton JCP and Edward Bromley BEx recommended that the equity of the cause should be considered in the Chancery. The Chancery's reply was to ask the two judges to make their consideration in both law and equity.[51] In *Watkins* v. *Farley* (1611) Croke JKB suggested that the equity of the cause was fit for consideration in the Chancery.[52] During the heated years of 1615–16 Warburton JCP was found assisting the court in a decision on a counterbond, and Croke heard a reference on a copyhold estate.[53] Croke, who in the previous years had shown himself a staunch opponent of injunctions after verdict, was also found upon reference reviewing whether an injunction should continue in force on behalf of the Chancery.[54] Nor was Egerton reluctant to send cases back to the common law for consideration. The same year that he dispatched *Manby* v. *Warrison* (1615) to the common law he also declared that the court would not help those in want of a surrender in cases of copyhold.[55] The masters of the Chancery might also recommend a case be sent to the common law, as in *Nurse* v. *Abdye* (1615).[56]

This evidence suggests not only a working relationship between the jurisdictions, but an intermeshing of their personnel and procedures. The participation of the judges in the Chancery's adjudication typified the overlap of practitioners. Historians have observed that the common lawyers occupied many of the masterships and most of the bar.[57] The participation of so many common lawyers in the work of the Chancery partly explains Coke's furore over *res judicata*; it also undermines claims about a fundamental division between the Chancery and the 'common lawyers'. Cases, litigants and practitioners moved back and forth between the courts. Lawyers were drawn to the Chancery because

---

[50] *Cases Concerning Equity*, vol. I, p. 374, no. 21. Williams was also active in *David* et al. v. *Maners* et al. (1611), C33/121, ff. 760v–761r.

[51] *Leighe* v. *Gattacre* (1611), C33/121, ff. 890r–v.

[52] *Watkins* v. *Farley* (1611), C33/121, f. 1,029r; *Langley* v. *Soprani and Barnardi* (1602), C33/103, f. 86r.

[53] *Hayne* v. *Bartlett* (1615), C33/129, f. 571r; *Nevell* v. *Albany* (1615), C33/129, ff. 140v–141r.

[54] *Baker* v. *Kerwyn* (1615), C33/129, f. 462v; and Sir Augustine Nicholls JCP in *Adams* v. *Webley* (1615), C33/129, f. 1,018v.

[55] *Manby* v. *Warrison* (1615), C33/129, f. 250r.

[56] *Nurse* v. *Abdye* (1615), C33/129, f. 496v.

[57] Knafla, *Law and Politics*, p. 180; Dawson, 'Coke and Ellesmere', 148; Holdsworth, *HEL*, vol. VI, pp. 455–6; Ogilvie, *The King's Government*, p. 119. Cf. Raack, 'Injunctions', 583, where the division remains.

its work was lucrative and necessary: clients could easily be drawn into litigation there once suit was commenced at the common law. While the struggle between Coke and Egerton had constitutional ramifications insofar as it sought to establish the priority of jurisdictions, it was not in origin a constitutional dispute.[58] It was a consequence of the patterns of coordination and practice that bound together both jurisdictions, and the anxiety of Coke and other common law judges about the certainty of their law.

Those trained as common lawyers were directly involved in the administration of the Chancery under Egerton, who was himself educated at Lincoln's Inn.[59] Egerton also served as master of the rolls, the second-highest office in the Chancery (1594–1603), and shared his common law background with his near successor Sir Edward Phelips (1611–14).[60] Between 1611 and 1616 six common lawyers served as masters in ordinary: Henry Thorsebye, Sir James Wolveridge, Sir Richard More, Sir George Carew, Sir John Tyndall and Sir John Hayward.[61] Nor were these marginal figures in the common law world: Thorsebye was prominent in Lincoln's Inn and served as the keeper of the Black Book (1603) and treasurer in 1608 (while he was a master in ordinary). Wolveridge was a bencher of Lincoln's Inn, while George Carew, who was also Egerton's secretary, was a bencher of the Middle Temple (1602). John Tyndall had served as the treasurer (1590) of Lincoln's Inn, where he was a bencher.

A common lawyer's practice in the two courts could produce conflicts between the jurisdictions, especially over the issue of *res judicata*. In 1588 Sir John Hele, who had an extensive Chancery practice, was indicted for praemunire by the opposing counsel, seemingly with the connivance of the judges, for preferring a bill into the Chancery after judgment at the

---

[58] *Pace* Hart, *Rule of Law*, p. 48.

[59] His successors throughout the seventeenth century were usually common lawyers, with the exception of John Williams and the Earl of Shaftesbury (who attended Lincoln's Inn); Michael McNair, *The Law of Proof in Early Modern Equity* (Berlin, 1999), p. 32.

[60] Julius Caesar (1614–1636) also occupied this office and though usually considered a civilian, he was a bencher of the Inner Temple from 1591 and treasurer in 1593; *DNB*, s.v. 'Julius Caesar'.

[61] Edmund Heward, *Masters in Ordinary* (Chichester, 1990). Several civilians, including Sir Matthew Carew (GI, 1589), Sir John Bennett (GI, 1590), John Amye (GI, 1590), John Hone (MT, 1605), Sir Charles Caesar (IT, 1610) and Francis James (GI, 1614) received admission, usually honorary, to the common law inns. In 1633 the Council reserved the majority of masterships for civilians in response to complaints about competition from common lawyers for offices; see Levack, *The Civil Lawyers*, pp. 60–6; cf. Terrill, 'The Application of the Comparative Method', 173.

common law.[62] Coke, citing Richard Crompton, reports that the indict-ment was quashed only because of a technicality.[63] While Hele's indict-ment reflected an attempt to protect common law judgments, it also revealed the problems that could emerge as lawyers moved between the jurisdictions in their practices. Hele's later elevation to the coif (1594) also points to the status of some common lawyers practising in Chancery. Sir Edward Phelips was a serjeant-at-law when he was appointed as the master of the rolls in 1611.[64] Phelips's presence in the Chancery signals a deeper pattern: the serjeants, who could act as judges at the common law on assize, were frequent practitioners in Chancery during the period of the greatest conflict with the common law. In one case it was recorded that if a serjeant were to disobey an injunction the lord keeper could not commit him for contempt: 'But my lord keeper, may ... bar such serjeant of his practice in Chancery.'[65] The threat was only significant because so many serjeants made their living in Chancery practice.

Data collected on injunctions from the Decree and Order "A" books for the years 1592, 1602, 1611 and 1616 reveal that, of those praying injunc-tions, serjeants obtained 111 of them, approximately 10% of the total recorded. Comparing the seventy-nine serjeants between the calls of 1577–1616 with the Chancery records shows that at least forty-two appear in Chancery, including John Dodderidge, Lawrence Tanfield, John Croke and Henry Finch (see Appendix). The call of 1614, in which only one of thirteen new serjeants did not appear active in Chancery, suggests a ten-dency to elevate common lawyers with practices there, a pattern possibly related to Egerton's influence.[66] Many of the serjeants were closely con-nected to Egerton and he had an extensive patronage circle of common lawyers.[67] Among the leading common lawyers litigating in Chancery were Henry Montagu, Francis Moore, Thomas Chamberlaine and Randall

---

[62] Richard Crompton, *L'authoritie et iurisdiction des courts de la Maiestie de la Roygne* (London, 1594), pp. 57–8. Hele's career is described by James Cockburn, 'The Spoils of Law: The Trial of Sir John Hele, 1604', in DeLloyd Guth and J. W. McKenna (eds.), *Tudor Rule and Revolution, Essays for G.R. Elton from His American Friends* (Cambridge, 1982), pp. 309–343; *Acta Cancellariae*, ed. Cecil Monro (London, 1847), p. 7. Hele's competition with Egerton is discussed in Jones, *Elizabethan Court of Chancery*, p. 92.

[63] 3 Co. *Inst.*, p. 124.

[64] J. H. Baker, *The Order of Serjeants at Law* (London, 1984), p. 176.

[65] *Cases Concerning Equity*, vol. I, p. 291.

[66] Robert Hitcham does not appear to have practised in Chancery.

[67] See also Louis Knafla, 'The "Country" Chancellor: The Patronage of Sir Thomas Egerton, Baron Ellesmere', in French Fogle and Louis Knafla (eds.), *Patronage in Renaissance England* (Los Angeles, CA, 1983), pp. 33–115, at pp. 62–8.

Crewe. They all became serjeants and were clients of Egerton. Thomas Chamberlaine was Egerton's steward.[68] Crewe had a long-standing association with Egerton, having been returned to the parliament of 1597 because of his patronage.[69] Egerton was also generous to Moore, who was his 'known favourite' and whom he had supported for admission to the bench of the Middle Temple in 1603.[70] At that time Moore praised Egerton as his protector.[71]

Egerton's immediate clientage proved highly successful after 1616, with Montagu himself succeeding Coke in his office as chief justice of the King's Bench. Chamberlaine became a justice of the King's Bench, and Crewe rose to become chief justice. Signs of division between Coke and this group are faint, but they do exist. The inscription on the rings Crewe gave away upon his call in 1614 read 'Rex lex loquens', a rejoinder to Coke's claim.[72] Yet these same men also made important contributions to the common law and the parliamentarian cause: Montagu argued against monopolies; Moore invented the lease and release, and his law reports circulated widely; and Crewe was the speaker of the parliament of 1614.[73] Despite any animosity that may have existed between them, Crewe could yet serve as his kinsman Coke's executor in 1634.[74] Such an outcome was entirely indicative of the mix of common lawyers with the Chancery.

The working relationship between the courts was driven and often defined by the writ of injunction, which was a command to individuals either to refrain from or perform particular acts. Since part of the equitable function of the court of Chancery was to relieve the strict course of the law or remedy inequities, injunctions were therefore vital to its work and might prevent expensive concurrent litigation.[75] Unlike the writ of *supersedeas*, they were not directed to the courts or their judges, but rather enjoined individuals *in personam*.[76] Some have assumed injunctions were

[68] Prest, *Rise of the Barristers*, p. 349.
[69] Hasler (ed.), *The House of Commons*, vol. I (London, 1981), p. 669. Crewe also praised Egerton at his serjeant's call; Hutton, *Diary*, pp. 77–85; Baker, *Serjeants*, p. 323; *DNB*, s.v. 'Randall Crewe'.
[70] Hasler (ed.), *The House of Commons*, vol. III, p. 74.
[71] Gareth Jones, *History of the Law of Charity* (Cambridge, 1969), p. 245.
[72] Baker, *The Order of Serjeants at Law*, p. 179.
[73] Hasler (ed.), *The House of Commons*, vol. III, p. 70.
[74] *DNB*, s.v. 'Randall Crewe'.
[75] Spence, *Equitable Jurisdiction of the Court of Chancery*, vol.1, pp. 670, 673; Holdsworth, *HEL*, vol. V, p. 336.
[76] Bryson, 'Introduction', in *Cases Concerning Equity*, vol. I, p. li.

given *de cursu*, the litigant merely requesting the writ from a clerk.[77] This would explain the traditional assumption of a proliferation of injunctions. However, Jones has written that injunctions were prayed by either including them in the original bill of complaint or afterwards by a motion.[78] In both cases this required at least passing judicial scrutiny.[79] Surviving bills show how the chancellor was petitioned to enjoin the other party, while the entry books reveal the court reviewing requests for injunctions and their issuance after an order of the court.[80]

Typically the court recorded that an injunction should be issued unless the defendant could show cause to the contrary. In default the writ would be issued, and this procedure was established by the 1590s.[81] It seems that the bar might be set low, however: George Carew recorded that the court granted an injunction to one party with a 'frivolous bill without a counsellor[']s hand'.[82] Injunctions often included a condition before they could be issued – in the case of debt this frequently required that the amount of the original debt be brought into the court. The injunction was extended to their lawyers, and it was not uncommon for unscrupulous defendants to shift their attorneys to avoid the injunction.[83] Another common form of condition ordered that an injunction would issue if the defendant failed to provide a sufficient answer by a certain date. The injunction would then be issued as a matter of course after that day. Often the injunction would last only until the defendant put in their answer, and sometimes the writ was used as leverage to force the defendant to answer.[84] From this answer the court could determine whether the complaint was actionable in Chancery and whether another injunction should be issued.

Injunctions could be irritants when litigants used them as a form of vexation. In 1592 a litigant described how two years previously the case had grown to issue at the common law and the injunction had been used to delay judgment and execution: injunctions could be held for three,

---

[77] *Ibid.*, p. xxxviii. Raack ventures no conclusion, citing the traditional view from Spence, in 'Injunctions', 568.

[78] Jones, *Elizabethan Court of Chancery*, p. 184.

[79] West, *Symboleography*, f. 185v; Powell, *The Attourneys Academy*, p. 32.

[80] West, *Symboleography*, f. 198v.

[81] Spence, *Equitable Jurisdiction of the Court of Chancery*, vol. I, p. 675.

[82] George Carew, *Reports in Chancery* (London, 1665), p. 152.

[83] *Courtney* v. *Marshall* (1592), C33/84, f. 146v; *Beddenham* v. *Parrye* (1592), C33/84, ff. 129v, 207v.

[84] Spence, *Equitable Jurisdiction of the Court of Chancery*, vol. I, p. 674; *Hunt* v. *Sibell* (1592), C33/84, f. 16v.

four or ten years.[85] Complaints of vexation and delay in Chancery were
frequent. They may have been used simply as pretexts in order to have
injunctions dissolved, but on occasion the actions of the court in punishing the offender supported the charge.[86] In *Goswolde* v. *Deerehaughe*
(1615) the defendant lamented that there had been three trials at the common law – and the plaintiff had revived the injunction once again. The
court ruled that if the cause was not procured by next term the injunction
would be dissolved.[87]

Litigants were sometimes determined enough to play the courts
against each other. In *Hughes* v. *Longs* (1611) the defendant complained
that a judgment had been obtained two years past for a rent charge, but
had been stayed by injunction. The plaintiff had failed to proceed in the
cause and had also sued a writ of error that 'meerlie delaieth his pro-
ceedinges both in this Courte and at the Comon Lawe'.[88] Sometimes the
plaintiff would begin concurrent suits at the common law, even while
enjoining the defendant.[89] Often this tactic was scattershot: the goal was
to attack the opponent in as many courts simultaneously as possible. In
one case three bills were preferred in the Chancery and five in the Star
Chamber. The Star Chamber referred the matter to the Council in the
Marches, which then cleared the accused.[90] In another case it was alleged
that twenty actions were sued at the common law against the defendant in the Chancery and the plaintiff had also sought an injunction. The
defendant's counsel reasoned that this was prima facie proof of vexation.[91]
Another case appears to have had three trials and judgments at the common law – yet the plaintiff revived the injunction.[92] Litigants joined with
others to pursue their ends in different courts.[93] While seeking injunctions, litigants might also be contending with prohibitions, or they might
be using injunctions where prohibitions had failed. Injunctions might

---

[85]   *Tarte* v. *Gifford* (1592), C33/84, f. 481v; *Bard* v. *Ascoughe* (1592), C33/84, f. 482v.

[86]   For an example of such suggestions, see *Snope* v. *Scott* (1592), C33/84, f. 246r.

[87]   *Goswolde* v. *Deerehaughe* (1615), C33/129, f. 497r.

[88]   *Hughes* v. *Longs* (1611), C33/121, f. 97v; *Pritherghe* v. *Horseley* (1611), C33/121, f. 440v;
       Mulcaster v. *Mulcaster* (1602), C33/103, ff. 18r–v; *Tey* v. *Warren* (1592), C33/84, f. 473v.

[89]   *Turnor* v. *Lawrence* (1611), C33/121, f. 193v; *Woodcock* v. *Chewe* (1615), C33/129, f. 25v;
       Stewkley v. *Pyke* (1615), C33/129, f. 713r.

[90]   *Westdon* v. *Steede* (1592), C33/84, f. 81r; *Goad* v. *Heydon* (1602), C33/103, f. 31r; and also
       Digbye v. *Parrot* (1592), C33/84, ff. 35r–v; *Turnor* v. *Lawrence* (1611), C33/121, f. 193v.

[91]   *Oskley* v. *Seaman* (1592), C33/84, ff. 83r–v; *Earle* v. *Falshurst* (1611), C33/121, f. 893r;
       Wistowe v. *Philippe* (1592), C33/84, f. 19r.

[92]   *Goswolde* v. *Deerehaughe* (1615), C33/129, f. 497r.

[93]   *Gardyner* v. *Wayte* (1602), C33/103, f. 95v.

also be used in highly tactical ways. One litigant claimed that he was only served with an injunction at the point when he brought the matter to trial, at 'great cost', though this may have simply been a coincidence. Another alleged that an injunction was obtained on untrue surmises merely to stop the trial at the assizes.[94]

The court responded by punishing those who misused or disobeyed injunctions.[95] Litigants could be determined – in *Winbe* v. *Mordant* the court informed the plaintiff that he would be punished corporally if he exhibited any more bills.[96] In *Snope* v. *Scott* the Chancery referred the matter to the common law courts with a condition that if the defendant were successful, the plaintiff would pay costs for wrongful vexation in the Chancery.[97] At times the Chancery might even expedite a case if it was felt that the parties would not be able to sustain the costs of extended litigation.[98] In other cases the court used the injunction to help litigants. In *Wistowe* v. *Philippe* (1592) the case had depended for fifteen years, and the plaintiff had joined with others to sue in both Chancery and Requests. The court issued an injunction to the court of Requests in order to prevent further vexation.[99] The Chancery also sought to end a multiplicity of suits through a single trial at the common law.[100]

Concurrency was therefore a major feature of Chancery litigation, and it was common for plaintiffs to begin a suit in Chancery and the common law at approximately the same time. Concurrency had the effect of drawing the defendant not only to increased charges, but greater hazards if he missed responding appropriately to any process. In *Hallway* v. *Pollard* (1602) the plaintiff took advantage of a lull in Chancery process to obtain a verdict at the common law against the defendant and proceeded with an attachment. The Chancery responded by discharging the attachment and dismissing the suit.[101] Tracing this concurrency also reveals how a single cause in the Chancery might have an extensive history in other

---

[94] *Marbury* v. *Fisher* (1592), C33/84, f. 725r; *Stratford* v. *Stratford* (1611), C33/121, ff. 318r–v.

[95] *Bostock* v. *Kemble* (1611), C33/121, f. 806v; *Evelenghe* v. *Yarde* (1615), C33/129, f. 501r.

[96] Jones, *The Elizabethan Court of Chancery*, p. 470; *Winbe* v. *Mordant* (1615), C33/129, f. 412r; see also *Smith* v. *Shepard* (1602), C33/103, f. 22v.

[97] *Snope* v. *Scott* (1592), C33/84, f. 246r; *Smyth* v. *Carter* (1592), C33/84, ff. 6v–7r. Other examples include C33/103, ff. 22v, 56r, 210v, 717v–718r; C33/121, f. 740v; C33/129, ff. 41v, 134r.

[98] *Faldoe* v. *Chamberlayne* (1592), C33/84, f. 540r.

[99] *Wistowe* v. *Philippe* (1592), C33/84, f. 19r.

[100] Though this strategy backfired in *Pye* v. *Goddard* (1592), C33/84, f. 473v.

[101] *Hallway* v. *Pollard* (1602), C33/103, f. 67v. Cf. *Hutt* v. *Bennett* (1602), C33/103, f. 128v.

courts: one case began in the sheriff's court of London and was lifted by *certiorari* into the Common Pleas and then the parties were enjoined by the Chancery.[102]

In response to these problems the court sometimes required an election or dismissed the suit altogether in cases of concurrency. Francis Moore, the counsel in *Bigge* v. *Seaman* (1615), attempted to secure this election when his client's case was dismissed from the Chancery for starting concurrent suits.[103] In 1592 a plaintiff was given the choice of whether to have his case dismissed or continued in the Chancery, since proceedings at the common law had also begun as part of an agreement to achieve a compromise.[104] Sometimes the plaintiff might respond that the suit was for a different cause or between different parties.[105] This latitude could lead some litigants to attempt to get around a restriction on concurrent litigation or innocently proceed at common law for matters that they believed were not determinable in the Chancery. In *Royman* v. *Royman* (1602) the plaintiff obtained an injunction of lands and sued at the common law for rents. The Chancery cautioned him against 'doble vexation' and required an election.[106] Litigants sometimes agreed to proceed concurrently in both courts, probably motivated by concerns about delay, as in the case of one octogenarian in 1611.[107] The court might on occasion demand sureties that the order would be followed and no execution sought.[108]

The Chancery did not always demand an election and suits might progress in tandem or waiting for resolution in the other court.[109] Concurrent litigation for the same cause was permitted when ordered or approved by the Chancery itself, a practice that imitated procedure on the Latin side. First, as we have seen, the Chancery often involved the common law as an aid in its adjudication. In *Lyte* v. *Eyres* (1592), a case over copyhold, it was decided that the cause 'semethe more meete to be tried and decided by the course of the comon lawe then in this courte'.[110] The Chancery continued an injunction for possession and then commanded a jury to try the case at assize. The order then continued 'And as the tryall shall fall out soe the

---

[102] *Besse* v. *Stowe* (1615), C33/129, f. 106r.
[103] *Bigge* v. *Seaman* (1615), C33/129, f. 456v.
[104] *Plandon* v. *Knightley* (1592), C33/84, f. 422r.
[105] *Gardyner* v. *Wayte* (1602), C33/103, f. 95v.
[106] *Royman* v. *Royman* (1602), C33/103, f. 387r.
[107] Though the Chancery might impose restrictions: *Carter* v. *Ashby* (1611), C33/121, f. 559v.
[108] *Crosse* v. *Weston* (1602), C33/103, f. 110v; *Betts* v. *Dyer* (1602), C33/103, ff. 192v–193r.
[109] See Moore's argument in *Bigge* v. *Seaman* (1615), C33/129, f. 456v.
[110] *Lyte* v. *Eyres* (1592), C33/84, f. 379v.

possession to be decreed by this Courte.' The Chancery may have opted for this procedure because of the fact-finding mechanism of the jury or to prevent subsequent litigation at the common law.

These interventions revealed how the Chancery often used the injunction to control the parties at the common law, beyond simply restraining their suits. This usually meant that the Chancery ordered the parties to proceed at common law up to a certain point, such as obtaining a verdict. They were enjoined to go no further than that point: '[to] forbeare to call for[,] take or procure by them selves or any other, any executions at the comon lawe upon any suche tryall or judgment'.[111] This referral to the common law court could result from a need to establish further proof before the matter could be resolved in equity: the validity of a will, title of land or legality of a local custom.[112] The mechanism could also be used 'to prove the Judges opinions for the lawe therein'.[113]

The procedure is detectable as early as 1592 and was doubtless of earlier origin.[114] It was sometimes used to speed the course of justice in either court, for example, threatening to dissolve an injunction in force if the plaintiff did not move the cause in the next term. In one case where Coke was counsel for the defendant, it was ordered that the plaintiff, notwithstanding an injunction, could proceed to judgment, but not execution.[115] The reason that the court gave was as follows: 'Soe as the plaintiff may proceede in this courte with effecte to get the cawse heard.' Later when the cause was heard again the court ordered the defendant to move 'the Judges before whom it was argued for their Resolution and Judgment upon the matter in lawe'.[116] In another case it was determined that the defendant could move for judgment in order to 'try the opinions of the said Judges of the comon pleas towchinge the premisses', though execution was prohibited.[117]

The Chancery might allow concurrent litigation as it proceeded to determine the equity of the cause. This was evident in *Kinge* v. *Ryden* (1592) where the matter having been preferred into the court, it was agreed that

[111] *Phelps* v. *Nevell* (1592), C33/84, f. 719v. Parties were also warned to avoid non-suiting; *Syms* v. *Franklyn* (1602), C33/103, f. 100r.

[112] *Cullyer* v. *Cullyer* (1592), C33/84, f. 128r; *Syms* v. *Francklin* (1602), C33/103, f. 100r; *Darcye* v. *Newdigate* (1611), C33/121, f. 476r; *Crawley* v. *Merydall* (1615), C33/129, f. 455r; *Dobbins* v. *Poole* (1615), C33/129, f. 483r; *Pannett* v. *Pallmer* (1615), C33/129, ff. 768r–v.

[113] *Zowche* v. *Thackerde* (1592), C33/84, ff. 748v–749r.

[114] Jones, *Elizabethan Court of Chancery*, pp. 474–6.

[115] *Boothe* v. *Hegge* (1592), C33/84, ff. 119v, 232r.

[116] *Boothe* v. *Hegge* (1592), C33/84, f. 351r.

[117] *Thorpe* v. *Jackson* (1592), C33/84, ff. 620r–v.

it could be heard there. Nonetheless the defendant was allowed to proceed to trial at the common law, 'But no judgment or execution shalbe taken ... untill the matter in equitye shalbe hearde and determined.'[118] The causes might move in parallel in both courts, so that if a case that was referred to the common law failed there, the Chancery might also dismiss it.[119] These arrangements could be complex, as in *Rowswell* v. *Cotteford* (1592) where the defendant had obtained a verdict and judgment at the common law contrary to an injunction then in force. A second trial in the Queen's Bench was ordered, and if the defendant should prevail, he would nonetheless relinquish the benefit of the previous trial. The defendant won the second trial by default, the plaintiff not being ready, but he had shown the jury the former verdict in disobedience to the Chancery's order. The Chancery responded by enjoining the defendant not to proceed with any of his verdicts and ordered the plaintiff to make a settlement. For this consideration and relief from the contempts, the defendant was commanded to discharge all his judgments.[120]

The Chancery at times created the situation where they might rule in equity against a verdict or judgment at the common law. In *Connyr* v. *Kingesmell* (1592) the court had ordered the parties to the common law with the condition that 'if the same did there passe for the defendant against the plaintiff, yet that the said defendant shoulde take no benefit thereof till this courte had heard the matter of equity'.[121] The defendant in this case having been successful at the common law, the court enjoined him not to call for execution. This procedure, in which the Chancery refrained from action until the judgment produced the 'injustice', gives credence to the Chancery argument that they could not provide relief in some circumstances until after judgment.

The Chancery might also use proceedings at the common law to obtain leverage over recalcitrant parties. In *Cullyer* v. *Cullyer* (1592) two brothers were litigating over copyhold. On account of their relationship Hatton thought it was appropriate that a commission should mediate their differences. The mediation having failed, the chancellor ordered 'that the said plaintiff shall forthwith bring an action at the comon lawe against the

---

[118] *Kinge* v. *Ryden* (1592), C33/84, f. 511v.
[119] *Hassellwood* v. *Bushey* (1611), C33/121, f. 233r; *Shoemaker* v. *Brooke* (1602), C33/103, f. 423r.
[120] *Rowswell* v. *Cotteford* (1592), C33/84, ff. 271r–v; and similarly, *Torperley* v. *Sherrington* (1611), C33/121, f. 76v.
[121] *Connyr* v. *Kingesmell* (1592), C33/84, f. 78v; and also *Pye* v. *Goddard* (1592), C33/84, f. 461v; *Darcye* v. *Newdigate* (1611), C33/121, f. 476r.

defendant'. By sending the parties to the common law and also enjoining them so that they could continue to participate in Chancery process,
Hatton hastened the resolution of the dispute.[122] That same year in *Caddor*
v. *Wyn*, in a case that the Privy Council had referred to trial at the common law over a lease, the Chancery sought to control the proceedings.
Allowing the defendant to proceed to judgment, but not execution, the
court stated its rationale: 'And soe that the plaintiff will become bownde
to this Courte to abyde the order thereof.'[123] Despite an injunction to
restrain the parties from proceeding upon a verdict, some did so nonetheless. In one case, the defendant in the Chancery succeeded at the common
law and took possession. The chancellor was incensed and ordered the
messenger of the court to apprehend the defendant and the under-sheriff
of Pembrokeshire to answer for the execution upon a Sunday.[124]

The development of the injunction was part of Egerton's reforming work
in the Chancery. Egerton had issued a number of ordinances, especially
those in 1596, 1598 and 1599, which imposed a more rigorous procedure,
tighter regulation of fees and a clearer definition of jurisdiction.[125] The
result may have been a smaller amount of litigation in the short term.[126] In
the long term, however, Egerton's achievement was the creation of a popular
court with a mandate as the keeper of the king's conscience – an association
traditionally ascribed to Hatton.[127] Egerton's streamlining of the Chancery
and his own desire to expand its jurisdiction was behind a dramatic rise in
litigation from 1603 onwards.[128] As Holdsworth and Knafla have argued,
Egerton was responsible for Chancery's emergence as a settled court, but
his reformed jurisdiction was on a course for conflict with the common
law.[129]

Amidst the complexity of jurisdictions, the Chancery used the injunction to provide justice to its litigants: none should leave the Chancery without remedy. At times this pursuit of justice was stated in cooperative terms
as a mission shared by the courts, and Anthony Benn in his lengthy defence

---

[122] *Cullyer* v. *Cullyer* (1592), C33/84, f. 128r.
[123] *Caddor* v. *Wyn* (1592), C33/84, ff. 166r–v. See also *Fyshe* v. *Johnson* (1592), C33/84, f. 323r;
     Greville v. *Tomlyns*, C33/129, f. 499r.
[124] *Barlowe* v. *Wegan* (1611), C33/121, ff. 53v–54r.
[125] Sanders, *Orders of the High Court of Chancery*, pp. 69–87. Knafla, *Law and Politics*,
     pp. 155–64; Raack, 'Injunctions', 587.
[126] Knafla, *Law and Politics*, p. 158.
[127] Jones, *Elizabethan Court of Chancery*, p. 44; Klinck, *Conscience, Equity and the Court of
     Chancery*, p. 89.
[128] Knafla, *Law and Politics*, p. 163.
[129] Holdsworth, *HEL*, vol. V, p. 236; Knafla, *Law and Politics*, p. 163.

of the court used this language.[130] But the Chancery made much of its duty as the keeper of the king's conscience to provide redress to those aggrieved by the course of the law. In particular, as Benn argued, the Chancery would remedy deficiencies in the operation of the common law: 'Freehold is in worse case than the beast fallen into the ditch if the Court of Chauncery for feare of giveing offence to the law should in this case lett it lye and not seeke to helpe it out.' Benn revealed his familiarity with the general criticisms of the common law when he dwelt on its shortcomings. He argued that the real cause of much legal uncertainty was innovation at the common law, such as ejectment: 'this is that which breedes confusion, this is it that makes the law to be taxed as causing uncertainty, multiplicity of sutes, besides excessive charge and vexation togeather with dangerous periury'. A municipal law such as the common law would over time no longer be 'just or proffitable to the state'.[131] Writing in defence of their jurisdiction Benn and Egerton explained that the work of the Chancery was necessary because of the parlous state of the common law.[132] In fact, although the courts had the same father, primogeniture made them unequal since equity was by far older and nobler. Benn explained that the Chancery 'refuseth ... to be set her limitts by her younger brother (for equity is auncienter then law)'. This, it was alleged, was common knowledge: 'very multitude and comon sort have it most familiar [in] their mouth, that Conscience and equity was before Magna Charta'.[133]

Much was made of the association of the Chancery with the king; in Egerton's words, equity was 'the moderation of the public law from the heart of the king'.[134] This claim to represent more immediately the king as justice-giver contrasted with the claims made by the judges. They argued that the King's Bench was the principal court of the king, since its proceedings were *coram rege*. The dispute was long-standing, and during a case in 1572 the authority of the King's Bench was asserted in argument: 'a judgment given in the Chancery which is before the King himself, it is to be reversed in the King's Bench, which is also before the King himself, and not in Parliament'.[135]

---

[130] BL Lansdowne MS 174, f. 206r.   [131] *Ibid.*, ff. 206v, 208r–v, 211r.

[132] Knafla, *Law and Politics*, pp. 326–7, 274–81.

[133] BL Lansdowne MS 174, ff. 212r, f. 211v. Coke referred to the Chancery as the 'little brother'; *L'Evesque de Bristoll* v. *Proctor* (1616), 1 Rolle 287, 81 ER 490.

[134] Ellesmere, 'A Breviate for the Kinges Councell', in Knafla, *Law and Politics*, p. 325; BL Additional MS 20700, ff. 13v–14r.

[135] *Anonymous*, 3 Dyer 315a, 73 ER 714; *The Case of Mines* (1568), 1 Plowden 393, 75 ER 595.

This jockeying for status intensified at the turn of the century, erupting in 1598 over the question of *supersedeas* from the Chancery to the King's Bench to stay proceedings there.[136] The Chancery claimed that the chancellor had power at his 'pleasure' to restrain the King's Bench through the use of the writ of *supersedeas*. Unlike the injunction, *supersedeas* was a command to the judges of the court, implying that they were an inferior jurisdiction.[137] The common lawyers were not slow to respond to the challenge. One writer declared that the King's Bench was the sovereign court for matters of the peace, and the Chancery was not to meddle in ordinary matters. No *supersedeas* could issue from the ordinary 'power' of the Chancery to the King's Bench since it was the highest ordinary court of justice, and the author cited the judgment in the Chancery in 1572 that was reversed in the King's Bench.[138] If the Chancery issued a *supersedeas* issued by its absolute power, then it should only be for an extraordinary circumstance; otherwise the King's Bench was not bound to obey it.

Another dispute over status occurred in 1604 in a debate over the precedence of masters of Chancery and serjeants.[139] The masters asserted that they were judges who represented the king in his justice seat, while the serjeants rejected their claim.[140] In 1612 Christopher Yelverton, a justice in the King's Bench, prompted another dispute when he sued an attachment of privilege against Paul Dewes, one of the six clerks of the Chancery.[141] A *supersedeas* issued out of the Chancery, and the legal issue arose concerning who should have superior privilege: a justice of the King's Bench or one of the six clerks in the Chancery? The King's Bench refused the *supersedeas*, claiming that it did not lie to their court since proceedings were *coram rege*, and threatened to fine the sheriff if he failed to attach Dewes.[142]

[136] Huntington Library Ellesmere MS 2920.
[137] Jones, *Elizabethan Court of Chancery*, p. 190. Powell, *The Attourney's Academy*, pp. 68–72; *FNB*, ff. 236r–239v; *Langdale's Case* (1608), 12 Co. *Rep.* 60, 77 ER 1339; *Case of the Marshalsea* (1612), 10 Co. *Rep.* 75b, 77 ER 1037; BL Stowe 415, f. 257v, For complaints that the writ was a source of abuse, see BL Lansdowne MS 167, f. 113v, and *Godscall v. Heyden* (1614), involving a servant of Coke's clerk; CUL MS Ii.5.26, ff. 77r–v; BL Lansdowne MS 44, f. 2v.
[138] Huntington Library Ellesmere MS 2920.
[139] Sir John Hayward and Francis Tate collected the opposing arguments; BL Additional MS 22587, ff. 33–6; BL Additional MS 22591; and Bodl. Barlow MS 9, pp. 1–10.
[140] BL Additional MS 12497, f. 172v; An earlier claim that the masters were judges appeared in *Halton's Case* (1588), Godbolt 141, 78 ER 86. Details of the broader dispute are given in Baker, *The Order of Serjeants at Law*, pp. 55–6.
[141] *Yelverton v. Dewes* (1612), *Cases Concerning Equity*, vol. II, pp. 399–400.
[142] Citing the granting of a special *supersedeas* in a Year Book case; YB Hil. 4 Edw. 4, pl. 4, ff. 43a–44b.

The claims of the King's Bench again relied on their relationship to the king, a logic that led to the reluctant admission that the Common Pleas was a lesser court.[143]

These tensions over precedence were among the fault lines of the daily interactions between the courts. But it was the injunction after judgment where Coke chose to draw the line. By suggesting that decisions from the bench were neither final nor certain, these injunctions eroded confidence in the common law. Moreover, the use of the injunction after judgment by members of his profession was a sign of the bad practice that was in need of reform. It had long been suggested that revisiting common law judgments had the effect of undermining the law by leading to unrestrained litigation: in the fifteenth century William Ayscough JCP had warned that 'infinite trial upon trial will be seen'.[144] St German had also cautioned similarly that 'the law should never have end'.[145] Before Coke the common law opposition to Chancery injunctions after judgment was sporadic.[146] In 1547 the petition to the Privy Council that led to the fall of Chancellor Wriothesley included complaints about injunctions 'aswel before verdictes, judgementes and executions as after'.[147] In 1572 in *Humfrey* v. *Humfrey* Serjeant Bendloe urged that: 'the Chancery after judgment could not enjoyn the party that he shall not sue forth execution'.[148] These precedents informed the praemunire threat against Hele in 1588, which J. P. Dawson considered to be the beginning of the troubles between the Elizabethan common law and the Chancery.[149] Coke's attempt to discipline common lawyers in the Chancery grew from both the competition between the courts and their pattern of cooperation.

In opposing Chancery suits after verdict, Coke and the other common law judges relied on two medieval precedents and the statute of 4 Henry IV, c. 23, which stated that 'after Judgment given in the Courts of our Lord the King, the Parties and their Heirs shall be thereof in Peace, until the Judgment be undone by Attaint or Error'.[150] The first precedent

---

143 HLS MS 118(b), f. 37r.
144 Trans. David Seipp, YB Mich. 19 Henry VI, pl. 82, ff. 39a–41a.
145 St German, *Doctor and Student*, p. 107.
146 Bryson, 'Introduction', in *Cases Concerning Equity*, vol. I, p. xl.
147 *CSPD, Edward VI, 1547–1550*, pp. 48–50; Baker, *OHLE*, vol. VI, pp. 179–80.
148 *Humfrey* v. *Humfrey* (1572), 3 Leonard 18, 74 ER 513.
149 Dawson, 'Coke and Ellesmere', 134; *Heale's Case* (1588), 2 Leonard 115–16, 74 ER 405; Richard Crompton, *L'authoritie et iurisdiction des courts de la Maiestie de la Roygne*, pp. 57–8. Coke mentions this case in 4 Co. *Inst.*, pp. 123–124, and 3 Co. *Inst.*, pp. 86, 91, and BL Harley MS 6686A, f. 226v.
150 4 Henry IV, c. 23, *SR*, vol. I, p. 142.

was *Russel's Case* in 1482 when the Chancery had stayed a verdict with an injunction. Chief Justice Huse offered the imprisoned suitor relief by habeas corpus.[151] The second was *Cobb* v. *Nore* (1465) where John Cobb won a case through 'false practice' and relief was denied in the Chancery.[152]

The Chancery viewed the granting of injunctions after judgment as a necessary part of their proceedings. Defenders of the practice argued that some cases could only be brought after judgment since the outcome of the common law trial produced the injustice.[153] Moreover, it was argued that the actual verdict or judgment was not under examination, but the conscience of the parties.[154] This analysis was especially relevant when parties acted quickly to obtain a verdict before an injunction could be granted.[155]

By the time of *Finch* v. *Throckmorton* (1591–8), considered the leading precedent for the subsequent dispute with the Chancery, the common law judges had already made clear their commitment to oppose equitable relief after judgment and were willing to entertain praemunire against those who did so. In *Finch* v. *Throckmorton*, the facts of the case were innocuous enough: in 1567 Throckmorton had failed to pay his rent within the required time when his servant ran away with the money.[156] Yet afterwards the Queen's receiver accepted late payment and made an acquittance, continuing to receive the rent until 1588. The question was whether the lease had been broken upon non-payment. The case was tried in the Exchequer and the barons determined that the lease 'was void immediately' upon non-payment and that Throckmorton had subsequently been held as a pernor of the profits. Significantly, as with several cases targeted later by Coke, the judgment was affirmed on a writ of error in the Exchequer Chamber.[157] Throckmorton then followed with a bill in

---

[151] YB Mich. 22 Edw IV, pl. 21, f. 37.

[152] Coke describes the case at BL Harley MS 6686A, ff. 225v–226r, citing Pasch. 5 Edward IV, rot. 35.

[153] Ellesmere, 'A Breviate for the Kinges Councell', p. 326; BL Additional MS 46410, ff. 117v–118r.

[154] Carew, *Reports in Chancery*, p. 4; Ellesmere, 'A Breviate for the Kinges Councell', p. 324.

[155] *Coytmore* v. *Robert* (1615), C33/129, f. 993r.

[156] The reports are *Finch* v. *Throckmorton*, Cro. Eliz. 221, 78 ER 477; *Moyle Finches Case*, 1 Anderson 303, 123 ER 485; *Sir Moyle Finch* v. *Throckmorton*, Moore 291, 72 ER 587; 4 Co. *Inst.*, p. 86; BL Lansdowne MS 1110, ff. 15v, 28v, reprinted in *Cases Concerning Equity*, vol. II, p. 441; Coke's manuscript report of the case is BL Harley MS 6686A, ff. 226v–229r.

[157] For injunctions to the Exchequer Chamber see the earlier cases of *Palmer* v. *Hassell* (1592), C33/84, ff. 304v–r; and *Barwell* v. *Estoft* (1592), C33/84, f. 116v; and also C33/84, ff. 444r–v.

the Chancery, seeking relief since the forfeiture of the lease resulted from an accident and the queen had accepted rent afterwards. The plaintiffs in the Chancery explicitly claimed that they did not impeach the judgment of the court, but rather sought to 'conform the corrupt conscience of the party'.[158] The case was referred to the judges and it was resolved 'that if a man has matter of equity and he first will try the [common] law, where judgment is given against him at the common law, he shall never be relieved in equity'.[159] The argument was extended even to recognizances, which acknowledged judgments that might later be used against the recognizee in court. In *Beverly's Case* (1603) the judges declared that relief in equity was not possible on recognizances entered into even by those who were non compos mentis. Relief in the circumstance would be 'against an express maxim of the common law ... in subversion of a principle and ground in law'.[160]

Coke recorded that if Throckmorton had prevailed, all the 'fruit and effect of the judgment would be taken away' and revealed what he believed was at stake:

> men after judgment and trials in law [will] then surmise matter in equity and by this put the one who recovered to excessive charges, and suits [by] these means would be infinite[,] and no one should be in peace for any thing which the law by judgment had given to him, but a contentious and able person who had an unquiet spirit he would be able to continually surmise matter in equity and thereby vex the one that recovered continually.[161]

He recorded in his notebook that 'it seemed to some' that praemunire might be applied against those who sought relief in Chancery after judgment. Against the objection that the Chancery was also a court of the king and therefore did not come within the scope of the statute of 27 Edward III, Coke argued that this was irrelevant so long as the actions of the Chancery were 'in destruction of the common law'.[162]

This commentary also hinted at a middle position that helps to explain why so many injunctions involving verdicts were otherwise tolerated: estoppel by election.[163] If a case had reached a verdict at the common law, but a suit on the same issue had already begun in the Chancery, there

---

[158] BL Harley MS 6686A, f. 224r.
[159] *Cases Concerning Equity*, vol. II, p. 442.
[160] *Beverly's Case* (1603), 4 Co. *Rep.* 124a, 76 ER 1119–20.
[161] BL Harley MS 6686A, f. 224r.   [162] BL Harley MS 6686A, f. 224v.
[163] Bryson, 'Introduction', in *Cases Concerning Equity*, vol. I, p. xxxix.

might be no opposition to the injunction. However, a suitor who 'first will try the [common] law' and not prefer their bill into the Chancery until after the verdict, unsettled the judgment, a point made in *Throckmorton*. In this analysis, the focus was on the litigant, who had implicitly made an election by not exhibiting a bill in the Chancery as the case was being heard at the common law. Popham in *Cardinal* v. *de la Brocke* (1606) explicitly identified this compromise position, which was formalized in an order by Egerton in 1614.[164] He allowed that the Chancery might proceed to decree so long as a bill had been preferred there before the common law judgment: 'if one has a bill pending in the court of equity and, before a decree made there the defendant procures a judgment against the plaintiff there at the common law, that notwithstanding this judgment, the court of equity may proceed to the decree'.[165] Popham's compromise reflected the realities of litigation: litigants often used the two courts together to obtain evidence, and at times parties might simply ignore an injunction and obtain a judgment at the common law.[166] But Coke, who was counsel in the case, took a harder line and retorted that Popham's opinion would render the statute of 4 Henry IV of little or no purpose and that once a judgment had been given in the 'king's court' the party should be in peace except in cases of error.

After Popham's passing, the next generation of judges became less well disposed towards injunctions that interfered with judgments. Thomas Fleming, whom Knafla has identified as a key figure in the use of praemunire to limit the Chancery, revealed his jurisdictional anxieties when he complained in 1611: 'There are too many causes drawn into the Chancery to be relieved there, which are more fit to be determined by trial at common law.'[167] The threat of equitable interference was revealed in a subsequent attempt by a remainder-man to defeat a common recovery. It was said that 'Coke ... Marvelled that they would meddle with such matters'.[168] The possibilities of Chancery interference in the main workings of the

[164] Sanders, *Orders of the High Court of Chancery*, p. 87.
[165] *Cardinal* v. *de la Brocke* (1606), *Cases Concerning Equity*, vol. I, pp. 344–5. Williams JKB was also in accord; IT Barrington MS 7, f. 210r; cf. Baker, 'The Common Lawyers and the Chancery', p. 209.
[166] This was the point adjudged in *Huet* v. *Conquest* (1616), *Cases Concerning Equity*, vol. II, no. 245, p. 470; see also C33/121, f. 422r; *The Case of Bradley and Jones* (1613), Godbolt 240, 78 ER 139; *Sir Francis Fortescue and Coake's Case* (1612), Godbolt 193, 78 ER 117.
[167] *Gollew* v. *Bacon* (1611), 1 Bulstrode 112, 80 ER 809.
[168] *Anonymous* (1613), *Cases Concerning Equity*, vol. II, p. 407, no. 209, and similarly *Markham's Case* (1620), *Cases Concerning Equity*, vol. II, p. 484, no. 258; *Stone* v. *Withypolls* (1588), 1 Leonard 113, 74 ER 106.

common law exacerbated Coke's anxiety, since it added to the problem of uncertainty in the law. Litigants would not have the benefit of their suits and 'the law should never have end'.[169] The conflict that broke out in 1615 was anticipated by the common law dispute with the Court of Requests. In 1611 the judges linked their assertion of *res judicata* against the Court of Requests to the Chancery.[170] Coke had even boldly suggested that prohibition might lie to the Chancery in *Jenoar and Alexander's Case* (1613) and *Wright's Case* (1614).[171] A bill in the ill-fated parliament of 1614 would have limited the examination of judgments at common law in other courts.[172] The scope of the clash widened in *Heath v. Ridley* that same year when Coke continued hearing a case after the plaintiff had disregarded an injunction. He took the occasion to cite the statutes of 27 Edward III, c. 1, and 4 Henry IV, c. 23, and encouraged parties to proceed with an information on the statute of 4 Henry IV whenever a bill was exhibited in Chancery after judgment.[173] He explained 'it is much to be wondered, that none will inform upon these laws in cases against the party that procures such injunctions after judgments at common law'.[174] His admonition acknowledged that the common law judges, if they were to respond to the Chancery, could only do so upon the initiative of litigants.[175]

---

[169] 3 Co. *Inst.*, p. 124.

[170] *Anonymous* (1611), HLS 114, f. 41r; see also *Orme v. Byrde* (1610), HLS MS 114, f. 24r. The issue of *res judicata* was pursued against courts other than Chancery and Requests throughout the period: see the custom in London involving the mayor rehearing cases in equity; *Anonymous* (1587), Godbolt 127, 78 ER 77; and also the chancery of Chester, *Vautrey v. Pannell* (1615), *Cases Concerning Equity*, no. 237, p. 451; and *Coats and Suckerman v. Warner*, 1 Rolle 252, 81 ER 469; 3 Bulstrode 119, 81 ER 101. On the other side, complaint was made that parties with decrees against them obtained prohibitions from the common law; BL Additional MS 46410, ff. 296r, 298v.

[171] *Jenoar and Alexander's Case* (1613), Godbolt 209, 78 ER 127; *Wright's Case* (1614), Moore 836, 72 ER 938. Coke relied upon the authority of Anthony Fitzherbert, *La Graunde Abridgement* (London, 1577), STC 10957, 'Prohibition', pl. 11 (13 Edward III); also Crompton, *L'authoritie et jurisdiction*, pp. 56–7.

[172] *Walts v. Hyde* (n.d.), *Cases Concerning Equity*, vol. I, p. 361; *Harwood v. Jewell* (1615), vol. II, pp. 447–8, no. 232; also *Vautrey v. Pannell* (1615), vol. II, p. 450, no. 236; 1 Rolle, 263, 81 ER 477; HMC, *Third Report*, appendix, p. 15; Thomas L. Moir, *The Addled Parliament* (Oxford, 1958), pp. 200–4.

[173] *Heath v. Ridley* (1614), 2 Bulstrode 194, 80 ER 1062; *Heath v. Rydley*, Cro. Jac. 335, 79 ER 286; *Cases Concerning Equity*, vol. II, no. 220; cf. *Cases Concerning Equity*, vol. II, no. 221. Probably the case in which Egerton declared that he would not 'meddle with the judgement, but I will deal with the corrupt conscience of the party'; *Browne v. Heath* (1614), BL Additional MS 25213, f. 159r.

[174] *Heath v. Ridley*, 2 Bulstrode 194, 80 ER 1062.

[175] Baker, 'The Common Lawyers and the Chancery', p. 211.

But by 1615 the outcome of four cases also revealed that the principal weapon, habeas corpus, was ineffective against the Chancery and so exposed the limit of the common law's reach. The common law judges had long used habeas corpus to review imprisonments by the chancellor, such as in *Astick's Case* (1592).[176] In 1614, however, the Chancery committed Richard Glanvill to the Fleet for a second time for defrauding Francis Courtney in the sale of fake diamonds that was secured by an obligation.[177] Courtney had unsuccessfully sought to reverse the judgment on the obligation by a writ of error, and had also exhibited a bill for relief in the Chancery. Though the terms of the decree passed against Glanvill were generous he chose to stand on his judgments and refused to abide by the decree.[178] For this Glanvill was committed, but then sued habeas corpus. Coke, citing *Cobb v. Nore*, declared that 'this decree and imprisonment, being after a judgment at the common law, was unlawful'.[179] The judges conceded that there was 'much matter of equity' in the case, but nonetheless urged priority: if Courtney had complained before the judgment, he 'should have been relieved'.[180] Arguably this was not possible since it was the original common law judgment that produced the injustice that needed relief, but the court discharged Glanvill absolutely. Nonetheless, the chancellor ordered Glanvill to be arrested again by a pursuivant to whom the court could not write.[181] This was one loophole that the Chancery had found to avoid having the King's Bench review its imprisonments by habeas corpus.

In *Apsley's Case* (1615), the chancellor had committed Michael Apsley to the Fleet in 1608 for exhibiting a bill into the Chancery after judgment in the Common Pleas that had been affirmed upon error.[182] *Ruswell's Case* developed upon more complex grounds. The decree in Chancery against him being contrary to the Statute of Wills, Ruswell chose to ignore it

---

[176] *Beddenham v. Parrye* (1592), C33/84, ff. 129r, 207v.

[177] BL Harley MS 1767, ff. 37r–39r; BL Lansdowne MS 163, ff. 223r–v; HLS MS 111, f. 47r. The published reports are *Glanviles Case* (1614), Moore 838, 72 ER 939; *Courtney v. Glanvil*, Croke Jac 343, 79 ER 294; *Glanvile v. Courtney*, 2 Bulstrode 301, 80 ER 1139. Previously unknown manuscript reports are published in *Cases Concerning Equity*, vol. II, pp. 440–4. The second committal is given in *Cases Concerning Equity*, vol. II, p. 443.

[178] PRO C38/20, *Courtney v. Glanvill*.

[179] *Courtney v. Glanvil*, Croke Jac 344, 79 ER 294.

[180] *Ibid.*, 295.

[181] *Cases Concerning Equity*, vol. II, p. 443. This strategy may already have been pursued in *Hele's Case*, *Acta Cancellariae*, p. 7.

[182] *Apsley's Case* (1615), Moore 840, 72 ER 940; *Apsley's Case*, 1 Rolle 192, 81 ER 424; *Cases Concerning Equity*, vol. II, pp. 463, 468–9. Elsewhere the date of his committal is given as 1604/5; *Cases Concerning Equity*, vol. II, p. 458.

and was committed to the Fleet on 30 May 1614.[183] A third case involved
William Allen, who later played a leading role in stoking the opposition to
the Chancery. Allen had taken advantage of the bankruptcy of his debtor
Edwards to obtain unscrupulously lands worth £2,400, after paying only
£400.[184] Allen refused subsequent decrees to return the lands, and he was
committed to the Fleet, seeking relief by habeas corpus from the overturning of judgments by decree.[185]

The use of habeas corpus tested confidence in the common law claim
to oversee imprisonments and to offer remedy against the misuse of legal
power. At the Bar George Croke explained that since the 'king sits in
person' in the King's Bench, the court had 'supreme jurisdiction of the
lives and liberties of men'.[186] Coke too asserted that the common law
had 'power to send for the body of a man in every place within England
and discharge him if the cause be illegal'.[187] The judges relied on several
precedents, especially *Mitchell's Case* (1576–7) where no cause had been
shown for the imprisonment on the return.[188] Relying upon this precedent and deeming the return invalid in *Glanvile v. Courtney* because it
failed to specify a cause for the imprisonment, Coke enlarged his remarks
and stated that the court should provide protection against a decree after
judgment.[189] How that relief might be offered was more problematic. Coke
admitted as much when he cautioned that the judges 'should not meddle'
with matters out of the return, 'but they were to meddle with that which
appears to them upon the return'.[190]

The very medieval law that they claimed to revere hampered the judges:
a Year Book case contained a clear dictum by Sir William Babington CJCP
in 1431 that the court would remand the prisoner if 'the cause appeared
to the Court sufficient in itself, notwithstanding that it was false'.[191] This

---

[183] Bacon later reversed the decree upon bill of review; *Cases Concering Equity*, vol. II,
p. 467.
[184] HLS MS 111, ff. 51r–v.
[185] BL Harley MS 1767, f. 43r.
[186] Rylands Library French MS 118, f. 282r; *Ruswell's Case* (1615), *Cases Concerning Equity*,
vol. II, p. 454.
[187] *Cases Concering Equity*, vol. II, p. 464; cf. *Glanvile v. Courtney*, 2 Bulstrode 301, 80 ER
1139; *Whetherby and Whetherley* (1605), HLS MS 118(c), f. 57r. See also *Perepoynt's Case*
(1609), Godbolt 158, 78 ER 96.
[188] *Henry Roswell's Case* (1615), Rylands Library French MS 118, f. 282r; *Cases Concerning
Equity*, vol. II, p. 465.
[189] *Courtney v. Glanvil*, Croke Jac 344, 79 ER 294.
[190] *Apsley's Case*, *Cases Concerning Equity*, vol. II, pp. 463, 464.
[191] 'quod Tota Curia concessit'; YB Mich. 9 Henry VI, pl. 24, ff. 44a–b. Coke cites the case
in *James Bagg's Case* (1615), 11 Co. *Rep.* 99b, 77 ER 1280. He had stated the position as

problem had recently been faced in the Common Pleas in *Sir Henry Lea's Case* (1612).[192] The Court of Requests had committed Sir Henry to the Fleet for disobeying a decree. The return at common law stated only that he had been committed for contempt. The Court was of the opinion that they could not deliver him, because no cause appeared in the return to warrant his delivery. The judges resorted to a prohibition, because the case might have proceeded upon the common law by an action on the case. During *Apsley's Case*, Coke was recorded as saying the following: 'And where the cause of the commitment appears upon the return to be legal, they must remand him according to 9 Hen. VI, 4.'[193] The Chancery was fully entitled to imprison for contempts and could craft the return so as to avoid an explanation of the actual nature of the contempt.

While the returns in *Glanvile v. Courtney* and *Apsley's Case* failed to specify a lawful cause of the commitment, and so were deemed bad, the return in *Ruswell's Case* was more exact, stating that the imprisonment was for contempt.[194] A comment of George Croke, who was counsel for the prisoner, revealed the strategy the Chancery was pursuing: 'this return was made by great advice and it was deemed that no one would speak against it'. He pressed the court to examine the grounds of the decree that Ruswell had disobeyed, arguing that the return must specify a 'certain cause', involving a description of the contempt. This was an attempt to reach the substantive issues in the case through the writ.[195] Since Ruswell had already been imprisoned for six or seven years, Croke also raised the issue of extended detention and urged the court to offer remedy to persons when their 'liberty is tortiously taken from them'.[196] When the return was deemed bad, the Chancery provided a different formulation on the next return that also revealed little of the substantive cause of the committal. Croke complained, 'the return is not good because he has not returned the

---

early as 1608–10 in *Wharton's Case*, Noy 149, 74 ER 1111; see Halliday, *Habeas Corpus*, p. 108n.42 and pp. 108–110, for discussion. The remedy, Coke suggested, was a writ of false imprisonment or action on the case for false return.

[192] *Lea and Leas Case* (1612), Godbolt 198, 78 ER 120.

[193] *Cases Concerning Equity*, vol. II, p. 464.

[194] *Ruswell's Case* (1615), *ibid.*, p. 453; *Henry Roswell's Case* (1615), Rylands Library French MS 118, f. 282r.

[195] *Cases Concerning Equity*, vol. II, pp. 454, 459, 461, 467 and see 462. He relied principally upon the precedent in *Astwick's Case* (1566–7) and the Year Book case of 9 Henry VI, 44. See also *Presidents Monstres En Bank Le Roy*, Moore 839, 72 ER 939–40; *Ruswell's Case*, 1 Rolle 219, 81 ER 444. No report of *Astwick's Case* has been found, but it is cited in *Ruswell's Case*, 1 Rolle 217, 81 ER 443–4; *Cases Concerning Equity*, vol. II, pp. 455, 457.

[196] An 'unreasonable thing'; *Cases Concerning Equity*, vol. II, pp. 463, 466. Coke cited Acts 25:27 in support, as he did again later in the context of imprisonment by the High

cause or reason of the decree'.[197] His argument did not overcome the technical learning around habeas corpus, and the court remanded Ruswell, 'quia curia advisari vult'.[198] The court was unable to look behind the return and examine the substantive merits of the case, a dilemma apparent again in *Doctor Googe and Smith's Case* (1615). According to the return, the chancellor had committed Googe and Smith 'for refusing to respond to a bill' exhibited in the Chancery that had sought to reverse the judgment in the *Earl of Oxford's Case* (1615). Coke was certain that if the bill was exhibited after judgment the parties should be relieved. There was, however, some hesitation: 'but I doubt how we are able to take knowledge upon this return that this is the same matter as [the *Earl of Oxford's Case*] because other persons are parties to this bill than those in the action in this court'.[199] Though he later dismissed his own objection and bailed the parties with sureties, he also encouraged them to settle the matter themselves.

Baker has observed that, 'Coke was unwilling to take a stand against Egerton on habeas corpus'.[200] The explanation is found in the limitations of the writ, an ineffectual tool to accomplish Coke's goals against the Chancery.[201] Even against a lesser authority, such as the College of Physicians, it was admitted in 1614 that discharging the petitioner would merely lead to his recommitment, and the College would amend and improve their return.[202] Though Coke and his brethren were ultimately judges of the returns and therefore set the rules, the reports betray discomfort as they sought to go beneath the surface of the writ, something that their medieval precedents suggested was beyond their powers.[203] A reporter suggested the remedies that the parties had available: an action for false imprisonment or an information on the statutes of 27 Edward II and 4 Henry IV, and here he may have been following Coke who had encouraged parties to inform as early as 1614.[204]

Commission; *Cases Concerning Equity*, vol. II, pp. 458, 461; *Codd* v. *Turback*, 3 Bulstrode 110, 81 ER 94.

[197] *Cases Concerning Equity*, vol. II, pp. 458, 461–2.

[198] *Ibid.*, p. 467; *Ruswell's Case*, 1 Rolle 220, 81 ER 445.

[199] *Googe and Smiths Case* (1615), 1 Rolle 278, 81 ER 487; BL Additional MS 25213, f. 180v.

[200] Baker, 'The Common Lawyers and the Chancery', p. 215. A summary of the outcome of these suits is found in Halliday, *Habeas Corpus*, p. 369, n. 123.

[201] It was recently argued that habeas corpus was 'extremely effective' against the Chancery; Hart, *Rule of Law*, p. 49.

[202] The court bailed, but did not discharge, the petitioner; *Alphonso* v. *College of Physicians* (1614), 2 Bulstrode 260, 80 ER 1106.

[203] *Cases Concerning Equity*, vol. II, p. 464, and again in another report, *ibid.*, p. 468.

[204] *Ibid.*, p. 458; *Heath* v. *Ridley*, 2 Bulstrode 194, 80 ER 1062. Popham had also noted that 'if a man libel in court Christian for a temporal matter action on the case will lie'; *Bray* v. *Partridge* (1601), BL Additional MS 25203, f. 341v.

The cases between 1614 and 1615 reveal another facet of the dispute and Coke's underlying motive to protect confidence in the common law. In *Googe* and *Apsley* a writ of error was either depending or had affirmed the original judgment. During the exchange with James in 1609, Coke had insisted that judgments given in the Exchequer Chamber must be respected; otherwise other decisions might be weakened.[205] These cases in Chancery drew into question the judgment of all the common law justices. Perhaps more significantly, in *Ruswell's Case* the issue was not *res judicata*. The sale by the executors was void by the Statute of Wills and the common law. The question was whether the Chancery might exempt parties from acts of parliament, and it was argued that the case was without fraud or covin.[206] The consequence of the decree was that a subject could be imprisoned indefinitely for following the common law, as Coke noted in his assimilation of *Ruswell* to *Astwick*.[207] Unsuccessful litigants would undermine confidence in common law adjudication by trying their luck again in the Chancery, as Tourneur recognized:

> And this is at present usual, that when the defendant at common law has tried his fortunes there and stood out at the course of the law and in the end the matter adjudged against him then will he exhibit his bill in Chancery and growned it upon points of equity for which he might have preferred his suite in Chancery before the judgment and so a double and infinite vexation.[208]

Without the confidence of litigants that their causes would reach a conclusion, the common law's authority would decay. After Coke's fall, Bacon with two common law judges as assistants revisited *Ruswell* and declared that the Chancery would subvert neither maxims of the law nor statutes, even though equity might relieve specific mischiefs caused by their operation.[209] In light of the stakes, Coke turned to a more drastic solution when the dispute reached a head in 1615: 'Glanvile and Allen relinquished the Course by habeas corpus because the King's Bench disliked it [and] Lord Coke misliked it [and] advised another Course and mentioned presidents as Glanvile saied ... he mentioned Myldemaies president.'[210] 'Mildmay's precedent' was praemunire.[211] Only a few years

[205] LRO 1953 D26/2595, f. 6r.
[206] *Cases Concerning Equity*, vol. II, pp. 462, 466.
[207] *Ibid.*, p. 465; *Beverly's Case* (1603), 4 Co. *Rep.* 123b, 76 ER 1118.
[208] BL Additional MS 35957, f. 55v.
[209] Baker, 'The Common Lawyers', p. 227.
[210] BL Additional MS 11574, f. 44r.
[211] *Hetley v. Boyer and Mildmay*, Croke Jac 336, 79 ER 287. The idea was firmly rejected in *King v. Standish* (1670).

earlier, another aggrieved litigant, Thomas Coe, had suggested such an attack on the chancellor.[212]

The outline of the story is well known.[213] It was alleged that while in prison for their contempts Glanvill and Allen prepared a plot to revenge themselves against Egerton and to curtail the power of the Chancery.[214] Much like the gathering of neighbours before a suit at law the conspirators urged others to join them in the legal assault against the Chancery.[215] First, Glanvill and Allen told others imprisoned by the Chancery for disobedience of their decrees that they could obtain release by habeas corpus.[216] They informed the other prisoners that the King's Bench could examine Chancery decrees 'and ment soe to doe'.[217] By offering the handle of a judicial sword, the conspirators hoped to begin a revolt against the Chancery. Glanvill brought to bear legal intimidation similar to the threats against the commissioners of sewers when he pursued actions of false imprisonment against the Warden of the Fleet and two other officers. These actions intended to bring 'that Courte into derision and to terrefye the masters and officers from doeinge theire service'.[218] The conspirators also seem to have sent a petition to the king, probably in Easter term 1615, in which they complained that the corruption of the Chancery had cost the king the remarkable sum of £500,000 and promised that £100,000 might be

---

[212] Huntington Library Ellesmere MS 5756. For details of Coe's litigation in the Chancery and his many contempts, see Ellesmere MSS 5726–93. Coe is probably the person referred to as 'C' and 'Coo' (an alternative spelling of his name) in a letter from Ellesmere to Salisbury in 1609 and described as that 'folishe and franticke fellow'. The indexer of the manuscript identified this person as 'Coke', an attribution that has been followed by Boyer, *Sir Edward Coke*, p. 204; BL Lansdowne MS 91, f. 98r. Coke at one point had indirectly warned Ellesmere that he might run into a praemunire for the lack of a patent; Huntington Library Ellesmere MS 418.

[213] The story is reconstructed from several documents, including BL Additional MS 11574, ff. 43r–58r; BL Stowe 298, ff. 210–12; *Glanvile and Allen's Case*, Hobart 115, 80 ER 264; *Glanvile v. Courtney*, 2 Bulstrode 301, 80 ER 1139; *Courtney v. Glanvil*, Croke Jac 343, 79 ER 294; *Glanviles Case*, Moore 838, 72 ER 939; PRO STAC 8/21/19; manuscript case reports in BL Additional MS 25213, ff. 162r, 176r–v; BL Additional MS 35957, f. 2v; Spedding *et al.* (eds.), *Works*, vol. V, pp. 249–54; Huntington Library Ellesmere MSS 5971 and 5973, printed in S. E. Thorne, 'Praemunire and Sir Edward Coke', in *Essays in English Legal History*, pp. 239–42.

[214] BL Additional MS 11574, f. 50r; Baker, 'The Common Lawyers and the Chancery', p. 216.

[215] BL Additional MS 11574, f. 57r.

[216] *Ibid.*, f. 53r; though Glanvill may have been first released on the grounds that the committal was before a pardon; BL Additional MS 25213, f. 176r.

[217] BL Additional MS 11574, f. 50r.

[218] They may have advised the other prisoners to bring similar actions of false imprisonment; *ibid.*, ff. 45r, 52v, 46r.

recovered from their property for the king's use.[219] These tactics – allegations of corruption, the manipulation of legal process, the undermining of confidence in judicial bodies – are familiar from the Fen dispute.

Like other effective litigants Glanvill and Allen sought to overwhelm their adversaries with several actions. The most significant legal weapon available to the conspirators was praemunire. How this idea occurred to them has been a long-standing subject of debate. Allen claimed that the idea had come to him as he was reading the statute. On the other hand evidence from a later deposition describes Coke's hand in the framing of the attack:

> he had directions from the Lord Coke to the Clerke of the Crowne to deliver him presidents and that the Lord Coke directed him to take that Course by Indictment and had tould him there were presidents in the Crowne office to warrant it and said that his Wife had byn with the Lord Coke and hee had perused one of the Indictments.[220]

Glanvill preferred his first bill for praemunire in Michaelmas term 1615.[221] The net of praemunire was cast widely against all attorneys, solicitors and counsellors who had helped impeach judgments of record. The first bill for praemunire aimed at Courtney and his lawyers. Already the conspirators discussed that a second bill would soon follow that 'ment to goe a strayne higher'. Glanvill later confessed to having framed a bill against Egerton, but hesitated to prefer it in order to proceed against lesser persons 'against whome they might have easier passage and so they might gayne a president to proceed against the Lord Chancellor'. Egerton himself in a letter to James I complained that he might be drawn into a praemunire prosecution.[222] Despite their initial hopes, a jury of Middlesex found *ignoramus* on the bill. Undaunted, the conspirators during the vacation approached members of the Privy Council and the servants of the king, attempting to enlist their support. They seem to have believed that the king and his servants might support their project in return for the financial rewards that would follow from the ruin of Egerton and his allies. During Hilary (1616) while Egerton was extremely ill, they preferred two bills for praemunire. A few days earlier John Croke JKB had suggested in a charge to the grand jury that they should indict 'any man, after a judgment given, had drawn the said judgment to a new examination in any

---

[219] *Ibid.,* f. 46r.
[220] *Ibid.,* f. 44r. On Coke's support of Glanvill, see also the deposition of John Cranfield, *ibid.,* f. 43r.
[221] *Ibid.,* f. 44r.   [222] *Ibid.,* f. 50r; IT Petyt MS 538/51, f. 40r.

other court'.[223] The first bill was similar to the bill against Courtney that had previously failed, while the second was against those who had counselled the plaintiffs in *Allen's Case* and officers of the Chancery itself.[224] This included Francis Moore SL who had served as counsel to Edwards' orphans *in forma pauperis*. The bill also embraced Sir John Tyndale, who had prepared the master's report in *Allen's Case*. At the assize Coke's involvement became more overt, though it was later relayed that 'the Lord Coke sayed secrettlie to the judges Wee must seeme to knowe nothing of this matter'.[225] Despite the efforts of Glanvill and Allen, the jury hesitated to return an indictment, explaining that, as the case was 'rare and leading', they should have more time to consider and consult with the king's learned counsel. Coke answered, revealing his partiality, 'the case was so cleere as they needed not once to goe from the barre'.[226] The jury was called to the Bar three times; during the second, Coke threatened to commit them if they would not indict. The jury returning to deliberate a third time. It was later alleged that Cotes, a servant of the court, slipped into their room and urged them to find for the bill and informed that they had nothing to fear, Egerton having died.[227] The ruse failed, because the jury returned, but this time firmly intending to find *ignoramus*.[228] Though both he and Dodderidge had earlier praised the jury as a 'verie sufficient and substantiall jurie', upon this return Coke began to heap scorn upon them declaring that they had been tampered with and that they were 'varlettes and knaves'. He then instructed Allen and Glanvill that they should attempt another indictment in the following term when 'hee would have a more sufficient jurie'.[229]

It was later on that same day that Coke made clear that the case was intended as a deterrent to other lawyers, saying

> openlie to the lawyers att the barre, Maisters looke to yt and take yt for a warninge that whosoever shall sett his hande to a bill into any Englishe court after a judgment att lawe wee will perclose him from the barre, for ever speaking more in this court. I give you a faire warning to preserve you from a greater mischiefe.

[223] Spedding (ed.), *Letters and Life*, vol. V, p. 251.
[224] BL Additional MS 11574, f. 51r; BL Additional MS 35957, f. 54v; Spedding (ed.), *Letters and Life*, vol. V, p. 251.
[225] Thorne, 'Praemunire and Sir Edward Coke', p. 239.
[226] *Ibid.*, p. 240.
[227] *Ibid.*, p. 241; later seen as a particularly egregious act.
[228] BL Additional MS 11574, f. 47r.
[229] Thorne, 'Praemunire and Sir Edward Coke', p. 241.

He then declared that 'Some must be made an example and on whome it lighteth it will fall heavy', and made the following warning:

> We must looke aboute, or the common lawe of England will be overthrowen. And sayed further that hee thought the judges should have little to doe at the assizes in their circuites by reason the light of the lawe was like to bee obscured. And therupon sithence this matter now mooved was after judgment, willed the partie to preferre an inditement of praemunire.[230]

Coke feared that litigants would eventually prefer the Chancery as the forum where judgments were final and incontestable.[231] The favouring of the Chancery raised concerns about the chancellor's absolute power and the possibility that it might one day devolve 'upon men of less judgment and integritie'.[232] The blame for this pattern of litigation fell not only on those who decided the rules in the Chancery, but the common lawyers themselves who pursued private legal victory at the public cost of eroding confidence in the common law.

Both Egerton and James I also explicitly identified the activities of lawyers and litigants as the source of the ongoing conflict between the jurisdictions. Egerton commented in *Grobham* v. *Stone* (1612) that 'he would [like to] know those lawyers that occupied their wits to jostle jurisdictions of courts together'.[233] In a speech in the Star Chamber in 1614 the chancellor blamed the problems in society partly on 'quarrelsome young lawyers'.[234] In the Star Chamber, in 1616, James I echoed the sentiment:

> He desyred that men[']s cases should be heard and judged with equitie, and he blamed the younge lawers, that did still sett on their clyents from court to court, from tryall to tryall and were not satisfied with decrees or trialls sayinge to their clyents, that their case was good ... It were better that some should suffer under the burden of an unequall sentence, then that ther should be noe end of controversies.[235]

---

[230] Huntington Library Ellesmere MS 5973, reprinted in Thorne, 'Praemunire and Sir Edward Coke', p. 242. Coke later admitted these words, but claimed that they were spoken in *Sir Anthony Mildmay's Case*, BL Stowe MS 402, f. 33r

[231] Though there were mechanisms of review, Coke considered the finality of decrees an issue with respect to both Chancery and Requests; *Orme* v. *Byrde* (1610), HLS MS 114, f. 24r and also BL Additional MS 25213, f. 266r; *Plowman* v. *Siternson* (1610), HLS MS 114, f. 11r; see also *Hetley* v. *Boyer* (1614), 2 Bulstrode 197, ER 1064.

[232] Chamberlain, *Letters*, vol. I, p. 604.

[233] *Cases Concerning Equity*, vol. II p. 397.

[234] Folger Shakespeare Library MS v. a. 133, f. 40r.

[235] Hutton, *Diary*, p. 12.

The competition between the courts was a struggle over contrasting views of reform. Coke desired certain process, finality of decisions and the pre-eminence of the common law as the king's law. Egerton aimed to see the Chancery as the forum where the king's justice-giving might reach its fullest expression. The intermeshing of the two courts brought these reform programmes into collision. Influenced by the context of reform, Egerton and other defenders of the Chancery believed that the common law was the cause of many problems that needed remedy in Chancery. Coke, on the other hand, claimed that the actions of common lawyers in Chancery and the use of the injunction after verdict introduced uncertainty into the law and eroded confidence in its adjudication. If parties should exhibit bills into Chancery after judgment, Coke claimed that 'either there should be no end of suits, or every Plaintiff would leave the Common law and begin in the Court of Equity, whither in the end he must be brought and that should tend to the utter subversion of the Common law'.[236] This subversion, as the next chapter will show, would ultimately undermine the king's duty to his subjects and his responsibility to preserve them and their property.

---

[236] 3 Co. *Inst.*, p. 123. Bacon imposed further rules to regulate injunctions, including those after verdict, in his orders of 1619; Sanders, *Orders of the High Court of Chancery*, pp. 112–14 (esp. nos. 32–4).

8

Delegation and moral kingship

'Such a judgment delights the honour of the king, whose person they represent as they sit in justice.'[1] So wrote the author of *Bracton*, the thirteenth-century treatise that appeared frequently in Coke's notes and the learned debate of his contemporaries.[2] The treatise was the source of the formulation of a powerful idea that spread across the pages of early Stuart treatises and informed parliamentary debates: the king ought to be under God and the law. Coke had used these words in response to James's anger in 1608 at the idea that the law defended the king.[3] To historians the citation of the passage has represented a sharpened belief in early Stuart politics that the law controlled royal power.[4] Those who advanced the common law, we are told, asserted that the law 'could not be abrogated by any claimant to sovereignty, whether king or Parliament'.[5] Coke, it is generally agreed, was fixated on protecting his beloved common law from royal meddling.[6] But *Bracton's* 'paradox' was ambivalent, like the text itself, which also declared that the king had no equal in the realm.[7] *Bracton* had declared that the king ought to be under the law, and the use of the subjunctive was an important qualification. Coke read the maxim subtly as part of a sophisticated conception of kingship and its relationship to the law. By probing this understanding it is possible to reconcile

---

[1] *Bracton*, vol. II, p. 307.
[2] Ian Williams has convincingly argued for *Bracton's* overlooked influence in the period; Williams, 'Bracton's authority', 50–64.
[3] *Prohibitions Del Roy*, 12 Co. *Rep*. 65, 77 ER 1343. The maxim appears at several points in Coke's notebooks; BL Harley MS 6687A, f. 64v; BL Harley MS 6687B, ff. 258v, 495r.
[4] Burgess, *Absolute Monarchy*, p. 212.
[5] Sommerville, *Royalists and Patriots*, p. 85.
[6] Burgess, *Absolute Monarchy*, pp. 173, 198, 204, 171n.31; Sommerville, *Royalists and Patriots*, pp. 81–104; R. A. MacKay, 'Coke – Parliamentary Sovereignty or the Supremacy of the Law?', *Michigan Law Review*, 22 (1924), 215–47; James Stoner Jr, *Common Law and Liberal Theory: Coke, Hobbes, and the Origins of American Constitutionalism* (Lawrence, KS, 1992), pp. 13–68.
[7] *Bracton*, vol. II, p. 33.

both Coke's elaborate claims for the common law and his commitment to the king's irresistible power. As Coke himself was to write, the king might be directed, but not corrected.

The path to unravelling Coke's reading of the paradox is through *Bracton's* notion of the delegation of power or its flow from the king downwards, so that it was the king himself whom the judges 'represent as they sit in justice'. Similarly Coke wrote that the 'the King is always present in Court in the judgment of law'.[8] The judges represented the king's duty to give law to his subjects, for which God had made the monarch his 'lieutenant on earth', and so Coke explained, 'the kingly head of this politic body is instituted and furnished with plenary and entire power ... to render justice and right to every part and member of this body'.[9] This idea of the distribution of power rested on delegation: God had delegated power to the king, who in turn assigned it to others in order to protect his people. This theory assumed that legal power did not inhere in the office of the delegate, but rather descended from the king, and indeed, the analogical relationship was taken to mean that the delegate might virtually represent the king. The system of delegation also implied how power should be used: for the preservation and security of the subject. This was the responsibility that came with delegation, a responsibility that coloured legitimate power with a moral hue. Law and its execution should conform to the law of reason and God. So it was said that one might be indicted if they claimed that the queen's law was not 'consonant or agreeable to the laws of God'.[10]

In those jurisdictional struggles with the High Commission and the Chancery, Coke and the other judges argued their pre-eminence on the grounds that the King's Bench represented the king more closely in his justice-giving capacity than any other ordinary court of law. The king was taken to be present in the King's Bench, because its proceedings were *coram rege* and it was traditionally identified as the court of the king. The judges guarded against the misuse of legal power not only to preserve the rights of the subject, but to protect the king from the corrupt or unlawful use of his delegation. As James I explained, he would account to God for his actions. Coke asserted the antiquity and rationality of the common

---

[8] *Prohibitions Del Roy*, 12 Co. *Rep.* 65, 77 ER 1343. The idea could also be used to argue that the king might judge in his own person, since the judges were merely 'delegates of the King'; *ibid.*, 1342.

[9] *Cawdrey's Case* (1591), 5 Co. *Rep.* 8b, 77 ER 10.

[10] *Lowe and Terry's Case* (1599), BL Additional MS 25203, f. 49r; *Address to the Serjeants*, Popham 44, 79 ER 1161; Callis, *Reading*, p. 7.

law in order quell uncertainty in the law and the misuse of legal resources. His jurisdictional warfare, for example, sought to prevent the judicial entrepreneurship that led to uncertainty (the Chancery) or usurpation (the High Commission). The law protected the king by preventing the usurpation or misuse of his legal authority.

Paul Halliday has recently described this tactic, 'prerogative capture'.[11] The judges insisted on the identification of the common law with the king's interest and indeed with the maintenance and enlargement of his authority. By claiming that they acted dutifully to protect royal power, Coke and the common law judges were able in good conscience to engage in activities that historians have subsequently considered oppositional. But Coke also thought of the prerogative in an enlarged sense, in a manner in which it could not be restrained. This conceptualization developed from his reading of *Bracton* and his interpretation of the roots and historical origin of kingly authority. Coke may well have been atypical in this sense – there were common lawyers such as Heneage Finch and James Whitelocke who thought of the prerogative in more limited terms.[12]

Coke had worked since his early career to protect and even amplify royal power and the prerogative. As a judge he sought to use the common law to continue his reformation of the misuse of the sovereign's power. Describing law and prerogative, Timothy Tourneur in his observations on Coke's fall acknowledged that the chief justice laboured 'to keep the balance of both even'. Tourneur elaborated on the real danger to the state that had disrupted the relationship between the common law and royal power: having convinced the king of his transcendent prerogative, the 'government in a little time will lie in the hands of a small number of favourites who will flatter the king to obtain their private ends, and notwithstanding the King shall be ever indigent'. Moreover, this misconduct was not simply a suppression or avoidance of law. Rather, the corruption that Coke apprehended and Tourneur observed was the control or misdirection of the law to the private ends of those favourites: 'and thus in a

---

[11] Halliday, *Habeas Corpus*, pp. 64–95. The judges might thus represent their actions as protecting the king's interest. For example, they argued that suits drawn from the common law to English bill courts removed fines that would otherwise go to the king; *Prohibitions* (1609), 13 Co. Rep. 32, 77 ER 1441; *Archbishop of York and Sedgwick's Case* (1612), Godbolt 201, 78 ER 122.

[12] Their more limited view of the prerogative was explicitly put forward in debates over impositions; see *PP 1610*, vol. I, pp. 109, 225–48, and Whitelocke's arguments are reprinted in *ST*, vol. II, col. 477.

short time they will enthral the common law'.[13] This sense of the vulnerability of the law to subversion was implicit throughout Coke's reforming
efforts, and it was the cause that ultimately undermined and then transformed his royalism.

Coke's understanding of the relationship between the common law
and the prince relied on a historical sociology drawn from his reading of
Fortescue, but mostly indebted to *Bracton*.[14] The relationship between subject and sovereign began primordially outside society in the law of nature,
'that which God at the time of creation … infused into [man's] heart, for
his preservation and direction'. This law encoded government, which was
necessary for 'preservation'. Coke relied on Aristotle for many of these
ideas: 'magistracy is of nature: for whatsoever is necessary for the preservation of the society of man is due by the law of nature'.[15] Human society
required government, a design prescribed by the law of nature. Yet society's form was dynamic, shifting and evolving. Coke followed Fortescue
by arguing that for the first two thousand years after the creation there
were no judicial or municipal laws: 'And certain it is, that before judicial
laws were made, Kings did decide causes according to natural equity, not
by any rule or formality of law, but did dare Jura.'[16]

The centrality of justice giving to kingship was archaic, and *Bracton*
had explained that, 'To this end is a king made and chosen, that he do
justice to all men that the Lord may dwell in him.' As Fleming CBEx
described in 1606, following *Bracton*: 'God had given to him power, the
act of government, and the power to govern.'[17] The duty imported a press-
ing responsibility, since the king sat in the place of God: 'he is the vicar
of God on earth, [he] must distinguish jus from injuria, equity from ini-
quity'. This responsibility implied an important consequence for the king
that was repeated throughout *Bracton*: 'He must surpass in power all

---

[13] Cited in Baker, 'The Common Lawyers and the Chancery', p. 222. Compare also the note
in the margin of the manuscript: 'this overthrew all at last and brought the whole nation
under a fewe into that slavery under which it now labours 1658'; BL Additional MS 35957,
f. 55v.

[14] There is no entry in his surviving notebooks specifically on Fortescue. However, Coke's
notes on his readings of *Bracton* span his notebooks. For example, the entry titled the
'king and his institution' is glossed almost entirely with passages from *Bracton*; BL Harley
MS 6687B, f. 260r. Pocock considers Fortescue's influence in *Ancient Constitution*, p. 33;
Burgess, *Politics of the Ancient Constitution*, pp. 77, 129 *et passim*. Coke's copy of *Bracton*,
with annotations, is Georgetown Law Library KD 600 B73.

[15] *Calvin's Case*, 7 Co. *Rep.* 13a, 77 ER 392.

[16] *Calvin's Case*, 7 Co. *Rep.* 13a, 77 ER 392, and 394, drawing from Fortescue, *De Laudibus*,
pp. 29–33.

[17] *Bate's Case* (1606), Lane 27, 145 ER 271.

those subjected to him, He ought to have no peer, much less a superior, especially in the doing of justice.'[18] Coke himself had made similar claims, described in Chapter 2, and in his notes observed that 'the king is the lieutenant of God' and cited Fortescue as his authority.[19] This supreme power enabled the king to protect and preserve his subjects by ensuring that no one could contest his justice. The claim remained authoritative, and so Fleming could cite Geoffrey le Scrope CJKB (who was citing *Bracton*) when he had declared that 'the king had no peer in his own land' and therefore could not be judged by parliament.[20]

Though kings preceded positive law, their justice-giving manifested as formal law as society progressed. Coke recorded how government developed 'from family to regal from regal to absolute from absolute to regal tempered with laws'.[21] The tempering of the regal state with laws was as much the work of kings themselves as parliaments or customs. The law was the means by which the king fulfilled his duty to provide justice to his subjects, to preserve and protect them. In a conquered kingdom, the king 'is able to constitute and appoint any such law for the good government of that place'.[22] The certainty of this protection ultimately bound his people to him. Coke was clear in *Calvin's Case* (1608) that loyalty to the king was a personal matter and not a consequence of his observance of the common law or the result of a subject's duty to an abstract 'Crown' or state: 'Now it appeareth by demonstrative reason faith, and obedience of the subject to the Sovereign, was before judicial laws.'[23] Allegiance, 'the mutual bond and obligation between the King and his subjects', was based on the law of nature and helped to preserve human society.[24] The subject gave the king obedience in return for protection.[25] Those aliens who entered England, by virtue of this protection, owed him 'a local obedience or ligeance, for that the one [protection] … draweth the other'.[26] In the *Case of Monopolies* Coke declared that

---

[18] *Bracton*, vol. II, pp. 305, 166, 33.
[19] BL Harley MS 6687B, f. 257v, citing Fortescue, *De Laudibus*, pp. 23–4. Coke also refers to the king as the lieutenant of God in the *Case of Magdalen College* (1615), 11 Co. *Rep.* 72a, 77 ER 1243.
[20] Trans. David Seipp, YB Pasch. 3 Edward III, pl. 32, ff. 18b–19a; *Watt* v. *Braynes* (1601), BL Additional MS 25203, f. 258r.
[21] BL Harley MS 6687B, f. 258v.
[22] *Nota* (1598), BL Harley MS 6686A, f. 274r; *Calvin's Case*, 7 Co. *Rep.* 18a, 77 ER 398.
[23] *Calvin's Case*, 7 Co. *Rep.* 13a, 77 ER 392, 388.
[24] *Ibid.*, 382, 392–3; Sommerville, *Royalists and Patriots*, p. 102.
[25] *Calvin's Case*, 388, 382.   [26] *Ibid.*, 383.

the duty of the queen towards the subject consists in protection ... the duty of the subject to the sovereign is loyalty and obedience. The protection of the queen of her subjects is to guard them in peace and plenty. The first is to be performed by the execution of justice which is the principal means to preserve the peace.[27]

The emphasis on protection and preservation explained the purpose of God's abundant delegation of power to the queen and was the kernel of the bond between her and her subjects.

Coke followed *Bracton*'s principle that the monarch was logically irresistible: that in order to preserve and protect his subjects it followed that the king could have no equal or superior. The only redress the subject had against the king was by petition.[28] Coke referred to the depositions of Edward II and Richard II as 'renunciation[s]', and declared that the 'renunciation' of Henry III was invalid because it was not before a parliament. Coke likened the Crown to an 'estate' of the king, drawing on the idea that the king could not be deposed by an inferior power and by definition a subject could not have greater power than their king:

> Note: the king has an absolute estate in the crown insomuch as the head is not able to be deposed by an inferior power, but it is able itself to demise the rulership of the kingdom ... and on account of this when Edward 2 and Richard 2, who were rightful and absolute kings, they were not deposed but the entry in the judicial records was ... dimisit.[29]

Coke later defined *dimittere* to mean 'a leaving of or cessation from government'. Kings might choose to abdicate their Crowns, but they could not be deposed. This opened the problem of the over-mighty vassal who defeated the king in the field. That the king might not be able to preserve his subjects or that the king might not be in command of their kingdom could lead to a distinction between de jure and de facto authority, a distinction that ultimately affected the bond of allegiance. In his discussion of Henry III, Coke described how the king, facing Simon de Montfort, 'would not release his subjects of the allegiance, and therefore he showed himself as absolute king and sometyme as fellow governor but there could not be 2 kings at one time so as de jure Henry the father continued king'.[30] The messy example of civil war yielded these tensions in Coke's thought: how could a hapless king be able to defend his subjects and to fulfil his side of the compact of allegiance? In his later discussion of the statute of

---

[27] *Darcy* v. *Allen* (1602), BL Additional MS 25203, f. 546v.
[28] BL Harley MS 6686B, ff. 634v–635r.
[29] BL Harley MS 6687B, f. 499v.   [30] BL Harley MS 6687A, f. 3v.

11 Henry VII, c. 1 (1495), Coke explained that obedience was owed to the de facto king and that 'if treason be committed against a king *de facto* and *non de jure*, and after the king *de jure* cometh to the crowne, he shall punish the treason done to the king *de facto*'.[31] This argument was fertile ground for later 'defactoist' claims, while also suggesting the priority that Coke placed on the king's duty to protect and the subject's consequent obligation to obey.[32]

Some of Coke's statements suggested that the common law bound the prerogative broadly, as when he wrote, 'the king hath no prerogative, but that which the law of the land allows him'.[33] While prerogative has been used as a byword for the royal power, the term was understood to have both an ordinary and an absolute form.[34] This distinction or 'double prerogative' has been discussed extensively in the historiography, with various theories as to its origin and significance for absolutism in England.[35] Popham CJKB explained that the king's absolute prerogatives, 'they are not examinable or determinable by any course of justice and only by the king'.[36] The law was taken to control the ordinary prerogative by its very definition, since no such prerogative could exist without the common law. The ordinary prerogative represented those special rights and privileges that the king held at common law as a consequence of his extraordinary position.[37] Prerogative was thus both included within and above the law – it was an exception to the ordinary course of the common law, which was allowed and accepted by that law. The ordinary prerogative was the king's participation at the law. The remainder of the royal power lay mostly in abeyance in a society that had advanced to 'regal tempered with laws'. This absolute prerogative made its appearance in the declaration of war or the minting of coins – these represented the vestigial powers of the

---

[31] 3 Co. *Inst.*, p. 6.   [32] Jones, 'Lawful Allegiance', 331.

[33] *Proclamations*, 12 Co. *Rep.* 76, 77 ER 1354; cf. Cope, 'Sir Edward Coke and Proclamations', 215–21.

[34] The idea of the double prerogative was a commonplace in the period; Holdsworth, 'The Prerogative in the Sixteenth Century', 561–3.

[35] Francis Oakley, 'Jacobean Political Theology: The Absolute and Ordinary Powers of the King', *Journal of the History of Ideas*, 29 (1968), 323–46; Burgess, *Politics of the Ancient Constitution*, pp. 139–62; Sommerville, *Royalists and Patriots*, pp. 96–8; J. D. Wormuth, *The Royal Prerogative, 1603-1649. A Study in English Political and Constitutional Ideas* (Ithaca, NY, 1939), pp. 54ff.

[36] *The Case of Swans* (1592), BL Harley MS 6686B, f. 592r, printed as 7 Co. *Rep.* 15b, 77 ER 435.

[37] William Staunford defines the prerogative as a 'privilege or pre-eminences'; *An Exposicion of the Kinges Prerogative* (London, 1567), STC 23213, f. 5r; Cowell, *The Interpreter*, ff. DDD3r–v.

primordial, pre-law king for the 'general benefit of the people'.[38] The logic of Coke's system of monarchy necessitated such a residual power, since in order to preserve his people the king might be required to take exception to the laws in emergency. These exceptions were not, as we shall see, merely a theoretical possibility.

Glenn Burgess's assessment of Coke's ideas on the prerogative has admitted that he may have held such an enlarged view of the prerogative. Burgess identified three slightly different positions on the prerogative in the *Institutes*, which he worked to reconcile.[39] He concluded that Coke believed that the prerogative was 'part of the law, and its scope bounded by law, but nor had he abandoned the view that this still left the king with certain "absolute" powers beyond legal control'.[40] The discretion inherent in these absolute powers, however, 'could be shaped and policed by the law and the courts'.[41] This approach, Burgess argued, allowed the common law to limit the misuse of the prerogative, while also avoiding 'the risk that it might be concluded that in consequence anything the king did was done per *legem terrae*'.[42]

In his manuscript notes, Coke gives a much fuller explanation of his understanding of the prerogative and by doing so offers an insight into his perception of the political order as a whole. In the manuscript version of *Darcy v. Allen* (1602) Coke discussed the prerogative extensively, recording that the court had stated that the king should summon the judges, not parliament, as arbiters of his prerogative.[43] Coke added, 'the king has 2 manners of prerogatives, the one absolute and the other ordinary; absolute it is thus called because it is not examinable or determinable by any course of justice but only by the king himself, as proclaiming war or making truces'. Coke's definition of the absolute prerogative was longstanding. In 1594 Coke wrote a long entry into his notebooks under the rubric 'Prerogative [of] the king' where he defined the prerogative:

---

[38] *An Information Against Bates* (1606), Lane 27, 145 ER 271.

[39] Co. *Litt.*, f. 344a; 2 Co. *Inst.*, pp. 36, 496; 3 Co. *Inst.*, p. 84.

[40] Burgess, *Absolute Monarchy*, p. 204.

[41] *Ibid.*, p. 198.   [42] *Ibid.*, p. 195.

[43] BL Harley MS 6686B, f. 592r. The 'constitutional' parts of the case were not printed by Coke, but must be sought in the manuscripts. The case is reported as *Case of Monopolies*, 11 Co. *Rep.* 84b, 77 ER 1260. Other reports are: *Darcy v. Allen*, Moore 671, 72 ER 830; *Darcy v. Allen*, Noy 173, 74 ER 1131; BL Additional MS 25203, f. 678v. The report in Coke's notebooks has been reproduced in Corré, '*Darcy v. Allen*', p. 1,270. Fleming's speech exists in SP 12/286, ff. 111–23. In a charge to Lincoln Assizes (not dated) Coke reiterated that the judges, and not parliament, should be the arbiters of the prerogative; Society of Antiquaries MS 291, f. 12v.

> Note that the king has 2 manners of prerogatives, one absolute and no one ought concerning this to argue or dispute, such as declaring war ... the other manner of prerogative is ordinary and this ought to be determined by the law and by the judges, and of this ... arguments are made in the courts of the king, as if the queen by her prerogative is able to give such privileges or liberties etc and of this prerogative Bracton says [in] book 1, chapter 7: Rex debet esse sub deo et lege[44] ... and note [that] truly it is said that Rex est solutus legibus quoad correctionem[45] for as Bracton said par in parem non habeat imperium multo minus superiorem[46] thus it is said in 22 Edward 3, 3,[47] the king does not have a peer in his realm ... and he ought not to be adjudged, but quoad directionem,[48] the king as Bracton said is sub lege.[49]

The passage acknowledged the two prerogatives and recognized that law might direct only the ordinary prerogative. Coke noted, in particular, that *Bracton's* paradox applied only to the ordinary prerogative and that 'as far as direction' the king would be under the law. This reference to Ulpian's civil law maxim indicated that the law might 'determine' or direct the king, but that he was not 'bound by the law as far as correction'. The king might be directed, but he could not be corrected – elsewhere Coke repeated this well-worn formula.[50] This was a logical consequence of the assumption that the king could have no equal in the realm, a point supported by *Bracton*.

Coke further defined the absolute prerogative with a citation to Sir Thomas Smith: 'In war time, and in the field the Prince has also absolute power, so that his word is a law, he may put to death, or to other bodily punishment, whom he shall think so to deserve.'[51] This opened the possibility that there were moments in the life of a society when the absolute prerogative of the king broke through. This prerogative was the remnant

---

[44] 'The king ought to be under God and law.'

[45] 'The king is not bound by law as far as correction.' This paraphrases the statement in *Digest* 1.1.31, 'Ulpian: Princeps legibus solutus est ...'; Fritz Schulz, 'Bracton on Kingship', *The English Historical Review*, 60: 237 (1945), 136–76, at 158.

[46] 'An equal cannot have command over an equal.' Cf. *Bracton*, vol. II, p. 33, c. 'Rex non habet parem'.

[47] YB Hil. 22 Edward 3, pl. 25, ff. 3a–b.

[48] 'As far as direction'.   [49] BL Harley MS 6686A, f. 95r.

[50] 'The law hath 2 powers coactive that concerne the subject only and direct[ive] and that concerne the king also'; Yale University Law School MS G R 24, f. 158r; perhaps echoed by Fleming, *An Information Against Bates*, Lane 27, 145 ER 271. For other references in the period, see Daly, 'Cosmic Harmony', 26.

[51] Thomas Smith, *The Commonwealth of England*, p. 56. Coke cites 'vide Sir Thomas Smith, lib 2, c. 3 et 4' as well as the *Register*, f. 191.

of the primitive origins of kingship: the absolute power of an individual who defended his people and gave them justice.

The exercise of this absolute prerogative – when the word of the prince was law – is found in Coke's report of the *Case of the Earl of Essex* (1601). The report from his notebook was never printed, and it revealed this exercise of the absolute prerogative and added further comments on its unlimited extent.[52] The example of the Earl of Essex also revealed the hazards and problems associated with the delegation of royal authority. In his report, Coke described how the 'archtraitor' Tyrone had rebelled in Ireland and in response the queen had dispatched Essex with a large army.[53] Coke, then attorney-general, construed the purpose of this expedition in keeping with the prince's role of protector: 'for the safeguarding of her subjects which the wars there had greatly diminished'. The queen had granted to the earl a commission under the great seal to suppress the rebellion giving him absolute power in the campaign. Elsewhere Coke had warned that 'absolute power ought not to be granted' and then continued: 'if it should be granted, it ought to be repealed at pleasure'.[54] This absolute power 'consisted in commanding or prohibiting', with no limits identified. In the case of Essex while the patent and letter included some instructions, the queen also verbally directed him not to give the Earl of Southampton command of the cavalry. While conducting the campaign in Ireland, Essex disregarded several of these instructions, including promoting the Earl of Southampton as general of the horse.[55] His disobedience and his return to England without leave were 'heynous and exorbitant tending to the hazard and danger of the kingdom'. Coke noted the extent of the earl's powers, while observing that the conditions of delegation were their only limit:

> [Essex] had the commission by letters patent under the great seal by force of which … he had absolute power without any restraint within them to limit him to any manner of proceeding just as he pleased[,] nevertheless it was a great misprision and contempt to disobey any command of the queen either by her mouth, letter, or instruction of any thing touching her martial authority.[56]

The queen could, and did, revoke this delegation of her absolute power at any time. As to her instructions, in matters of the absolute prerogative

---

[52] The report is found in BL Harley MS 6686B, ff. 408v–410r.
[53] Coke at one point claimed that the King's Bench might control common law proceedings in Ireland; *Vaudry* v. *Pannel* (1615), 3 Bulstrode 117, 81 ER 100.
[54] Holkham MS 732a [n.f.].   [55] BL Harley MS 6686B, f. 409r.
[56] *Ibid.*, f. 409v.

the very word of the prince had the force of law, and Coke here cited the maxim from the *Digest*:

> because the queen had 2 manners of prerogative, the one absolute and the other ordinary. In the first the commandment of the king is to be obeyed without disputation principis placitum legis vigorem[57] and epistola Regis vim habet legis[58], the other is ordinary and that is able to be disputed because it is to be decided by the laws of the realm.[59]

Coke exempted the absolute prerogative from control by the laws, as he clarified when he continued: 'no subject ought to dispute and these high matters of estate are not to be directed by the ordinary rule of the common law, but in these the commandment of the queen ought to be obeyed'.[60] But the citation by Coke of that absolutist maxim – 'what pleases the prince has the force of law' – most starkly revealed his understanding of the absolute prerogative. He was again to paraphrase the maxim in a case in the Star Chamber in 1606 against Lords Stourton and Mordaunt, suspected of involvement in the Gunpowder Plot, for failing to obey their summons to the opening of parliament: 'Causa legationis, epistolae regis habent vim legis.'[61]

Yet duty conditioned the exercise of this irresistible power. The queen participated at the law in her ordinary prerogative, and Coke understood how the law limited the queen by again interpreting *Bracton*.[62] In his preface to the *Fourth Reports*, Coke recorded how the king, 'whose commandement being to me Suprema Lex', had ordered him to record the judgments of the court, which were the 'sweet and fruitful flowers of his Crown', and then cited *Bracton*: 'therefore let the king attribute that to the law, which from the law he hath received, to wit, power and dominion: for where will, and not law doth sway, there is no King'.[63] *Bracton*'s dictum here captured the circular logic of a theory of kingship that both necessitated an absolute power in the king while explaining that power as a consequence of duty and moral responsibility. Law was a means for the king to delegate and distribute his justice-giving authority. The law also provided the mechanisms to protect the king from the consequences of that delegation. The dangers of those consequences can be seen most

---

[57] *Digest* 1.4.1 and *Institutes* 1.2.6.
[58] 'The letters of the prince have the force of law.'
[59] BL Harley MS 6686B, f. 409v.   [60] *Ibid.*, f. 410r.
[61] Hawarde, *Les Reportes*, p. 288. Cf. Burgess, *Absolute Monarchy*, p. 200.
[62] For discussion of the paradox, see Charles McIlwain, *Constitutionalism: Ancient and Modern* (Ithaca, NY, 1958), pp. 67–74.
[63] 4 Co. *Rep.*, p. xix.

spectacularly in the delegation to the Earl of Essex and also in the lesser abuses and corruptions of legal power that have been detailed throughout this book.

The law did not control the king, but as the king chose to participate in the law, it directed his power towards his responsibilities. Coke explained that 'the common law admeasures the prerogative of the king', and this bounding by the common law was necessary to the king's justice-giving.[64] When making this claim Coke drew from a number of authorities, including a Year Book case from 1461 on whether the king might grant a protection for one 'on the high seas' for an indeterminate period.[65] Walter Moyle JCP warned that the king should grant a protection for no longer than one year, since 'the king is held (as a matter) of right to administer law to each of his subjects'.[66] Coke commented: 'note in what way the law admeasures the prerogative [of] the king [which] should not [give] prejudice to the subject'.[67] Finally he glossed another Year Book case from Henry IV and recorded that 'the ancient sovereignty of the king is bounded within what is permissible by the common laws of the realm'.[68] Coke cited a passage from *Bracton* as an authority. This passage explained that the prince should be just, for the 'government of the wise man is stable … but if he lacks wisdom he will destroy them'. The goals of preservation and justice controlled the admeasuring of the ordinary prerogative even as they might permit the intrusion of the absolute prerogative.

The hard case for such an analysis is the seventeenth-century insistence on an absolute security of property, described with such eloquence by Whitelocke who claimed that property rights were 'a question of our very essence … whether we shall have any thing or nothing. If the king's claims are true, we are but tenants at his will of that which we have'.[69] This insistence on these rights may well have been tied up with the erosions of property rights found in the misuse of authority or uncertain law. The most significant obstacle to security of property, however, was not so much the ambitions of Stuart monarchs, but the problem that the common law often favoured the prince's authority over his subject's

---

[64] BL Harley MS 6887A, f. 101v.
[65] Coke also cited other cases, including YB Hil. 34 Henry VI, pl. 1, f. 25a, and YB Mich. 21 Edward IV, pl. 6, f. 47b.
[66] YB Hil. 39 Henry VI, pl. 3, ff. 38b–40b.
[67] BL Harley MS 6687A, f. 101v.
[68] BL Harley MS 6687A, f. 101v; YB Mich. 2 Henry IV, pl. 45, ff. 9b–10b. Coke cited as further authorities *Willion* v. *Barkley* (1562), 1 Plowden 223, 75 ER 339, and *Bracton*, vol. II, p. 306.
[69] *ST*, vol. II, p. 479.

property, a point illustrated in *Bates's Case* (1606).[70] Coke and other common lawyers conceived of the king as the protector of property, and property was related to his duty to preserve his subjects. While the law of each individual nation defined the exact form of its tenurial system, God's granting of the fruits of the earth to Adam was often taken as a type of property grant: 'that greate charter of the whole earth to men bestowed on Adam and confirmed to Noah'.[71] Property was an 'instinct', as an anonymous writer commented in 1601: 'the lawe of propertie [was] in parte ingrafted by naturall instincte, and fullye established by the tables of Gods Comandements'.[72] Similarly although Coke does not elaborate on a theory of property, he acknowledged that it was given by God so that humans might preserve themselves and prosper.[73] Property and the contention it created were attached to the origins of kingship, as Davies declared: 'the first and principal cause of making Kings, was to maintain property and Contracts, and Traffique, and Commerce amongst men'.[74] In a sense property created kings and their duty to protect and preserve: they defended against its unlawful seizure and adjudicated disputes that arose from property. When the common lawyer and parliamentarian Sir Thomas Hedley insisted that security of property affected personal liberty he added that without property the subject would wither and 'grow both poor and base-minded'.[75]

Security of property produced one form of society, while insecurity and servility produced France, a nation of slaves.[76] Coke used the commonplace of France as a seigniorial despotism when he declared, 'an idle justice is like to the king of France'.[77] Thus as *Bracton* had stated, the king was the preserver of his people and their property, 'by a just award each be restored to that which is his own'.[78] The sentiment was widespread: Fitzherbert wrote in his *Natura Brevium* that 'the king is held of right by the laws to defend his subjects and their goods and chattels, lands, and tenements, and thereby each loyal subject by the law is held to be within

---

[70] A survey of early Stuart attitudes towards property can be found in Sommerville, *Royalists and Patriots*, pp. 134–53.

[71] BL Harley MS 4708, f. 194r; Genesis 1:28–30.

[72] 'Concerning Entayles and Perpetuities' (1602), BL Additional MS 25206, f. 115v.

[73] Co. *Litt.*, f. 4a; cf. St German, *Doctor and Student*, p. 57.

[74] John Davies, *The Question Concerning Impositions* (London, 1656), Wing D407A, p. 29; *Le Case de Mixt Moneys* (1604), Davies 18, 80 ER 507; Davies, *Le Primer Report*, f. *6r.

[75] *PP 1610*, vol. II, p. 194, repeated on p. 196; Davies, *Le Primer Report*, f. *6r.

[76] Fortescue, *De Laudibus*, pp. 25–7, 49–54, and especially pp. 81–7 on governance in France.

[77] Society of Antiquaries MS 291, f. 10v. [78] *Bracton*, vol. II, p. 305.

the protection of the king'.[79] The king's protection of his subjects' property distinguished him from the tyrant, and it is well known that Englishmen of the period lauded their commonwealth as a 'monarchy royal' whose subjects were free 'and have property in their things'.[80]

If the king protected property as a consequence of his responsibility rather than in response to an abstract right, this complicated the common law understanding of property. Coke often spoke of an individual's 'absolute property' in land, but various exigencies gave the king even an ordinary power to quash these rights.[81] Real property was conceived as a right to hold land that was held mediately or immediately from the Crown, an assumption that was taken as a 'ground or Maxime in our lawes'.[82] As a consequence the king was ultimately the guarantor or technically the warrantor of that right 'for the conservation of the people of this realm in unity and peace, without rapine or spoil'.[83] The king's duty to preserve his people through justice-giving or war, however, produced the most important limitation on property rights, since the king had rights in the property of his subjects by his ordinary prerogative. These rights would inhere even where a subject conquered a foreign land, because the subject was merely 'the means of the conquest', and the land would belong entirely to the king.[84] The king's prerogative allowed him to mine for gold and silver even in the lands of his subjects.[85] Since saltpetre had only recently been discovered for use in gunpowder, its supply could not be an 'ancient prerogative'. Coke thereby admitted that the king's prerogative could enlarge as it suited the king's need to defend the realm.[86] The argument from preservation was used again when Coke explained that the king's right to

---

[79] Fitzherbert, *La Novel Natura Brevium*, f. 232v.

[80] Staunford, *An Exposicion of the Kinges Prerogative*, ff. 36v–37v; *Le Case de Tanistry* (1608), Davis 41, 80 ER 528.

[81] Co. *Litt.*, f. 145b. Coke refers to 'absolute property' in *Packman's Case, Manning's Case, City of London Case, Hensloe's Case, Lady Billingsly* v. *Hersey* and *Waller* v. *Hanger*. Examples where a 'man maye loose his propertie and right in land' are described in 'Arguments Against the Queenes Majesties Prerogative and Interest in Lands ... with Answer', BL Additional MS 25206, ff. 14r–20v, at f. 17v. These takings might also be explained as a consequence of an 'implied consent' on the part of the subject, as in the arguments following *Bates's Case*, BL Stowe MS 497, f. 49v.

[82] BL Additional MS 25206, f. 14r; *Case of Stannaries* (1606), 12 Co. *Rep.* 10, 77 ER 1293.

[83] *Cawdrey's Case*, 5 Co. *Rep.* 30a, 77 ER 34.

[84] *The Case of the Isle of Man* (1598), BL Harley MS 6686A, ff. 279r–283v; possibly referred to in *Bret* v. *Johnson* (1605), Lane 9, 145 ER 256, and HLS MS 118(a), f. 6v.

[85] *The Case of Mines* (1568), 1 Plowden 314, 75 ER 477.

[86] *The Case of the King's Prerogative in Saltpetre*, 12 Co. *Rep.* 13, 77 ER 1295; BL Harley MS 4817, f. 213v; see also BL Harley MS 6687B, f. 102v; BL Harley MS 6686B, f. 391v.

butlerage was given to him by the common law 'for his prerogative that he was able to take the goods of any man for the necessary provision of his household'. The reason was that the king 'preserves his subjects in peace and safety', and being busied with the affairs of government the law 'gave power to him for taking of the goods of his subjects'.[87]

Coke's theory both naturalized property while conceptualizing it through its relationship to the king and allegiance. The king had distributed and given a warranty for the subjects' property for his preservation and he might take it back for the same reason – even by process of the common law. But he should not go against his warranty and disseize his subjects without cause. Finch, for example, commented in this vein that: 'the power of God is alwais joined with Justice and truth: for to doe wrong, to deale untruly, is not omnipotencie, but a thing of weaknesse and impotencie. So it is with the King, he cannot be a disseisor, he can be no wrongdoer: for he is all Justice'.[88] Coke reported that it was a 'rule' that the king by his grant 'cannot make a discontinuance or wrong'.[89]

This maxim that 'the king by his power or prerogative ought not to make a wrong or an injury to any' gained prominence in the sixteenth and seventeenth centuries. Clayton Roberts has connected its importance with the emergence of ministerial responsibility.[90] Similarly Janelle Greenberg has observed that before Charles I the maxim reflected the king's immunity from legal process and the liability of his agents.[91] But the maxim also served a logical function within a system of delegation that depended on the moral character of royal power. It was a commonplace that the 'prince is tyed by oath aswell to abolish corrupt and unlawfull customes, as to maintayne good, and lawfull'.[92] Coke wrote that the king could do no wrong because 'the king derives his royal power from God'.[93] Coke cited this interpretation in his notebook as a reading from *Bracton*, where it was written that the king's power was

---

[87] R. v. *Vavisor and Haughton* (1598), BL Additional MS 25203, f. 22v; the same rationale was given for purveyance; BL Harley MS 6686B ff. 684r, 651v.

[88] Finch, *Law*, p. 83; cf. p. 85.

[89] *The Case of Alton Woods* (1595), 1 Co. *Rep.* 52b, 76 ER 119; *Attorney-General* v. *Bushopp* (1600), 1 Co. *Rep.* 45a, 76 ER 103. The *Case of Alton Woods* is reported in Coke's notebooks at BL Harley MS 6686B, f. 384r ff.

[90] Clayton Roberts, *The Growth of Responsible Government in Stuart England* (Cambridge, 1966), pp. 4–10, 115.

[91] Greenberg, 'Our Grand Maxim of State, "The King Can Do No Wrong"', 216.

[92] BL Additional MS 25206, f. 14v.

[93] Coke also wrote that 'the king by his prerogative is not able to do wrong ... rex superiorem non habet nisi deus'; BL Harley MS 6687A, f. 102r.

that of *jus*, not *injuria* and since it is he from whom *jus* proceeds, from the source whence *jus* takes its origin no instance of *injuria* ought to arise ... for that power only is from God, the power of *injuria* however, is from the devil ... Let him, therefore, temper his power by law, which is the bridle of power.[94]

In reading *Bracton*, Coke had derived a theory of moral kingship: the king's politic capacity had a body that was 'royal power' and a soul that was justice.[95] Law harmonized the two, 'because power is to do justice', and so 'by laws are kings, without law tyrants'.[96] It was the design of the common law to prevent the possibility of the misuse of royal power: 'And although, by the common law the King has many prerogatives touching his person, his goods, his debts and duties, and other personal things, yet the common law has so admeasured his prerogatives that they shall not take away nor prejudice the inheritance of any.'[97]

Historians have acknowledged that it was widely understood in the period that the king was bound by a moral sanction aimed at limiting his power.[98] W. H. Greenleaf has analyzed the idea of 'moral kingship' or what James Daly termed 'harmonist' political thinking.[99] At its core, Greenleaf believed, it was a medieval mode of analyzing the relations between king, law and subject.[100] It promoted the authority of the king, the 'final source of positive law' by connecting the source of that authority with divine power. Yet 'harmonism' also limited the actions of the king by implying that they required moral sanction. The problem then arose, by whom and how should the king be judged? According to Greenleaf, Coke's answer, as an 'opponent of royalism' was the ancient constitution.[101]

But Coke conceived of this moral restriction in a more nuanced form. He believed that the primary threat to the integrity of royal authority was not the misuse of the law by the king, but rather by those to whom he delegated his power. The danger was the subversion of the law either

---

[94]   *Bracton*, vol. II, p. 305.
[95]   BL Harley MS 6686B, f. 592v; Schulz, 'Bracton on Kingship', 136–76.
[96]   BL Harley MS 6686B, f. 591v; Yale University Law School G R 24, f. 158r.
[97]   *Willion* v. *Berkley* (1562), 1 Plowden 236, 75 ER 359.
[98]   Sommerville, *Royalists and Patriots*, pp. 43–6; Greenberg, 'Our Grand Maxim', 215.
[99]   Greenleaf, *Order, Empiricism and Politics*, pp. 44–57; Daly, 'Cosmic Harmony', 10–30; Franklin le van Baumer, *The Early Tudor Theory of Kingship* (New York, 1966), pp. 11, 195–210; most recently discussed in the context of absolutist theory by Sommerville, *Royalists and Patriots*, p. 45.
[100]   Greenleaf, *Order, Empiricism and Politics*, p. 33.
[101]   *Ibid.*, pp. 184, 187.

through error or for private purposes. The misuse of the law both compromised the moral obligations inherent in delegation and eroded confidence in the law. The common law operated to protect the king from this danger. In *Darcy* v. *Allen* (1602) Coke recorded that, 'the law is the most high inheritance that the king has, because by the law he and all his subjects are ruled and if there is no law then there is no king nor no [*sic*] inheritance'.[102] When Coke described the law as the king's 'inheritance' or his 'estate' in the Crown he was referring to the idea that the prince's title was analogous to 'an estate in the Crown' protected by the common law. The issue was more than academic. In a challenge to the title to the throne in favour of Mary Queen of Scots, the Bishop of Ross had suggested that the common law could not buttress Elizabeth's claim.[103] His work sparked a response from Robert Glover, Somerset Herald, who alleged that Ross's claim was an attempt to undermine the law of the realm and dissolve it into confusion. The common law, Glover claimed, guided the title to the realm.[104] Similarly Coke noted that the title to the Crown was by descent and not by any ceremony or act.[105] However, it was the common law that defended that right of descent, and Coke advised that kings by succession ought not to change the laws on account of his reliance on them to protect their own titles.[106]

The law also protected the king from judging in his own person and possibly erring. Repeatedly throughout his career Coke urged the maxim that 'no man is wiser than the law', and warned that untrained individuals might tend away from the 'stiff cord' of the law towards discretion and then affection in their judicial decision-making.[107] The king's removal from the sole administration of justice was a means to immunize him morally from doing wrong. The system of judicial delegation was sketched out by Coke:

> the King himself is *de jure* to deliver justice to all his subjects; and for this, that he himself cannot do it to all persons, he delegates his power to his Judges, who have the custody and guard of the King's oath. And forasmuch as this concerns the honour and conscience of the King, there

---

[102] BL Harley MS 6686B, f. 592v, quoting John Fray CBEx in YB 19 Hen. VI, pl. 1, f. 63a.

[103] John Leslie, Bishop of Ross, *A Defense of the Honour of the Right Highe, Mightye and Noble Princesse Marie Quene of Scotlande and Dowager of France* (London, 1569), ff. 50v–119r.

[104] Bodl. Carte MS 105, f. 26r. Another copy of Glover's treatise can be found in Bodl. History MS C 272.

[105] *Calvin's Case*, 7 Co. *Rep.* 18a, 77 ER 398.

[106] *Ibid.*, citing inheritance in *Bracton*, vol. II, p. 184.

[107] Folger Shakespeare Library MS v.b.303, 'The Somme of My Lorde Cookes Charge', p. 2.

is great reason that the King himself shall take account of it, and no other.[108]

Coke and other common lawyers explained that this structure of delegation emerged when the king had been overcome with suitors at a pre-historical point.[109] The biblical model was Jethro's advice to Moses to appoint others as judges, and so the 'king being unable to determine all matters appointed others to minister justice as sheriffs etc'.[110] To conceptualize the process of delegation the common lawyers called upon the image of the fountain. Royal power was theorized to flow downwards like a stream from a fountain that was the king.[111] Robert Snagg observed that 'As all justice floweth from the King or Queen, as from the Fountain, and no authority or jurisdiction in England is lawfull that is not drawn from thence.'[112] Bacon in his address at the sessions of the Court of the Verge asserted that the justices were nearer to the king in their duties, 'who is the fountaine of justice and governmente'.[113] The metaphor was more than conceptual, it had practical effect. In *The Case of Praemunire* (1607) Davies asserted that all jurisdiction being derived from the king 'it remaineth in him as in the fountain' and he could therefore punish or correct the ecclesiastical judge.[114] Coke in his charge to the Bury Assizes in 1609 praised James I, declaring to those present to 'observe your authoritye deryved and extended from the great kyng of England'.[115] The king was 'the fountain of all dignity'[116] and elsewhere Coke described him as 'the head of the commonwealth ... the fountain of justice and mercy'.[117] The metaphor

---

[108] *Floyd and Barker's Case* (1607), 12 Co. *Rep.* 25, 77 ER 1307; BL Stowe 423, f. 140v; Baker, *OHLE*, vol. VI, p. 119.

[109] *Calvin's Case*, 7 Co. *Rep.* 14b, 77 ER 394; BL Additional MS 11405, f. 5r; Bodl. Barlow MS 9, f. 34v; BL Cotton MS Vespasian C VIX, vol. II, f. 52r; *PP 1610*, vol. II, p. 152.

[110] Exodus 18:13–26; *Bullen* v. *Godfrey* (1607), BL Additional MS 25209, f. 103r.

[111] This metaphor was a commonplace: see, BL Stowe MS 297, f. 38v; BL Additional MS 48986, f. 126r; BL Additional MS 58218, f. 22r; BL Additional MS 48053, ff. 224r–v; and it appears in other petitions; CUL MS Dd.3.64, no. 21. It could also be used by the government; BL Lansdowne MS 174, f. 219v; Ellesmere, 'Observacions Upon Cookes Reportes', in Knafla, *Law and Politics*, p. 305.

[112] Reprinted from the manuscript account of a reading in 1581 as Snagg, *Antiquity & Original*, pp. 50–1.

[113] BL Additional MS 73087, f. 147v; Davies, *Le Primer Report*, sig. 7v.

[114] *The Case of Praemunire* (1607), Davies 98, 80 ER 582.

[115] Folger Shakespeare Library MS v. b. 303, 'The Somme of My Lorde Cookes Charge', p. 2; *Baggs Case* (1615), 11 Co. *Rep.* 100a, 77 ER 1281.

[116] *Nevil's Case* (1604), 7 Co. *Rep.* 33b, 77 ER 461.

[117] *The Prince's Case*, 8 Co. *Rep.* 18b, 77 ER 502; *Hugh Manney's Case* (n.d.), 12 Co. *Rep.* 101, 77 ER 1377.

was attached to the ideal of moral kingship and the belief that the king might do no wrong: 'because he is the fountain of justice and common right and the King being God's lieutenant cannot do a wrong'.[118] It could also be used as a vehicle for a biting criticism about the corruption of law, in this case the common law, by Archbishop Bancroft: 'He is the fountaine of all justice from whence who so immediately draweth is sure to receive the same with all cleanes and purity, whereas often tymes beinge derived throwgh pipes and Cesternes not soe cleane as they shuld be it is tainted and looseth a great parte of the vertue it had.'[119]

The metaphor of the fountain explained how power flowed through the body politic. Royal power was passed to the administration of officers who acted in the king's name, and sometimes in his own person, by the mechanism of statutes, patents, commissions and charters.[120] The entire thread linked the mundane exercise of royal power to its origin in God: 'judges sit in the seat of the King as in the throne of God. The king is the vicar and lieutenant of God and his iudgments are not the judgements of men, but of God'.[121] Delegates represented the grantor, so that Coke might describe the petty constable as 'a finger of the grand officer, the Lord High Constable of England'.[122] The Earl Marshal was the body of the king within the Verge, and the king was taken to be present in all his courts at once. The king, Coke wrote, was 'always present in law'.[123] Yet this delegation must be used appropriately: its misuse by error or design would undermine the moral foundation of the king's power. The king was held not to be able to grant something that would undermine his duty to do right to his subjects.[124] In 1603 in a case over wild swans, Popham explained that 'it is a maxim in law that the king through his power and prerogative is not able to make wrong or injury to any ... and the reason for this maxim is that the king derives his royal power of God'.[125]

---

[118] *The Case of the Master and Fellows of Magdalen College in Cambridge*, 11 Co. Rep. 72a, 77 ER 1243; cf. *ibid.*, 1245, 1246.

[119] BL Cotton MS Cleopatra F II, f. 122r.

[120] The source of the magistrate's power was disputed extensively on the Continent. Myrone Gilmore, *Argument from Roman Law in Political Thought, 1200–1600* (Cambridge, MA, 1941); Stein, *Roman Law in European History*, p. 60.

[121] Saltern, *Of the Antient Lawes of Great Britaine*, f. Mv.

[122] *R. v. Earl of Shrewsbury* (1600), BL Additional MS 25203, f. 183v; *Floyd v. Barker* (1607), 12 Co. Rep. 25, 77 ER 1307.

[123] BL Harley MS 6686B f. 576v; *Prohibitions Del Roy*, 12 Co. Rep. 65, 77 ER 1343; Finch, *Law*, p. 81; cf. *Marsh's Case* (1591), Croke, Eliz. 225, 78 ER 481.

[124] BL Harley MS 6687A, f. 101v, citing YB 39 Henry 6, f. 40b. Coke again stated this rule in *The Case of Alton Woods*, 1 Co. Rep. 45–52, 76 ER 103, 105, 117, 119.

[125] BL Harley MS 6686B, f. 592v.

This system meant that legal authority was exercised on behalf of the king. This was true of borough magistrates and even of the lowest courts, such as the court-leet, which also was the 'King's court'.[126] The common law judges made use of this structure to assert their superiority over the other ordinary courts of law and legal authorities, claiming that 'the King's bench is the supreme court in England to superintend all the others, and to reform all injuries etc'.[127] This oversight was directed not just to the 'prerogative' courts, but also to those municipal and corporate bodies scattered across the kingdom. For example, James Bagg, who sat on the common council and served as a magistrate in Plymouth, carried himself contemptuously and even threateningly towards several mayors. Warned for his conduct, Bagg nevertheless remained disruptive and intervened in a dispute over the customary payment of a wine duty to the borough. The borough council then removed him from the council and disenfranchised him. Despite Bagg's questionable character the King's Bench sided with him, declaring: 'that to this Court of King's Bench belongs authority, not only to correct errors in judicial proceedings, but other errors and misdemeanors extra-judicial ... so that no wrong or injury, either public or private, can be done but that it shall be (here) reformed or punished by due course of law'.[128] Coke's report with its broad claims for the King's Bench infuriated Egerton, who suggested that there would be 'little or no use either of the King's Royal Care and authoritye exercised in his person ... nor of the council table'.[129]

This super-eminence was a consequence of the king's presence in their court, their 'sitting in the seat of the King', for proceedings in the King's Bench were *coram rege*: 'the King [*sic*] Bench which is in persona Regis et coram justiciariis domini Regis; and [thus] coram domino Rege, et coram ipso Rege'.[130] This relationship was buttressed by medieval authorities that described the King's Bench as the 'place where the king has his court' to

---

[126] *Anonymous* (1586), Godbolt 71, 78 ER 44; BL Harley MS 5265, f. 186v; 11 Co. *Rep.* 100a, 77 ER 1281; cf. BL Additional MS 25203, f. 372r.

[127] R. v. *Earl of Shrewsbury* (1600), BL Additional MS 25213, f. 183v.

[128] *Bagg's Case* (1611), 11 Co. *Rep.* 98b, 77 ER 1278; BL Additional MS 25213, f. 176v; BL Additional MS 35957, f. 7r. Bagg also intervened in a dispute in 1607 on behalf of a local vicar against the High Commission, Plymouth Record Office, 1/359/42.

[129] Ellesmere, 'Observacions', in Knafla, *Law and Society*, p. 307; Halliday, *Habeas Corpus*, p. 81.

[130] *Cox* v. *Gray* (1607), 1 Bulstrode 208, 80 ER 894. Croke was echoing traditional language. See, for example, a case in 1470 where it was observed that *supersedeas* from the Exchequer would not lie against the King's Bench 'for they are not able to make

emphasize the immediacy of the king in their proceedings.[131] Coke wrote: 'It is truly said that the Justices De banco Regis have supream authority, the king himself sitting there as the law intends.'[132] Their aim was to review delegated power, to make sure it operated in a manner consistent with the king's moral duty. Their strategy of alignment with the king and his prerogative was a means of reform to control the delegation of power.

These claims and their underlying reasoning were explicitly stated in two cases that debated the jurisdiction of the Cinque Ports over an appeal for murder. The judges assumed jurisdiction and the Queen's Bench punished the accused. Their assertion was partly for practical reasons, since the Ports could not apprehend the felons beyond their liberty, resulting in a restraint of justice. But the judges in *Cripse* v. *Viroll* (1602) also appealed to the pre-eminence of the King's Bench, 'the highest court of justice, and of greatest sovereignty; and although the kings have heretofore granted conusance of appeals to the barons of the Cinque Ports, yet that does not give away the queen's interest concerning herself'.[133] The delegation to the barons did not exhaust the jurisdiction of the queen, and if the plaintiff non-suited in the prosecution the defendant would be arraigned 'at the suit of the queen'. In these circumstances, 'it appertains to the prerogative of the queen in such cases of necessity to see that justice should be done'.[134] The authority of the Queen's Bench to reach into a liberty was explained in an earlier case, which was cited by the justices in *Crispe* v. *Viroll*. In *Watts* v. *Braynes* (1600) Popham declared 'that this is the most high court of the queen to give justice to her subjects', and continued that it would be 'greatly inconvenient' if a subject were barred from their ordinary remedy.[135] Later in the case Fleming in his argument explained that this was a question of the priority of jurisdiction, a question that should be resolved in favour of the common law. He began by distinguishing the source of the court's authority, 'For the jurisdiction of this court is not derived from

supersedeas to the king, and the plea is there held coram Rege'; YB Hil. 9 Edward IV, pl. 18, ff. 53a–53b; 2 Co. *Inst.*, p. 21, 46; *Searle* v. *Williams* (1619), Hobart 288, 80 ER 433–4. The claim that the king had sat in the court was repeated by laymen such as Richard Robinson; see Harvard Houghton Library MS Eng 976, f. 4v.

[131] *Bracton*, vol. II, p. 301; H. G. Richardson and G. O. Sayles (eds.), *Fleta* (London, 1955), vol. ii, 137; Francis Nichols (ed.), *Britton* (Oxford, 1865), vol. i, 2–4.

[132] 4 Co. *Inst.*, p. 73.

[133] *Crispe* v. *Viroll* (1602), Yelverton, 13, 80 ER 10; Croke Elizabeth 910, 78 ER 1132; BL Additional MS 25203, f. 375r. Other reports include BL Additional MS 25203, f. 589r, and BL Additional MS 25213, ff. 15r, 50r; 2 Co. *Inst.*, p. 557; 4 Co. *Inst.*, p. 223.

[134] *Crispe* v. *Viroll*, BL Additional MS 25203, f. 373r.

[135] BL Additional MS 25203, f. 221r; BL Harley 6686B, ff. 402v–403r; *Park* v. *Lock* (1613), 2 Bulstrode 123, 80 ER 1002.

the queen as all the other jurisdictions within the realm are, but it is the jurisdiction of the queen, because in this court she is always said to be present in intendment of law.' The Queen's Bench was superordinate because of the presence there of the queen, and Fleming continued by making expansive claims for that authority:

> For the jurisdiction of this court is above all other jurisdictions and has power to allow or disallow of all franchises within the realm, for they all can be brought into question in this court ... but the jurisdiction of this court is supreme and absolute. For though all jurisdiction of inferior courts and officers are derived of the crown, yet the crown is not diminished nor loses any of its original jurisdiction, but with all things it retains its supreme authority and preeminence ... and all inferior jurisdictions and authorities they are well compared to stars that receive all their light of the sun and despite this the sun does not lose any of its original light.[136]

Only a few years later in 1605, Coke, arguing as counsel, can be found echoing Fleming's words. In a report of a case over the jurisdiction of the Council in the Marches of Wales, Coke justified the supremacy of the King's Bench by arguing for the king's presence in the court. Coke acknowledged that some had argued that it appeared nowhere in writing that the King's Bench possessed the authority of using habeas corpus to review the imprisonments of other legal authorities. Coke explained that regardless of whatever power the king had delegated to others or to other courts to hear causes or imprison, nonetheless the review of their decisions remained in his supreme power and 'in his bench [the King's Bench], which is his proper seat of justice'. He made the following declaration:

> All courts of justice in the dominions of the king they are subordinate, this court only excepted in which the king is always by the law intended to be present, and which is restrained to no one place but extends to all his dominions. Therefore alone this court has examination of all the other courts of justice, and as the king gives authority by his commission or the law by act of parliament to any man to execute justice, yet the examination of them will be by such authority that remains in the absolute and supreme power of the king in his Bench, which is his proper seat of justice.[137]

Popham and the court responded with 'great approbation' and claimed that any opinion that habeas corpus not be used to review the

---

[136] BL Additional MS 25203, ff. 255v, 256r.
[137] *Whitherby and Wetherley's Case* (1605), HLS MS 1180, f. 69v. The background of the case is discussed in Halliday, *Habeas Corpus*, pp. 11–13.

imprisonments of other legal authorities was 'a derogation of the real prerogative of the king and a depriving of the subject of his natural freedom and the benefit of the law'.[138] This logic explaining the oversight of the King's Bench was repeated again by Christopher Yelverton JKB in 1608: 'by the jurisdiction of this court it is intended that the king sits here in his proper person, and he is to have account why any of his subjects are imprisoned and for this cause his judges do this court they are able to send for any prisoner within any prison in England'.[139]

A close association to the king justified these claims, a strategy found in the common law use of praemunire. In origin the offence involved appeals to Rome in derogation of the king's authority, which led some to question its continued applicability to the Church courts after the Reformation.[140] In 1606 Coke described the offence in a charge to Northampton Assizes, suggesting that it applied broadly. He urged indictment, for example, against those who penalized those people who obeyed the king's laws, but 'suffer those that is [sic] the Cause of his not keepinge the lawe to be unpunished'.[141] In this way, Coke emphasized praemunire's association with legal malfeasance, a characteristic that had led to its use against those who derogated from the common law in the previous century. Praemunire was brought against individuals who sought to undermine common law judgments in 1567, 1588 and 1589.[142] In 1603 creditors complained that special commissions to relieve debtors were examining causes after judgment and threatened the commissioners with praemunire.[143] In explaining praemunire, Coke claimed that by derogating from the common law, ultimately the offender diminished the authority of the king.[144] A similar argument had been made in 1590 in Coke's presence when it was claimed that a suit heard in the Admiralty court was examinable at the common law, 'which is a matter of the crown and thus in derogation of the

---

[138] *Whetherby and Wetherley's Case*, HLS MS 118(c), f. 57r.

[139] *Maunsell v. Onon*, HLS MS 105, f. 86r; see also *Cox v. Gray*, 1 Bulstrode 208, 80 ER 894; *Penson v. Cartwright* (1614), Croke Jac 346, 79 ER 296; 2 Bulstrode 207, 80 ER 1071.

[140] 27 Edward III, st. I, c. 1 (1353), *SR*, vol. I, p. 329; 16 Richard II, c. 5 (1392), *SR*, vol. II, 84–6; 2 Henry IV, c. 3–4, *SR*, vol. II, 121–2; Helmholz, *OHLE*, vol. I, pp. 177–80; Ridley, *A View*, pp. 110–12; Dalton, *Countrey Justice*, pp. 200–2.

[141] BL Harley MS 6055, f. 47v; BL Sloane MS 1664, f. 47r.

[142] Fitzherbert, *La Graunde Abridgement*, f. 105r, s.v. 'praemunire', no. 5, citing a case in Paschal 11 Henry VII; against a court baron hearing a case of debt if it interfered with the common law; Fitzherbert, *Natura Brevium*, f. 185. It was also applied more broadly against the the Bishop of Norwich for attempting to interfere with local custom; *Attorney-General v. Nix, Bishop of Norwich* (1534), *The Notebook of Sir John Port*, pp. 75–7.

[143] BL Royal MS 18 A 36, f. 8r.   [144] 3 Co. *Inst.*, pp. 120–1.

crown and the dignity royal'.[145] Ironically after his fall it was claimed by an anonymous author that Coke himself had committed praemunire for detracting from the king's sovereignty and (citing the case of Magdalen College) for having 'given judgment upon the king'.[146]

Coke explained this line of reasoning with a technical argument, noting that praemunire had applied to litigation in 'the Court of Rome, or elsewhere'. Coke interpreted 'elsewhere' as meaning any court that was not the 'king's court' or the common law.[147] The wording therefore extended the reach of the statute to those courts that 'proceed by the rules of other lawes, as by the Canon or Civill law … or by other trials, then the common law doth warrant'.[148] By drawing those causes that were properly examinable in the king's court away 'ad aliud examen', the wording of the writ itself, these courts drew subjects away from the common law.[149] When causes were wrongfully removed from the king's courts, this trenched on the Crown and the monarch's obligation to give justice, since the subject 'ought to have his cause ended by the common law, whereunto by birthright he is inheritable'.[150] In making these claims, Coke once again cast the common law as the defender against those courts that might 'usurp jurisdiction' and the spiritual court especially, which was 'alium forum'.[151] When Thomas Ridley objected that praemunire should not apply to the ecclesiastical jurisdiction, Coke replied by reminding his readers of the past encroachments of the Church courts. Coke warned

---

[145] *Buckeleye and Mathew's Case*, BL Harley MS 1633, f. 168v; *Sir Richard Buckley's Case* (1589), 2 Leonard 183, 74 ER 461–2; and the related case, *Buckley v. Wood* (1591), 4 Co. *Rep.* 14b, 76 ER 888.

[146] SP 9/209, f. 55r.

[147] Coke relied on 27 Edward III, c. 1 ('en autri Court'), and 16 Richard II, c. 5 ('in curia Romana, vel alibi'); *SR*, vol. I, p. 329; *SR*, vol. II, p. 85; 3 Co. *Inst.*, pp. 120–1. According to J. H. Baker, by 1465 the common law judges had decided that this language brought English ecclesiastical courts within the purview of the statute; Baker, 'Introduction', in *The Reports of Sir John Spelman*, p. 66n3; John Rastall, *An Exposition of Certaine Difficult and Obscure Words, and Termes of the Lawes* (London, 1598), f. 149a; *Murrey v. Anonymous* (1614), 2 Bulstrode 206, 80 ER 1071. For the argument *contra*, see Cosin, *An Apologie*, pp. 126–7.

[148] 3 Co. *Inst.*, p. 120. Coke elsewhere included the Chancery among the 'king's courts', following a Year Book case. In this same Year Book case, however, it was also concluded that the chancellor's subpoena could be ignored if against law, implying the priority of the common law; 2 Co. *Inst.*, p. 22; YB Hil. 9 Edward IV, pl. 18, ff. 53a–53b.

[149] *Hetly v. Boyer* (1614), 2 Bulstrode 199, 80 ER 1066; Smith, *De Republica Anglorum*, p. 117; *Parret and Doctor Matthews Case* (1586), 3 Leonard 139, 74 ER 592. Similar language was used discussing prohibitions; BL Hargrave 33, f. 114r; HLS MS 1003, p. 422.

[150] *Praemunire*, 12 Co. *Rep.* 39, 77 ER 1320.

[151] BL Harley MS 827, ff. 2r, 17v.

that 'Every oppression against Law, by colour of any usurped authority, is a kinde of destruction.'[152] For this reason Coke had perceived in Ridley's argument a threat to the common law itself, and it was said that he 'undertook from thence to prophecy the decay of the common law'.[153] At stake in praemunire, Coke later explained, was the restraint of those practices that led to, 'First, the prejudice and disherison of the King and his Crowne ... the disherison of all his subjects ... [and] the undoing and destruction of the common law'.[154]

The judges' assertion that they acted as the 'king's court' to protect the king from the errors of his delegates justified their extensive claims of review. Coke and others were able to make their arguments firmly within a royalist framework. The common law was the king's instrument to ensure the appropriate use of his delegated power. This opened a wide, and still unexplored, aspect of their jurisprudence. Their efforts to defend the king led to the supervision not only of other courts and their jurisdiction, but the behaviours of patentees and officers. As Coke wrote in his discussion of libels against magistrates:

> for what greater scandal of Government can there be than to have corrupt or wicked magistrates to be appointed and constituted by the King to govern his subjects under him? And greater imputation to the State cannot be, than to suffer such corrupt men to sit in the sacred seat of justice, or to have any meddling in or concerning the administration of justice.[155]

The exercise of patents that delegated royal authority attracted the concern of the common law judges and led them directly into the problem of reform. For example, it was claimed that if the king were to grant a new market with a toll this would be 'burthensom' and therefore could not be justified except by statute or prescription.[156] Coke compiled notes under the heading 'Patents', with entries on relevant Year Book rulings, and from the bench restrained purveyors of saltpetre.[157] While he acknowledged that the patent was necessary, Coke insisted that the officers who executed it should do the least harm in their work, so they could not undermine

---

[152] 2 Co. *Inst.*, p. 48.
[153] Lloyd, *State-Worthies*, p. 423. The ecclesiastics also mentioned the slander against them that they sought the 'overthrowe of the Comon Lawe'; see BL Cotton MS Cleopatra F II, f. 121r.
[154] 3 Co. *Inst.*, p. 120.
[155] *Case de Libellis Famosis* (1605), 5 Co. *Rep.* 125b, 77 ER 251.
[156] *Heddper* v. *Roullz* (1609), BL Additional MS 25213, f. 96v. Only prescription or act of parliament could support the toll.
[157] BL Harley MS 6687A, ff. 44r–48r.

walls with their digging. These restrictions seem partly meant to prevent extortions: they could not dig in the floor of a barn where corn was kept. The need to prevent these abuses was again connected to the preservation that was the aim of royal power: 'my house is the safest place for my refuge, safety and comfort, and of all my family; as well in sickness as in health … and it is very necessary for the weal public, that the habitation of subjects be preserved and maintained'. The prohibition that the officers must work during daylight was justified 'so that the owner may make fast the doors of his house, and put it in defense against misdoers'.[158] Patents that enabled private monopolies, but were unrelated to inventions, were also major grievances heard before the courts.[159] In *Darcy* v. *Allen* the common law judges voided the grant to Darcy, and the recurrent statement that the common law 'abhorred' monopolies was connected to the need to preserve the subject. Monopolies restrained the freedom of the subject from engaging in trade, which 'maintains his life'. Public good alone justified exceptions to this rule. It was crucial that monopolies unrelated to original inventions were denied, because they misused the law: 'for the end of all these monopolies is for the private gain of the patentees'.[160] Thus, once again, the judges had demonstrated their disapproval of the bending of public power to private interest.

The review of delegated legal power might extend to the monarch herself, so that the queen would be prevented from committing a wrong. Under Elizabeth, Coke had written that the queen might prohibit by proclamation, 'for the good of her people'.[161] In the next reign Coke reversed this endorsement, urging instead that proclamations be used to admonish subjects.[162] The justification reveals the workings of Coke's theory of power, for historical example had revealed proclamations 'which are utterly against law and reason, and for that void'. They were voided because similar to custom and other sources of legal authority, such decrees that were repugnant to reason were of no force. A power to create offences by proclamation might cause the prince to err, since where there was an absence of legal precedent for an offence: 'there is heed of great consideration, before that any thing of novelty shall be established'.[163]

---

[158] *The Case of the King's Prerogative in Saltpetre*, 12 Co. *Rep.* 14, 77 ER 1296; BL Harley MS 6686B, f. 643r; BL Harley MS 1576, f. 186r.
[159] For later evasions, see Zaller, *Parliament of 1621*, p. 128; Baker, *IELH*, p. 452.
[160] *The Case of Monopolies*, 11 Co. *Rep.* 87a, 77 ER 1263, 1266.
[161] PRO SP 12/276, f. 126v.
[162] *Proclamations*, 12 Co. *Rep.* 76, 77 ER 1354; cf. Burgess, *Absolute Monarchy*, pp. 201–2.
[163] 12 Co. *Rep.* 76, 77 ER 1353.

Coke also asserted that the king could not delegate some powers. A forest could not be granted to a subject, since a forest allowed the creation of a justice-in-eyre, and only the king himself might create a justice-in-eyre.[164] Nor could the queen, opined Popham, grant to another to make justices of the peace, and also debated was whether butlerage could be delegated.[165] Deputation raised important issues of confidence: could subordinates be trusted as much as their superiors? Sheriffs might indemnify themselves from the actions of their underlings to whom their authority had been delegated.[166] Was a further delegation precluded because the original grantor did not know the deputy and therefore could not have confidence in them? The judges also imposed limits on the ability of bailiffs to delegate their power.[167] Coke reasoned that a stewardship, as an office of trust, might not be deputed where no words existed to that effect in the original patent.[168] The same emphasis on confidence and trust recurs in Coke's report on a conference on penal statutes where the judges decided that the king could not grant over the 'penalty, benefit, and dispensation' of a penal statute to a subject. Coke reported that this prohibition arose from the trust 'committed to the King by all his subjects for the good of the commonwealth'.[169]

Delegated power was an expression of confidence that would be violated by the misuse of that authority. While the common law judges might need to correct errors of ignorance – the perception of a court that their jurisdiction extended beyond its traditional bounds – the other danger was that delegated legal power would be used corruptly. In the *Case of Monopolies* this reasoning is explained: the judges will control the grant for the 'benefit of the king' and 'for justice sake' using their 'rules of law'.[170] In a system of delegation infused with moral obligations, the common law benefited the king by preventing his authority from being used to commit

---

[164] *Rex v. Briggs* (1614), 2 Bulstrode 296, 80 ER 1134, following YB Mich. 1 Henry IV, ff. 4b–5a.

[165] *Acton v. Wall* (1599) and *R. v. Vavisor* (1598), BL Additional MS 25203, ff. 61r, 22ff; see also Hartley (ed.), *Proceedings in the Parliaments of Elizabeth I*, vol. III, p. 386. Though Baker notes that this position differed from the medieval law and that some boroughs might appoint JPs (private communication with the author).

[166] HLS MS 1192, ff. 164v, 183r. Reported as *Norton v. Simmes*, Hobart 12, 80 ER 163; and *Norton and Symm's Case* (1613), Godbolt 212, 78 ER 129.

[167] *Taylor and James's Case* (1607), Godbolt 151, 78 ER 92.

[168] *County of Rutland v. Count of Shrewsbury* (1610), HLS MS 114, f. 6r. Cf. *Denis v. More* (1609), 2 Brownlow and Goldesborough 299, 123 ER 953.

[169] *Penal Statutes*, 7 Co. Rep. 36, 77 ER 465.

[170] *Darcy v. Allen* (1602), Noy 175, 74 ER 1133.

a wrong. That law could be used to occasion a wrong was unreasonable, as Coke explained: 'it is not reasonable that one should take advantage of his own wrong; and if the law should give him such power, the law would be the cause and occasion of wrong'.[171]

At stake in maintaining the integrity of the law was the entire conceptual edifice on which the theory of the system rested. The duty of the prince, himself the delegate or lieutenant of God, was to see that the law was used justly and that his deputies behaved appropriately. Failure would bring that power and ultimately the king himself into disrepute. In *Floyd* v. *Barker* it was implied that accusations of judicial corruption would rebound onto the prince, and so the judges warned against that which tended 'to the slander of the justice of the King, which will trench to the scandal of the King himself'.[172] Indignation over the misuse of royal power by delegates fuelled criticisms of the prerogative, such that Hedley had declared: 'And if for one subject to take from another by force without color of law be robbery, that prerogative that without law taketh away the subjects' good must needs be thought an exorbitant prerogative and to trench rather to the breach than support of justice.'[173] Sandys in the parliament of 1621 during the debate over dispensing with penal statutes warned, 'this regall power ought not to be putt into the hand of a person that hath not a Regall mind'.[174] Arguing whether certain powers might be delegated, Coke drew attention to the frailties of ordinary persons: 'the king is honorable and should be trusted by his subjects for they have committed their lives to him, but that is not a reason that so great a trust should be given to another person [who is] common'.[175] When Walter Chute petitioned the king for a new office to register aliens in the kingdom, it was observed by Coke that the office was 'for a private man to have private ends' and objected to its creation.[176] The discussion of Coke's experience as attorney-general in an earlier chapter demonstrates his experience of that problem. When discussing the authority of the commissioners of sewers, Coke similarly warned against the misuse of the law: 'and that by colour thereof a private be not privily intended, when

---

[171] *Coulter's Case* (1598), 5 Co. *Rep.* 31a, 77 ER 99.
[172] *Floyd* v. *Barker* (1607), 12 Co. *Rep.* 25, 77 ER 1307; *Lord Cromwell's Case* (1581), 4 Co. *Rep.* 13a, 76 ER 880.
[173] *PP 1610*, vol. II, p. 194.
[174] Notestein (ed.), *Commons Debates 1621*, vol. V, p. 54; reported elsewhere to have been a statement about the impossibility of redelegating such power; *Commons Debates 1621*, vol. IV, p. 173.
[175] BL Additional MS 25203, f. 23v.
[176] *Chute's Case* (1614), 12 Co. *Rep.* 116, 77 ER 1392.

the publick is openly pretended'.[177] Coke argued that the delegate must be prevented by rules and clear instructions from abusing their discretion: 'although the words of [a commission] gives authority to the commissioners to act according to their discretion, their proceedings ought nevertheless to be limited and bound within the rule of reason and law, for discretion is a science … and they are not to act according to their wills and private affections'.[178] As he spoke to the assembled, including JPs and other royal officers, he repeated the sentiment in his charge to the Lincoln Assizes.[179] Both as attorney-general and as a judge Coke had attempted to develop this framework of rules.

The delegation of legal power to commissioners, officers and local courts has generally been taken as a positive aspect of self-government. The policy imparted flexibility to communities and regional elites to manage their affairs, and reflected the limitations of a central government that was chronically short of money. The numbers of those who held such delegated authority in a local capacity increased over the sixteenth century. Coke's jurisprudence and that of his immediate predecessors on the bench focused on the oversight of this dissemination of legal power and sought to rationalize the legal system.[180]

While Coke disagreed with royal policies, this does not mean he believed himself in opposition to the king or even to his authority. Aware that his authority both as law officer and judge depended on the king, he made the conservative case that the common law protected the king and advanced his duty and power. The king protected property as God's delegate, and the common law directed his use of that authority and bound its re-delegation. The theory of delegation allowed Coke to maintain that the king's power was ultimately absolute and irresistible, while moving to limit its exercise by delegates. If there was a dispute over the constitution leading up to 1616, Coke identified the culprit not as an overreaching king. Instead Coke looked to his fellow subjects who misused, manipulated or misunderstood legal power. Only wise kingship and an active common law would protect against them.

---

[177] 10 Co. *Rep.*, p. xx.   [178] *Rooke's Case* (1598), 5 Co. *Rep.* 100b, 77 ER 210.
[179] Society of Antiquaries MS 291, f. 11v.
[180] For a contemporary survey and list of the numerous officers appointed to judicial commissions from 1606 to 1620, see PRO C181/2.

~

Conclusion

In his speech to the assembled judges on 20 June 1616, the king reminded them that they were his deputies: 'the seate of Iudgement is properly Gods, and Kings are Gods Vicegerents; and by Kings Iudges are deputed under them, to beare the burden of government'.[1] Even though Coke shared James's belief in this relationship, delegation worked very differently in his mind. Their difference of perspective on the problem of law reform and delegation ultimately led to Coke's dismissal in November 1616, though the proximate causes are easier to identify.[2] The first was Coke's dispute with the Chancery. In June 1616 the Archbishop of Canterbury had been appointed with other commissioners to resolve the conflict. Coke denied their oversight: on a copy of the commission he wrote that it was 'against lawe to examine the proceedings of the judges of the kings benche etc'.[3] Their report, unsurprisingly, sided with the Chancery as did the king who declared that the 'Chancerie is undependant [sic] of any other Court, is onely under the King'.[4] That same month another dispute came to a head over the king's request to stay proceedings in the *Case of Commendams*. On 6 June the judges were summoned to explain their conduct in that case, and then on 26 June charges were laid against Coke. These allegations included his handling of a debt of Sir Christopher Hatton when he was attorney-general, 'speeches of heigh contempt' for claiming that the common law might be overthrown, and for 'uncomely and undutifull carriage' during the meeting of 6 June.[5] By 30 June he was suspended from

---

[1] James I, *Political Writings*, p. 205.
[2] Chamberlain attributed Coke's fall to the 'fowre Ps ... that is, Pride, Prohibitions, Premunire, and Prerogative', while Sir Richard Hutton also cited Coke's reports of several cases; Chamberlain, *Letters*, vol. II, p. 34; Hutton, *Diary*, p. 13.
[3] Society of Antiquaries MS 79, f. 45r. The events immediately following the clash with the Chancery are described by Baker, 'The Common Lawyers and the Chancery', pp. 225–6.
[4] BL Lansdowne MS 107, ff. 183r–187v; BL Stowe MS 415, ff. 63v–67v; James I, *Political Writings*, p. 215.
[5] *APC, 1615–1616*, p. 645.

riding circuit and ordered to review his book of *Reports* where 'there bee manie exorbitaunt and extravagant opinions sett downe and published for positive and good lawe'.[6]

This command suggested the deeper cause behind Coke's fall that was a recurring theme in the king's sometimes scolding and often admonitory speeches. On 20 June, James presented himself in the guise of a reformer who would 'purge' the common law 'from two corruptions, Incertaintie and Noveltie: Incertaintie is found in the Law it selfe ... The other corruption is introduced by the Iudges themselves, by Nicities that are used'.[7] The former might be remedied by parliament, but the latter needed the intervention of the king himself. He told his judges that the common law should be intelligible to laymen: 'that your interpretations must be always subject to common sense and reason. For I will never trust any Interpretation, that agreeth not with my common sense and reason, and trew Logicke ... it must not be Sophistrie or straines of wit that must interprete, but either cleare Law, or solide reason.'

He disparaged the 'foolish Querke of some judges' in the Union project.[8] The judges were not to 'incroach' on the prerogative and instead keep to their own bounds, a rule that the king would enforce personally.[9] In other censures of Coke's conduct the theme of the law's obscurity is returned to repeatedly. The warrant to scrutinize Coke's *Reports*, was justified so 'that our crown and people be not secretly snared by conceit of laws'.[10] Bacon in a speech to the judges in 1617 put it more succinctly: 'That you shall drawe your learning out of your bookes, and not out of your Braines'.[11] Ellesmere, combing the *Reports* and reflecting on *Bonham's Case*, wrote that the judges 'advanceth the reason of a particular Court', and in his speech to Coke's succesor Sir Henry Montagu, he identified what was at stake: 'your grandfather wold not take upon to challeng so much [Authority] to his Court as to reforme all abuses Judiciall and extrajudiciall ... I speake of Law and reson that shold be construed by some few

[6] *Ibid.*, p. 649; *CSPD, James I*, 1611–1618, p. 400.
[7] James I, *Political Writings*, p. 211. James indicated that he had provided the judges with an 'epitome' of their 'bad interpretations' that 'he wished to reform according to reason'; BL Additional 35957, ff. 55r–v. This was possibly Ellesmere's 'Observacions', reprinted in Knafla, *Law and Politics*, pp. 297–318.
[8] James I, *Political Writings*, pp. 208, 212.   [9] *Ibid.*, p. 213.
[10] John Hardy (ed.), *Report on the Manuscripts of the Earl of Verulam* (London, 1906), p. 27.
[11] BL Sloane MS 3522, f. 27v.

against the whole kingdom'.[12] By making these accusations it was possible to paint Coke and the judges as exercising a discretionary authority that was not bound by rules except their 'quirks of law' and 'sophistries', so that 'my Lord Coke, to magnify his science of law, draweth every thing, though sometimes improperly and unseasonably, to that kind of question'.[13] The danger was not only to the king's prerogative, but to the entire commonwealth: as James had pointed out, the judges administered an uncertain law.

The natural consequence of such pride was contemptuous behaviour, and Coke's high-mindedness led him into trouble even if his actions may not have amounted to an uncompromising defiance.[14] The road would end at the *Case of Commendams*, but already there was anticipation in *Peacham's Case* (1615) when Coke refused to offer an opinion on the treason to the attorney-general. This attempt to obtain such a private opinion, Coke claimed, was 'new and dangerous'.[15] Bacon continued to press the king's privilege in *Brownlow* v. *Cox and Michil*, a case begun in Easter term 1615, when he presented a writ *de non procedendo rege inconsulto* to stop proceedings and have the case heard on the Latin side of the Chancery.[16] In Bacon's view the case touched the king closely, and to have the matter heard in the Chancery would favour the royal interest, since the chancellor 'is ever a principal counsellor and instrument of monarchy, of immediate dependence upon the King'.[17] However, serjeant Thomas Harris for the plaintiff moved that the writ did not lie. Bacon argued that the allowance of the writ was not open to debate, but Coke, who noted that 'these writts are usuall', rejected this claim.[18] Yet in late January 1616 Bacon, writing to James, believed that Coke had nonetheless privately reassured him about the case. Referring back to the preceding November when he had written to the king urging a delay in the debate over the writ, he advised 'so as for

---

[12] CUL MS Additional 335, f. 31v, recorded slightly differently in *The Lord Chancellors Speech to Sir Henry Mountague* (1616), Moore King's Bench 828, 72 ER 932. See also Hutton, *Diary*, p. 13.

[13] Spedding (ed.), *Letters and Life*, vol. XII, p. 237. As early as 1607 James had warned that common law prohibitions extended suits, putting 'the subjects to Tantalus pain, that, when he thought to take the fruit of his suit, it fled from him'; *ibid.*, vol. IV, p. 90.

[14] Chamberlain, *Letters*, vol. II, p. 34; Wilbraham, *Journal*, p. 117.

[15] Spedding (ed.), *Letters and Life*, vol. XII, pp. 108, 107.

[16] *Brownloe* v. *Cox* (1615) Moore 842, 72 ER 942; 3 Bulstrode 32, 81 ER 27; 1 Rolle 205, 81 ER 434; 1 Rolle 188, 81 ER 421; Spedding *et al.* (eds.), *Works*, vol. VII, pp. 687–725.

[17] Spedding (ed.), *Letters and Life*, vol. XII, p. 236.

[18] 3 Bulstrode 33, 81 ER 28; Spedding *et al.* (eds.), *Works*, vol. VII, p. 688. This debate was objected to by Bacon and Ellesmere; *The Lord Chancellors Speech to Sir Henry Mountague* (1616), Moore King's Bench 828, 72 ER 932.

the present your Majesty shall not need to renew your commandment of stay'.[19] The case was resolved by the compromise of the parties and no judgment was given.

Meanwhile, in April 1616, word that argument in the overlapping *Case of Commendams* was touching on the royal prerogative pinched the king's anxieties over his prerogative. The Bishop of Winchester was sent to attend a hearing and he returned with the report that Charles Chibborne SL had claimed that the 'Kinge had noe power to graunt commendams, but in case of necessitie'. Chibborne supposedly added that there would be no situation where there would be such a necessity. James responded with angry remarks about lawyers debating his prerogative in parliament, and it is clear that Chibborne had touched a nerve.[20] The king directed Bacon to write to Coke to inform him that his 'Majestie bee first consulted with, before the Judges proceeded to argument'.[21] Bacon later recalled that the precedent for this command was *Brownlow v. Cox and Michil*, and he may have been referring to the king's order to adjourn the case to the next term that Coke had obeyed.[22] In the *Case of Commendams*, however, the judges refused to obey and wrote back to the king to explain that the case was 'betweene subjects for private interest', and stood upon their oath to ignore letters 'contrary to lawe'.[23] The matter escalated from there, and the king's letters revealed his concern that the judges were allowing lawyers 'a greater boldness to dispute the heigh pointes of his Majesty's prerogative' before them.[24] After a second, peremptory letter to them, the judges were summoned on 6 June. At the conference James repeated his dislike that 'ever since his comeinge to this Crowne the popular sorte of lawiers have ben the men that most affrontedly in all Parlaments have troden upon his prerogative'.[25] He tied this meddling with the prerogative with the observation that the 'Common Lawe were grown soe vaste and transcendent' as to deal with his absolute prerogative and encroach upon other jurisdictions.[26] If James perceived the case partly through the lens of his unhappy experiences with his parliaments, Coke preferred to mollify the king's concern by explaining that 'the case (as they meant to handle it) did not concerne his Majesty's prerogative'.[27] When asked by James whether they would stay a suit touching the king 'in power or profitt' and

---

[19] Spedding (ed.), *Letters and Life*, vol. XII, pp. 237, 225; *CSPD, James I, 1611–1618*, p. 330.
[20] *APC, 1615–1616*, pp. 599, 602.
[21] *Ibid.*, p. 596.   [22] Hargrave (ed.), *Collectanea Juridica*, vol. I, p. 2.
[23] *APC, 1615–1616*, p. 598.   [24] *Ibid.*, pp. 599, 601.
[25] *Ibid.*, p. 602.   [26] *Ibid.*, pp. 602–3.
[27] *Ibid.*, p. 605.

consult with him, all the judges agreed that they would, except for Coke who equivocated 'hee would doe that should bee fitt for a Judge to doe'.[28] This response, he later explained, was because 'the question included a multitude of particulars'. However defiant or circumspect Coke may have been in this answer, nonetheless 'all' the judges then continued their surrender assuring the king that they would not do anything to risk the prerogative in *commendams* and would correct those who had drawn it into question at the Bar 'and all promised soe to doe'.[29] The conference closed with James once again admonishing the judges to 'apply themselves to the studie and practize of that ancient and best lawe, and not to extende the power of anie of their Courtes'.[30] Though Coke may have made a passing resistance, the judges had otherwise capitulated. Their motives for their conduct in the case are still unclear: they may have always believed that the prerogative in *commendams* was never in danger or they sought to oppose a pattern of interference by the attorney-general in their proceedings.[31] Coke's oblique answer, however, was among the pretexts for his removal from the bench. Yet even during the time when he was defending himself he looked to the king: 'I knowing the security of his Majesty's justice … And ever persuade my self that they which had infourmed against me should not be my iudges, and therefore his Majestie was pleased to vouchesafe the hearing of it himselfe.'[32] Given Coke's subsequent reputation as an opponent of the royal prerogative, it is also revealing that two of his most important protectors were the Queen and Prince Charles.[33] Though the king thought him misguided, he nonetheless admitted that Coke was nonetheless an 'uncorrupt and a good justicer'.[34]

Coke's perspective on reform was the ultimate cause of his fall. From the king's point of view it was Coke and the judges who were creating problems in the legal system: a year earlier, before the Chancery praemunire, he had warned Coke to refer matters in dispute with Chancery to him.[35] Their esoteric claims about reason were suspect, and even Coke himself

---

[28] *Ibid.*, pp. 607, 646.   [29] *Ibid.*, p. 608.   [30] *Ibid.*, p. 646.

[31] Baron Altham in his notes clearly disapproved of those who 'Arguing att the Barr did labour to weaken or blemishe the kings prerogative in this behalf did err exceedingly and unadvisedly'; Lincoln's Inn Hale MS 80, f. 244v.

[32] Bodl. Tanner MS 74, f. 63r.

[33] Chamberlain, *Letters*, vol. II, p. 32.

[34] *CSPD, James I, 1611–1618*, p. 407; Chamberlain, *Letters*, vol. II, p. 38; Whitelocke, *Liber Famelicus*, pp. 50, 51; BL Harley MS 6687A, f. 18v; Holkham MS 727; James, *Chief Justice Coke*, p. 44. Coke proudly recorded in his notebooks that he had obtained his offices 'neither by entreaty or purchase'; BL Harley MS 6687A, f. 18v.

[35] *CSPD, James I, 1611–1618*, p. 381; SP 9/209, no. 42.

had admitted problems in the common law. Nor was James impressed that autumn with the conduct of Warburton JCP, who hanged a Scot despite the king's command to stay. Making matters worse, Sir Humphrey Winch JCP and Randall Crew SL executed persons falsely accused of witchcraft – the king himself uncovered the plot.[36] Coke, meanwhile, had a different perspective shaped by his career and his perception of the effects of the growth of the legal system. He was well aware that the profession did not have a consensus on these changes: lawyers practised across jurisdictions and some found lucrative possibilities in Chancery, the development of perpetuities or the obtaining of injunctions after judgment. Many lawyers were aware, as this book has shown, that the common law attracted criticism for its perceived uncertainty. This was not the only context that affected Coke's thinking about the law. The Reformation had reshaped jurisdictional relationships, and those who opposed the government's religious policies endangered the state. Coke's own professional advancement led him to engage with these problems: he experienced the uncertainty of the law as a litigator and pursued its abuses as attorney-general. As a judge he worked to protect confidence in the common law and prevent what he perceived as the encroachments of other jurisdictions.

In order to defend the common law and the government, and to guard against the unjust use of the law, Coke pursued a provocative agenda of reform. His jurisprudence, focused on reason and method, would guide practitioners to settle controverted questions within the law and review the exercise of legal authority outside the law. In doing so, the reason of the common law that had been tested over time would spread to protect the rights of subjects and preserve the prerogatives of the king. Coke's belief that the King's Bench was the court of the king justified these broad claims for the common law. But history also validated them: the common law had protected the king in the past from the usurpation of his legal authority, and it was the tool that would limit encroachments in the present.

Coke's belief that the judges acted as the king's deputies in their exercise of judicial authority both complicated and justified his project. God's grant to the king of absolute power came with an obligation to see that this power was used morally. But as this authority was granted to others, it needed to be controlled to prevent its use as an instrument of oppression that would violate the king's responsibility to see his power well used. The expansion of the early modern judicial state's legal apparatus

[36] *CSPD, James I, 1611–1618*, p. 398.

brought with it the challenge of retaining confidence in its operation. To that purpose Coke wedded himself. His work was both defensive, aiming to protect confidence in the common law as the instrument of this reform, and offensive, asserting the common law as the forum to review the exercise of legal authority and to restrain those who opposed the religious settlement.

The reforming efforts of the period were retarded in many ways: disagreements over the course of reform, the practical interests of lawyers and their clients, and the difficulty of establishing claims about corruption and misuse. But for Coke the gravest threat to his own efforts was James's lack of confidence in the common law as it was practised. The king's doubts are usually ascribed to his high opinion of the regal office, which certainly sensitized him to some of Coke's claims. But these doubts, as this book has argued, were in sympathy with those of many others of his time. This led James to interpret common law jurisprudence and its ideas of artificial reason as obscurities that contributed to the problem of uncertainty and served the judges' turn to extend their influence over the system. This lack of confidence limited Coke's reforming work even as it exposed the tension in his political thought. Hampering the common law to quiet the misuses of the law increased the risk that the king's authority would be abused for private purposes. While much attention has been given to misguided royal policies under James and Charles, Coke perceived from his own experiences, accurately or not, that the use of law among subjects also created abuses. The failure to remedy these oppressions was detrimental to the king's moral duty.

In effect, perhaps paradoxically, the attribution of so much authority to the king had also placed too much responsibility on him for its use. There were many reasons for Coke's insistence on the separation of the person of the king from the exercise of the law. Among them, however, was the inherent problem in the system of moral kingship that the king could not err. The perception that legal authority was used as a means of oppression invited increasingly assertive claims that the law was misunderstood or misapplied. Such assertions drew both on the English constitutionalist tradition, but even royalist ideas contained the means by which the king might be opposed.

This book has attempted to explain how Coke remained committed to royal authority even while he seemed to oppose aspects of its exercise. His claims up to 1616 were not supported by a belief in the autonomous constitutional status of the common law. In fact, as earlier chapters have argued, he claimed an intimate connection between the common law and royal authority. What bears explaining is how individuals who held strongly royalist views were drawn to oppose the government of Charles I. The early motivation, in Coke's case, came from 'below' in his interpretation of how the law was used, rather than from an assumption that the prerogative and the common law were inherently in tension. If an insistence on constitutional restrictions on the king emerged from Coke's beliefs, then this was because of his commitment to the king's sovereign authority and the insistence that his delegates should exercise this power fairly.

Forces within the law as well as without could lead people to insist on better protections for their property, clearer recognition of their rights, and the accountability of those who used royal authority. It has been easy to blame James I and Charles I for the grievances of their subjects, but one should not overlook how private individuals cheated government and oppressed one another. The significance and scale of their behaviour remain elusive: did the rackets of informers, for example, amount to a sizeable indirect tax? The functioning of the early modern judicial state was more fluid than paradigms of centralization and the dichotomies of prerogative courts and common law have allowed. Characterized by competitive entrepreneurship, yet structured by ideas of complementarity and functional specialization, the system was both dynamic and unsettled.

The purpose of this book has been to suggest a different approach to Coke's jurisprudence, one that reconciles his devotion to royal authority with his insistence on its limitation. This is not to deny that individuals in the period directly opposed royal policies or believed that they were illegal. Coke, however, has been used as a straw man for the constitutionalism of the period, and his jurisprudence a crude axe that he used to attack 'prerogative'. The diversity of opinion and variety of debate among the common lawyers has also been reduced in concepts such as the ancient constitution and the 'common law mind'. In favouring their engagement with political questions, we have overlooked their experience of the everyday problems of early Stuart society. Attending to the problems of the workings of legal power is one way to gain greater insight into, yet momentarily think outside, the paradigm of the conflict between prerogative and law that has dominated the analysis of the period. As James, through the Earl of Salisbury, declared, 'the marriage between law and prerogative is inseparable and like twins they must joy and mourn together, live and die together, the separation of the one is the ruin of the other'.[37] So it was in Coke's thought prior to 1616.

[37] *PP 1610*, vol. II, p. 50.

APPENDIX: SERJEANTS CREATED BETWEEN 1577 AND 1616 WITH PRACTICES IN THE CHANCERY FROM 1592 TO 1615

(in order of their creation)

William Fleetwoode
Thomas Snagg
John Puckering
Christopher Yelverton
Francis Beaumont
Edward Drew
Thomas Owen
Thomas Hannam
Thomas Harris
John Glanvill
William Daniel
George Kingsmill
John Spurling
John Hele
David Williams
Edward Heron
Edward Phelips
John Shurley
George Snigg
Lawrence Tanfield
John Croke
Thomas Foster
Thomas Harris
James Altham
Henry Hobart
Robert Barker
Richard Hutton
John Dodderidge
John Davies
Henry Montagu

Randall Crewe
George Wilde
William Towse
Leonard Bawtrey
Henry Finch
Thomas Chamberlaine
Francis Moore
Thomas Athow
John More
Francis Harvey
Charles Chibborne
Thomas Richardson

Source: survey of TNA C33 'A' books for the years 1592, 1602, 1611 and 1615.

INDEX

absolute monarchs, 199, 254
absolute power, 18, 84, 233, 247, 256–8, 259, 283
absolute prerogative, 255–60, 281
absolute property, 262
absolutism, 12, 45, 116, 255
abuses, 10, 14, 23–7, 49, 52–3, 60–2, 66–7, 94–5, 283–4
accountability, 29, 71–3, 285
acts of parliament, 44, 99, 103, 165–8, 171–4, 243, 270
administration of justice, 265, 273
administration of the oath ex officio, *see* oath ex officio.
Admiralty, 37–9, 271
adultery, 179–80, 207–8
Alford, Edward, 56
Alford, Francis, 53
Alfred, 121, 125–7
aliens, 79, 134, 253, 276
Alkynton, George, 52
allegiance, 7, 61, 74, 78–88, 134, 253–4, 263
Allen Ball's Case, 193
Allen, William, 240, 243–6, 256, 265, 274
allies, 24–5, 117, 214, 245
ancient constitution, 5, 10–12, 115–16, 264, 285
ancient constitutionalism, 5, 10–12, 116
Anderson, Sir Edmund, 61, 69, 92, 98, 149, 162, 189, 218
antiquity, 135, 250
application, 16, 22, 79, 139, 145, 160, 211
apprehensions, 17, 44, 155, 184, 210

Apsley's Case, 239–43
arbitration, 24, 110, 219
Archer's Case, 33
Aristotle, 141, 147, 160, 252
arrest, 37–9, 81, 185, 193–4
Articuli Cleri, 198, 200, 204
artificial reason, 17, 153–5, 177–8, 284
Ashley, Sir Francis, 123, 138
assizes, 31, 104, 133, 150, 223, 227–8, 247, 266, 277
assumpsit, 30–1, 38
attachments, 185, 193, 227, 233
Attorney-General v. *Nixen* et al., 64
attorney-generals, 9, 14, 21–4, 59–64, 70–1, 191–4, 203–4, 207, 276–83
attorneys, 41, 63, 67, 225, 245
authority, 65–71, 81–5, 93–6, 175–9, 182–4, 188–99, 260–4, 266–71, 275–7
   common law's, 93, 116, 127, 139, 175, 243
   discretionary, 29, 206, 280
   of the monarchy, 1, 61, 89, 135, 260, 271, 284
   residual, 180–1, 192

Babington, Sir William, 240
Bacon, Sir Francis, 22–3, 40, 54–6, 86, 93, 107, 159, 214, 279–81
Bacon, Nicholas, 52–4
Baker, J. H., 28, 34, 187, 242
balance, 4, 59–60, 209–12
Bancroft, Richard, 177, 198–200, 204, 267
Bar, 9, 20–1, 48, 119, 221–3, 225, 246, 282
Barnes, T. G., 20, 23, 37